The
Junak
King

1940: young and idealistic.

The Junak King

Life as a British POW, 1941-45

Sydney Litherland

First published 2014 by Spellmount,
an imprint of

The History Press
The Mill, Brimscombe Port
Stroud, Gloucestershire, GL5 2QG
www.thehistorypress.co.uk

British Library Cataloguing in Publication Data.
A catalogue record for this book is available from the British Library.

ISBN 978 0 7509 5560 7

Typesetting and origination by The History Press
Printed in Great Britain

Contents

Foreword

An account of the experiences of No. 4805024 Lance Corporal Sydney Litherland during the Second World War

I am writing this account of my life during the years of the Second World War in the hope it will be of some interest to my children and grandchildren, and perhaps to others who want to know what life in a working prisoner-of-war camp was actually like.

I also write as a tribute to those many colleagues who were incarcerated with me in prisoner-of-war camps of the German Third Reich – sometimes referred to as 'the University of Life'. None of us 'other ranks' had ever been briefed on what to do if we were taken prisoner, nor on how to escape: that briefing was, apparently, confined to commissioned officers. We had to do manual work for the Germans, often in difficult conditions. We made it a point of honour to do as little as possible whilst seeming busy: in short to be as obstructive as we could be. We did what we could to hinder the German war effort through many minor acts of sabotage and to undermine our captors' morale whenever possible. I am convinced that, although imprisoned, we managed in no small way to assist the Allied war effort. Never, even in the darkest days, did we contemplate defeat and our indomitable belief in victory confounded and puzzled our captors. So this account is dedicated to my 'muckers' of those days.

Sydney Litherland
Written in 1999 at the age of 80
Revised in 2011

The war memorial, Burton-on-Trent, designed by my father, Richard Litherland.

1

Prelude

I was born in 1919, the second youngest of six. My two brothers were some fourteen years older than me, born before the First World War. My father died at the early age of fifty-three on 11 August 1937 when I was nearly eighteen. I had been educated at Burton Grammar School and had just left, having taken my Higher School Certificate in zoology, botany and chemistry without much success because of a mix-up in my sixth-form education. I had wished originally to go to university to study marine biology, but father announced, quite out of the blue, that he was negotiating a pupilage for me with a Burton firm of solicitors, Messrs Talbot, Stein and Evershed, a well-regarded local practice whose senior partner became Master of the Rolls as Lord Evershed. My father was also the honorary umpire for the Burton Cricket Club of which the Eversheds were prominent members and players.

I discussed the pupilage with my form master who advised me that scientific subjects would be of little use, so he proposed I should switch instead to Roman history, English and maths. Two terms later, father was informed that these solicitors no longer had a vacancy for a pupil. I switched back to zoology, botany and chemistry with subsidiary English, again with the aim of going to university. However, those missed terms meant I did not do particularly well in my Higher School Certificate. I was still sixteen at the time, so there would have been plenty of time to retake it – in fact I could have done another two years and still been in the usual age group for the Higher School Certificate. However, I had become disillusioned and had made up my mind to quit school. Looking back, I realise that I got little or no advice on my future career either from school or from my family. One very left-wing master, Charlie Brown, said my future was as a Labour Member of Parliament. He was one of two masters who used to heckle my father when he spoke at Conservative political meetings.

I saw an advertisement for an assistant at the local opticians who had their shop in the High Street near father's office. Without telling my family, I applied for the post, was interviewed and offered the position. This put me in a quandary as I did not really want to work there and had only applied in reaction to my disappointment with my Higher School Certificate results. It was not that I was unhappy with school life – I even went to voluntary sessions on Saturday mornings. I decided to turn down the offer and, on the spur of the moment, I went to father's office at 10 High Street in Burton and announced I was leaving school and was coming to join him in the architectural practice. Father seemed very pleased. At the time he was very busy and, perhaps, welcomed an extra hand.

My first weeks were spent practising lettering for architectural drawings as my father insisted that all lettering on plans should be clearly legible. I found the work at the office alternately interesting and tedious. The hours spent checking specifications and bills of quantity which had to be absolutely correct in every detail were very boring. The more interesting part was helping to supervise building works in progress: checking on the builders, the number of men working, the weather, testing samples of concrete, mortar mixes and so on. My father was a strict disciplinarian who expected builders to stick to the terms of their contracts. We were all very much in awe of him as he was such a strong character, but he could also be very kind and considerate.

My elder brother Dick worked in the practice. A few years earlier he had privately designed a house for a friend of his, without telling my father. He said he had done it to get some pocket money. When father found out he was livid. He told Dick that the business was a family one in which all commissions were to be shared, that what he had done was underhand and deceitful, and immediately threw him out of the office. This was during the 1930s depression when jobs were very difficult to find and Dick spent several months looking for work without success. Sometime later, when I was with father on my way to school, we came across Dick walking towards the railway station. My father stopped the car and asked where he was going. 'To Derby to look for a job,' came the reply. 'Jump in', said father, 'I think you've learned your lesson, come back to work.' It had been a hard lesson.

My father in a relatively short life had become very successful. He had started as a junior apprentice in an architectural practice. By working hard, he qualified as a member of the Royal Institute of British Architects (RIBA) eventually taking over the firm he had joined as a school leaver. The firm prospered under his leadership. He was exceptionally politically and civic-minded, becoming a county councillor for Staffordshire and a Justice of the Peace. The law courts in Burton and the war memorial are examples of his skills as an architect and also serve as a memorial to him. In politics he was a Unionist (now Conservative), a prominent aide to Colonel John Gretton (later Lord Gretton) the Member of Parliament for Burton-on-Trent. In my idealistic youth, I thought they spoke a lot of nonsense on the hustings; now I am not so sure!

My world was shattered by my father's early death in 1937 and my future appeared to be in limbo. My brother Dick took over the practice. One day soon afterwards I overheard my second brother Charles, who was paying a visit to the office, discussing my future prospects with Frank Johnson. Frank was the son of a close cricketing friend of father. He was a paid assistant and studying for his architectural diploma whilst I only got pocket money. Charles said, 'What do we do with the youngster, has he any future in architecture?' To which Frank replied that, if I worked hard, I could probably qualify as an architect by the time I was twenty-six or twenty-seven. I thought they were pretty condescending and was annoyed. I decided I would show them by qualifying by the time I was twenty-one. Looking back, I realise Charles had a genuine concern for my future, but at the time I was just cross. I enrolled for a correspondence course for the RIBA Intermediate Examination with Prof. L. Stuart Stanley of the Bartlett School of Architecture, London University and worked very hard.

After Father died, it was decided (presumably by elder brother Dick in consultation with mother) that Barton House, our home, should be sold as it was now too big for mother, younger sister Ruth and me. Instead, we would build a new smaller house on part of our land which was designed by Dick and me. I did the layout and planning while he designed the elevations and details. Whilst it was being built, Mother, Ruth and I, plus Zilpah our maid, moved into a rented house. By this time, both of my elder brothers had long married and departed the family nest. Then Betty had married and left home and Mary, the one next to me, had taken a course in hotel management and left to be a hotel receptionist in Leamington Spa.

The new house was duly finished and provided a comfortable home for Mother until her death in 1946.

My father had had a subscription to the *Intelligence Digest*, a review of international affairs. It was anti-fascist, detailing the spread of Falangism in Spain, Fascism in Italy and National Socialism in Germany. For the first time I read how the Germans and Italians were using their aid to General Franco during the Spanish Civil War to test their aircraft and other military equipment in preparation for their planned aggressions. I also learned that the Soviet Union were doing much the same thing in their assistance to the Republicans in Spain. Like many others in England, I became more and more concerned about the aggressive activities of Hitler's regime in Germany, where he had been freely elected as chancellor. I learned much more about what was going on in Europe from the *Intelligence Digest* than the national newspapers. The daily paper we took was the *Morning Post* (later taken over by the *Daily Telegraph*). I suppose that living in a country town made us somewhat parochial in our outlook, somewhat detached from world affairs; we rarely left the Burton area except for our annual holidays at the seaside.

I felt strongly that the government should be doing something to halt Germany and Italy. First there was the blatant occupation of Abyssinia (now Ethiopia) by the Italians under Mussolini and the fiasco of the inept efforts of the League of Nations to take any effective action against it. I thought the league was quite hopeless, as did many others. The German reoccupation of the Ruhr followed, unopposed by the French. Germany was also increasing the size of its navy in contravention of the Treaty of Versailles. In 1938 Germany succeeding in annexing Austria into Greater Germany following the *Anschluss*; Bohemia came next.

Even in Burton – hardly a hub of world affairs – many felt that both Britain and France needed to act to stop the Axis Powers of Germany and Italy. I wrote to Col. John Gretton, our MP, to express my concerns. He was a member of the House of Commons' Foreign Affairs Committee and had been a close friend of my father. He replied, assuring me that the government (then under the premiership of Neville Chamberlain, who had succeeded Stanley Baldwin in 1937) was equally concerned with the gravity of the situation, but that after the disastrous period of disarmament brokered by the League of Nations, it was necessary for the country to build up our armed forces, armaments industry and improve our defensive capabilities again, before we could be in a position to take any effective counter-action. It seemed ironic to me that Hitler was also building up his armaments industry, enlarging his army, navy and air force and most probably at a faster rate than we could achieve at the time, as he had had a good start on us. At this time, the United States of America was pursuing isolationist policies and was not very interested in our problems. Indeed, their ambassador in London, Joseph Kennedy (father of the later President Kennedy), was clearly anti-British and expressed the opinion later on that we would lose the war.

As the months of 1938 and 1939 passed, the clouds of war grew thicker and so did the desire of my school friends and young people in general to join the coming fight against Hitler and Mussolini. These volunteers were at first part-time, but ready to be called up permanently when required. Most of us wanted to join the Royal Air Force and become pilots and some of my friends succeeded. I was turned down because of my shortsightedness. The Royal Navy, my second choice, did not want me for the same reason, except as a pen-pusher on land, which I did not relish. I was still determined to play my part. Frank Johnson had joined an anti-aircraft unit of the Royal Artillery. I decided to volunteer for the same unit. I went to the recruiting office and volunteered, signed on, took the oath of loyalty and prepared to join the unit.

When I arrived at the camp, the CO (commanding officer) seemed a little concerned. It turned out he was a friend of my brother Dick with whom he had discussed my enlistment. I was called to his office and told that, as I was planning to take my RIBA Intermediate Exams in November 1939, I would be well advised to take them. If I passed, I would be useful to the Royal Engineers. He then tore up my enlistment papers and told me to go back home and resume my studies, which I did with renewed zeal.

During this 'waiting period', we had some interesting commissions in the office. We surveyed country mansions taken over by the Army as training camps and gleaned some idea of Army life from the regular units who ran them. We also did a survey of a factory in Derbyshire which manufactured 'patent plaster' from gypsum obtained from adjacent mines which went horizontally into the hills. The factory was haphazard in the extreme; the buildings, caked in white dust, were tropically hot in the furnace rooms, so that the conditions for the workmen were pretty torrid. We battled away to measure it all and set our survey on paper, producing the only record of the factory layout, its buildings and the entrances to the mines. During the war these mines were used as ammunition dumps for the RAF and a massive explosion did immense damage with considerable loss of life. After the war, I was told that our plan was the only record of the site and proved of great value in the rescue work.

The international situation worsened month by month. Hitler famously told Chamberlain, 'I have no more territorial claims in Europe.' Chamberlain returned from a meeting with Hitler in Munich, stepped from the plane waving his umbrella and said, 'Peace in our time.' How wrong he was. Hitler then turned his attention to Poland. First it was over access to Danzig (now Gdynia) which had once been part of Prussia. Having signed a mutual non-aggression pact with Stalin, he ordered German forces to invade Poland on 1 September 1939, whilst the Russians occupied, 'temporarily', the eastern half. Chamberlain issued final ultimatums to Hitler which were ignored and so, on the morning of Sunday 3 September, we were at war.

Although we had all been expecting it, the actual declaration confused us ordinary people: we did not know quite how we ought to react. At first I think we felt we should all stay at home and wait for something concrete to happen or to be told what to do and that some major changes to our life would quickly unfold. The first confirmation that things were different was the trial sounding of air-raid warnings followed some minutes later by the 'all-clear' sounding. Very quickly we realised there would be no immediate changes to the flow of our daily lives. On that fateful afternoon I announced to the family that I intended to go out to play tennis in order to show some sign of normality.

Indeed, we quickly resumed our normal routines: going to the office, playing tennis at the weekends and badminton some evenings.

There were some indications of change: Anderson Air Raid Shelters were made available, issued in packs containing sheets of corrugated iron. A hole had to be dug, so that about two-thirds of the sheets when fitted together were underground. Then earth was heaped over the curved corrugated roof and entrance steps made to the door at one end. Inside a wooden bench ran along one side and lighting was provided by electric torches or paraffin lamps. I never had to use the shelter and doubt if my family ever did; many people used them as a convenient tool store. The shelters were named after Sir John Anderson, the then home secretary. Gas masks were issued in cardboard boxes about 8in by 7in by 6in, with string to hang them round our shoulders; we were required to carry them at all times but we never, thankfully, needed to use them.

The main inconvenience for households was the order to black out all windows at night. Covers for windows were made of thick black material and put up at dusk each evening. Air raid wardens were appointed, part of whose duties was to patrol their area and see that there were no chinks of light showing. There were some air raids on industrial towns and cities; none of this remotely affected Barton-under-Needwood or Burton during these early days of the twilight war (as Churchill later called it). Cars were not allowed to use their headlights, which were fitted with light metal covers that had a horizontal hooded slit about one inch wide across the light. They made driving at night very difficult and slow.

In April 1939 the Conservative government had introduced conscription for twenty-year-olds, although it was opposed by both the Labour and the Liberal parties. Most of my contemporaries at school had volunteered for the Royal Air Force and gradually the remainder of us were called up for service; even so, the process of call-up was slow. I was one of those who awaited my call; I was twenty that September. In the meantime, life went on quite smoothly. We had a number of dances at Barton village hall to which many friends from Burton came. Now a number of them were in RAF uniform; often we would nip out to the pub nearby, the Bell. One of these was Geoff Hall, the only surviving school friend I met after the war. Most of my closest friends were killed. In November 1939 I was called to London to sit for my RIBA Intermediate Examination held at 66 Portland Place. I had previously submitted my testimonies of study, all of which had been approved. This was only my second visit to London, the earlier one being a school trip to see St Paul's Cathedral. On this occasion, I stayed at St John's Wood with Arthur and Muriel Page. Muriel was the sister of Zilpah our maid and a much nicer person. I confess I was rather apprehensive at being on my own in this huge metropolis. I had little difficulty with the various written papers, but became somewhat nervous when it came to the oral exams. I got into a mild argument with the examiner in structural design. The question had been to calculate the size of beams required to support a water tank. The diagram showed the tank eccentrically placed, so I took this into account; the examiner said this was not necessary – it was not a trick question. I insisted I was right and I must have convinced him as I passed.

The most interesting interview was with Prof. Allen of Leeds University. I arrived at his table just before lunch to be questioned on my paper on the history of architecture. One question had asked for a cross-section drawing of one of Wren's churches and I had chosen St Stephen Walbrook. He told me that only two students had chosen this example, one had got it right and the other wrong, but he could not remember which was which as he did not have our papers with him: they had been posted to London but had not yet arrived. He then handed me a piece of paper and a pencil and asked me to draw it again. After drawing just a few lines, he told me to stop, saying I was certainly the one who got it correct. We broke off for lunch and when we met again afterwards, the papers had turned up. He looked through them, asked a few questions and said, 'A very good paper indeed.' That really made my day! I had a snack at the Quality Inn, one of a chain of cafés whose great appeal to impecunious students was the free top-ups of coffee. Sometimes I would go for light meals to The Lyons Corner House, a chain which was also very popular and reasonably priced. The waitresses wore black and white uniforms with white lace caps. They were called 'nippies' because of the speed of their service. This led to a corny joke: 'Why did they put the central heating on in Lyons Corner House?' The answer: 'To prevent you feeling nippy!'

I returned home and in due course was informed that I had passed the examinations in all subjects. This was very pleasing as I had achieved the first half of my goal by the age of twenty, and had high hopes of being fully qualified as an architect by the age of twenty-one or twenty-two, but it was not to be.

Soon, rationing of food, clothing and other items was introduced. Everyone was issued with a ration book which had different weekly coupons for various foods such as butter, meat, eggs, sugar, sweets and chocolate, the shopkeeper detaching the coupon when you made a purchase. In time, as supplies became more difficult there was not enough food available for shops to honour the coupons. Some foods were not rationed such as vegetables or offal from the butcher. However, for me rationing had very little impact because, soon after it was introduced, I was in the army. It was not until after the war that I was really affected by rationing.

2

Into the Army

My call-up came in February 1940. I was ordered to report to a recruitment depot in Derby for enlistment. First there was a somewhat cursory medical examination; I duly coughed as required and was pronounced A1, fully fit for service. There were a number of other recruits there. Following the medical, we were all lined up to have a variety of vaccinations; I think the main ones were for TAB, typhoid and paratyphoid A and B, and tetanus. Because they were free, one or two men decided to go round twice and passed out!

After the medical, I was interviewed by an elderly colonel. He asked me which unit I would wish to join. I told him I was a half-qualified architect and had experience in land surveying, and therefore wished to join the Royal Engineers. Incredibly, he said he had never heard of surveyors or architects in the Royal Engineers, hummed and haa'd a bit and dismissed me. I went home to await my fate. I did not have to wait long – a week or so later I received orders to report to the Burton Road barracks in Lincoln to join the Royal Lincolnshire Regiment, an infantry regiment. So much for my request to join the Royal Engineers! My army soldier's service and pay book shows that I 'attested' at Lincoln on 15 February 1940.

The Lincolnshire Regiment was known as the Yellow Bellies and their regimental march was 'The Lincolnshire Poacher'. They were one of the few regiments permitted to wear a cap badge at the back as well as the front, an honour bestowed on them after the wars in the Sudan when they fought with the enemy behind them as well as in front.

My soldier's service and pay book.

On arrival, we were marched off to the quartermaster's store to be kitted out with battledress, boots, puttees, forage caps, shirts, underwear, socks, haversacks, kitbags, water bottles, billycans and 'housewives' (the army sewing kit). We were also issued with old Lee Enfield 303 rifles, together with a cleaning kit which included pieces of cloth known as a 'four by two' (its size in inches) and army gas masks. Our civilian clothes were parcelled up and sent back home. I was also issued with my army pay book, identity tags (these were duplicate fibre/plastic red-brown discs to be worn round the neck, one to be buried with you and the other to be returned to your next of kin). I was also allocated my service number: 4805024 Private Litherland. One never forgets one's army number. I had no reason to use it after the war, but can still recall it immediately.

Our quarters were in a large hangar-like building with a concrete floor. We had metal beds with mattresses made of three 'biscuits'; in the mornings, these had to be placed on top of each other at the head of the bed for inspection with the grey army blankets neatly folded on top. We had rough pillows but no sheets: not at all comfortable. The weather was very cold and there was no heating. I do not recall anything about the food but assume it was basic and sufficient.

Discipline was very strict – in my opinion stupidly so. The officers and NCOs (non-commissioned officers) were all regular soldiers who had recently returned from a tour in India. Before the war, the general opinion seemed to be that men only joined the army if they could not get a job anywhere else and so were widely considered to be a rather low class of person. I discovered that some of the recruits who joined in my batch were also, in my view, a rough lot. The regular NCOs were a bullying group, who clearly enjoyed shouting at and trying to belittle us. We could do nothing but accept, or be given extra duties; the worst of these was to clean the latrines. It was from these regular soldiers I first came across really crude and lewd language.

My greatest difficulty was with drill on the square. I found marching extremely difficult, as I just could not keep in step easily; perhaps I have no natural sense of rhythm. I, among others, got constant bollockings for this ineptitude. There was one man who was worse than me as he could only march with both arms swinging at the same time. However, when it came to weaponry I was interested and learned quickly, and was soon proficient in stripping down and re-assembling a Bren gun. I will always remember the instructor telling us to feel for the catch underneath, saying, 'If it had hairs on it you'd soon find it'. I was also quite good at shooting, except when we had to fire whilst wearing gas masks, as the mask did not fit properly over my spectacles and I could not see well enough to aim properly. Gas masks fitted over army spectacles, but none were available then. Army boots took some getting used to; they were very hard on the feet at first and we had to be careful not to get blisters. It was said that urine was very good for breaking them in and I recall one drunken soldier urinating in his boots rather than stagger to the latrine. We were also required to polish the boots to a high gloss. This was done by 'boning' them: we were issued a regulation 'bone', a piece of bone about five inches long and two wide, with which we rubbed the boots for hours until they were highly polished.

Apart from the drill sessions I began to enjoy my infantry training, even though the RSM (regimental sergeant major) often referred to me as 'Creeping Jesus'. On Sundays we had to parade through the town to church behind the gaily clad regimental band.

Despite settling down to infantry life, I was still annoyed with old Colonel 'Blimp' at Derby who had sent me to the infantry rather than the Royal Engineers. I still felt I would be of more use in the engineers. I decided to write to Col. John Gretton to explain my feelings. He replied, saying he agreed with me and sympathised with my situation. He said he would make enquiries on a general basis but felt he could not ask for intervention on an individual case, so he did not give me much hope. Time went on and I started to enjoy life at Lincoln. I put the matter out of my mind and resolved to do well in my infantry regiment.

One day we were out on the ranges when a messenger arrived in a truck asking for Private Litherland. He said, 'Are you the bloke who is being transferred to the Royal Engineers?' After just a moment's hesitation, I replied, 'Yes, that's me'. I jumped in the truck and we sped back to the barracks. I was told to tidy up and get ready to see the CO. I arrived at the regimental office only to get a bollocking from the RSM for having mud in the welts of my boots. I was then marched into the CO's office. 'Left right, left right, halt, salute, stand at ease, remove forage cap,' and all that bullshit.

I had not spoken to the CO before; I doubt whether I had really seen him. Officers were, to us, rather remote figures to be admired or feared from a safe distance. On this occasion he was, in fact, quite friendly. He told me he had received instructions from the War Office that I was to be transferred to the Royal Engineers with immediate effect. He explained that the attitude to soldiers was now very different from that in the First World War in that every effort was being made to place them in the branches of the Army where their skills would be used to the best effect, and because of my architectural qualification it was correct for me to go to the Royal Engineers. I merely replied that I understood, with my tongue in my cheek. Then he said, unexpectedly as I hardly knew him, how very sorry he was to lose me. He added that he had been monitoring my progress closely and indeed I was on his list of those to be recommended for a commission in the regiment. He wished me well and said he was sure that before long I would be selected for a commission in the Royal Engineers. He then dismissed me and told me to report to the orderly room to receive further instruction and details of the move. The orderly clerk informed me I was to leave the next day, to get my kit ready and report early in the morning for my various instructions and papers and be ready to depart.

The next morning I received a personal letter from Sir John Grigg, the Under Secretary of State for War, informing me that, having talked to Col. John Gretton, he had ordered my immediate transfer to the Establishment for Engineer Services of the Royal Engineers at the Southern Command office in Salisbury, Wiltshire. It came with a covering letter from John Gretton – good old Col. Gretton! So much for the army placing men where they were of best use to the war effort! It had taken a minister of the government to achieve the move.

I reported to the orderly office where I was issued with various documents, my pay book, the travel warrant, a regimental route and a subsistence allowance for the journey. Amazingly, the regimental route gave very precise details for my journey. I wondered who had worked it all out so quickly. It gave the time of the train I was to take from Lincoln to King's Cross in London, the underground route across London to Waterloo and the time of the train I was to catch from Waterloo to Salisbury. On arrival at Salisbury I was to report immediately to the Establishment for Royal Engineers, Southern Command, at their office on Fisherton Street in Salisbury. I have also wondered why such detailed instructions were given, which allowed no latitude for delayed trains. At the time they were often delayed by bomb damage to the tracks.

Next morning I was taken by truck to Lincoln station; I do not recall any fond farewells to my infantry colleagues as I had not made any lasting friends. I followed the timetable scrupulously; luckily none of the trains were delayed by air raids. On arrival at Salisbury, I asked for directions to Fisherton Street, fortunately less than half a mile away. I arrived at Salisbury just before 5.30 p.m. with all my kit, including my rifle. I am not certain of the exact date but it must have been mid- to late-April. I eventually found the right place in a small, requisitioned school. I knocked, but no one replied so I walked in complete with all my kit: pack, side-pack, kitbag and rifle.

I was most surprised to find the only two people in the office were middle-aged civilians. They told that me that they were civil servants, seconded to the army from the Ministry of Works. I handed over my papers which they scrutinised casually and at length announced they had been told to expect me, but not for another week or so, so no arrangements had been made for me. As they were just about to close the office for the day, would I please come back in the morning when they would sort things out? I asked them to direct me to the barracks where I could get a bed for the night only to be told there were no barracks and all soldiers working for the engineers were billeted with civilians and I would have to find a billet. This put me in a quandary. I explained that I had just arrived from Lincoln having travelled all day, had never been to Salisbury before, did not know anyone there, so how could I be expected to find accommodation? They were in a hurry to get off home and somewhat disgruntled at my sudden arrival at such an inconvenient time. However, they decided rather reluctantly that they must help and got in a huddle to discuss what to do. Eventually one said the only possibility was a Mrs Eades who lived on Devizes Road. They would take me to see if she would give me a room, at least for one night. They said she did billet some Royal Engineers from the office and might possibly have a vacancy. Luckily Mrs Eades did and straightaway made me very welcome. So began my few months' stay in Salisbury; a stay which was to have the most immense effect on the rest of my life.

The next morning I went off with the other couple of sappers billeted with Mrs Eades and reported to the same office at the school on Fisherton Street. I was told I would be working as an architectural draughtsman in the Establishment for Engineer Services (a branch of the Royal Engineers) drawing office, situated above a shop, further down Fisherton Street.

I was taken there and handed over to the chief draughtsman, a Mr Green, a civil servant from the Ministry of Works. He was an elderly man who must have been near retirement; he was kindly, but very old-fashioned. In his architectural design work he was very outdated and met with little success when he tried to steer the young army personnel into the same mould. He told me that he had a son who was a regular soldier and a warrant officer in the Royal Engineers and so was well disposed to us and in his way tried to be a father figure. I was put into a large room overlooking Fisherton Street. There was a drawing desk running the whole length of the street-side wall with windows overlooking the street and places for four draughtsmen. Of the four who occupied them, three were army and one a civil servant. There were a few other rooms in the offices which were allocated to other draughtsmen, mostly soldiers, but there were also three or four civilians. There was a separate 'den' for Mr Green.

Amongst my fellow architects/draughtsmen that I remember well were Reg Pianca whose family was connected with The Café Royal in London; Tom Ellis, also a Londoner and already fully qualified; and Harry Foyster, also qualified, not in the RIBA but some other architectural society not recognised by us as the real thing. These three will feature later in the story. There were also one or two student surveyors.

When I arrived at the office, I was informed that the lowest rank for an architectural draughtsman was lance corporal, so I was automatically promoted and put up my single stripe: it turned out to be my only promotion during the whole of my service.

The summer of 1940 was quite good; we got lots of warm sun through the office window. One of my army colleagues suffered from hot feet, so he would remove his boots and socks, get two buckets of water and sit at his desk with one foot in each bucket. The civilian in the room was the first civil servant with whom I had worked. He was engaged in preparing a working plan for a building – it seemed to be half-finished when I arrived. He did not appear to make much progress and it was nowhere near completion when I left Salisbury some four months later. He showed no interest at all in the war effort, only in his own retirement. This coloured my impression at the time of the Civil Service as a lazy lot. Although some certainly did the minimum of work, I later came across many dedicated, hard-working civil servants.

Soon after I arrived, we were asked individually to prepare plans for a new ATS (Auxiliary Territorial Service) headquarters, setting up a sort of mini-competition. The scheme I submitted was for a modern building with the whole emphasis on a layout which was simple and functional, with the disposition of offices in the correct sequence for medical routine and the service rooms – bathrooms, toilets, kitchens, etc. – grouped together for ease of water supply and drainage. Old Mr Green produced his own scheme, based on the idea that you first designed the elevations of the building and thereafter devised the internal arrangement to fit in them. The result was, to me, a complete hotch-potch of a plan with rooms fitted into a fixed shell – quite awful, and it would be far more expensive to build than any of the other designs. But he was head of the office and only put forward his own design. We all felt it would just be a waste of valuable scarce materials and would be functionally unsatisfactory.

Sometime during that summer, the Southern Command took over Wilton House, at Wilton just outside Salisbury – the home of the Pembroke family and a major historical building. There were no floor plans of the house, so the office was told to make a survey and prepare floor plans of the whole house, so that the rooms could be allocated their new military functions. A team of four was selected by Mr Green: himself, another civilian and two soldiers: Harry Foyster and myself.

When we arrived we were greeted by the Countess of Pembroke who said we were free to go anywhere we liked in the house to carry out the survey. Mr Green decided that Harry and I should start on the ground floor whilst he and his companion would measure the first floor. This was the first time I had been in a stately home, and I found it quite magnificent. What struck us most was the immense thickness of some of the walls; up to six feet thick, some with two sets of doors, often double doors, one on each side of the wall. There were even doorways within the thickness of these walls – one thought of them leading to secret passages for fugitives and assignations. Harry and I set about our task with great enthusiasm; it was so good to be working in such delightful, classical and sumptuous sur-roundings. We worked hard and by the time we had completed measuring up the ground floor found that the civilians had nowhere near finished the first floor (maybe they spent some time trying the beds) so we were asked to survey the second floor, which we completed to find that they still had not finished, so we carried on by surveying the cellars.

In due course, all the field work – as it was called – was completed, and we took all our survey sheets back to the office and set about pre-paring the plans of the building. We had done our work thoroughly and accurately; the test was whether the ground, second and cellar floor plans fitted over each other, which they did exactly. But Mr Green's plan of the first floor did not fit with ours: there were large discrepancies. We were immediately accused of being inexperienced and inaccurate surveyors which, they said, was only to be expected from young soldiers barely out of their teens. He then condescended to allow us to examine his plan. To our amazement, we found they had drawn all the rooms quite accurately but had not bothered to measure the thickness of the walls, assuming that they were, as was the twentieth-century norm, all eleven inches thick with plaster. Considering that the walls varied from two feet to six feet thick it was no wonder their plan did not fit with ours. We pointed out their errors with great satisfaction and received a grudging apology.

Away from the office, my outside life centred on my digs, that haven with Mrs Eades. There were then four of us billeted with her including Harry Foyster and Jack Cheetham. Mrs Eades was a widow with three sons, the eldest of whom joined the RAF and was later killed in action. She fed us quite adequately, even though many of the evening meals consisted of sandwiches and/or soups. I cannot really remember, but assume we handed over our ration cards to her. The semi-detached house was comfortable and we shared rooms.

Mrs Eades worked in a shoe shop in town and so knew a number of young shop assistants, some of whom she would invite round to meet her soldiers. Harry, although he was married, soon made a liaison with one and would frequently go off to meet her, always armed with his ground sheet. I must say I disapproved but said nothing. Then one evening another girl appeared at the house, a most attractive young lady about two years younger than me. Her name I soon learned was Stella Sparks and there was fierce competition for her company. I was told she had been very friendly with one of the previous soldiers billeted with Mrs Eades, Ian McCulloch – also an architect. He had been with the BEF (British Expeditionary Force) in France, and had been safely evacuated from Dunkirk. Luckily for me, he had disappeared from Stella Sparks's life and been posted elsewhere. After the war he became one of the senior planners for the rebuilding of Basingstoke.

Another who was already quite friendly with her was Jack Cheetham, a year or two older than me and unbeknown to her, also married. Slowly and perhaps shyly, I showed my interest in her. My patience was rewarded when she finally consented to go out with me.

We often went to the Odeon cinema where we saw *The Wizard of Oz* for the first of many times, and a film with Nelson Eddy and Jeanette MacDonald in which they sang 'The Donkey Serenade'. We had a favourite tune: 'The Woody Woodpecker Song'. The Cadena Restaurant, just opposite the Salisbury marketplace, was a favourite place for tea and cakes. We went for long walks to Harnham and across the water meadows or to Old Sarum, the site of ancient Salisbury. When the weather was fine, we used to take a boat out on the River Avon and row up river and anchor in a quiet spot under the willows. There I would present her with a box of Fortune chocolates.

One day I bought her a string of pearls from one of the jewellers. I kept it in my pocket waiting for a suitable opportunity to present it. I remember rather surreptitiously passing it to her in the darkness of the back row of the cinema. After these outings I would walk her home along the river by the County Hotel, along St Ann Street, St Martin's Street and into St Martin's Terrace where she lived at No. 2. I never got beyond the gate and did not meet any of the family until after the war.

One incident sticks in my memory. Stella and I were walking arm in arm along a street in Salisbury; I think I was escorting her home. There was a sudden shout from a young officer across the other side of the road, a second lieutenant, who said, 'Why have not you saluted me? You are aware you must always salute officers.' He gave me a bollocking in front of Stella. It was most embarrassing for her and humiliating for me and, to my mind, quite uncalled for. What a little prig he was! Unfortunately there were a few like that, just throwing their newly acquired rank around.

When I left Salisbury to go on draft overseas we continued to correspond and did so throughout the long years of the war; her letters were a tremendous support to me, especially during the long years as a POW (prisoner of war). She wrote more frequently than my family and I still have some of the letters she wrote to me to then, and some of mine to her from Chatham, during the Blitz and from Naumburg–Saale after our escape to areas under American control in May 1945.

3

Off to War

During my few months in Salisbury, the phony war came to an end and the real one began. It was called phony because the war had yet to affect much of Western Europe. There had been air raids but no activity on land. It certainly had not been phony for the poor Poles and others in Eastern Europe, who had suffered terribly at the hands of both the Germans and the Russians.

Then on 10 May 1940 the German armies invaded Belgium, swept through and into France round the western end of the 'invincible' Maginot Line. The Maginot Line was the main defensive line between France and Germany but unfortunately had not been extended to the coast because of disagreements between the Belgian and French governments. The German panzer divisions just went round the end of it, whilst the bulk of the French army was underground manning its useless defences.

The BEF became cut off in north-east France and as many as possible were evacuated from the beaches at Dunkirk, that supremely heroic action by ships and boats of all descriptions which brought back the bulk of our soldiers. Many ordinary people manned their little boats and sailed across the Channel to help bring back our boys and there were innumerable instances of outstanding bravery. This miraculous evacuation was completed by 2 June 1940. When the forces came back they were given a short leave and then sent back to barracks to be retrained and re-equipped. Incredibly, most of them soon recovered from the trauma and just got on with the war.

For us stationed in Salisbury, life went on as usual as we had not been involved in the catastrophe. We came across a few of the returning soldiers as they made their way back to their units or went on leave, but it seemed a distant event to us. I think the general feeling of the soldiers in England was that more of us should have been sent over to France to help. The success of the German Blitzkrieg now meant that the whole of Western Europe, apart from Britain, Ireland, Spain, Portugal, Switzerland, Norway and Sweden, was occupied by the Nazi armies. There were immediate fears that Hitler would invade England, especially as air raids increased in frequency, with warnings every day and night leading up to the Blitz and the Battle of Britain. All efforts were now directed to the defence of the eastern and southern coasts of Great Britain.

Towards the end of July several of us were transferred to Chatham on the north Kentish coast to await posting overseas. There we were accommodated in some Royal Engineer barracks, called Kitchener barracks. By the design and condition of them they must have been in existence since the Crimean War or even the Napoleonic period. These were certainly the worst I came across in England; in fact I had better conditions in some POW camps in Germany. Our barrack room was on the first floor, approached by the most dismal staircase, at the half-landings of which were the filthy toilets and ablutions. Quite a change from the comfort of Mrs Eade's house! I do not think the barrack room had been decorated for decades; it was cold and miserable even in mid-summer.

We were put on standby to go to Norway as the Germans were expected to invade Norway at any time. This fell through because of the disaster at Narvik, which was followed by the German occupation of that country. We were stood down and had no idea where we would be sent.

Early September saw the height of the Blitz on London and its surrounding areas. Every night there were massive air raids by the German Luftwaffe. It was tremendously noisy with the explosion of bombs and anti-aircraft fire. There were fires all around, mostly caused by the showers of incendiary bombs dropped by the German planes. I can vividly remember the great fires raging day and night when the oil storage tanks at Thameshaven were hit and set alight. Luckily our barrack block was not hit by any bombs, although we had to extinguish some incendiary bombs which fell on the roof. There was plenty of devastation all around. I quote from a letter I wrote to Stella around 4 September:

About 2.00 am of Tuesday morning we were awoken by a terrific amount of anti-aircraft gunfire and machine gunning, we went down stairs, returning when it died down. We had not been in bed 10 minutes when it started again; this time we saw the German bombers picked out by the searchlight beams. Actually we went down three or four times during this period. It was rather terrifying at first with shrapnel dropping all around and yet no warning sounded … We had five warnings here yesterday and there was lots of gunfire, we saw two or three planes hit, and saw one pilot come down by parachute.

I also recorded seeing a Messerschmitt, the German fighter plane, on display in Chatham. At one stage I had a twenty-four-hour pass, went up to London and stayed the night with Muriel and Arthur Page in Abbey Road, St John's Wood, during which the Baptist priest with whom they lived put on a film show. On another occasion, Tom Ellis, Reg Pianca and I went out one evening for dinner at The Café Royal.

As we awaited our posting, life became rather boring. Occasionally drill sessions were organised on the parade square which I hated. During one of these drill exercises, I came over very faint, felt really ill and knew I would pass out if I carried on, so I dropped out and went to sit on a seat at the side of the parade ground. This was against regulations, although it seemed entirely sensible to me – but no, I was instructed that I was expected to continue marching around until I actually collapsed: how stupid! I was given a tremendous bollocking from the NCO in charge.

Apart from these occasional parades there was very little to do. Sometimes we were put on fatigues in the barracks. We, that is, the Establishment for Engineer Services men, decided we ought to get out of barracks and go into town to a café, cinema or just to walk around, so we decided to form a false working party. We formed up outside our barrack block, with one corporal in charge, then marched to the quartermaster's store and drew out some picks and shovels. We re-formed, about eight of us, marched to the gates, reported to the guard that we were a working party going into Gillingham to clear up bomb damage. There was never any problem with the guard; no one would ever question men going off to work! So off we went into Gillingham, to a local café for tea and cakes. We were still lumbered with the picks and shovels, but had no difficulty in persuading the friendly café owner to store our tools in the back of the café, to be collected later. Then having agreed a time to meet up again, we went off on our various jaunts. Generally we would go to the cinema or wander around the town. I do not recall ever trying to make liaisons with the local girls. At the agreed time we met up at the café, formed up again and marched back to camp as if our day's work was completed. The ruse never failed; we were cheerfully greeted by the sentries on duty, returned our tools to the store; our little (non) working party became a daily feature of the barrack routine.

Off to Egypt

Towards the end of August 1940, we were at last informed we would shortly be going overseas and were sent on embarkation leave for a few days. I was issued with my railway warrant to Burton-on-Trent and off I went to Barton-under-Needwood, to Berry Brow, to take leave of my mother, sister Ruth, sister Betty and her baby Michael, Dick and his family, Grandfather Litherland, and Aunts Olive and Pat. This was the last time I was to see my grandfather. He had rejected me as a baby because he said my parents already had too many children: I was number five. Later he became very fond of me, especially when I designed a brick sundial for him which he then built himself and very much enjoyed. When I became a POW, I was told that he had expressed a wish to live to see me again. Sadly he died a few months before my return.

On our return, we were kitted out with tropical clothes and topees, so it seemed likely we would be going to the Middle East or possibly, but less likely, India. We were ordered not to divulge any information about our movements to anyone. This was quite easy as we did not have any. In due course we were entrained and set off with our topees strapped to our packs, a clue to any observers that we were going somewhere warm. As the train journey progressed, it became clear we were going north-west, especially when we passed through Burton-on-Trent and then Barton station. I saw grandfather's bungalow at Branston from the train and waved goodbye as we passed by.

In due course we arrived at Liverpool docks and embarked immediately on HMT *Britannic*. My embarkation card – see opposite – says I was on deck C, cabin 5 and berth 3 (of four), that I messed in the third salon at the first sitting. At the bottom of the card it says, 'IMPORTANT – it is essential you RETAIN THIS CARD': I guess I have complied.

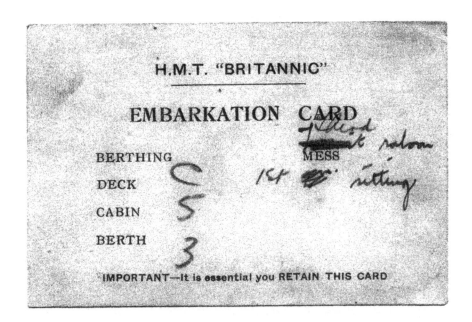

The *Britannic* had only just been requisitioned as a troopship and still had many of her civilian crew, including stewards, and a large quantity of food left over from her last cruise. In 2000 I showed the card to our friend Philip Cratchley. He said, 'She sailed from Liverpool on 12 September 1940.' 'How do you know?' I asked. He replied, 'I was on board.' Another of life's coincidences: he had also been in the Royal Engineers and was later taken prisoner in Greece.

Four of our group – myself, Tom Ellis, Reg Pianca and Harry Foyster – were allocated a cabin complete with four bunks, very lucky because most of the troops had to put up in the lounges. The stewards on board naturally only served the officers, but we became friendly with some of them and so were able to augment our meals with ice-cream, roast chicken and other delicacies.

Our small group of Royal Engineers were part of what was known as the Establishment for Engineer Services. We found out that there was an Army Command instruction to the effect that Engineer Services personnel were to be kept for twenty-four hours of the day exclusively for engineering services and were completely exempt from all regimental duties. This was most important and useful information; we all committed the number of the instruction and its contents to heart. I feel sure it was Tom Ellis who dug out this information; he was always on the ball when there was some advantage to be had.

Our cabin gave us a considerable amount of privacy. As soon as we had settled in, a muster was called on deck by the CO on the ship and his RSM. The CO welcomed us on board then handed over to the RSM. He immediately set about organising duties and detailing people to carry them out. These included fire pickets, guard duties and various fatigues. It was at this stage we produced our Army Command instruction, although it was probably not designed for this kind of situation, and declined to undertake any of the regimental duties. The RSM was quite disbelieving until he actually saw a copy of the instruction, which Tom Ellis produced, even then consulting with the CO before having to accept it as authentic. In the end he took it well and asked if we would please help him to run the ship by volunteering to do other duties. We agreed. I was asked to regulate the queues which formed outside the NAAFI before it opened.

We soon sailed from Liverpool and it was then that we were informed we were bound for Egypt. Although there was no way of telling by looking at the sea which way we were going, the sun's position, when it appeared, indicated we were travelling north-west. Our route took us all round the north coast of Ireland and into the mid-Atlantic, where we eventually changed course southwards. For me and many others who had not been to sea before, all we saw was a lot of water and waves. The whole journey was relatively calm, so there was very little seasickness amongst the troops. There were a number of other non-naval ships in our convoy but we had no idea what ships they were, what they carried or where they were going. We had an escort of naval ships, no doubt cruisers and destroyers. I have to admit I knew very little about the ships of the Royal Navy. Our escort moved about amongst the ships they were protecting.

Every day we had boat drill for which we assembled on deck at our allotted stations and donned our life jackets. The life jackets were made of four blocks of cork, each side sewn into a rough canvas cover and tied at the sides with tapes: there were then no top-up valves, no whistles and no water-activated lights. The alarm was sounded before boat drill. One day I just happened to be resting on my bunk and did not hear the alarm sound. I was roused out of my doze and ordered onto deck by someone doing the rounds, just before the all-clear sounded. It turned out that it had been a real alarm. We were told that there had been a U-boat attack on the convoy.

I then realised that it was the thud of depth charges detonating which had eventually woken me. There was no sign of any damage to any ships within our sight. As far as I know there were no further attacks on our convoy.

The weather soon began to warm up and some days later the convoy anchored off Freetown in Sierra Leone. We were not allowed to go ashore, but had our first sight of tropical Africa with rows of palm trees along the distant shore. There was some contact with the local people who came out in canoes to sell fruit and souvenirs. This was also an opportunity to send letters home, headed 'at sea'. I duplicated mine in case of loss; just one of them has survived, written to Stella's mother. The *Britannic* took on water and provisions, and we sailed on southwards. Soon afterwards was the 20 September, my twenty-first birthday. There were several who also had their twenty-first birthdays around the same time. Our friendly stewards provided us with roast chicken, ice-cream and some wine. To celebrate we had a sing-song around the piano in one of the lounges, with beer flowing freely. I did not drink beer but I enjoyed the wine. We all made the best of it and had a jolly time. Sadly there were no cards or greetings from our families as no one knew our whereabouts. By the end of the war our coming of age had long been forgotten.

The voyage was pleasant and leisurely. We had great fun and games at the ceremony of 'crossing the line'. All we saw were the other ships in the convoy, lots of sea and the occasional flying fish. I do not recall seeing any dolphins, whales or other large fish.

The most memorable event of the whole voyage was the visit to Cape Town. We docked there for about three days to take on supplies. After all the port formalities had been completed we were issued with shore passes. The weather was quite perfect and there were glorious views of Table Mountain. We had no idea what to do or where to go once on shore. We need not have worried because there were a large number of people lining the quay to welcome us and entertain us: it really was a marvellous surprise. I went down the gangway with Reg Pianca and almost before we stepped off, a couple came up to us and said they would be delighted to entertain us. They introduced themselves as Morna and Tom Frew. Only the few who wished to go off alone were left to their own devices. Amongst my souvenirs is a card frosm the Methodist Church of the Cape Peninsula inviting us to the Metropolitan Methodist Hall saying, 'We really mean it when we say "Welcome".'

The Frews were very kind and hospitable. First they took us on a tour of Cape Town then to the Kirstenbosch Botanical Gardens where the marvellous display of plants was largely unknown to us. Mrs Frew took a few photographs, we were able to give her our BFPO address and in due course she sent them on to us. I still have one or two of them, complete with the POW *Geprüft* (examined) stamps on the back, wonderful mementos of our happy visit to Cape Town. They also took us for a stupendous meal at the Café Royal and did not allow us to pay for anything: what marvellous people!

I saw no evidence of opposition to the war, but was given to understand that some sections of the Boer community were against it and some even pro-German. Tom Frew, who was a journalist, told us of a recent visit to Cape Town by a troopship of Australian soldiers on their way to the UK. It seemed odd to me that they were going in the opposite direction to us, running the risk of U-boat attacks in the Atlantic, when they could have gone straight to the Middle East and we could have stayed in England. It seemed illogical, almost as if the right hand of those organising the movement of troops did not know what the left hand was doing. Tom told us that the Aussies caused mayhem in Cape Town with their boisterous and drunken behaviour. Some of them even commandeered a fire engine, careered down the streets in the centre of town smashing into shops, other vehicles and anything which got in their way. Yet, amazingly, the effect

Methodist Church of the Cape Peninsula

SOLDIERS and SAILORS

We extend a very hearty welcome to the Metropolitan Methodist Hall, at the corner of Burg and Church Streets, near the centre of the town.

Refreshments, Writing Materials, Magazines, etc. will be provided.

We really mean it when we say " Welcome."

Just jump into a car marked " Metropolitan Hall."

Mrs Frew, Reg Pianca and me at Kirstenbosch.

on the local population, especially young men, was the opposite to what might have been expected. Their visit resulted in a massive increase of volunteers from Cape Town to join the South African Forces and take part in the war!

Having enjoyed an occasion of a lifetime, we sadly said goodbye to Cape Town and the Frews, re-boarded the *Britannic* and sailed off around Africa. I had the idea we would hug the coast and perhaps see Durban and other places, but we did not see anything. There was another celebration and jollification when we re-crossed 'the line' going north. The troops organised various entertainments including a concert on the promenade deck. The weather once again became much hotter; this must have been when we approached the Red Sea. We were now into mid-October.

One day we suddenly had an air-raid alarm. We all went up to our boat stations, looked up and, almost invisible as they were so high, were four or five Italian planes. They dropped some bombs from their great height which all hit the sea a considerable distance from the convoy, then flew off and we saw no more of the Italian Air Force.

Sometime in the latter half of October we finally reached our destination. It was only when we docked that we were informed that we were in Port Suez in Egypt at the southern end of the Suez Canal. We arrived in the early evening and it was just getting dark as we disembarked, loaded with all our kit and wearing our topees for the first time. We were immediately marched to the railway station where a train was waiting to take us away into Egypt.

The whole atmosphere was alien; the sky absolutely clear, full of brightly twinkling stars and there was an eerie feeling and sand everywhere. At the side of the road palm trees wafted in the breeze, and there were ghosts all around us: local people clad from head to foot in flowing white robes and headgear, with myriads of flies buzzing around. But the main unforgettable impression was the smell of Egypt; an entirely new and unexpected experience, made up, I suppose, of the odour of camels, donkeys and goats – and their droppings – and of the people. There were occasional wafts of perfume from scented shrubs, a really heady amalgam, difficult to describe but never forgotten.

Having reached the station we were immediately entrained amidst the usual chaos of getting our kit into a carriage, finding a seat and space for our kit in the overhead racks. All this went on whilst hordes of local Arab vendors were trying to sell trinkets, souvenirs, fruit and the ubiquitous 'eggs and bread'. Eggs and bread, we soon learned, appeared to be the universal snack to sell to the troops. In due course the train got up steam and off we went. Some vendors continued to cling to the doors before eventually dropping off as the train gathered speed. We travelled overnight across the flat sandy desert; not that we saw much of it, just sensed it. In the morning the train steamed into Cairo; we scrambled off the train and, without ado, were formed up and marched away to the Kasr-el-Nil Barracks. I have only a rather faint recollection of the barracks as a huge red brick complex of several storeys, dull, dark and forbidding amidst the brightness of the sky and the heat of the day. We settled in, were told this was only temporary and shortly we would be posted elsewhere.

The Kasr-el-Nil Barracks from the air, *c.* 1938.

We were allowed to go out into Cairo and were warned of the preva-
lence of pickpockets and thieves, and told always to bargain before buying
anything. One day several of us took a horse-drawn gharry and set out to
visit the Citadel and the Dead City of old Cairo. We were told that many
years ago the whole of the old city was stricken by the plague that had
killed most its inhabitants. A decision was made to abandon the whole city
and develop a new one some miles away to the north. The Dead City, as
we saw it, had no residents, only the abandoned shells of buildings and
their internal gardens, which were still cleaned and tended. There seemed
no rationale to this, unless it was for visitor attraction. We found the place
creepy and eerie. We also had the opportunity to see the Great Mosque
and to do some shopping in the street markets. I bought a few things for
souvenirs and presents to take home in Cairo and later in Ismailia. These
included a copy of the New Testament with olivewood covers, the wood
said to be from the Mount of Olives; a silver filigree butterfly brooch and
an Alexandrite tie pin: Stella still has these. I also bought a fob watch with
a black case and black braided cord with the intention of giving it to Stella.
This I kept for a few years until I was persuaded to sell it in POW camp to
another prisoner at a good profit.

After several days absorbing the atmosphere of Cairo and Egypt, our postings came through. I had not really liked Cairo: it was too big, complicated and congested with unfamiliar people. I was posted to the CRE (Commander of Royal Engineers) at Moascar Barracks near Ismailia on the Suez Canal. I do not recall the name of the CRE, a lieutenant colonel, but he was very reasonable and I got on well with him. Moascar Garrison was situated on a level desert site not far outside Ismailia, one of the main towns along the Suez Canal. The Moascar Barracks were spacious and well planned; there had been some attempt at planting trees and growing grass to relieve the monotony of the universal sand. There was a pleasant, stone-built Anglican church which I attended regularly. We were all expected to attend but there was no church parade.

It was a great relief to have no regimental duties. I considered we achieved a considerable amount of useful work for the army without them. There was a large NAAFI with restaurant in the camp called the Allenby Institute. I had lots of light meals there, usually fried eggs on toast or baked beans on toast. It was surprising how very small the eggs were, as if the chickens were underfed. Our barrack block was quite large with, probably,

Drawing office at Moascar with Don Luckett, February 1941.

some twenty beds, ten along each side; the ceiling must have been about 14 or 15 feet high with large ceiling fans that rotated quite slowly, moving the air around rather than cooling it; not particularly efficient, but better than nothing. The office working hours were unusual for us British, from 7 a.m. to 12 noon and then 5 p.m. until 8 p.m., so there was a long siesta after lunch. The rule during siesta was 'in bed or out of barracks'; this was to ensure that those wishing to rest or sleep had quietness and were not disturbed by the others who wished to be active.

In the office there was a considerable workload: lots of drawings and designs to prepare for a great variety of projects. These were mostly for the new army bases being built on the Great Bitter Lake to the south of Ismailia. One particular small project I remember was to prepare a plan for a special kitchen and store for the Sikh soldiers which had to meet their religious ritual requirements. This entailed discussions with them, my first close encounter with non-white people. I found I had no problem getting on well with them; they approved my design and I hope it served them well. In the not quite three months I was there, I made drawings for over two hundred separate projects. I kept a notebook recording them, but destroyed it when I was captured on Crete, in case it gave information to the Germans, though I doubt it would have been of any real value to them.

My most important project, which I clearly remember, was a design for a field hospital to be erected at the new camps at the Great Bitter Lake. I had been supplied with a plan of the standard field hospital and asked to prepare just the location plan for the proposed building. Looking at the set of plans, I decided the design was so awful as there was no logical sequence of rooms for the hospital procedures or needs. I went to the CRE and explained my views, telling him how I thought it could be improved and made much more efficient and workable. He listened to my ideas and agreed with me, suggesting that I prepare an alternative design for these hospitals. I willingly and enthusiastically did so; the colonel liked it and approved the layout. He then told me to prepare the working drawings so that he could send them to the engineer-in-chief in Cairo for approval. So I got down to work and prepared a complete set of working drawings, which were duly signed as designed by LCpl S. Litherland and approved by the CRE. The colonel sent them off to Cairo for approval by 'head office'. Some weeks later our office received a set of plans of the new standard field hospital to be used for all future hospitals: they were my plans in every detail, but redrawn and signed as being designed by someone in Cairo. I was livid! I felt they should have had the decency and courtesy to acknowledge my work. How naïve I was in those days!

There was a considerable amount of construction work going on for the army in Moascar and out at the Bitter Lakes where new training camps were required. This required very large amounts of materials, especially bricks. The purchase of these was in the hands of the army clerks of works. It was widely rumoured that contracts for the supply of materials depended on large hidden payments to the clerks of works. I have no actual proof of this, but am absolutely certain it went on, reflected in the lifestyles of some senior NCOs employed as clerks of works. The camp cinema at Moascar was run by two men named Shafto and Jamil, widely rumoured to have been ex-quartermasters from the First World War who made enough money to set up a chain of cinemas for the army all over the Middle East.

What worried me quite a lot was the lackadaisical attitude of many of the office staff, more especially the junior ranks. They did not give a damn whether they did any work or not. My attitude was in the minority: to do as much as possible, quickly and efficiently, in order to help the war effort. I enjoyed my time at Moascar; the work was very interesting and there was plenty of sport and a reasonable social life.

One part of the social life in which I had no interest whatsoever was visiting the local brothels. Quite a number of the men did and related many lurid details and accounts of sex shows they had seen. In fact, the Royal Engineers had the task of examining the brothel buildings on behalf of the medical corps, before they were given approval for use by the soldiers. I did not take part in any of these inspections; they were probably in the hands of the WOs and sergeants. I do remember the men singing a ditty which went:

I am Bedalia from Ismailia the fan dance girl,
You'll always find me willing,
Five piastres to the shilling.

I suppose it was at this time that I came across many of the old army bawdy songs such as: 'A Troopship was leaving Bombay', 'The Quartermaster's Store', 'I'll tell you Bible Stories you've never heard before', 'Eskimo Nell', and 'As she wound up her little ball of wool'. There was also a topical one in Egypt which started, 'Here's to you King Farouk, hang your bollocks on a hook'.

Quite a lot of sport was played at the garrison including football, rugby, hockey and tennis. All the pitches were hard, compacted clayey-sand, a very good surface for fast hockey, good for football but very hard for rugby. I did not see any grass pitches at all. I mostly played hockey. We held inter-unit games, some of which were against Indian teams. The 4th Indian Division was then stationed at Moascar. The Indians, in particular the Sikhs, were excellent hockey players and we rarely, if ever, beat them. They were always agreeable to umpire matches for us when we could not find our own umpires; they were splendid men. I remember well an officer who played hockey at Moascar: Freddie Brown, who played for the Royal Army Service Corps and who, after the war, captained the Marylebone Cricket Club. In fact I came across him again on Crete at Suda Bay where he was supervising the unloading of a supply ship.

There was a New Zealand division in the garrison and quite understandably they played a lot of rugby. The Maoris amongst them played barefoot; they even place-kicked barefoot. The abrasive sand caused a great deal of painful grazes whenever someone was tackled, but in spite of this I did play some rugby.

I decided to try and learn Arabic so I bought Hugo's *Teach Yourself Arabic* and made some progress in learning to count; I almost mastered the Arabic script which, with some application, proved easier than I had expected. Unfortunately I did not stay long enough in Egypt to become proficient. Naturally everyone picked up some phrases in the language which were in everyday use amongst the soldiers, much of which was rather rude and lewd.

We were advised to be very careful not to have things stolen by the locals who worked in the garrison. Stories abounded: for instance, an Arab could steal a revolver from under your pillow whilst you slept by breathing gently on your cheek which made you automatically turn over. As I was not issued with a revolver, I was not worried about this. It would have been rather uncomfortable to sleep with a rifle under the pillow. Our rifles were chained and locked up in the barrack room. From time to time we had to oil and clean them, but by and large they were forgotten. I cannot say I came across much pilfering by the local Arabs, in spite of all the stories to the contrary.

Mohamed.

The dining room and cookhouse were in hutted buildings and separated by an open 'courtyard'. We had to collect our food in the cookhouse then walk with our dixies, in the open, across to the dining room some 60 feet away (another example of incompetent army planning). There were always a number of birds hovering over, kites or hawks, known to the troops as 'shite 'awks'. Sometimes one swooped down and took a sausage from a man's plate or dixie.

I remember very little about the food except the fried eggs which were always very greasy and the grease congealed; it was quite cold early in the morning so food soon cooled. The bacon also was greasy and fatty, and came out of tins. We also had a brand of tinned stews called MacConachies. It was said that some of the tins were left over from the First World War. We had plenty of fresh fruit, especially oranges and fresh ripe dates. I liked these greenish dates which were so succulent and entirely different from the preserved ones we get in England.

Our laundry was done by the local dhobi. We wore khaki shirts and knee-length baggy shorts. The laundering was quite good with plenty of starch applied before ironing. The method of applying starch was interesting: the dhobi-wallah would take a mouthful of starch and blow it from his mouth in a very fine spray over the shirts or shorts as he ironed them. It must have taken a great deal of practice to achieve such a fine spray. The ironing was done with flat irons heated on braziers, the handle of which had to be held with a cloth as there was no insulation. The dhobi-wallah had to wipe the bottom of the iron first to remove any dirt from the brazier, then test the heat on a sample piece of cloth to ensure the clothes would not be scorched. This was not completely strange to me because all ironing at home was still done with flat irons heated on the top of the cooking range. Electric irons did not come into general use until after the war.

The office had a local messenger, Mohamed, who was a pleasant, helpful man; amongst other things, he took me to a shoemaker. Although, in general, only officers were permitted to wear shoes when in uniform, the CRE allowed us to wear shoes in the office and when out in town. So I went with Mohamed to the shoemaker who produced an old piece of brown paper and asked me to stand on it wearing just my socks. He then drew round my feet to make the pattern for my shoes which were ready in a couple of days; they were brown leather and amongst the most comfortable I have ever had.

Drawing office staff, November 1940: L/Cpls Luckett, Deadman, Litherland, Dvr Shaw, L/Cpls Foyster and Sampson.

Fred Waite, Dougie Davis and John Little, Moascar, December 1940.

I have the names of some of my fellow sappers from those days because I still have a number of rather faded photographs of them. Among them were Lance Corporals Don Luckett, Hartop, Harry Foyster, Deadman, Fred Rodriguez, John Little, Bernard Sampson, Fred Waite, Dougie Davies and Driver Shaw, a very amusing cockney lad. I became friendly with one of the warrant officers, Fred Bray, an architect from Cornwall. As a qualified architect he automatically was given the non-commissioned rank of warrant officer. Later on – too late – I found out that with my RIBA Intermediate I was entitled to be a warrant officer class 2, but when I enquired I was told that the rule only applied to regular soldiers. An example of discrimination against wartime soldiers! Socially I was unable to mix very much with Fred Bray because senior NCOs had their own quarters and mess. Fred was soon offered a place at the Royal Engineers' section of the Middle East OCTU (Officer Cadet Training Unit), but he declined. He reasoned that he was better off and of more value as a warrant officer architect in the Establishment for Engineer Services than as an officer with a field regiment. I met Fred, briefly, after the war in a camp at Doncaster; he had spent most of the war in Cairo and was still a warrant officer.

Another Fred – Fred Rodriguez – was French, or half-French; I have no idea how he came to be in the British army. He was a staunch Roman Catholic. On Christmas Eve 1940 he told me he would like to attend Midnight Mass at the Roman Catholic Cathedral in Ismailia. As he did not want to go alone, he asked me if I would be willing to accompany him and I agreed. I knew very little about Roman Catholics, or 'left footers' as they were known in the army. Thinking about this, I realise that coming from Barton-under-Needwood I had only known the Church of England and the Methodist Chapel, the latter considered rather lower class. The only Catholics I had ever met were boys at Cotton College in North Staffordshire, not far from Alton Towers, against whom we played cricket and rugby. At that time I had not met any Jews or Muslims either. Because of this, I had little knowledge or perception or prejudice against other religions and religious differences. So I went along with Fred Rodriguez to attend my first Mass. The Cathedral was packed, but we managed to squeeze into a pew. I was a little nervous not knowing the form of the service and not understanding much of it because it was all in French. It was an interesting experience and Fred appreciated my presence.

Rue Negrelli, Ismailia, 1940.

On other occasions we went into Ismailia, down the Rue Negrelli (the only street name I can remember, and that from an old photograph I still possess) and wandered around the shops which were all completely open to the street, sometimes stopping at a café for a glass of mint tea, which was the most popular drink – cooling in the heat of the day. The Blue Kettle Club was run by some elderly English ladies who lived in Ismailia, for the soldiers, who said it was a sort of English haven in a foreign land, a home from home. Those who visited the club were provided with free tea, sandwiches and cakes and conversation with the ladies on duty. I enjoyed these visits immensely, but the place was much too staid and dull for most soldiers.

At other times we would walk through the French Gardens, oases of green amongst all the surrounding sandy, ochre landscape. The gardens were well tended, sprinklers constantly irrigating the grass with water drawn from the Sweet Water Canal; the grass was really green and there were lots of trees, palms and flowering shrubs. The other side of the gardens was Lake Timsah where we could sit and watch the sailing dinghies, a very pleasant place to relax, although the Sailing Club itself was out of bounds to non-commissioned soldiers. In the gardens was a statue to Vicomte Ferdinand de Lesseps,

the man who promoted and organised the building of the Suez Canal. The Sweet Water Canal (see above), I recall, ran from the Suez Canal westwards to Cairo. It was used for irrigation and was the sole water supply for people living alongside, who used it for bathing, drinking water and as a rubbish dump; it was not unusual to see dead bloated animals in the water. It no doubt contained lots of sewage as well: it was sweet only by name. We were warned to avoid it because of the danger of being infected by some disease or other. It was a source of leptospirosis, a deadly disease which came from rat urine. If anyone accidentally fell into the canal he was immediately hospitalised and treated for this disease. Generally I and most of our men kept in good health, apart from the occasional 'gyppy tummy'.

There was a Shafto and Jamil open-air cinema called 'The New Garden, United Services Cinema' in the garrison in Queens Road, Moascar. I still have a ticket, marked Cash Pesetas 3 (opposite).

In Ismailia there was a normal indoor cinema called The Majestic. Here the films were usually in French with English subtitles. I have a cinema notice giving the programme from 'Mardi 19 au Lundi 25 Novembre 1940'.

One incident I must relate. One day we were in the camp assembly hall where some Egyptian workmen were attempting to move a piano off the stage at one end of the hall and take it to the other end. They were all grunting and chanting as they strained to lift the piano and when they did, lo and behold, it was lifted onto the back of one little man who amazingly staggered across the room with it whilst the rest carried on their rhythmic chanting.

A major event for me was a visit to El Arish in the Sinai Peninsula. A survey project was required there, so Bernard Sampson, who was a surveyor, and I, with my limited surveying experience, were chosen to go there. We went by train to El Kantara, where we crossed the Suez Canal by ferry and caught another train on the other side for El Arish. The journey was in a packed train; I think all trains in Egypt were always overcrowded. It was very hot and sticky during the overnight journey from El Kantara to El Arish. I must have dozed off when suddenly I was shaken awake by a very irate sergeant and given such a dressing-down (as only sergeants can give) for sleeping and leaving my rifle vulnerable to theft. He informed me that I was very lucky not to be put on a charge, which would have been a bit difficult for him to arrange because he was going on to Palestine. I have no idea who he was or from which regiment.

Eventually the train arrived at El Arish. My impression was of a miserable village with an encampment of army tents nearby. We were allocated quarters in a tent. This was the real desert: very hot by day, coldish at night and very dusty when there was any wind. There were lots of camels and donkeys. The men rode the donkeys, sitting right on the tail, whilst their women walked behind.

We were then informed that our task was to trek out into the desert accompanied by a water diviner whose job it was to locate a source of water so that wells could then be excavated and a water supply pumped and piped back to supply the camp.

We set out early the next morning and trekked and plodded mile after mile southwards into the desert, up and down sand dunes, halting from time to time in a wadi for our water diviner to twiddle his forked stick to see if it would react to any water below the surface. To me it all seemed a rather hit-and-miss way to locate underground water supplies.

The sun rose and it soon became extremely hot – this was one of the times when we really appreciated wearing our topees. It was very hard going walking in the desert, so our progress was relatively slow. Eventually we came to a spot in a wadi where the diviner's stick twitched and he announced that there was a plentiful supply of water below. I must say I was very sceptical: I would have thought a test well would have been dug to check on his divination! But no, he was absolutely convinced the water was there. We never knew if it worked as we were soon returning to Moascar. Our task now was to mark the location, fix a compass position and then survey and mark a route back to the El Arish camp. This we did; it was very hot and sticky work and we did not arrive back in camp until dusk, dusty, drenched with perspiration and very exhausted. We quickly washed and changed into dry clothes and made for the NAAFI tent.

We were very thirsty, so Bernard, naturally, suggested we needed plenty of cold beer. I was at first hesitant; I had never tasted beer before. This sounds incredible coming as I did from Burton-on-Trent – the beer capital of England – but as a teenager I had seen quite a lot of drunkenness and had vowed not to drink beer. This time I relented and so at El Arish, and very parched, I had my first beer. Quite appropriately the beer was called 'Stella'. I enjoyed it; it really quenched my thirst and so I downed a number of beers. Then suddenly I had to go out of the tent into the desert, not to urinate, as was the common practice, but to be violently sick. I retired to kip in the tent in a very sorry state. The rumour circulating had it that Stella beer was not brewed from barley and hops, in the usual way, but from onions. Having completed our assignment and plotted out the route for the proposed pipeline on a map and handed it over to whoever was in charge of the little camp at El Arish, we returned by train to Ismailia. This time I took great care of my rifle, although I never discovered how, on a long train journey, one could manage to sleep and also safeguard one's rifle.

Not long after I arrived at Moascar, an officer came round to look for prospective cadets for the Middle East OCTU. I was asked if I was pre-pared to apply for a commission in the infantry: if I agreed I would almost immediately be sent to OCTU. I was told that there was a great short-age of officers. It seemed a retrograde step having transferred from the Lincolnshire regiment to the Royal Engineers to go back to the infantry. Therefore I declined, but told the officer I would be interested in a commis-sion in the Royal Engineers, which was noted.

Bernard Sampson also refused the offer of an infantry commission and indicated he was only interested in one in the Royal Engineers. Shortly afterwards we were informed that we would be considered for commissions in the Royal Engineers, but that before we could be accepted, we would have to be interviewed personally by the chief engineer, Middle East, and told this would be put in motion. Bernard Sampson, who was qualified as a land surveyor, was older than me and senior in length of service, so it seemed that his application would be dealt with before mine. Sometime in January 1941 Bernard was called to Cairo for his interview and he was accepted for the Royal Engineers OCTU. He came back with the good news and very soon afterwards he left Moascar to go to Cairo to start his course. That was the last I saw of him during the war. Amazingly, during the 1950s, I met him in Salisbury in Southern Rhodesia where he was working as a land surveyor with the Southern Rhodesian government. A few days later, before my turn for a formal interview with the chief engi-neer, Middle East, could happen, I was informed that I was being sent to Cairo to await a new posting elsewhere.

So, in early February 1941, I got my kit together and set off by train to Cairo. On arrival, I once again reported to the Kasr-el-Nil Barracks and as always in the army spent a few days in limbo, during which I took the opportunity to see more of the city. I was told that I and a whole crowd of others would shortly be leaving for Alexandria to await transport to

Piraeus. We were going as part of the British Expeditionary Force being organised to go to the assistance of Greece.

A day or so later we were trucked back to Cairo railway station and entrained for our journey north to Alexandria. The usual confusion reigned at the station as we fought to get on the train, get seats and our kit stowed overhead. As usual there were dozens of hawkers trying to sell souvenirs, fruit and food with their cry of 'eggs and bread' (pronounced 'brid'). The space on the overhead racks was limited because some squaddies decided to climb up and use them to sleep in as a sort of hammock. There was continuous noisy bargaining with the hawkers though the windows and doors – some soldiers hanging on to souvenirs until the train started moving and then whipping them away from the hawkers without paying, whilst the hawkers ran alongside the moving train demanding payment. Some even clung to the moving train and only got off at the first stop some miles further along the line. Many of the soldiers considered it fair game to cheat the hawkers whom they considered were all thieves and cheats.

The journey, which was by day, was quite pleasant as the railway line ran through the Nile Delta which is flat, green and very fertile. There was a lot of human activity on the land as the people tended their crops and rode about on their donkeys. We arrived at Alexandria and were immediately trucked away to our transit camp. We did not go into Alexandria at all because we were confined to camp. The most I saw of Alexandria was from the docks when, later, we went there to embark for Greece. However, from the camp personnel we heard stories of the fabulous brothels in Alex known as 'the Cages' and of the good life enjoyed by those able to visit the city.

We were taken to a large transit camp at El Amiriya, to the west of Alexandria. There we were accommodated in Nissen huts which were extremely hot during the day. The camp was set in the middle of the desert and a very bleak place it was. As everywhere in Egypt, there were lots of flies which were incredibly annoying as you spent much of the time brushing them off your face. They did not seem to bother the locals; it was rather horrifying to see little children with their eyes almost covered with flies and they, literally, did not bat an eyelid. There was little to do except frequent the NAAFI. We could not even go to the Shafto and Jamil camp cinema because it had been burned down by some Australian soldiers who were frustrated at the non-arrival of promised films.

Whilst I was in Egypt the Italians had invaded the western edge of the country and occupied parts of the Western Desert. It was easy to see that the Egyptians were not interested in the war, except, of course, the traders who were making lots of money from the troops. We soldiers did not consider or appreciate that Egypt was their country and we were interlopers. This was reflected in their newspapers which blew hot and cold as the military situation fluctuated. At the time of the Italian invasion, they became noticeably anti-British but many Egyptians were quite scared and were contemplating fleeing from Cairo and Alexandria. The newspapers forecast the occupation of the country by the Italians. Then General Wavell made his unexpected offensive and chased the Italian army right out of Egypt and halfway across Libya. Overnight the mood changed; they all became friendly towards the British. No doubt they were even more volatile when later, sometime after I had left, the Germans came to North Africa and advanced into Egypt as far as El Alamein. Later on in a POW Camp I met a gunner from the Royal Horse Artillery who had been in Wavell's push. He had become separated from his unit and came across a group of disorientated Italian soldiers who immediately surrendered to him. He marched them back to camp, handed them over and, poor man, was immediately put on a charge because he had forgotten to put the bolt in his rifle when he went out – no kudos for having captured so many Italians!

At Amiriya I met up with the group of engineer services personnel who were going to Greece. We were addressed by the officer in command of the group, Major Ralph Carr. He told us we were to be divided into a small advance headquarters and a larger rear headquarters. The advance headquarters would be the first group to go to Greece and were to set up an office in Athens; they would be accompanied by advance groups from other regiments and would prepare for the later arrival of the main party. The senior NCO in charge of the advance party of all units was an RSM of the Scots Greys who became known to us as 'Bonehead'; probably undeserved as later events showed.

The Royal Engineers' advance party comprised Brigadier Hutson, Major Carr, Lieutenant Bailey (as interpreter – he spoke fluent Greek), Sergeant Idwal Pugh, myself, Lance Corporal Smith (known always as Smithy) and Driver Dougherty, the brigadier's driver, plus one or two other drivers and one or two Cypriot muleteers, although I do not remember them ever fulfilling that role. I suppose it was envisaged that we might need mule transport in the Greek mountains. Major Carr told me that the brigadier had personally selected me to be his draughtsman and map reader. The main party of the Royal Engineers was to follow us, headed by a full colonel (whose name I have forgotten); their personnel were organised by RSM Morris, soon to become my *bête noire*.

Whilst waiting to go to Greece we were allocated camp duties. One day I was ordered by old Bonehead to be guard commander. This rather horrified me as I had never done it before and was completely ignorant of the procedures for mounting and changing guards. Thinking quickly I decided to take refuge under the Army Command instruction that engineer services were not permitted to do regimental duties and I told old Bonehead that I refused to do the guard duty. All hell was let loose: Bonehead was furious, said he'd never heard such nonsense, and threatened to put me on a charge. In due course I prevailed on him to consult my officer, Major Carr, who confirmed that I was correct. The RSM had to back down. I was saved the embarrassment of making a cock-up of guard duty and that for me was the essence of the episode.

This is an appropriate moment to say something about Major Ralph Carr. He was a delightful man and very easy to work with. It was rumoured that he was a member of the Carr's Biscuit family. I always thought this was true until in 1996 I read his obituary in the *Daily Telegraph*. He had in fact been born in Burma to an army family. He was awarded an MBE in Wavell's first desert campaign during which some 130,000 Italian prisoners were captured. After the Greek campaign he served in Syria and the Lebanon fighting against the Vichy French. He commanded the 21st RE Field Squadron at the Battle of Alamein. Later in the desert campaign he was wounded by an anti-personnel mine near the Mareth Line. Afterwards he was posted to the 51st Highland Division as CRE for the Normandy landings, his tank was blown up, his driver killed and he again was wounded. Sometime afterwards he was awarded a bar to his DSO for his bravery in establishing a bridge over the River Nier, south of Kessel. Then at Goch he was wounded in the head, thought to be dead and prepared for burial when it was noticed he was breathing. He was sent to hospital in Oxford where eventually he recovered and was invalided out of the army in 1951 and later farmed near there. I feel it an honour to have known such a remarkably brave man.

Whilst at Amiriya someone gave me a slip of paper taken from the pocket of a dead soldier (see below). On it was a poem: I have often wondered who Peter Nicol was.

At last we were given orders to move and we left the forlorn, dismal camp at Amiriya, feeling somewhat sorry for the staff left behind. We went by truck to the Alexandria docks where we embarked for Greece on, I think, HMS *Hyacinth*. The main body was to sail a few days later, scheduled to arrive after we had made arrangements for them in Athens. This was at the beginning of March 1941.

In passing.........

To you who pass life's highway once
Here's wisdom from another
As long as God will give you life
Be kind and good to mother.

For when she's gone beyond recall
Your sorrow and your tears
Will not bring back that life again
Re-live those childhood years.

To you who pass life's highway once.
Here's wisdom from another
One of God's most priceless gifts
Is gone when you've lost mother.

peter Nicol Sgt.

4

Greece 1941

We sailed in brilliant sunshine with calm seas, but within a day or so the weather changed completely. It grew much cooler, the sea became very rough with massive waves and a gale-force wind. Eventually and thankfully we steamed into Piraeus harbour.

Trucks took us to some very ancient Greek army barracks situated somewhere just behind the royal palace. They were quite dreadful: cold, dull and dismal with primitive toilet facilities ('squatters'). There was nothing we could do but settle down for the night on the stone floor wrapped in our blankets. We were very disillusioned, more especially when we discovered that the main rear headquarters had already arrived; no doubt they had travelled in larger, faster ships which were not slowed down so much by the turbulent seas.

The next morning the situation was soon sorted out. We were removed from the Greek barracks; apparently we should not have been taken there in the first place – just a cock-up – not at all unusual. Our small group were taken to the Grand Bretagne Hotel which had been allocated as the Royal Engineers headquarters by the Greek government. Here the headquarters was divided into the two distinct groups, the advance headquarters and the rear headquarters.

The intention of the Army Command was for Brigadier Hutson, who had joined us in Athens, and whom I found out was in fact the chief engineer, Middle East, to stay with rear headquarters and for the second-in-command, the full colonel, to take charge of the advance headquarters. However, the brigadier soon made it quite clear he had no intention of staying in Athens. He said he could not stand the officers' messes with all their protocol and pecking order. So he decided to take charge of advance headquarters and the colonel was ordered to stay in Athens.

We stayed at the hotel for a couple of weeks whilst the two headquarters were set up and began to function. I did not have much to do at this stage as we were waiting to move forward. It was here I first came into close contact with officers and found out how much they varied in temperament and attitude, both to their work and to their handling of the non-commissioned soldiers serving under them. For example, our two senior officers, Brigadier Hutson and the colonel, were as different as chalk and cheese.

The colonel was what I considered to be a typical, hidebound regular army officer, who organised his life and those under him absolutely by the rule book. In his immaculate uniform he set up his immaculate office. He had a great number of army manuals and reference books which were neatly stacked, all in precise order, in a bookcase; a leather-topped desk precisely set out with in- and out-trays, blotter, pen rack, telephone and so on, all in their correct positions, which he constantly re-aligned. Of course he had a leather upholstered chair and did nothing without consulting the appropriate authority from his library. To me he was a real pain in the neck.

On the other hand, the brigadier had a simple office with a plain, trellis table holding only his briefcase and sat on a folding chair. He slept in the office on a camp bed, disdaining the officers' mess. He did not need any manuals or reference books as he had all the knowledge he needed in his head. He asked me to make a notice to put on his door with his name on. He had a number of decorations: DSO, OBE and MC. He came along one day whilst I was preparing the notice and remarked, 'It looks as if you may be short of space, so if there is insufficient room just put the MC (that's the one I might have earned) – the others came up with the rations.'

One day an officer arrived from the north with some booby traps and a mine which he had obtained from behind enemy lines, probably the Italian lines in Albania. I am not certain who he was, but have in the back of my mind that his name was Peter Fleming. We were requested to examine and strip them, then to make drawings of the components for despatch to the War Office. While we were waiting to do this, it was decided to store them in a bathroom which just happened to be next to the colonel's room. He was scared stiff and moved out of the hotel until we had completed the job.

The rear headquarters which was to stay in Athens was organised by RSM Morris – their guardian angel! We took an instant dislike to each other. Whilst still in Athens we shared part of their offices and I got to know a number of their staff, becoming quite friendly with a few of them, in particular some of the clerks who were about my age. One was Bill Whittingham, a rather quiet and reserved man, very keen and conscientious in his work. As soon as papers appeared in his in-tray he dealt with them, and having done so he would pop across for a chat with someone else, only to return to his desk to find his in-tray full again, usually with another clerk's work – but he always got a bollocking from RSM Morris for slacking. He was clearly being put on by Morris and the other regular soldiers. I remonstrated with Morris about picking on Bill, for which I got a dressing-down from him, but he could not take any real action against me because he had no jurisdiction over me and our mutual dislike continued.

Pugh, Smithy and I were allocated a room in the hotel as sleeping quarters. I cannot call it a bedroom because there were no beds and we had to sleep on the floor. There was no central or other heating in the room and Athens was very cold at night then. One of the regular soldiers gave us an invaluable tip that really worked: to keep warm it is best to put most of your blankets underneath rather than on top of you.

I enjoyed the week or so in Athens before we moved north. It had only been a year before that I had been studying Greek and Roman architecture for my architectural exams, so I was pleased to have the opportunity to actually see some of the buildings of Ancient Greece. I was determined to visit the Acropolis and other archaeological sites, if I could find them. Off we went, Pugh, Smithy and I, to visit the Acropolis. Smithy was a real pain in the neck, continually grumbling, or crooning Bing Crosby style. I must admit he had a good voice, and on occasions entertained us well, but he never stopped. At last I was able to go all around the Acropolis, seeing the Parthenon, the Propylaea, the Erechtheum with its caryatids, the Temple of Athena Nike: it was all so very different from the textbooks. We posed for photographs on the steps of the Parthenon, taken with my old box camera (see over). At my insistence – and to Smithy's annoyance – we wandered around to find two other buildings I had studied: the Temple of the Winds and the Choragic Monument of Lysicrates. I eventually found the latter tucked away in a dreary side street. I felt such a charming little gem should have been more prominently displayed. Sadly, I got the impression that some of the ancient buildings did indeed look better in the illustrations in books.

We spent some time exploring the centre of Athens. We visited the King George Hotel (also requisitioned by the BEF), saw the royal palace and watched the changing of the guards: the quaintly dressed Evzones in the style of Gilbert and Sullivan, with their embroidered shoes with turned-up toes, white tunic shirts and long tassels from their hats. Quite attractive ceremonially but quite hopeless if they had to deal with any disturbance or unrest! We went to cafés for snacks or to enjoy the rich, custardy cakes; many British soldiers ate them accompanied by a glass of beer – typical! We also sampled the Greek wines: a white Asprodaphne, the quite sweet red Mavrodaphne, and retsina, that exclusively Greek wine with the resinous taste which I found quite revolting. Then there was the anise-flavoured liqueur 'ouzo', in Crete called 'raki', whilst in Egypt it was called 'arak': it played havoc with a lot of the soldiers. When we wanted a light meal, we chose a café/restaurant displaying a notice 'English spoken'. The waiter would give us the menu, which was 'Greek to us'; the

Pugh, Pierce and Smith on the Acropolis, 10 March 1941.

waiter rarely spoke any English, so we would just point to what seemed a likely item. Away went the waiter and invariably, no matter which item we had pointed to, we were served with eggs and chips – a change from the 'eggs and brid' of Egypt.

The public transport in Athens was by trams, very handy for getting around and quite intriguing, as always there seemed to be as many people clinging on the outside as there were inside, something which would not have been tolerated in England, but was quite the norm in Athens. I recall one incident: the conductor came round for our fares and I fished in my pocket taking out first a clip of 303 bullets, whereupon he just signalled that we did not have to pay. Maybe he thought I was preparing to shoot him even though I did not have a weapon with me.

As we walked around, we would be approached by touts, mostly quite young boys, asking, 'You want my sister, very cheap?' When we declined and tried to shoo them away, the question changed to 'You want my young brother?' This was all very new to me, a quiet country lad. I had no interest at all, but some of the staff did pick up these casual acquaintances or visited brothels. In Athens I first encountered a case of VD. The soldier from our rear headquarters who contracted VD was immediately shipped back to Cairo for treatment. It was considered to be a 'self-inflicted wound' and subject to disciplinary action. In our view, he neatly, unintentionally, avoided the fighting in Greece.

All this time our forces, British, New Zealand, Australian and others, were moving forward to take up positions to counter the expected moves of the Germans and to assist the Greek forces on the Albanian front in north-west Greece. The Italians had occupied Albania, overthrowing King Zog, then attacked Greece but had been repelled; retaliating Greek forces had now occupied significant parts of Albania. They felt they were able to take on the Italians at any time and beat them. But to the Greeks, the Germans were a different kettle of fish, and they were very worried about the prospect of defending their country against them. We were given to understand that one of the aims of the BEF was, if possible, to move northwards through Greece into Yugoslavia and link up with the King of Yugoslavia and his forces to help them resist any German invasion. This may sound simplistic and unrealistic in the light of what followed in the Balkans shortly after, but I can assure you it was the strategy as we understood it at the time.

Our turn came to move forward and set up the advance headquarters of the BEF somewhere behind the front line. We set out from Athens in a convoy of three ten-ton trucks and the brigadier's station wagon and pro-ceeded up and over the Thermopylae Pass. We travelled through the night. Pugh, Smith and I, 'the office staff', were in the back of a truck with the tailgate down; we had to sleep with our legs out on the tailgate as there was so little room inside. We were in our greatcoats and wrapped in blankets – it was bitterly cold and uncomfortable.

The journey northwards towards the Mount Olympus area during day-time was very pleasant: the countryside was quite lovely with many spring flowers and blossoming trees, mostly almond. The attitude of the Greek villagers interested me because it varied significantly from village to village and town to town. In most places the people lined the streets to cheer and wave, presenting us with garlands of flowers, bread, fruit and wine or ouzo, seemingly very pleased to see us. But in a few villages the people appeared sullen and almost angry, showing clearly that we were not welcome or wanted. I am not certain if they were just anti-British, or pro-German as some factions undoubtedly were, or resentful of the effects of war on their lives, or possibly because they had already lost friends or family in the fighting on the Albanian front. On the whole, though, we had a most warm welcome.

Our convoy was only one part of the advance headquarters and we travelled independently of the other units, rendezvousing with them most evenings. We travelled by day and slept in the back of the lorry at night. I clearly remember one evening when we stopped in an attractive place surrounded by olive trees. Brigadier Hutson decided to sleep in the back of his station wagon. Shortly after settling down, he got up and shouted to his driver, 'Dougherty are you sleeping in the front of the car?' 'Yes sir,' said Dougherty. 'Have you taken your boots off?' asked the brigadier. 'Yes sir,' came the reply. 'Well in that case,' said the brigadier, 'I am not sleeping in here with your smelly feet.' He got out and slept under a tree. Most officers would have ordered their driver out of the car, but our brigadier was different.

Two of the main towns we went though were Lamia and Larissa. Around 1936, I think, Larissa had been hit by a massive earthquake and largely destroyed; it was still in ruins, just gradually being rebuilt. It was a humbling experience to see such total devastation by natural forces. Our journey passed through a series of fertile plains separated by mountain ranges over which we passed, winding round the hairpin bends on not very good roads.

At last we reached the location which had been selected for the whole headquarters, just outside Tirnavos just south of Elasson and on the slopes of Mount Olympus. The camp was a tented one. We had a large tent divided into compartments to provide separate offices for the brigadier and Major Carr. Captain Bailey never seemed to be in the office and so did not need one. There was a general office for Pugh, Smith and myself; we had a table each, mine I converted to a drawing table. In fact, I did very little drawing, my work was mainly with maps and map interpretation. The officers slept and messed in the central officers' mess. We had no separate sleeping quarters, so we slept on the floor of the tent. There was a central cookhouse and dining tent, and an ablution tent with portable wash basins and cold showers. The toilet we used was a village one with a primitive surrounding wall and no roof. There was a hole in the ground with roughly flat stones round it leaving a triangular opening, not very large; one had to squat down and hopefully aim straight into the 'long drop' below; what with the occasional fouling on the stones, it was not very salubrious.

The working arrangements were relaxed and free and easy. I recall meeting the brigadier the first morning on the way to our mess; I said, 'Good morning' and saluted him. On the way back I met him again and saluted him. He called me across and said he did not want me spending all my time saluting him, once a day was enough and even that, he said, did not particularly matter. I got to know the brigadier quite well. When he asked me why I had not applied for a commission, I told him I had applied but had been informed I had to wait for an interview with the chief engineer, Middle East, and had been posted to Greece before it could be arranged. It was then he informed me that he was the chief engineer, Middle East. He said I could take the interview as read and that as soon as I returned to Cairo I could immediately go to the Royal Engineers' Middle East OCTU. But I never did get back to Cairo.

As things turned out, the BEF were too late to move to King Peter's aid in Yugoslavia. The Germans had decided it was necessary to invade the Balkans in order to safeguard their flanks and gain control of the Romanian oil fields. With the Italians floundering in Albania, facing defeat there and the arrival of Allied troops in Greece, the Germans decided they had to invade Greece. It has been said, and in my view quite correctly, that the campaign to conquer Greece, followed by the battle for Crete, crucially delayed Operation Barbarossa, the German onslaught on their erstwhile ally, Russia.

Undoubtedly the most fascinating event of the day for us was the arrival, first thing every morning, of the 'Most Secret' intelligence reports. They were received and opened by Sergeant Pugh. Although, no doubt, intended for the eyes of the brigadier and Major Carr only, we always had a look at them first. I found them most interesting and revealing and was astounded by the amount of information received daily: the wide scope of it and, as events later proved, the accuracy of the intelligence gathered. It gave one pause to ponder as to how the information was gathered, who gathered it and at what risk. Once gathered and collated, all these military details were then passed along the lines of communication to arrive typewritten each morning on Sergeant Pugh's desk.

One report stated that advanced units of Germans, masquerading as civilians, had arrived at specified aerodromes in southern Bulgaria and were upgrading them for military use. Another report went on to give precise details of the numbers and arrival times of planes landing at the aerodromes in Bulgaria, their types and the times of their departure from Germany and other parts of occupied Europe.

Another report forecast absolutely accurately the date on which the Germans were expected to commence the now inevitable assault on Greece: 6 April 1941. Amongst the last reports we had was one which stated that the Germans were assembling parachute regiments in Germany with the intention of sending them to the Peleponnese region of southern Greece to establish a base for airborne forces. When, later on, we left Greece and were told we were bound for the island of Crete, I realised that the Germans must be preparing for an airborne invasion of Crete. We should all salute the many unknown women and men who must have constantly risked their lives to obtain and pass on this mass of good, accurate, intelligence about the Axis powers.

In planning for the defence of Greece against the forthcoming invasion, my task was to study the available maps of northern Greece and identify the bridges over rivers. The main rivers were the Vardar which flows southwards through the Macedonian part of Yugoslavia, from Skopje, to discharge into the Mediterranean at Salonika (Thessalonika), and the Aliakmon, which flows south-eastwards from Albania and then turns north-eastwards to reach the sea to the west of Salonika. Having, as far as possible from the limited maps available, located all the bridges and recorded their map references, the brigadier in consultation with other officers had to decide which ones should be destroyed. Having made the decisions, instructions were sent to the field units of the Royal Engineers to carry out the demolitions. I believe a few of them were destroyed by bombing from the air, but our air force in Greece was pitifully small. I remember seeing a few Wellingtons, Blenheims and fighter planes. They carried out reconnaissance flights taking photographs to show that the bridges had been destroyed.

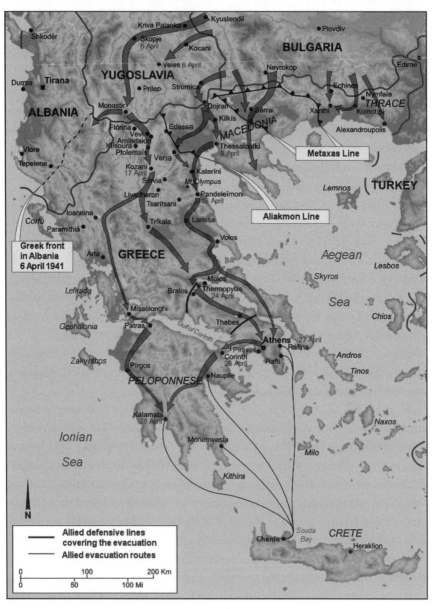

Map showing the German advance into Greece, April 1941.

These efforts did little to impede the German advance down the Vardar valley, as instead of coming down the eastern bank, as we had expected, and then crossing the river by bridge they just came down the western side of the river.

During our time at Tirnavos, Easter arrived and we wished to have a church celebration, so the local Greek Orthodox priest was asked if we could use their church; he was very pleased and eager to allow us to have our service. This date did not clash with their Easter which is celebrated some two weeks after ours. So on Sunday, 13 April 1941, we had our Easter service in the village church. It was a typical Greek Orthodox church, quite small, cruciform in plan, with a dome over the crossing, and whitewashed inside and out, a plain, simple church. We had a good service with lusty singing of the Easter hymns. What I do remember clearly is the Greek priest and his acolytes standing in the entrance vestibule peeping round the pilasters to observe our service, for them, no doubt, an unorthodox service; from their gestures they obviously found it most fascinating. Later we saw the Greeks observing their own Easter celebrations with processions around the outside of the church, so much more colourful than our simple ceremony.

It was at Tirnavos I first witnessed the effects of ouzo. One day an Australian soldier staggered into our camp; he was completely and utterly intoxicated and quite incomprehensible. He collapsed, so we bedded him down for the night. The next morning he awoke out of his stupor. After establishing from us his whereabouts, he said he felt much better and would get back to his unit although he did not seem to have the faintest idea of its location. He said he was absolutely parched and gulped down lots of water. Amazingly this reactivated the ouzo and within minutes he was almost as drunk as when he arrived. It took him another whole day before he sobered up. The next morning he wandered off to rejoin his unit. Apparently that was a quite usual reaction when drinking water after a session of ouzo.

Another new sight for us were the storks, lots of them, which built large untidy nests of sticks on many of the chimneys and roofs of the houses; they and their nests were to me one of the distinctive features of rural Greece.

One day orders were given for everything to be spruced up, as far as could be done in a village encampment, because 'Jumbo' Wilson was due to pay us a visit with his entourage. General Sir Henry Maitland Wilson, later field marshal, an Old Etonian, was apparently the General Commanding the BEF Greece. It was a flying visit. He went into conference with the senior officers of the advance headquarters, and within half an hour or so he had disappeared back to Athens and on to Cairo. There was considerable resentment amongst the other ranks that the general in charge of the campaign in Greece was running it from Cairo. It was some time after the war I found out that at the same time as handling the Greek campaign, he was also commanding all land forces in the Middle East. In hindsight he had probably come to order the commencement of the withdrawal from Greece. Perhaps we thought that the general in charge should be there at the front, on the spot and not far away. I now realise that I knew very little about Army Command and strategy.

I have referred to our presence as the 'Greek campaign', but in fact neither this nor the battle for Crete has ever been officially recognised by the British government as a 'campaign' and has consistently refused to award a campaign medal. The Greek government has awarded a medal for the Allied forces – British, Australian and New Zealand. The lack of official recognition by the British government has been a very sore point with the British veterans of these battles.

Even before the invasion by the Germans, when it was clear that it was imminent, we noticed a column of Greek soldiers passing through Tirnavos and moving southwards away from the fighting. This seemed rather odd. On enquiry they told us they had been fighting on the Albanian front and had been sent home on leave. Later, other columns passed through, also apparently on leave. Rumours were prevalent that although the Greek army was quite prepared to continue fighting the Italians and knew they could defeat them, they were not prepared to take on the might of the Nazi forces. They had heard of the Blitzkrieg in Western Europe and how the German forces had so easily destroyed the French army and forced the British out at Dunkirk. Many, possibly most, soldiers in the Greek army thought the Germans were invincible. It appeared to us that there were cracks in the defence of Greece even before the invasion started. It also became apparent that a substantial number of Greeks had pro-German feelings and were not prepared to fight on. It was well known that their dictator head of state, General Metaxas, was sympathetic to the Fascists and Nazis. I must emphasise that those Greeks who continued to fight the Germans did so valiantly and heroically.

The German invasion of Greece from Bulgaria began on the morning of 6 April 1941, as predicted in the intelligence reports, and proceeded rapidly.

Shortly after Easter we were given orders to move and reassemble further south. Each unit of the headquarters was ordered to move separately and independently. Our small convoy set off having been given a map reference for the next location. And so we began our withdrawal. Pugh, Smith and I were, as usual, travelling in a ten-ton truck with a driver and all our equipment. We were the last group to set off and we had not been travelling long when a large staff car appeared going in the opposite direction. The car stopped and the driver asked for directions to a village further north where he said he was going to collect his commanding officer; the driver was the only person in the car. We knew the village he mentioned had already been captured by the Germans. When we told him the news he was undecided what to do, but after some discussion he agreed the only sensible option was to accompany us to our rendezvous and then ask for further orders; thus he decided to join our little convoy.

What was the point of us travelling in an uncomfortable lorry when there was an empty staff car with pennant flying? So Pugh, Smithy and I piled into it and had a very comfortable journey to the new camp site. When we arrived most of the headquarters were already there, setting up tents in their allocated positions. Directing operations was none other than RSM 'Bonehead'. As we drove up to the entrance, he approached our car, came smartly to attention and saluted us. We opened the window and he peered in only to find he had saluted his un-beloved corporals. All hell was let loose. How dare we travel in a staff car without any authority! It was almost as if he felt that we had fouled the car by travelling in it. Luckily he soon got over his rage, which had clearly arisen from having made a fool of himself for saluting his inferiors. Nothing further was heard of the incident and we never learned what happened to the staff car and the driver or whether he ever found his CO and unit. We were allocated a large tent for sleeping quarters. The only lighting we had came from hurricane lamps. No sooner had we had a meal from the cookhouse tent and all settled down to kip when some idiot accidentally set fire to the tent by tipping over a hurricane lamp. We all had to gather our possessions and scramble for safety, but the tent was destroyed. We spent the night wrapped in our blankets under the stars which, as it happened, was quite pleasant.

One of the tragedies of the Greek campaign – I insist it was a campaign – was the almost complete lack of air support. The RAF could not be blamed – they were as valiant as ever; the problem was that they just did not have enough planes. There was a shortage throughout the Middle East and planes could not be spared from the Western Desert where General Rommel with his Afrika Korps had arrived to bolster the Italians. Naturally the bulk of planes being produced were required for the defence of Britain and for bombing occupied Europe. All the supplies for the Middle East were sent by ship, the convoys having to go all the way round Africa via the Cape. It was said that at the very beginning of the war in the Western Desert there were so few planes that the bombing of Italian positions in Libya had to be carried out with Valencias, the bombs being carried in the plane and manually heaved over the side when the plane was over the target and hopefully hitting it or something of importance nearby.

At Larissa, near one of our overnight camps, we saw that the few operational aircraft were moved under the olive trees for camouflage and safety, whilst wooden dummy ones were placed near the runway. However, when the German planes came over the aerodrome they bombed and strafed the real planes, ignoring the dummies; it was rumoured that 'Fifth Columnists' amongst the Greek population were giving information to the Germans. It must be said that with very minimal resources the RAF did a marvellous job in Greece, against overwhelming odds, until they were completely eliminated.

During our travels in Greece, we had been amazed to see that road construction and maintenance was mainly carried out by women – this was the first time I had seen women undertaking such manual work – and all done by hand; maybe it was a normal practice in Greece or because the men were away fighting in the war. Years later, I found it was the norm for Chinese women to be employed on road and building work. Another common feature of the rural scene in Greece was to see men riding their donkeys seated well back, almost on the tail of the animal, whilst the women and children trailed behind on foot carrying loads on their backs; certainly it was a male-orientated society, quite alien to us.

The retreat now began to gain momentum. As we continued to move further south the pattern of the land and road communications became very clear: a series of flat cultivated plains with high mountain ranges separating them. The roads wound round the mountains in a series of hairpins to cross the passes and then ran straight across the plains, sometimes elevated with quite large open drains on each side.

We were not the only ones retreating southwards: there were hundreds of civilians, people of all ages and Greek soldiers, sometimes whole units of them. There were also individual soldiers, no doubt deserting. The roads were congested and conditions chaotic, more especially across the plains; presumably people could disperse more when going over the passes. During daylight hours, as we crossed the plains, there was almost continuous harassment from the Luftwaffe: their Messerschmitts strafing and the Stukas dive bombing. The Stukas were very frightening as they dived with their sirens at full blast screaming at us, an experience never to be forgotten.

The refugees were fleeing with as many of their belongings as they could manage to carry on their backs or on whatever transport they had. There were mule and donkey carts loaded to the hilt, handcarts of various types and sizes, prams, wheelbarrows, some cars and lorries; but the majority were struggling along on foot carrying what possessions they could. The crowded roads slowed down our progress, more so when carts or vehicles broke down. I felt so very sorry for these poor people and wondered what would happen to them. Where were they going? How would they handle their lives? Would they ever get back to their own homes and if they did, what would they find? This was my first experience of mass panic in the face of expected tyranny and enslavement; it was a most unhappy and terrible phenomenon. In 1945 I was to see similar scenes, but this time the refugees were German, fleeing from the advancing Russian hordes. One has to be personally involved in and experience the movement of refugees to realise the misery, distress and suffering of people fleeing their homes and roots in the face of oncoming repression.

We had to make progress towards our next rendezvous, forcing our way in our trucks through the mass of humanity, sometimes pushing obstructing carts off the road into the ditches at the side, feeling, rightly or wrongly, we had precedence over them in their own country. Very frequently we had to stop and get out of the truck to take cover in the drains at the roadside as the Messerschmitts and Stukas flew along the roads seeking out appropriate targets. Numerous vehicles were hit and some burst into flames; these also had to be pushed into the ditches to clear the road. Very luckily our little convoy escaped being hit. It seemed unfair to have to push refugees, their carts and other forms of transport off the road to allow us to pass, giving us an unfair advantage over them; this in their own country where we had been generally made very welcome. I was, I supposed, one of the few in our group who had a sense of guilt and some shame at our heavy-handed actions, but this was a full-scale war with not much room for sentiment.

During our progress southwards in the direction of Lamia we came across RSM Bonehead in his vehicle, which had been shot up by a Messerschmitt; the windscreen and side windows had been shattered by bullets. The whole vehicle was pockmarked with bullet holes and had to be abandoned. Luckily none of the occupants was wounded but the poor RSM was utterly shell-shocked. We dragged him out, made him comfortable and consoled him until we safely reached our next rendezvous, by which time his condition was greatly improved. He was very quiet and visibly shaken by the experience, but thanked us for our help and said how much he appreciated us coming to his rescue. Beneath all the loud bluster, which he deemed necessary for his rank, he was a decent, likeable man.

We again received mixed receptions from the local villagers and townspeople. Some as before were rather antagonistic, blaming us for attracting the Germans to their country, being of the opinion the Germans might not have bothered about Greece if we had not interfered. However, our intelligence had clearly shown that the Nazis wished to occupy Greece as part of their strategy to dominate the Mediterranean, and would have done so whether we were there or not. But in general the people were still very friendly and well disposed to us, giving us food and wine and presenting us with bunches of flowers as we passed through.

Our last encampment before Athens was near the northern base of the Thermopylae Pass. From there officers had to send dispatches to our rear headquarters in Athens. The driver who was instructed to take them asked us if there was anything we wanted from Athens. Naturally some requested beer, but several, including me, said we would like some of the custard-cream cakes we had so much enjoyed before. Off he went and, true to his word, came back with a whole box of these scrumptious cakes. Sadly, they were to be our last cakes in Greece.

The decision was now made for us to withdraw over the Thermopylae Pass under cover of darkness. As in Britain, the headlights of vehicles were partially blacked out, covered with a metal cover, having an open horizontal strip about an inch wide, shaded from above by lifting up the piece of metal cut to form the opening, this meant the amount of light let out was so little that the driver had to be most careful and proceed quite slowly. We asked our driver if he would be all right negotiating the many hairpin bends at night with such limited light. He replied that he would have no difficulty, then confided that he had never driven at night! In the event all went well and we slowly crawled up the pass and down the other side, surviving all the dangerous hairpin bends; perhaps being in the dark and not being able to see much, we escaped seeing any hazards or near calamities there may well have been awaiting us. As dawn broke, the truck negotiated the lower slopes of the pass and the driver drove on into Athens on a clear, bright sunny morning.

The plan was for us to go first to the Grand Bretagne Hotel to join up with our rear headquarters staff and then decide on the next move. As we wound our way through the streets of Athens everything seemed quite orderly; here and there we saw Allied units formed up, presumably preparing for further withdrawal or for rearguard actions and then evacuation; some were moving in the direction of Piraeus harbour. We arrived at the Grand Bretagne Hotel only to find it completely deserted.

The rear headquarters staff had already left, no doubt at the instigation and on the orders of their jittery colonel. The indications were that they had left in a great hurry, maybe in a panic, because the offices had been left intact, all the records and files still in their cabinets or on the desks and quite a lot of equipment including theodolites and other surveying instruments left lying around. The brigadier was horrified, as were the rest of us. He felt their flight irresponsibly selfish and their leaving everything intact unacceptable. So we set about destroying all the records which might be of use to the enemy, burning them and the colonel's library, which had also been left behind. Then we took all the surveying instruments and any other pieces of equipment we felt might be of use to the Germans and dumped them in the sea. Maybe this was a small gesture but it was an indication of our determination not to assist the enemy in any way. Nevertheless it was a symbolic one to register our disgust that the rear headquarters had fled ahead of us, without even leaving a message for us. I never heard what had happened to them. Later I did meet up with RSM Morris, but I was not inclined to ask him.

The evacuation of Greece was now in full swing. I must mention the gallantry of the troops who fought the rearguard, especially the New

Zealanders, the Australians, the British and the Royal Engineer field units. These rearguards would take up defensive positions in the mountains over-looking the plains, wait for the German columns to approach and inflict very heavy casualties on them, then quickly withdraw down the other side of mountains, move across the next plain and quickly take up positions in the next range of mountains to repeat the process and inflict further casu-alties on the advancing German troops, whilst overall suffering very few casualties themselves.

Brigadier Hutson then told us the plan was to retreat southwards through Piraeus, along the coast to the Corinth Canal, cross the bridge over the canal, if it was still there, and continue southwards. I remember crossing the Corinth Canal very well; that spectacular waterway so very deeply cut into the hills, forming a deep straight arterial way through the red earth, which I presume is red sandstone; the cuts were straight as was the line of the canal. Having crossed the undamaged bridge, we again headed south. Here the road was still crowded but not nearly as bad as on the plains fur-ther north. There was evidence of the Stukas and Messerschmitts having been active: a great number of broken carts and other vehicles, some dead bodies and many dead mules and donkeys. Luckily we were not hit in any of the strafing attacks we endured during our journey to the evacuation ports. Slowly we made our way to the port of Nauplion, not far from Argos and Mycenae, which was to be our evacuation point.

We drove straight to the dockside where a Royal Navy corvette was moored, a relatively small ship. She was being loaded with evacuating soldiers, quietly and very efficiently by her crew. Orders were given that we could take on board only one piece of baggage plus a rifle or revolver; everything else had to be left behind so that as many men as possible could be evacuated. I had to offload all my books – I had a number of archi-tectural and engineering textbooks which had been sent out to me by my mother whilst I was in the Suez Canal camp at Moascar, to enable me to continue with my studies – not that I had done much studying in Greece. What did amuse us and gave us deep satisfaction was seeing some of the toffee-nosed officers attempting to take all their numerous items of bag-gage on board, arguing it was essential for them to do so, only to see the sailors on the gangway unceremoniously grabbing the excess and dump-ing it in the sea amid protests from the officers concerned. However, my most vivid impression on getting on board was the large number of red hats; these were officers above the rank of lieutenant colonel who wore red bands round their hats, and red tabs on their epaulettes, officers of staff rank. They seemed to outnumber all the other passengers. Sergeant Pugh, Smithy and I were amongst the very few NCOs on board.

Then Brigadier Hutson and Captain Bailey came up and said they were leaving the ship, they wished to say goodbye, and hoped we would have a safe voyage to wherever we were going. When we asked why he was not coming, the brigadier replied that whilst he had some of his field units left in Greece, it was his duty to stay on and do his best to direct their rearguard operations and take what action he could to look after them. He said it was unnecessary for us to be with him and ordered us to stay on board; he suspected our destination would be Crete and hoped to see us there in due course. Brigadier Hutson was an amazingly good man, one I am proud to have known.

The ship was very crowded but the crew immediately got round to looking after their 'guests', first bringing round mugs of hot cocoa. We found what space we could, sleeping on deck and being fed, but I remember little else of the 'cruise'; we must have escaped any attacks by the Luftwaffe and the Italian Navy and we had reasonable weather. We sailed during the night in order to clear Greece and be out of range of the Luftwaffe by dawn, the date I think was 24 or 25 April 1941. Of the 53,000 or so troops in Greece almost 19,000 were evacuated to Crete and over 10,000 directly to Egypt. Of the ones who arrived on Crete about 7,000 were later taken on to Egypt.

I only had experience of my small part in the evacuation of our forces from Greece, which was carried out very smoothly and most efficiently. There was no sign of any panic; it almost seemed as if it was just a routine exercise by a highly disciplined Royal Naval crew. Reading about it long afterwards and learning of the large number of troops successfully evacuated to Crete, I can only have the very highest praise for the Royal Navy.

5

Crete: The Island of Doomed Men

We landed at Suda Bay, the large sheltered harbour on the north coast of Crete. Suda Bay is towards the western end of the island of Crete and just a short distance from the then capital Canea (now usually spelt Chania). Having disembarked and stretched our legs, we were formed up in groups and marched away westwards through Canea and a few miles further on, where we camped in some olive groves. Having arrived at this temporary camp site, the priority was to sort people out into their own units. This took quite some time but in due course a rather ragged group of sappers were gathered together and allocated their own site amongst the olive trees. I was amused, at the time, with the constant talk of olive groves because in the 1930s and 1940s there was a famous soprano named Olive Groves, so I always associated olive groves with her. We had, as far as I can remember, just one officer, who immediately took overall charge: Major 'Dicky' Lorraine. The senior NCO turned out to be none other than my old antagonist, RSM Morris.

'Dicky' Lorraine was a couple of years older than me, had first joined the Royal Navy but for some reason which I forget, had transferred to the Royal Engineers, obtained his commission and had, he said, been very lucky to get promotion to major in the field during the Greek campaign. He was very friendly and easily approachable, perhaps because he was the only officer.

We had very little to do. RSM Morris ordered some cleaning up, smartening of dress, rifle maintenance and cleaning, then started drill sessions and a system of inspections. This, we felt, was the usual regular army bullshit, the type of useless – in wartime – exercises only pre-war NCOs would arrange. Of course, there was some sense in trying to bring some discipline to a ragged, tired and rather forlorn group of soldiers. As always, the drill irritated me – clearly I have some genetic fault in my sense of rhythm. It appeared to us that Morris just did not know what else to do with us; maybe he was not receiving any instructions from whoever was in command in Crete.

Brigadier Hutson, accompanied by Captain Bailey, visited us. He told us that the two of them had eventually left Greece in a caïque, a small Greek fishing boat with sails, which they had commandeered and then sailed across to Crete; this in itself was a remarkable feat. The brigadier said arrangements had been made for him to return to Egypt on a cruiser which was then docked in Suda Bay. He said he understood the ship was full but as he would like us to continue on his staff he would do his best to get us on board. He returned to say it had not been possible, but he hoped we would get a passage back to Egypt soon, and he told me that as soon as I arrived, I was to go to the Royal Engineers' section of the Middle East OCTU.

I had learned from Brigadier Hutson that there was a CRE (Commander of Royal Engineers) on Crete who was stationed in Canea. It occurred to me that he might welcome the addition of some engineer services people in his office. I discussed the idea with Major Lorraine, who agreed that Pugh, Smith and I should walk into Canea, locate the CRE's office, and offer our services. We walked the few miles back into Canea and found the office easily. We made ourselves known and were taken in to meet the CRE himself. I cannot ever forget his name, which was Lieutenant Colonel P.I.G. Wavish (a name somewhat similar to Wavell, but with such interesting initials). He was delighted with our offer of help, said he would like us to join his staff as soon as possible and gave us a note for Major Lorraine detailing this.

We strolled back to our olive grove in high spirits, knowing we would soon be away from RSM Morris, only to enter a hornets' nest. Morris was waiting to confront us: he had noticed our absence and threatened us with dire punishments for leaving camp without his permission. We enjoyed it all. We referred him to Major Lorraine who confirmed that it was he who had given us permission to go into Canea to see the CRE. Morris was still boiling under the surface, but had to back down. We handed Lieutenant Colonel Wavish's note to Major Lorraine who agreed we leave for Canea as soon as we were ready. We could not get away quickly enough, thankful to be getting away from RSM Morris for what we hoped was the last time.

We were welcomed by the staff at the CRE's office and allocated sleeping and messing quarters with them in the house next to the office. The CRE's office had been set up some six or seven months before our arrival. What surprised and amazed me was the lighthearted way the whole of the garrison on Crete carried on. They appeared to treat it as a kind of holiday camp on a beautiful island with its good weather and glorious golden beaches. As far as I could ascertain, the main task of the CRE's office seemed to be the provision of creature comforts for the troops. One of the main achievements had been the design and erection of portable shower units to provide freshwater showers. No doubt they did some other useful things, but I saw little evidence myself. I got the feeling there was a lack of any real preparation to defend the island. Surely they must have considered the possibility of an invasion? The last intelligence reports I had seen in Greece indicated that the Germans were sending parachute regiments to the Peloponnese and establishing bases for them. Thus on the balance of probabilities it seemed likely that they would in due course attempt an invasion of Crete.

My thoughts were that any attempt to invade by sea would be effectively dealt with by the Royal Navy, in whom I had great faith. There seemed to be no evidence that the Germans could quickly assemble an invasion fleet in the Greek ports, a prerequisite to making a successful seaborne invasion. The most likely strategy, if the Germans were to succeed in invading Crete, was by an airborne invasion, and this could only succeed if their parachute troops first captured the aerodromes thus enabling them to land more troops and supplies by air transport. I gathered there were three (two large and one small) aerodromes on Crete. The main aerodrome was at Maleme to the west of and fairly close to Canea, the second at Heraklion and the smallest at Rethymnon, a town between Canea and Heraklion. I concluded their primary attacks would be aimed at the Maleme and Heraklion aerodromes, which they would have to capture in order to sustain the invasion because their troops would have to be supplied by air and the aerodromes used to bring in more troops. Therefore the priority for our garrison must be the defence of the aerodromes.

I was told by members of the CRE's staff that nothing had been done to build any defensive works at Maleme aerodrome. With all this in mind, I, very presumptuously, prepared a long memorandum to the CRE setting out the position as I saw it and suggesting that immediate steps be taken to build defences for the aerodromes. Lieutenant Colonel Wavish read my memorandum with interest and thanked me for submitting it to him. Presumably he then discussed it with the commanders of the island, because very shortly afterwards an instruction was given for the design of concrete gun emplacements and ancillary works for the defence of the aerodromes, also for improved access to them and alternative routes into them. How I wish I had been able to keep a copy of my memo! After the war I read that the Command on Crete had been of the opinion that any invasion of the island would come by sea and troop dispositions had been made predominantly on that assumption. Little or no thought seemed to have been given to the aerodromes as the crucial locations for an attack. How wrong they were! Possibly they were not privy to the intelligence we had had in Greece; if so it was a glaring omission.

One day there was considerable activity and commotion a few houses away from our office. This was, we gathered, due to the arrival of members of the Greek royal family, headed by Prince Paul who was acting as Regent of Greece. They lived in the house near us for several days – we saw them coming and going – then, just as suddenly, they left, presumably to go to a place of greater safety.

Our relatively short stay in Canea was quite comfortable and, at first, enjoyable. During their several months on Crete, the staff at the CRE's office had had considerable contact with the Cretans, especially with firms in the building trade. They had become quite friendly with some and their families, in particular with the daughters. Pugh, Smithy and I were soon included in these social events and friendships. The one Sapper I remember most is Dave Raynor, a stockily built young man of medium height and with a ruddy tanned face who could almost have been taken for a Cretan. Dave had got down to learning Greek, becoming very fluent, so acted as interpreter. His prowess was to come in very useful later on. We used to wander into Canea town in the evenings and at weekends and go to cafés along the Venetian harbour and drink Mavrodaphne wine or beer.

In the office I was kept very busy designing concrete gun emplacements for the Maleme aerodrome and simple reinforced concrete slab bridges to cross the small streams on the access routes being constructed to the aerodrome. It was not long before the Luftwaffe began to take an interest in Crete: there were an increasing number of daytime sorties and reconnaissance flights by Messerschmitt fighters and the Stuka dive bombers over Canea and bombing raids on Suda Bay, targeting the ships in the harbour. The Messerschmitts would fly straight down the street at a very low level, strafing as they went; they were so low I could clearly see the pilots – almost see the whites of their eyes. They also dropped small bombs as they passed along.

One day a small bomb dropped near the office; the blast from it blew out the window in front of me which fell over my head – framing me! Luckily I had my head down as usual working at the drawing board, so my face was protected and all I got was a few scratches on the top of the head from the broken glass. On another occasion, as we got up in the early morning, a small bomb hit the protruding balcony, facing the road, on the first floor of the house in which we were billeted. I was still in bed. The house shook so much I was, literally, blown out of bed. One outside wall, on the first floor of the house, was blown completely out. At the time, one of the men was shaving in front of the mirror which was fixed on that wall; both just disappeared in front of his eyes. Quite remarkably he was not hurt, just shaken. Luckily no one was injured.

On another occasion we had to go down to the docks at Suda Bay to collect some supplies. The sheltered harbour housed the principal port of Crete into which almost all supplies came. It was one of the most dangerous places to be in because throughout the day the Stukas made their screaming, diving attacks on any ships in port and on the warehouses. The only defence our army had against them were one or two batteries of light anti-aircraft guns, sited on the hills to the west of the bay. These, I was informed, were Italian Breda guns captured from the retreating Italians during Wavell's first campaign and victory in North Africa. In order not to reveal their positions, the gunners told us that they only fired into the planes after they had passed over. I am not certain how many, if any, they managed to hit. There were very few RAF planes on Crete and most of these were small fighters of early designs: twelve Blenheims, six Hurricanes, certainly no Spitfires, twelve Gladiators, and six Fulmars and Brewsters of the Fleet Air Arm; of the latter most were unserviceable. Aeroplanes were in very short supply: the defence of Crete was a low priority. The planes which were there fought on valiantly – I think they were all eventually destroyed

– but the air crews did their best against impossible odds. Almost all of them must have been killed in action. One memory of our visit to the docks at Suda Bay was once again meeting Freddie Brown, whom I had played hockey against at Moascar and who captained the MCC after the war. He was, I gathered, an RASC officer in charge of the port.

If we did not go into Canea, we would gather in the sitting room of the house after the evening meal and listen to the wireless, trying to get the BBC on a rather primitive set. More often than not we would get 'Lord Haw-Haw', with his 'Jairmany Calling' broadcast from Berlin. He gave dire warnings to the British and Allies saying how we were losing the war, especially listing the many ships both naval and merchant sunk by the U-boats and German surface raiders. At this time he turned his attention to Crete, telling us we were on 'the island of doomed men'. He was quite correct, but in fact it turned out to be doomed for both ourselves and the Germans, as statistically their losses were much larger than ours. So he warned us of the imminent invasion, which we already knew was coming. He was executed as a traitor at the end of the war.

A few days before the now expected invasion, the office staff were told to prepare their rifles for action. As the Establishment for Engineer Services did not have any regimental duties, parades, inspections or weapon training we hardly ever looked at our rifles. Indeed, some like Harry Foyster had never had any training at all in weaponry and had never fired a rifle. Some had even put a cork in the end of their rifles to try to prevent it rusting. So now all the rifles had to be cleaned; in some cases wire wool had to be used to remove the rust in the barrel. Then they had to be oiled and polished using the piece of four-by-two pulled through the barrel. We even had to give some of the men, including Harry Foyster and Smithy, instructions on how to hold, aim and fire their rifles. As a non-combatant unit, this was our sole preparation to help repel the forthcoming invasion. At no time were we given any instructions as part of the battle plan for the defence of Crete. Other, mainly infantry, units were strategically placed for the defence of the island, generally along the coast for the assumed seaborne invasion.

In the early morning of 20 May 1941 the Germans began their invasion of Crete by air. The first we knew about it was when someone shouted that the sky was full of parachutes. We went out to look: there were hundreds of them, some white and some grey, a very impressive sight – in other circumstances one would say a beautiful sight – in the clear sunny sky. The white

German paratroopers landing on Crete.

parachutes carried the soldiers whilst the grey ones carried equipment of various kinds. Some pieces seemed very large, which prompted one wag to shout, 'Look they're dropping bloody battleships.'

One of the staff was a keen photographer and immediately started taking photographs. I have just one memento of him, an earlier photograph of the Cretan countryside with the mountains in the background. It is, of course, a black and white one as there was very little colour photography in those days. I had only come across colour transparencies – now called colour slides – just before the war.

From the direction of the falling parachutes it was clear that the objective was Maleme aerodrome. I have been asked what our immediate reaction was to this sight. It was certainly a mixed one: some exhilaration at seeing this rather beautiful scene of hundreds of parachutes gracefully drifting down to earth, and then a realisation of how vulnerable they were to anyone within range of them, followed by a sinking feeling in the gut that the invasion had at last started and everyone would now be involved in the fighting. What we had not expected – I cannot remember seeing them in the air – were the silent gliders.

Then suddenly, out of the blue, one of them landed about a hundred yards from our office. I am not sure how many Germans were in the glider

– about ten or twelve, I think – but they all scrambled out only to be met by our rifle fire; all but one were killed as they tried to move to cover. The one who had managed to get clear climbed into a tree, opened fire and killed one of our sergeants but then was himself quickly shot and killed. We had just witnessed our first casualties of the invasion. We saw no more action that day; everything was quiet except for the sound of distant gunfire.

I have no personal knowledge of the battle strategy of the Army High Command for the defence of Crete, or the execution of the defence. I have since read a number of accounts. The brief account in Churchill's *The Second World War*; Antony Beevor's *Crete: The Invasion and Resistance; The Fall of Crete* by Alan Clark and one by a New Zealand medical officer. This last chimed most with my recollections of the battle.

Our orders were to stay put in the house and prepare to help to defend the vicinity. Rumours soon began to circulate about what was happening, mainly wrong, but some with a grain of truth. We heard next that the Germans had captured Maleme aerodrome. The story was that a New Zealand, mostly Maori, battalion had wanted to counter-attack during the first night to retake the aerodrome but were denied permission by the local commander of the sector. Instead they were ordered to regroup ready for an attempt to retake the aerodrome the next morning. I had confirmation of this later on in a POW camp from the New Zealanders themselves. Their opinion was that the aerodrome could most certainly have been retaken before the Germans had time to consolidate their positions, had they been allowed to counter-attack that first night. As it was, the Germans were given the opportunity to prepare for the defence of the aerodrome. Without holding the aerodrome the invasion would not have succeeded, it is as simple as that. We also heard, probably on the third day, that the Germans laid out coloured sheets as markers for the drop of supplies to their troops on the ground, at which the New Zealanders and other Allied troops, having observed this, got hold of some of the sheets, placed them in their own positions and thus received some German supplies.

It soon became apparent to us that the Germans still held the airport because we observed an almost continuous stream of Junkers aeroplanes coming in to land. We heard that such was their determination to resupply their ground troops as quickly as possible that some planes were belly-landing on the adjacent beach. There was virtually no hindrance to this flow of men and supplies because, as I have mentioned, our few aircraft were soon out of action and the only anti-aircraft fire was from the infantry, which was ineffectual.

It was now we heard that the overall command of our forces on the island had been taken over by General Bernard Freyberg, the New Zealand VC. He had arrived on the island only a day or so before the invasion, and, poor man, had not had much opportunity to reorganise the forces at his disposal.

On the fourth day, I think, we were ordered to withdraw eastwards in the direction of Georgioupolis and then to move southwards. We met General Freyberg who was travelling on a motorcycle and who stopped to give us a few words of encouragement before speeding off to visit one of the local headquarters. During all this early period we heard constant gun and rifle fire and there was continuous strafing of our positions by the Luftwaffe fighter planes.

After we had withdrawn southwards some miles we came to a small rocky plain where we found the remains of one of our small aeroplanes, I think it was a Brewster, which had been shot down. Beside the plane wreckage were the bodies of the crew who had been thrown out of the plane and had been exposed to the hot sun for sometime. They were bloated and had turned almost black; the stench was nauseating. This was my first experience of bloated bodies: an awful scene that haunted me for a long time afterwards.

It must be remembered that the British forces on Crete, apart from the small garrison which had been sent there as a token force some months before, consisted by and large of the remnants of the BEF to Greece. They had lost most of their equipment in the evacuation, or had it taken from them on arrival at Suda Bay, as Antony Beevor records in his book. Our little party had not had our rifles confiscated when we arrived at Suda Bay. The men were tired from the gruelling campaign on mainland Greece, the units were severely depleted, lacked equipment and now had to face fresh German Parachute and Alpine troops, the cream of the German Army, supported by the Luftwaffe, which had soon established complete domination of the skies.

Despite all these basic deficiencies, our troops put up a magnificent defence of Crete, most ably assisted by the local Cretan soldiers and many civilians. We should never have lost Crete and would not have done so if the aerodromes had been properly defended. To place the troops along the coast indicated to me a lack of faith in the ability of the Royal Navy to intercept any invading ships before they reached shore. It seemed sensible to assume that no attempt would be made to bring in troops by sea before the bridgehead of the aerodromes had been secured. I still cannot understand why the Command on Crete ignored the intelligence reports which clearly pointed to an airborne invasion. Even so, in the first day of the airborne attack, the German parachutists suffered very heavy casualties and were to a large extent in disarray. Had the counter-attack proposed by the New Zealanders on the first night been permitted by the area commander and the Maleme aerodrome retaken, Crete would not have been taken. In my considered opinion, Crete was lost by the misinterpretation of intelligence and the incompetence of the local commander on the first day. I learned later from the Germans that, even towards the end of May, the German Command were considering withdrawal from Crete and that some of their senior officers had already been withdrawn before our surrender.

As was undoubtedly known to British Intelligence, Hitler was involved in planning Operation Barbarossa, the invasion of Russia. Preparations for the attack were well advanced with large numbers of army divisions being moved to the east. A seaborne invasion of Crete which would have required large numbers of ships and landing craft in the Greek ports would have been unlikely. He already had his parachute regiments in southern Greece with their support bases. Hitler had already given up the idea of invading England by sea, and for that there had been months of planning. Shipping had been available and the English Channel was only twenty miles wide, but he had decided it was unlikely to succeed. In any case the date of the fall of Greece could not have been forecast with any accuracy, so the planning of any seaborne invasion of Crete could not be done in any detail before ports in Greece became available; it is certain that the necessary shipping was just not available.

It has been said (and I firmly believe it to be true) that the diversion of some twenty-five German divisions to the Balkans and the heroic resistance in both Greece and Crete by the British, Commonwealth, Greek and Cretan forces delayed the commencement of the German onslaught on the Soviet Union, Operation Barbarossa. The effect of the delay was that the onset of winter prevented the Germans from taking Moscow and completing the conquest of Russia. As the German failure in Russia marked a major turning point in the war, it could be argued that the Greek and Crete campaigns played their part in bringing this about. Attending the sixtieth anniversary of the Battle of Crete in 2001, it was hurtful that Britain did not even send a member of the government, whereas the President of Greece, the Prime Minister of New Zealand and a senior minister of the Australian government attended.

Our little group had hardly any news of how the various sectors of the battle were proceeding. Each day we were ordered to withdraw to new positions for defensive purposes and it was not long before we realised that we were in retreat before the Germans' advance out of Maleme. We knew absolutely nothing about the position at Heraklion and Rethymnon. At first our journey took us through the lovely lowland valleys with many fruit trees, olive groves and exotic shrubs and flowers. We had to take shelter in the olive groves to avoid the constant strafing. I vividly recall being in one olive grove when we were strafed by three Messerschmitts. They flew in from one side then turned and came back from the other direction, so we lay with our heads against the tree trunks to shield us from the bullets which whistled through the foliage, turning to the other side of the trunk when they came back. Then someone shouted, 'Let's get out of here, we are lying on an ammunition dump,' which was absolute nonsense but there are

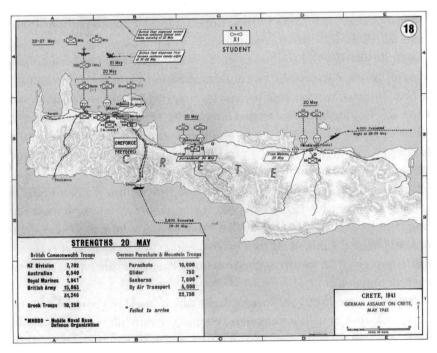

Map of Crete.

87

always some who panic at the least opportunity. There was no way there could have been an ammunition dump in a place which a few days before had been a quiet olive grove miles away from any fighting.

So day by day we moved further south. Gradually the vegetation became less lush and we climbed higher and higher into the mountains. The tree cover thinned out until there were just occasional scrubby trees and shrubs, many aromatic, and there were still a few late spring flowers. The going now became very rugged and difficult, rations we picked up at various points became smaller and water began to become scarce. Shelter from the continued strafing by the Messerschmitts became tricky. As we got higher, we came across large rock formations and the occasional cave, welcome as shelter as the nights were cold. The weather was fine, sunny and dry, getting very hot during the day. There was very little water in the mountains and this became a major problem. We, that is Idwal Pugh, Smithy and I, travelled rather independently, but constantly met other groups who were also retreating and sometimes officers who told us to continue moving south.

It was now a general retreat and we were told to make for the south coast of the island and try to find the proposed evacuation point at a place called Sphakia (or Sfakia). On the upper slopes of the mountains there were no roads, just the occasional track on which sometimes we would meet a shepherd with his sheep or goats; otherwise it was a lonely, desolate terrain. As we started the descent from the mountains we were reduced to our few hard rations kept for emergencies and, if we were lucky, had our water bottles full. The last two days before the descent were the worst; we were exposed to the fierce sun and had to ration the last of our water, having just enough to moisten our lips, but we had to keep going. Our mouths were parched and our lips began to swell. Thirst is a terrible sensation and there is nothing one can do to relieve it, just grin and bear it – and you cannot even grin. This was accompanied by non-stop moaning from Smithy. We had no water at all the day we started the descent into the Imbros Gorge (identified on the visit to Crete in 2001). We had no officers with us, received no further orders and just followed the general movement towards Sphakia.

We were now moving mostly by night which made the going down the steep rocky slopes without any lights even more difficult. Then, suddenly, there was a shout from someone that he could hear water. Further down the rocky path we stumbled across the source, a tiny spring coming out of

The Imbros Gorge in 2001.

the rocks at the side of the path, not much more than a trickle. There was a lot of shoving, pushing and jostling to get at it and be able to relieve our thirst. Although Pugh, Smithy and I were still together we had been joined by all sorts of other soldiers and it became difficult to stick together in the dark. There was quite a crowd trying to get at the water. In the dark it was not possible to see to fill water bottles, so we did the next best thing: we took off our steel helmets, which were pretty sticky and mucky inside, and filled them from the trickle of water. It tasted better than champagne.

The path down the gorge was hardly wide enough to take two abreast, when there came a shout from behind, 'Make way for the Layforce.' As they passed, they said they were going through to take up defensive positions to form a rearguard to safeguard the evacuation from Sphakia. We let them go ahead of us; it was only then we began to think it strange for the rearguard to be at the bottom of the gorge rather than higher up, behind us, at the entrance to the gorge. I have often thought about this and am pretty certain that they were just endeavouring to get to the evacuation point ahead of us. Later on in POW camps I met some of them; they were the Middle East commandos under the command of Colonel Robert Laycock, a force of some 750 who had landed at Suda Bay on 26 May. They had certainly made their way pretty quickly to Sphakia as the date they passed us was probably 28 May. At dawn, as we were still moving down the gorge, we came across an old man with his donkey. Being very hungry we decided to take the donkey and cook it but were met with such absolute fury from the old man that we gave up the attempt.

Eventually that morning we came within sight of the coast and seeing a level area in the hillside with a cave behind it we decided to rest there and await developments. Some rations were issued – I am not sure where they came from – but we were able to brew some tea and have something to eat. News was passed along to us that the Royal Navy would be coming in during that night to evacuate troops. Our group, now grown to around thirty men, was drawn from various regiments. Like others, we were an orderly group and prepared ourselves for the short march down to the beach and waited for the arrival of the ships.

About 11 p.m. orders were given to march down to the evacuation point where we joined the queue and moved down towards the beach in an orderly fashion. The ships anchored offshore and the soldiers were taken off in the lifeboats which came in silently to the beach. Gradually we moved forwards and in due course came in sight of a boat. I was within four or five of the boat when the sailors said it was full and and that there would be no more that night as they had to get well clear of the coast before dawn to avoid being attacked by the Luftwaffe. So, very disappointed, we made our way back to the shelter of our cave to await the coming day and hoped to get off then. So near and yet so far, never was that saying more true.

Throughout the next day more and more soldiers came down the gorge to the Sphakia area. During the morning an order was issued that all troops were to regroup into their own units. Up to now we had organised ourselves quite smoothly into groups of twenty to thirty men ready to go to the beach when required and in our opinion there was no need to regroup for evacuation. What thick-headed army officer, in typical bureaucratic manner, devised the idea of regrouping into our own units for evacuation I shall never know, but it was absolute stupidity and undoubtedly led to fewer men getting off and probably to a greater loss of life. So throughout the day there was chaos as men tried to locate their own units, with locations for each unit to be established and bickered over. This idiotic scheme of regrouping went on all day and was still incomplete at nightfall. The result was that no one, certainly no one from our vicinity, went down to the beach that night. We learned that the navy came in and waited and waited but had to go away empty, much to their disgust. I have since been told that the navy did take people off that night but as far as we knew, and we were on the spot, no one got off. The naval ships had taken all the risks of coming to Crete only to find gross bloody incompetence by the army officers handling the land side of the evacuation.

The Royal Engineers regrouped at the same spot which we had first selected. Major 'Dicky' Lorraine was the senior officer and my *bête noire*, RSM Morris, was the senior NCO. It was announced that the Royal Navy would be coming in that night and it would be for the last time. Early that afternoon, Harry Foyster arrived, completely exhausted and in quite a bad way. Just at that very moment RSM Morris called a parade. I and (I think) Smithy decided we must bed Harry down, make him comfortable and give him something to eat and drink before joining the parade. Quite rightly we decided his needs were paramount and the parade could wait for us; Harry certainly was in no condition to go on parade. As a consequence we were a few minutes late going on parade, which was noted with disdain by the eagle eye of Morris.

He then officially told us that the navy would be coming in, that night, for the last time. He said it had been decided that each unit would be allocated a fixed number of places on the ships. This was an effort by those in command to deal fairly with the situation, a quite acceptable idea in the circumstances of the regrouping. Then RSM Morris went on to announce that places for the Royal Engineers to get off would be allocated according to rank: officers first, then warrant officers, staff sergeants, sergeants, corporals, lance corporals and lastly sappers. He added that, being late on parade, Lance Corporal Litherland would be considered last amongst the lance corporals. In fact, with the number allocated to the engineers I would certainly have got a place. I was deeply concerned that this method of selection by rank was grossly unfair to the bulk of the sappers who would be left behind. It seemed wrong that the Command having made an effort to be fair to the different units, our unit was going to discriminate against the lower ranks. I noted that Major Lorraine had not attended the parade.

I was so incensed with RSM Morris's decision that I went off and sought out Major Lorraine to express my misgivings about the arrangements. He said it was the first he had heard of it and was clearly upset. He told me that he, for one, would not be going off: it was his duty to stay behind and look after his men. After some consideration, Major Lorraine told the RSM to call another parade at which he announced that he had decided places to go on the boats would not be allocated by rank but by ballot. Everyone, irrespective of rank, would have a chance to be evacuated except for himself who would not take part as he was staying on the island. He instructed RSM Morris to organise the ballot. There were a number of papers with 'Yes' on them, representing the number of places allocated to us, and the remainder were blank. The papers were put in a steel helmet and we all filed past to take our chance. Harry Foyster drew a 'Yes', but Pugh, Smithy and I drew blanks as did, ironically, RSM Morris. There was no fuss about the results of the ballot which were accepted quite calmly by all concerned. I heard of no complaints and everyone present seemed to agree that Major Lorraine had acted very correctly. To me it was just one of those things. I have no idea what the inner thoughts were of the others being left behind. For those lucky enough to be going off there were dangers to face: the ships might be attacked by the Luftwaffe and sunk or they might even be sunk by Italian submarines: evacuation carried its own risks.

In the end my decision – and it was mine alone – to challenge RSM Morris on the allocation of places led, a day later, to my being taken as a prisoner of war. I never learned of the immediate reaction of RSM Morris nor the fate of any of the men evacuated that night. However, I never got back to Cairo to go to the Middle East OCTU and so ended my chance of being commissioned. I did hear after the war that Harry Foyster got back to Egypt safely.

The next morning was Whitsunday, 1 June 1941; it was a bright sunny one with hardly a cloud in the sky, but there were other clouds. We were informed that all senior officers had been evacuated. We were told that it had been decided to surrender the island to the Germans. We were ordered to give ourselves up.

What is interesting is that a few days later we came across a group of German officers from an Alpine regiment, who asked us what had happened to all our staff officers and commanders. On being told they had already left Crete, they told us that they also were on the point of abandoning the struggle and leaving the island, so they were very surprised to hear of the British surrender. It seemed to me rather unlikely but it was what they told us. One of the German officers was Max Schmelling, the German heavyweight boxer.

I did not know what happened to Major 'Dicky' Lorraine after the surrender, but years later in 2005 I read *The Colditz Myth* by S.P. Mackenzie in which the author refers to the exploits of a Major Richard Lorraine in Oflag IXA (Rotenburg) in planning escapes from that camp.

6

In the Bag

Pugh, Smithy and I were still together. Pugh had heard a rumour that just along the coast to the east there was a boat hidden in a creek so we decided to try to find it. We set out along the top of the cliffs; this was open country covered in scrubby grass and lots of small stones. The German Luftwaffe had, I suppose, not been told of the surrender and cessation of fighting because as we were halfway across the cliffs we were strafed by three Messerschmitts who turned and repeated the strafing from the opposite direction before flying off. This was a particularly frightening experience because the largest stone we had for cover was not much more than fist-sized. We spread out and lay down lengthwise to the line of the attack covering our heads as much as possible, turning round the other way when they came back. Very luckily no one was hit – we were not the only ones on the cliff – it certainly was a very narrow escape.

When the planes had gone, we continued eastwards and scrambled down a ravine to find a cave which had an inlet from the sea. There was the caïque, completely sheltered from view but already full of soldiers with others trying to get on board. It was obviously overcrowded already, even dangerously so. We decided there was no option but to leave. What happened to the boat I shall never know: a voyage in it to Egypt would have been hazardous in the extreme and it would have been very vulnerable to air attack. There was quite a lot of struggling to try to get on board and quarrels were breaking out. We left and decided to go westwards towards a village we could see in the distance. I recollect that it was at this stage we decided to get rid of our rifles to prevent the Germans getting them, so we threw them down a ravine into the river at the bottom; perhaps a foolish gesture. It did not even occur to us that they might have been useful to the Cretan Resistance. We had no idea that there might be a resistance movement by the Cretans to the German occupation. At that time I had not heard anything about resistance movements in other occupied countries.

As we were approached the village, following the line of a stone wall about five feet high, a German plane suddenly appeared, flying low over us and dropped a string of small bombs. We immediately dropped flat to the ground; one bomb dropped just the other side of the wall. Luckily for us the wall took all of the blast; we got up covered in dust and debris but uninjured. That was just another bomb without our number on it.

We then bumped into a German foot patrol who had already occupied the village and were rounding up prisoners. So, Pugh, Smithy and I went 'into the bag' on a beautiful bright Whitsunday morning, 1 June 1941.

We had never been given any information whatsoever about the possibility of being taken prisoner of war, nor instructions or advice as to how to handle the situation should we be captured; nor that it was a soldier's duty to try to escape. As we saw the situation, Crete was an island in the middle of the Mediterranean Sea and a long distance from anywhere, so where would one escape to?

British soldiers surrendering to German paratroopers.

I had no knowledge of my rights or duties as a POW – that had not been in our army curriculum. Neither did I know of the existence of the Geneva Convention on the treatment of prisoners of war, to which I much later discovered both Great Britain and Germany were signatories. Many years later I read M.R.D. Foot and J.M. Langley's book *M19 Escape and Evasion 1939–1945*. This book gives the impression that great efforts were made to help POWs to escape, providing them with information on routes, safe houses, sending them maps, compasses and other escape material. No doubt this did happen on a limited scale and, I suggest, was primarily targeted at officer POWs and smuggled into their camps. The vast bulk of British and Commonwealth other rank POWs in German hands had absolutely no knowledge of the existence of M19 or any other organisation aiding prisoners to escape and received no assistance whatsoever to help them do so. I came across just one example: half a map turned up in a camp in Germany. Any attempts to escape by POWs lower than sergeant in rank were, in my experience, made solely on their own initiative.

The German soldiers who captured us were quite ordinary men who shouted orders at us, in German of course, but they were, I would say, rather gruff and rough, not brutal, nor very cultured. The order was soon given to start moving northwards in groups of around thirty or forty men. Individual guards varied, but there were always some German soldiers around as we trudged back north.

What was my reaction was to being taken prisoner? I think there were a number of different feelings all muddled together. The first was of anger (shared by most of us) towards those senior officers who had got themselves off the island, leaving behind the men they were supposed to command, and had ordered the surrender instead of staying on to fight. The second was a sort of relief that the fighting was over, mixed with apprehension as to where we would now go and how we would be treated and what would it be like to be a POW. The third was concern for my mother, family and Stella: how would they know what had happened to me when my letters ceased to arrive?

I think most of us were quite stoical. I personally did not come across anyone having any sort of mental breakdown. The great British trait of 'it's happened, so let's get on with it and make the best of it' came to the fore. We may have felt apprehensive, but I do not remember anyone feeling guilty or ashamed at being captured; after all, we had been ordered to surrender. Soon the other British trait of 'grumbling' surfaced, although

Captured British soldiers on Crete, June 1941.

rather muted in the circumstances so as not to get on the wrong side of the guards. But we clung to the idea that although we were prisoners, all was not lost and the thought that somehow our side would persevere through to victory was always with us and buoyed us up during the years ahead. It is important to know that throughout our time as prisoners, never did we lose our faith in final victory over the Germans, even if from time to time we did have rather low moments.

We were not a column of soldiers, but groups of stragglers, chivvied along by our guards from time to time. There were halts about every half hour to rest, to allow others to catch up and see to the calls of nature. We soon got to know the German phrase for these halts: '*pinkelpause*', pronounced 'powz-a', i.e. a pause for a pee. We were not told where we were going but assumed it was back to the north coast. At intervals we met other German soldiers, some in trucks, some on foot, and a number on motor cycles, some of which had sidecars. When we enquired about food, were always told it was available a couple of miles ahead, but it rarely materialised. Thinking about this later, I realise it must have been a huge task for the Germans to have to provide food and drink suddenly for thousands of prisoners; this would have taken some organising. At the time we were just bloody hungry.

Pugh, Smithy and I stayed together. Once out of the gorge onto the higher land the going was somewhat easier, but we were very hungry, and food from the Germans did not appear for some time. I remember my sole sustenance one day was a couple of spring onions taken from a hillside garden. Some of the plains, relatively small ones, seemed very fertile. We had not seen them on the retreat because we had been much higher, crossing the mountains. In fact the going on 'the way back' following the road was the easier route.

Water was also a big problem. I clearly remember on one occasion coming across an isolated well whose water level was about eight to ten feet below and surface was covered with green weed whilst numerous flies and other insects hovered above. Our problem was how to reach the water. We managed to find some string which we tied round the necks of our water bottles and gingerly lowered them down and filled them; we had to be careful that the string was secure so we did not lose the bottle and water down the well. That day we certainly learned the value of the army water bottle. Having drunk our fill we refilled the bottles and set off again. The water tasted like nectar, and as far as I know no one suffered any ill effects from drinking it.

As we moved further north, the Germans did provide some sustenance consisting of pieces of dark brown rye-bread and black ersatz coffee which was said to be made from acorns; not a pleasant drink but warm and better than nothing. We slept in the open at night with guards on patrol but I think we were too weary to escape; it would have been relatively easy but into very inhospitable mountains.

The journey back to Canea took four or five days. Having reached the town, we marched westwards for three or four miles to arrive at our first prisoner-of-war camp. We referred to it as Maleme, but it was in fact about halfway between Canea and Maleme. The site was between the road and the sea, and had been fenced off from the road with a tall barbed-wire fence which also ran down each side to the sea, but was not fenced along the shore. Guards constantly patrolled outside the fence, but not along the beach. The site itself was in an idyllic position with golden sand and unimpeded access to the sea: ideal for the holiday centre it now is, but now spoilt by ribbon development and hordes of tourists. Much nicer then! On my return to Crete in 2001 I tried to locate the site of the camp without success. In 2005 I returned again, with my elder son and daughter, on the

Sir/Madam,

I regret to have to inform you that a report has been received from the War Office to the effect that (No.) *1605024* (Rank) *L. Cpl*

(Name) *Litherland. Sydney*

(Regiment) ROYAL ENGINEERS.

was posted as " missing " on the *2nd June 1941*

The report that he is missing does not necessarily mean that he has been killed, as he may be a prisoner of war or temporarily separated from his regiment.

Official reports that men are prisoners of war take some time to reach this country, and if he has been captured by the enemy it is probable that unofficial news will reach you first. In that case I am to ask you to forward any postcard or letter received at once to this Office, and it will be returned to you as soon as possible.

Should any further official information be received it will be at once communicated to you.

I am,

Sir/ok Madam,

Your obedient Servant,

[signature]

Colonel Officer in charge of Records.

IMPORTANT.

Any change of your address should be immediately notified to this Office.

The letter sent to my mother, informing her that I was missing, which arrived before my card. This was sent through the Royal Engineers, rather than directly by the War Office. She had to wait until September to know that I had not been killed or injured, but had been taken prisoner.

'Heroes Return' scheme. We booked, from a tourist brochure, at the Hotel Palazzo, Porto Platanias in the town of Platanias between Canea and Maleme. As we arrived at the hotel I noticed, in front of the hotel, a small island off the coast and immediately recognized it as Ag. Theodoris. Thus the hotel itself must have been on the site of our prison camp; I had solved my problem – what a coincidence! The management at the hotel had no idea the site had been a POW camp; they were most intrigued and impressed.

It was here we learned the German for POW camp: *Kriegsgefangenenlager*. Our camp was for non-commissioned soldiers only. The officers were sent elsewhere; we never saw any of them again.

On arrival we were allocated, or rather scrambled for, accommodation in white tents, about eight men to a tent. One would have expected army tents to be camouflaged but these were gleaming white. Pugh, Smith and I managed to keep together, the only other occupant of the tent I remember was Sapper Dave Raynor – the one who had learned Greek and spoke it fluently. In retrospect I suppose it was quite an achievement for the Germans to provide tented accommodation so quickly. We slept directly on the sand and used our haversacks as pillows. We were quite comfortable because the nights were warm. The weather was glorious, so we soon settled down to our new life in the 'holiday camp', sunbathing and swimming. We had unrestricted access to the sea.

At this stage we were not officially registered as prisoners of war. In fact, while we were at the camp on Crete the Germans took no steps to take our names or even to count us; there were no parades, *'Appells'* as they called them, to check on us. Indeed, it was not until we arrived in Germany that we were registered, photographed and given identity tabs.

Some three weeks after arriving at the Maleme camp, we were given postcards, reddish in colour, to write home stating we were prisoners of war in German hands and were in good health. Mine was written on 26 June 1941; I addressed it to my mother – I still have it. It has a date stamp of 16 October 1941, whether British or German I do not know, but it indicated the length of time it took to get to my mother. The card reads:

Dear Mother, I am a 'Prisoner of War' in German custody. I am unwounded and quite well. Please do not write to me until you hear from me again as I am at present only in a Transit Camp. Love Syd.

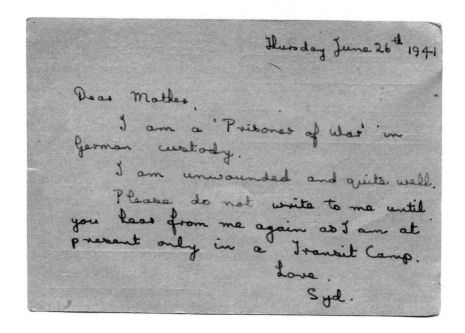

Thursday June 26th 1941

Dear Mother,

I am a 'Prisoner of War' in German custody.

I am unwounded and quite well. Please do not write to me until you hear from me again as I am at present only in a 'Transit Camp.

Love,

Syd.

She had received a notification from the Royal Engineers' record office in Brighton informing her that I was missing, dated 23 June 1941. Later she had a card from the War Office dated 11 September 1941 informing her I was a prisoner of war. This gives an indication of the time the family had to wait to learn my fate: it must seem incredible in these days of instant communication. It seems a little ironic that those left on Crete were posted as 'missing' when in fact we had been abandoned and they knew jolly well where we were. There was certainly a long period of worry before learning that I was safe and well.

The Germans referred to Crete as Kreta, so we thought that after the war we should form an ex-servicemen's society to be called the ExKreta Society – this because we felt we had been dropped in the shit.

The main food dish we were given was a thin rice soup, not particularly appetising or filling, and at first, a small ration of rye bread. Then a camp bakery was established which produced quite a good white bread with sultanas in it. When the bakery opened, one of the prisoners who had managed to get a job working there gorged himself with so much new bread that he was taken very ill and died. To drink we were given the same ersatz coffee (without milk or sugar of course); most of us preferred water. Very infrequently we were issued with small tins of meat or fish.

I suppose it was two or three weeks after arriving at the camp that I discovered there were little white insects in the seams of my shirts and trousers; I had no idea what they were, but was soon told by the others that they were lice. I was quite horrified: I had never seen lice before, but I had heard of them and associated them with dirty people. Since then I have heard that in medieval times people ate cabbage to keep them free from lice! But here I was now infected with lice and I began to feel very unclean. Of course, everyone was infected with them; we spent hours and hours crushing them between our fingernails. Daily we went into the sea and washed our clothes in the salt water, scrubbing at the seams with the hope of killing or drowning them. However, they were most persistent and always reappeared. In the end I suppose we were resigned to having them. There was talk that lice carried typhus, so there was always the thought in the back of our minds that we might get infected with the disease, but thankfully it never happened. Lice remained our close companions until we were in a camp in Staaken in Berlin. Infestation, I understand, is often a result of malnutrition, and probably this was a factor in our circumstances.

Perhaps the most embarrassing feature of the Maleme camp was the latrines. They were placed in the open air along the fence by the main road leading past the camp. There were several, consisting of wooden structures each about sixteen feet long. The seats were oval holes made at intervals in the wooden top. There were boards along the front of the latrines, but none at the back. They were placed over a deep trench which received the 'offerings'. When using them one sat with one's back to the road from which there was an uninterrupted view to passers-by, who could watch, if they so wished. It was always most embarrassing for us and presumably unpleasant for passers-by. We had to use the latrines frequently because from time to time we all had bouts of diarrhoea and dysentery. One of the biggest problems was the complete lack of toilet paper. We scouted around to find bits of paper blown against the fence – we had no newspapers – or we could occasionally use leaves if, that is, we could find ones big enough. An alternative was to get a piece of rag which could then be washed out in the sea (early recycling!) but which resulted in some contamination of the sea water. Since then the availability of toilet paper has been an obsession with me – I always carry sufficient in my pocket for a couple of visits!

The Germans soon erected some outdoor showers and wash basins with rudimentary canvas screens round them, provided with water piped from overhead tanks, most probably taken from our Royal Engineers' stores. Luckily the pit latrines did not contaminate the water supply. We did our best to keep clean, spending hours in the sea; the water was warm so we could swim and frolic around without getting cold. Surprisingly the German guards did not bother to patrol the beach but kept mainly to the perimeter fences while there were always a few wandering about the camp. The guards did not worry us very much and we had minimal contact with them. Our main contact was when they supervised the issue of rations. We had much closer contact with the ubiquitous companionable lice.

We had not been in the camp very long when some visitors began to arrive at the gate. These were local Cretans, mostly women, bringing food and sometimes cigarettes and tobacco for us. They were mainly the ones who had had contact with those of the garrison who had been on the island for several months. They enquired about them and usually were able to make contact. The guards on the gates tried their best to supervise the prisoners because there was always a clamour from the men trying to get hold of any extra food, so there was always a certain amount of squabbling going on. Quite early on, three teenage girls arrived with a basket of food; they were the daughters of one of the building contractors who had been employed by the CRE in Canea. I knew them by sight, but Dave Raynor knew them well. At the gate they asked for him and he told the guards, or at least indicated to them, that he was the acquaintance the girls were seeking and so the basket of food was for him and his friends. As he did so, up pushed RSM Morris and a couple of other warrant officers who occupied a tent together. They pulled rank with the guards, insisting the basket of food was for them and despite the protests from the Cretan girls and Dave, the guards decided that Morris and his buddies should have the food.

Dave and the others in our tent were livid at being cheated by these sergeant majors who, in fact, did not know these girls. Morris presumably took his cue from the fact that we were Royal Engineers who knew the girls and that he was our superior. The problem now was how to outwit the 'thieves' when the girls came again. Very luckily Dave was able to discuss with them the date and time of their next visit, speaking in Greek, which our ignoble WOs could not understand. He told us, in a whisper, but intentionally loud enough for Morris and co. to overhear, that they would return with more food the next day at, say, 11 a.m. and we returned to our tents very disillusioned with our seniors. Actually Dave had arranged to meet the girls much earlier. He managed to vary the times of subsequent visits and in this way we outwitted the warrant officers every time. I have never forgotten the blatant cheating by men who were supposed to set us an example. I suppose that hunger changes people's behaviour. And so every few days we would receive basketsful of extra food which was shared around the men in our tent. There were slices of extremely hard bread which could keep forever, but had to be well soaked in water then dried again when it became like new bread before we could eat it: no doubt this was what the shepherds took with them to the mountains. Then there was a dried powdered goat's cheese, also reconstituted by mixing it with water; most useful, because like the bread, it kept forever. The girls also brought fresh fruit including oranges and apricots. And it was here I was introduced to halva, a sweetmeat in slabs and made mainly of honey and ground almonds; the type we received were quite crisp. There were also fresh bread rolls, but I do not recall there being any meat. These were marvellous additions to the basic rations supplied by the Germans and certainly helped to keep us fit.

There were some working parties sent out from the camp who were given extra rations for working, usually in the form of tinned food. The parties were selected by the Germans and tended to be sergeants and warrant officers. I was never selected but Sergeant Idwal Pugh was and as we had a reasonable amount of food from our Cretan friends, he saved his tinned food for later emergencies. I must admit I was somewhat relieved at not being selected to go on the working parties because the work mainly entailed the collection of soldiers' bodies killed in the fighting, both German and British, and burying them: not a very pleasant task.

I do not recall any medical facilities at the camp but I am sure they were available. The only illnesses really prevalent were diarrhoea and dysentery and these we allowed to take their course.

Then came the day when Dave Raynor said he had been talking to the Cretan girls about the possibility of escaping and was beginning to make plans. They had told him they would be able to look after him and hide him until there was an opportunity to get him off the island. They pointed out that just off the coast at the eastern end of our camp was an island (Ag. Theodoris, although we did not know its name at the time) which had a cave on the western side of it, which went into the hill for a long way and eventually emerged, we were told, on the mainland. So, they said, it was possible to escape through the cave and they could arrange for him to be met at the other end. Dave spoke good Greek and was stockily built with a deeply tanned face: he could easily pass himself off as a Cretan. He asked if I would go with him, but the drawbacks were that I spoke hardly a word of Greek, I was tallish with a rather pale complexion and in no way could be passed off as a local. We discussed this at great length and finally decided that I would be a hindrance to his successful escape and so it was agreed that he would go alone.

We began to make plans and preparations and packed into two haversacks the things Dave needed to take with him. To get to the cave he had to swim across to the island, without attracting the attention or suspicion of the guards. It would be more difficult to go at night as there was greater possibility of being seen; the guards were likely to pick up movements after 'lights out' and there was the problem of swimming in the dark and being able to locate the cave on the island. During the day there were lots of prisoners in the sea swimming about or just playing about in the shallows; usually the few guards around paid them little attention. We picked a time when the sea was fairly full of men, carefully going in a group so as to screen the haversacks from view. We lowered them into the water and, still screened, strapped them to our ankles. Dave bade farewell to the men from our tent who wished him well, then he and I waded into deeper water and began to swim out slowly towards the island, whilst the others created some diversion further along the shore to attract the attention of the guards away from us. Dave and I had to swim breaststroke slowly across to the island with the haversacks dangling from our legs; it was quite an arduous swim but we got to the island and crawled into the shelter of the cave. I wished him well and he disappeared into the cave with his soaked and dripping haversacks. I swam back to the camp, wondering whether I should have gone with him; had I just funked it? I had mixed feelings and a little guilt at leaving him to cope on his own, yet felt I was right that I would be a liability. I never saw him again, but after the war whilst at Doncaster, I heard he had eventually got off the island after having been well looked after by his Cretan friends, had reached Alexandria and continued his service in the Middle East. For my part, I got safely back to shore without the German guards being aware of the escape.

There was one rather amusing incident at the Maleme camp. Amongst the men rounded up and put in the camp were a small number of Chinese sailors from Hong Kong who had been on board a freighter in Suda Bay. The Germans were at a loss as to what to do with them and, of course, they could not understand a word the Chinese were saying. They asked if there was anyone in the camp who spoke Chinese and could act as interpreter. After a while a soldier named Lofty Pierce stepped forward and said he thought he could probably help as he had served in Hong Kong. However, it transpired he could not speak any Mandarin or Cantonese but claimed to know a little pidgin. So there was a hilarious episode with the Germans shouting in German, the Chinese sailors chattering in, I think, Cantonese and Lofty occasionally adding a few words of pidgin; no one appeared to understand what the others were saying. It did not advance the Germans' dilemma one iota; they eventually seemed to give up on Lofty's attempt at interpretation. I have no idea how they resolved the problem, they certainly did not want the sailors, but later they were sent away from the camp; we never knew what happened to them.

Towards the end of August 1941 (I do not recall the exact date) we were informed we were to move, ordered to get our paltry belongings together, lined up in columns and marched off in groups to Suda Bay. We soon realised that we were going somewhere by sea. We were not told of our destination. We were issued with some rations for the trip, inadequate as always, but we still had some food remaining from the gifts of our Cretan friends and the tins Idwal Pugh had saved, which helped.

We were embarked on a rusty old freighter, most probably requisitioned from the Greeks. She was certainly no oil painting, very much in need of some repainting and rust removal, which seemed fairly normal for old cargo boats, especially Greek ones. Once on board, we were herded down into the hold, crowded in and we jostled to find sleeping/living space. Pugh, Smith and I remained close together at all times. We were shut in the hold for the journey. We soon began to realise what being a prisoner of war was actually going to be like. The only time we were allowed on deck was to visit the toilets which had been especially improvised for the prisoners. On the deck at the stern of the ship a wooden platform had been built out beyond the stern rail with oval holes for our bums and a straight drop down to the sea below: this really was the longest of long drops. It was a simple and effective system, bearing in mind that many of the men still had diarrhoea and dysentery, the experience being quite exhilarating when our backsides were sprayed from the breaking waves. Had we had to use loos inside the boat I am sure they would have soon become horribly fouled; instead we just added a little to the pollution of the sea.

In addition to the bread and little tins of meat or fish we had been issued for the journey, we were also given watery soup once a day and the now usual ersatz coffee. The ship was not marked in any way to indicate it was carrying prisoners of war, so we were very apprehensive throughout the voyage, aware that Royal Navy ships and submarines were active in the Mediterranean. They would probably consider this freighter a legitimate target, and so we listened for anything which might indicate their presence. Luckily for us there was no attack as we would almost certainly have perished, locked in the hold as we were. The journey took some four or five days until we eventually crept into the port of Salonika.

7

Salonika and Onwards into Germany

Having docked, we were soon disembarked and lined up in columns of four by the German guards who had arrived at the dockside to take us away. The weather was gloriously sunny, but the atmosphere was entirely different from that on Crete. The guards were older men, non-combatant soldiers I think, aggressive and difficult. On Crete the guards had been frontline soldiers and there was a certain amount of camaraderie, *esprit de corps* and mutual respect, but these 'unfit for active service' guards were a different kettle of fish. I found it to be true throughout my years as a POW that the guards who had seen active service were invariably the ones who treated us well.

We were marched through the streets of Salonika, which were thronged with people very interested in us as we passed by. Some of them waved and shouted greetings and tried to pass food and fruit to us. We were quite surprised how openly welcoming they were, especially as we felt we had let them down. The German guards took a dim view of this friendliness, shouting at the Greeks and quite brutally knocking them out of the way with their rifle butts to stop them making any contact with us. In particular, I was upset to see them using their rifle butts on some nuns who tried to greet us and give us fruit. It was my first encounter with the German bully who, having been given some measure of authority, perhaps for the first time in his life, made full use of that licence to oppress other people. These men were quite different from the elite and arrogant officers and soldiers of

The Germans enter Salonika, April 1941.

the SS and other Nazi regiments who gloried in war and their own superiority especially when, as at that time, they were winning on all fronts.

We eventually arrived at a large barrack complex which the Germans had taken over from the Greek army and turned into a transit prison camp. It was a gruesome place. We were accommodated in a large barrack room like a warehouse. Brick built with a cold stone floor, it must have been built at the time of the Crimean War, if not before. No beds or bedding were provided, so we slept on the floor packed together like sardines. At one end were the toilets and ablutions; stark, cold and miserable with everything discharging into open drains. The whole place was infested day and night with large rats. One night I was woken up by screams from a man who found a rat was biting his ear. As we used the ablutions and toilets, there were always rats running along the open drains.

The food at this camp was very meagre, just a bowl of watery soup with a minimum of rice or millet at midday and part of a loaf of bread. For the first time in my life I felt really hungry. Outside the kitchen block there were refuse bins and I and others would search them for scraps of food; it felt very degrading to have to do this, but we were starving. One day as the soup was ladled into my dixie I really thought I was lucky, for there floating in it was a large white object – had I been given a dumpling? – so very tempting; my mouth began to water. When I turned it over I saw it was a cow's eye.

There were a large number of prisoners in this camp, I suppose well over a thousand. Occasionally a few were selected to go out on working parties but these, again, were restricted to sergeants and other senior NCOs. I have no idea what work they did, but luckily Pugh often managed to get himself on them. They were given extra rations, usually small tins of meat or fish and were sometimes given bread and fruit from the local Greeks who were very friendly towards them. Pugh was a very good companion, who always shared his extra food with Smithy and me. There were rumours, as always, that we would soon be moved to Germany, so quite wisely Pugh decided to keep back some tins of food in case we needed extra food on the journey.

I did not have the energy to explore the whole camp complex even if it had been possible: there were always guards wandering around. We heard on the grapevine – commonly known as 'shithouse rumours' – that some prisoners had managed to escape through the system of main sewers leading out to the sea, that is until the Germans found out and guarded the entrance to them.

There were always new rumours. I recall one that Russian gunfire had been heard in the distance and they would soon be coming to liberate us. We had heard whilst still on Crete that the Germans had invaded Russia. They had in fact, unknown to us, done so on 22 June 1941 and were advancing deep into Russia but we knew nothing of this or any other war news, as we had no access to newspapers or a wireless. This period from our capture until we were in 'settled' prison camps in Germany was a period when we had virtually no news of the progress of the war, and so it was a fertile time for rumours of all types, very few of which turned out to be true. Nevertheless, there was no sign of any defeatism amongst our ranks. Later when we reached Berlin, for the first two years our news came entirely from German sources such as the camp newspaper they supplied, or from the guards and occasionally from the odd German newspaper we managed to get our hands on – often the *Frankfurter Allgemeine Zeitung*. Naturally that was biased, so we had to read between the lines carefully. It was only from 1943 to 1945 that we managed to get BBC news and towards the end of the war, news from leaflets dropped by the Allied air forces.

It was now mid to late summer and mostly very hot. I had my khaki battledress but no greatcoat. Quite a number of men only had tropical uniform; some only had short trousers and very few had coats. This was fine for the moment, but autumn was approaching and we were expecting to move to Germany where it would be much colder. The Russians never arrived to free us.

I have learned since that Clive Dunn – Corporal Jones in *Dad's Army* – was in the camp at this time and that there is a photograph taken there of him in the nude. However, I did not meet him. Clearly he had not been told that I was there!

Eventually the day came when we were called out on to the parade ground. I suppose there were about three hundred of us on parade that day. We were ordered to form up in columns of four, not three as in the British army; we were a pretty motley crowd. The parade was called to attention when three German officers arrived in their immaculate uniforms. They told us we would shortly be going to Germany. Then they gave their first order which was, 'Fall out the Jews'. This was repeated several times without any response whatsoever. It seemed to me rather stupid of the Germans to expect any Jews to reveal themselves; it was already well known how the Nazis persecuted the Jews, although at this time we did not know about the extermination camps. We had had one Jewish sapper with us and as soon as we were captured we had told him to destroy his pay book and anything which might indicate he was Jewish and to change his name; from then on he was Sapper Brown, and was still Sapper Brown when I lost touch with him somewhere in Germany; I cannot even recall his original name.

Having failed in their efforts to find any Jews, the next order was, 'Fall out the Irish'. The orders were, of course, given in German and translated into English by one of the British RSMs who helped with the administration of the camp. This led to some very quick thinking: we knew that the Republic of Ireland was neutral in the war, so we thought the Irish might be treated better than other prisoners and might even be sent home – it seemed a good idea to be an Irishman. Certainly many thought so, and a whole host of would-be Irishmen stepped forward, probably about half of all those on parade. Most conspicuous amongst them were Australians in their bush hats, New Zealanders in their distinctive hats, some Sikhs in their turbans, small, tanned Cypriots, Scots wearing their tartan berets, lots of English and others, including some who really were Irish. This seemed to take the German officers by surprise and baffle them. There was a lot of shouting and gesticulating as they tried to cope with the ludicrous situation. They dismissed the Aussies, Kiwis, Sikhs and Cypriots and then attempted to select the real Irish. When they had selected the men they accepted as Irish they formed them up separately and marched them away. In fact they were sent to a special working camp in the Berlin area for Irish POWs. I learned their story when their camp was broken up and some of them were sent to our camp at Staaken in Berlin.

Those remaining on parade were told that the journey to Germany would take four or five days and that we would be issued with rations which were to last the whole journey. We were dismissed from parade and told to get our goods and chattels ready for the journey. The rations consisted of one large loaf of rye bread and four small tins, two of meat and two fish. We were clearly informed that there would be no more food issued until we arrived at our destination.

In due course we were assembled with our luggage: some with kitbags, some back packs, some haversacks, some with virtually nothing to carry and a few still clothed only in shorts. We were formed up in fours and marched off to a railway marshalling yard and were subjected to a great deal of shouting and bullying by the guards. We were divided into groups of forty alongside the train. The goods train was composed of cattle trucks, clearly labelled in French, '10 horses or 40 men'. We were then ordered, assisted by some rifle butts and more shouting, to climb up into the truck allocated to us. Having counted forty into the truck the sliding door was closed and padlocked.

The trucks were of timber with plank floors. We were completely enclosed, apart from two small openings on each side which were situated near the corners. These were about 18in by about 12in high covered by an iron grille and were about 5ft 6in from the floor, so that standing by them one could just see out. They provided the only light and ventilation. We were very crowded in our 'Orient Express'. There was not enough room for everyone to lie down at the same time so we had to take it in turns. At any one time there would be some lying down, very cramped, some squatting down and the others standing. As can be expected, there was considerable jostling for places; everyone wanted to be by a wall and have something to lean against. There was a certain amount of squabbling with the biggest and strongest as usual getting the best positions. This scramble was repeated after each time we were let out to relieve ourselves, which was generally two or three times a day.

During the four- or five-day journey most of us were pretty lethargic. There was a lot of chattering, plenty of arguments and occasionally some-one would try to start a sing-song, not that there was much to sing about. As we were passing through Eastern Europe and places I had not seen before, I wanted to take the opportunity to look out at the countryside and see what it was like. Quite surprisingly, there were only two or three of us out of the forty who were interested enough to do this; the others, including my two companions, Pugh and Smith, were not. So I spent hours look-ing out, watching farmland, villages and small towns pass by; possibly because I was a country boy and loved the countryside. I happened to have some paper and a pencil – I do not recall where I obtained them – and made some sketches of buildings we passed. I was particularly intrigued by the churches with their bulbous onion-shaped domes, often gilded, on the towers and whitewashed walls: not at all like any churches I had seen before. Unfortunately none of my sketches survived.

We were not told our itinerary for the journey, but I was able to pick up the route from the towns we passed through: Skopje, Belgrade, Zagreb, Klagenfurt, Villach, Bischofshofen, Salzburg, Regensburg, Leipzig, and finally our destination, Luckenwalde – a town some miles south of Berlin which was to be the site of my first prison camp inside Germany, albeit a transit camp. The names of towns in stations had not been blacked out as they had been in England.

The first large town I remember was Skopje, the capital of Macedonia. Rumbling across the plains of Yugoslavia, we passed field upon field of ripening maize – I had not seen maize growing before – and also fields of giant sunflowers. All this was quite new to me and I got a lot of satisfac-tion from seeing it. It helped pass away the time on this tedious journey. We passed through Belgrade at night with just a slowing down through the station, sufficient to be able to identify the name on the platforms. The town we did stop at was Zagreb, where we were, surprisingly, permitted to get out onto the platform to stretch our legs. We were most amazed that the crowds of civilians on the platform were very friendly towards us and gave us bread, small cakes and fruit, and more surprisingly, on this occasion, the guards did not try to interfere. We were also provided with some ersatz coffee, which must have been arranged beforehand by the Germans and possibly the Red Cross or a similar charity was involved. This, apart from earlier in Salonika, was the only time we were offered food by the local people. At the time I knew little of Yugoslavia and, I suppose, imagined they were all one people: I had no idea of all the different ethnic groups in the country. I now know that Zagreb is the capital of Croatia, and that during the war it was the Croatians who supported the Nazis. So why were they so friendly to us as we passed through? Another of life's enigmas!

One place I quite clearly remember is Bischofshofen. We stopped a while at the station there and then passed through a long tunnel; this was the first alpine scene I had ever seen. The other memory is of the jolting of the train from time to time as we were shunted into sidings to let other trains go past, this happening frequently after we entered Germany.

Unfortunately our deluxe compartment did not boast of any lavatory or washing facilities. About three times a day, once early in the morning, once about midday and then in the evening, before dark, we were let out for calls of nature. The train would slow down and shudder to a halt at some remote country spot and amidst a great deal of shouting from the guards the doors would be unlocked, everyone would be ordered out to perform, if they could, their natural functions. The guards would cock their rifles and keep an eagle eye on us in case anyone tried to escape; there was much shouting and threatening and we were beginning to accept this was a natural characteristic of many Germans – loudmouthed bullying. Despite these comfort stops, there were occasions in the sealed trucks when men still with diarrhoea or dysentery simply just had to 'go'. The Germans did not supply chamber pots; the only containers available were empty jam tins, the two pound size, or dixies. So those who had to go just had to use these containers. It was most embarrassing for them and for those of us who could not avoid watching. There was naturally a terrible stink as the poor men 'performed'. Having used the containers there was then the problem of disposing of the contents as soon as possible or waiting until the next stop which might be hours away, and there were times when the person could not stop and the tin overflowed. Someone spotted a knot hole in the floor and managed to open it so they then tried to pour the contents through it; this was only partially successful and there was always some spillage which they had to try and clean up. They also tried throwing it through the window openings but it tended to blow back into the truck. That was the most unpleasant aspect of the journey. Very thankfully I was constipated for the whole time I was on the train and did not have to perform in front of the others.

Pugh, Smith and I had some extra food which Idwal had hoarded in addition to the rations which had been issued to us all at the start for the whole journey. The three of us pooled it all and divided it into rations for each day of the journey and no matter how hungry we felt, we stuck to our ration plan. However, quite a few of the men were not so prudent or thoughtful and consumed all their rations in the first two days and thereafter had nothing to eat for the remainder of the journey. They were envious of those of us who had spaced out our rations to last the whole trip and some of the more loudmouthed demanded we share our food with them. This caused a lot of tension and unpleasantness. We felt it was their own fault that they had not listened to the instructions and had scoffed their food too quickly, but they indicated quite venomously that we were utterly selfish in not sharing with them. There were also tensions about smoking; there was not very much tobacco, and those who were lucky enough to have cigarettes were expected to share them with those without or give them a 'drag' of the one they were smoking. As a very occasional smoker, this did not affect me, but smoking was a drug to many soldiers and any shortages gave them real problems.

The train finally halted immediately outside the fence of the transit camp at Luckenwalde. My Grand Tour of Eastern Europe was over. The journey had been pretty grim from the cramped space, little chance of sleep, constant grumbling, the occasional fight and the most unhygienic conditions. We were very dishevelled on arrival at Luckenwalde. However, I had seen some of Eastern Europe, however scant, and I have always been glad I had taken the opportunity to look out.

We alighted from our trucks with our few bits and pieces amidst the now normal shouting from the guards. As we stretched our legs, a number of French prisoners came up to the inside of the camp's barbed-wire fence to see who had arrived, all smoking Gauloise cigarettes. As soon as our men saw this, many clambered over to beg for cigarettes from the Frenchmen. They grovelled to them, quarrelling when one got a cigarette and another did not. The French prisoners were really enjoying the way our men were demeaning themselves. I felt ashamed of them and thought they were letting the side down. I was disgusted and that scene has remained with me ever since. Such is the power of addiction.

We were lined up and marched into the camp where we were allocated quarters in wooden barrack blocks. The beds, the first for months, were two-tiered wooden affairs, and even had mattresses or palliasses. The palliasse is a long sack made of hessian and filled with straw and was to be our standard mattress throughout our years as prisoners.

The process of properly registering us as prisoners of war or *Kriegsgefangenen* now began. The first part was 'de-lousing': we were taken to the shower rooms, our clothes were taken away to be disinfested by putting them in a sort of hot oven; we were then showered, and had to stand about to dry off as there were no towels. Then we were disinfected by a guard with what looked like a 'lavatory' brush dipped into a bucket of disinfectant and shoved under our armpits and then around the genitals; men joked that they would like this job of disinfecting in a female camp. Then our clothes were returned to us, still warm from the disinfection process and we were taken to be photographed and our fingerprints taken.

We were issued our POW identity tags, made of some sort of aluminium alloy about two inches by one and a half inches with a sort of perforation across the middle so they could be divided into two if the prisoner died – then one half would be buried with him and the other sent to the next of kin. I still have mine (see below). The identity tag was engraved with the

number of the Stalag (short for *Stammlager*) to which one was to be sent, ours was Stalag IIID, together with one's *Kriegsgefangener* number; mine was 11207.

The Stalag numbers related to the various areas or regions into which Germany was divided for the POW system. We soon were to find out that IIID was the Berlin district. It was at Luckenwalde that the prisoners were sorted out into workers and non-workers. Officers did not work and were sent to Oflags. Of the non-commissioned officers, sergeants and above were also sent to non-working camps. I think the senior NCOs did have the option to go to working camps and a few removed their stripes so that they could. Some of the warrant officers were sent to take charge of the working camps, but in an administrative capacity, not as workers.

So it was in this sorting process that Sergeant Idwal Pugh and I parted company. He had been a very good companion, a very level-headed sensible Welshman with a charming, lilting Welsh accent; sadly I never saw or heard of him again. We had been close buddies since we first met at Amiriya and went through the campaigns in Greece and Crete together and then in the early prison camps on Crete and at Salonika, not to mention the Grand Tour from Greece to Germany. Smudger Smith had also been with us over the same period; he was sent to a different working camp and I did not hear of him again either.

And so at Luckenwalde another phase of my life ended. I do not remember the date of our arrival at this camp; it must have been towards the end of September or early October. We had lost count of days and dates over the past few months: we had no calendars and kept no diaries. I must have passed my twenty-second birthday completely unnoticed. Thinking back, I do not recall birthdays being celebrated or even remembered in prison camps. Thus my twenty-second, twenty-third, twenty-fourth, and twenty-fifth birthdays passed without being noticed, let alone celebrated.

8

Teltow - Berlin

The Senior NCOs, usually RSMs, who were sent as camp leaders of working camps were referred to by the Germans as *Vertrauensmänner* or 'men of confidence'. Not only were they camp leaders, but one of their duties was to represent the prisoners in any dealings with the International Red Cross Society. Both Great Britain and Germany were signatories to the Geneva Convention on the treatment of prisoners of war. Their treatment of POWs was monitored by a neutral power and in our case it was the Swiss Red Cross Society as part of the International Red Cross Society, referred to as the 'protecting power'. A Red Cross representative was supposed to pay regular visits to camps to monitor what was going on, but in my experience if they did, we certainly did not get to meet them and had no opportunity to air any grievances directly with them. As far as I can recall, there was only one visit to any camp I was in by the Swiss Red Cross and that was over a fatal shooting incident.

The men of confidence were permitted to communicate with the protecting power but through the Germans. I believe that on rare occasions some did meet the Swiss representatives. More often the Germans, the 'detaining power', would try to resolve any problem themselves rather than have the representative of the protecting power involved. As the representative of the prisoners in the camp, the man of confidence had to have the confidence of the men and if not satisfactory, could be replaced. The rule was that he should be elected by the prisoners of each camp, but the Germans had a power of veto if they disagreed with the choice. However, in all the

American Red Cross map showing locations of POW camps and hospitals.

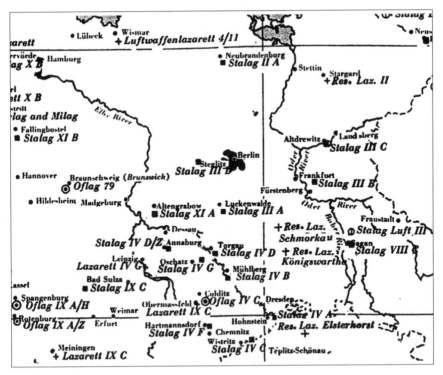

Detail showing the camps in the Berlin area.

camps I was in except one, he was in fact appointed by the German commandant and in all cases was also camp leader. The system worked very well. I knew nothing of this whilst at Luckenwalde and only really found out all about our 'right' to have a man of confidence when I arrived at my second working camp at Staaken.

Many of the men were short of warm clothing. This was rectified to some extent at Luckenwalde by the issue of army clothing which the Germans had captured from the French and Belgian armies. I remember being issued with a Belgian greatcoat, very thin and of poor quality compared with our British ones, but it was better than nothing. Mine was quite voluminous and tied around the waist with a cord. A number of the men had poor footwear and they were issued with wooden-soled shoes. At some stage most of us had to have these wooden-soled shoes when our own boots wore out.

We stayed at Luckenwalde for about a week before being selected to go to working camps in or around Berlin. I assume that the prisoners were chosen randomly. The size of the camps in the Berlin area was usually around 250 to 400 men, although in the last two camps I was in we had only around 100 prisoners, but that was in a different Stalag. The last one I was in, in the Berlin area, had well over a thousand prisoners. In fact the size of the camp was probably determined by the amount of labour required by the Germans, so that over Germany and the occupied countries their size must have varied considerably. I understand that the work on which we could be employed was not to be directly connected to the production of war materials, but at the time we were quite ignorant of the existence of the Geneva Convention, let alone any of its terms.

At Luckenwalde we first became acquainted with the *Appell* system. The Germans were always obsessed about counting the number of prisoners to check that we were all there; we could not have cared less, but the continual counts were an ever-present nuisance for us. We would be paraded for the count, the *Appell*, lined up in four ranks and called to attention when the commandant arrived, then be solemnly counted by an NCO, usually a *gefreiter* (corporal) who reported to the commandant that all were present and correct. Fairly frequently there would be a recount if the first was wrong. On occasions we could be kept for hours on parade when the commandant was bloody-minded and took his time to turn up. Normally there were two of these 'check parades' a day, one in the morning and one in the evening; in addition, each working party was checked in and out of camp.

Camp 714, Stalag IIID, Berlin

Having been assigned to go to a working camp, I and some two hundred and fifty others were assembled, counted and marched to the railway siding where we again got into the ten horses/forty men type of railway wagons and set off for an unknown destination. We were never told where we were going. The journey this time was much shorter, about three or four hours. We disembarked at a siding and were marched a short distance into our first working camp. We soon gathered that this was in a suburb of Berlin called Teltow – it was here we learned that we were in the Berlin area. We also soon learned we were to work for the German railways and later were informed that the camp itself was owned by the railway company.

The camp was rectangular in shape surrounded by a barbed-wire fence about 15ft high with the upper 3ft or so sloping inwards. There was one searchlight at the corner of the camp near the gate which moved in an arc and at nights swept a moving beam continuously backwards and forwards across the camp. It was affixed to the single watchtower near the gate with one guard manning it at night. Two guards patrolled the camp perimeter at night, outside the barbed-wire fence: it must have been really cold for them. The entrance was in one corner: double gates clad with barbed wire. The whole site was flat except for a raised area at the end nearest the gate, about 4 or 5ft higher than the rest and approached by steps. On this raised area were the buildings housing the cookhouse, food stores and storerooms for furniture, tools and so on. We later learned that all the contents of the camp also belonged to the German railway company. On the lower main area, the prisoners' barracks were placed around a central grassed open space and there were concrete paths around the perimeter giving access to the barracks. The open space was used for the parades; it was not really large enough for a football pitch. In fact there was no football pitch at the Teltow camp, but this grassed patch was, when a football was obtained, used for kicking a ball around. Generally speaking, football was the game played by the majority of prisoners although at my last two camps in the Berlin area we also played a lot of rugby.

All the buildings in the camp were constructed of timber, with boarded walls and floors, the roofs (also built of boards) were covered with roofing felt, the floor levels were about 2ft above ground level with timber steps at the doorways. Coming into the camp from the gates, there were two buildings on the left-hand side. The first was a multi-purpose barrack, at one end the sick room and doctor's quarters, a storeroom and the canteen combined with a recreation room, and at the other end the room for the man of confidence, the camp leader. The camp leader soon made his presence felt; he was an RSM from the Black Watch Regiment. The recreation room was hardly ever used as such except for church services which were organised on an *ad hoc* basis by two of the prisoners; we did not have a padre. Next to that block was another barrack with four rooms; each pair of rooms had a common entrance with a small open porch set into the building. At the end of the camp and at right angles was another similar block of four rooms. Then to complete the square on the fourth side were, first, two more barrack blocks of four rooms each, and lastly completing the square a block with the toilets, ablutions and showers together with the boiler room and storage for fuel, which was coke. Outside the gates was another block with

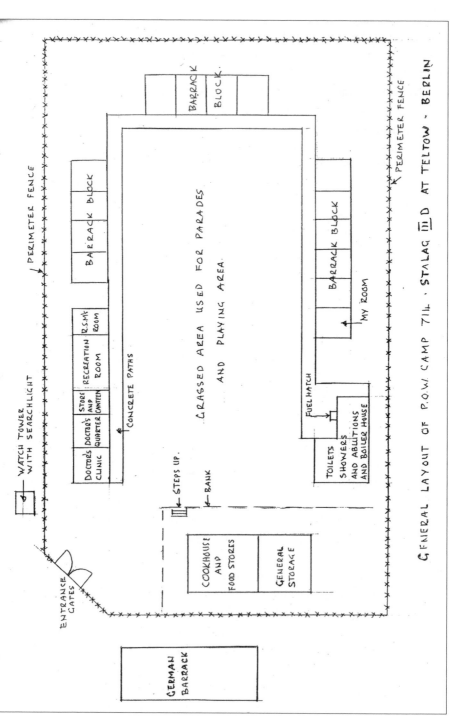

The general layout of Camp 714, Stalag IIID, Tetlow, Berlin.

a guard room and quarters for the commandant and the guards. I have no idea of its layout as I never went inside. The land around the camp had been cleared for some thirty yards or so, after which it was woodland, thus the camp was quite secluded (see camp plan opposite).

I cannot remember any other development nearby and the only civilians we came across during our time at Teltow were the foremen and gangers at the work sites.

The men in the camp were all complete strangers to me. Pugh and Smith were the only ones I had really known and now they had disappeared elsewhere. On arrival we were lined up on the 'parade ground'; the RSM introduced himself, and proceeded to allocate us to barrack rooms. I was sent to the barrack block next to the ablution block and indeed to the room at the end of the block nearest the ablutions. The room had two-tiered bunk beds, six on one side of the room and five on the other, housing twenty-two men. As expected, there was a scramble for places, most preferring the upper bunks; I ended up with a lower bunk, approximately in the middle of the row of six. The bunk was quite low down, only about 12 to 15in off the floor, and with around 3ft 6in headroom between it and the bunk above. There was about 18in of space between the bunks so it was cramped and allowed access for only one person at a time. The central space, our living area, was 7 or 8ft wide, heated by a round cast-iron stove in the middle, called a 'tortoise stove' with a removable lid and a curved door in the middle which opened to put fuel in. There were two rectangular tables and a few wooden stools, insufficient for everyone to sit down at once, so we spent much of the time lying on our bunks. There was a window at each end of the room, giving adequate light, but as it was now approaching winter we never ever opened them. The entrance door to the room was from the little recessed porch serving our room and the adjacent one.

It did not take very long to get to know the other men in the room and something of their backgrounds. They included Robert Atkinson, Don Campbell, Jack Cousens, John Denham, Bob Jennings, John Stevenson and Charles Lusted. The latter I found I remembered from the train journey to Germany as he had stood by me to look at the scenery and we had discussed some of the buildings we passed en route. I still have my old address book, a good *aide-mémoire*. They were a friendly group from diverse parts of the British Isles and from different regiments. A number were from the Liverpool area and others Geordies from Northumberland. We all got on

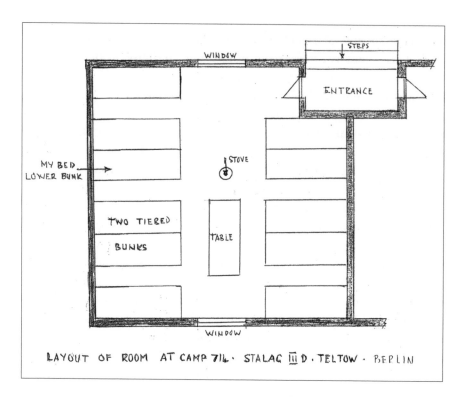

LAYOUT OF ROOM AT CAMP 714. STALAC III D. TELTOW. BERLIN

well together; thankfully there were no really awkward characters and no barrack-room lawyers.

Gradually we began to learn about real POW life. We were told what contacts we were allowed with home by letter cards and postcards and that we were allowed to receive clothing parcels from our families. However, at this time we knew nothing at all about Red Cross food parcels, and I do not think we received any of them at the Teltow camp. The Germans made no attempt to inform us of any of our rights or about the Geneva Convention. We learned gradually as we went along, from snippets of information picked up here and there. My recollection is that we were not, at that stage, particularly concerned about our rights; it was sufficient just to be alive and adjusting to the regime and routine.

Our bunk beds were wooden with palliasses for mattresses. The palliasse was supported by a series of loose boards, known as 'bed-boards'; each was about 5in wide, and filled the whole length of the bed. They were supported on each side by a wooden runner and were easily removable. There were no pillows or sheets, instead we were issued with just two rather thin grey blankets. None of us had pyjamas so we slept in our underwear. Usually we folded our greatcoat for a pillow, unless it was needed, as often that winter, as an extra blanket. The room was lit in the evenings by one single light in the centre of the room, operated from the German barrack and very promptly switched off at nine o'clock in the evening.

The room was heated, more or less – rather less than more – by the tortoise stove. The fuel we were issued with was in the form of coal briquettes, about 9 by 4in and 2.5in thick, made of compressed coal dust with some sort of a binder. The daily ration was ten to twelve briquettes, dependent on availability. We did not light the fire until we had returned from work in the evening; the briquettes were sufficient to give about three hours' heating which did not reach the whole room, so we tended to cluster as close to the stove as we could get or otherwise lie on our beds with the blankets and/or coats on to try to keep warm. We were given no kindling or paper to start the fire and had to pick up what we could – paper, twigs or bits of wood – whilst out at work. Matches we could buy in the canteen.

The weather became much colder as winter drew nearer, and we spent a lot of time devising ways of supplementing the fuel supply for the stove. The first option was to scrounge bits of wood, and the odd lump of coal whilst out on the working parties; this provided a small amount of extra fuel but never enough to keep the fire going through the night. In desperation, we decided that the bed-boards would make an excellent source of fuel, so each one in turn was asked to give up a bed-board. This kept us going a little while, then a second board was given up, then another and on and on. So from being solidly supported there became gaps in the support for the palliasse. There was, of course, a limit to this supply and we had to stop at the point where there were just enough boards left to support the palliasse. These boards were good fuel but burned all too quickly. We then had to look for other sources, one of which was the furniture in the recreation room. This also was a limited supply and had to be removed surreptitiously hidden inside our coats. The barrack rooms closest to it were in the best position to benefit so they got the most; our room got very little.

The store room next to the recreation room also contained a quantity of blankets which gradually disappeared; they were 'acquired' and then cut up to make linings for the very thin greatcoats. Keeping warm was our chief concern during the 1941–42 winter, which was exceptionally cold – the coldest in Europe in the twentieth century.

The boilers in the ablution block were heated by coke. When it was periodically delivered to the boiler room, we had been able to get a few odd pieces and this helped a lot because coke burned much longer than the briquettes. We noticed that the deliveries of coke were tipped down an outside chute which had a pair of wooden lids which were always kept padlocked. Naturally our thoughts turned to getting hold of a supply of coke. The padlock was inspected – we must have had a lock-picker amongst us – and it was decided the lock could be opened and access gained to the chute. As our room was nearest to the ablution block, we were the best placed to raid the coke store. The next problem was how to store any coke we acquired out of sight of the guards who made fairly frequent visits to our room. It happened that at the time one of the men in our room was away in hospital, so someone suggested we could store the coke in his palliasse. It was emptied and, the straw distributed and put in other people's palliasses. The raid was then planned – of course it had to be at night – and we told no one else about the scheme, not even those in the room immediately next door.

Our door was not locked at night because occasionally someone needed to go to the loo. There were two guards patrolling, moving singly in opposite directions, until they met when they stopped to exchange a few words and have a cigarette. It must have been a lonely, weary, monotonous task for them, night after night walking around in the cold and nothing ever happening. I do not think there was ever any attempt to escape from Teltow camp, so it was likely they got very bored and were not completely vigilant. Thus the raiding party had, first, to dodge the guards and the sweep of the searchlight to get to the chute and secondly, to force the lock without making too much noise. But there was a third problem which we had not appreciated: this was the noise made by the coke whilst it was being shovelled into the palliasse. A raiding party of four of us undertook the task. We crept out of the room, one by one, and keeping to the shadows we managed to avoid the guards and the searchlight and assembled silently at the chute. We opened the padlock easily. Three of us went down with the empty palliasse and the fourth remained on guard outside. There was a certain amount of noise down below as the palliasse was filled, which then had to be manoeuvred out, the hatch closed and the broken padlock put back in position. Then we had to get back to the room carrying the now heavy palliasse between us, which we managed without being spotted.

The palliasse was placed on the empty bunk, a top one, smoothed out and covered with a blanket. We now had fuel for several weeks. It was not until the next delivery of coke arrived a couple of weeks later that the Germans discovered the broken padlock. They surmised there must have been a break-in to the coke store, obviously by the prisoners, although they were not quite sure what had happened. The commandant ordered a thorough search of the camp.

There had been some heavy falls of snow which had to be cleared from the paths around the camp. Our RSM called for volunteers. Generally the men were not interested in volunteering, but a number of us from our room did so, calculating that it might prove useful to be on the right side of the guards who supervised the work and seemed quite pleased with us. The ploy seemed to work as the same guards conducted the search for the missing coke. Their search of our room was fairly cursory: the guards looked under the beds, in our kit and in the stove for evidence of coke. We had been careful to cover any remains with briquettes as soon as we learned of the search. We also kept a few briquettes at the ready at all times in case a guard came around. There was one tricky moment when the guard came to the alley between the beds where the coke was hidden. One of the men stood in the alleyway looking away from the guard as if he had not seen him. After a little hesitation the guards went away saying we were a good room and they had not expected to find anything. Of course we had to be vigilant until the coke had been used up. I think this was our first deliberate and successful deception of the Germans: over the years there would be many more.

From time to time the coal wagon arrived to deliver the briquettes which were tipped out onto the ground and then had to be stacked in a heap outside the camp gate near the Germans' barrack block, very sensibly from their point of view. The call would come for volunteers to help with unloading and stacking the briquettes. There was never a shortage of volunteers for this! As soon as sufficient men were let through the gate it was closed. As we were as close to the gate as any, we usually managed to get four or five in the unloading party. Our plan, of course, was to pinch a few briquettes and this was where the very loose voluminous greatcoats came in useful. With the cord tied tightly around the waist there was room to get a few briquettes inside – a dusty black bosom. It must have been obvious to the guard on duty what was going on, but he always turned a blind eye;

maybe he considered it one of the perks for volunteering. We used to return to the room to unload the swag to the acclaim of the other men, shook our coats out and repaired to the ablution block to wash our filthy hands. Thus we had another small supply of fuel for the stove and very helpful it was; we were always perished with cold.

One day there was a clarion call for everyone to get out on parade. We duly formed up and were called to attention by the RSM when the commandant accompanied by other soldiers and a couple of civilians arrived. Our Black Watch RSM was wearing his glengarry; he had a large black moustache and made a splendid figure. He announced in stentorian tones, 'Gentlemen, the day of reckoning has arrived.' He told us that the railway representatives had come to take an inventory of everything in the camp. He then explained that the camp was owned by the railway company and this included all the contents including beds, furniture, blankets, kitchen equipment and so on. He knew for a fact that we had been burning any wood we could get hold of and had also taken blankets for coat linings and was of the opinion that this would be revealed and we were for the high jump. He expected the railway people would find large discrepancies so there would be recriminations with some as yet unknown punishment for the whole camp.

However, it soon transpired that there was some disagreement between the commandant and the civilians. The commandant apparently told the civilians he could allow them to inspect the cookhouse and store area but that our barracks and the German barrack were under military control and no way could the civilians go into them, let alone inspect them and their contents. He told them that, whether or not they owned the buildings and their contents, military regulations took precedence and he would not let them enter the prisoners' barracks. The civilians argued that the whole camp belonged to them and furthermore the prisoners worked for them. They said the whole purpose of the camp was to serve the railways and demanded to inspect it entirely. The commandant was adamant and got very annoyed. There was a complete stand-off and in the end the civilians stalked off and left the camp. The idea of an inspection was dropped; we never heard any more about it. The parade was dismissed and we all heaved one huge sigh of relief.

During that winter temperatures dropped to -40°C. It was so cold we had about half an inch of ice on the inside of the windows in our room, the moisture to form the ice presumably coming from our combined breath. We slept with all our clothes on. Using our greatcoats as either an additional blanket or even sleeping with them on, we still could not keep warm. Even with our augmented fuel supply we could not keep the fire in the stove going all night. No one would dare to venture out to the toilets during the night although the cold made us want to pee a lot, so we had to improvise and get 'potties' to use during the night. I was lucky enough to get hold of a large empty jam tin about 10in in diameter and about 6 or 7in tall, which just fitted snugly under my bed. Even so it was extremely cold getting out of bed during the night to have a pee. In due course I found I could lift the tin up to the bed and have a pee without getting out of bed. The men in the top bunks were not so lucky and had no option but climb down from their beds. One had to be careful not to overfill the receptacle and of course in the mornings we had to venture out into the morning cold to empty them in the toilet block.

In one way it could be said the cold winter was a godsend because it was also dry and despite the poor food, there were virtually no cases of flu or the common cold. In this sense it was healthy weather and I do not recall any cases of hypothermia (a term not yet in use then or at least unknown to us).

However, there was one illness which almost always required hospitalisation and this was beriberi. Beriberi is caused by deficiency of thiamine (vitamin B1), often from poor diet. There were a number of cases, including me. We had a doctor in the camp who had arrived two or three weeks after us. Dr Rana was Indian; a small man with a round face and of a very dark complexion, probably from southern India, and a very pleasant man. He did his best but was seriously handicapped in having only the very limited range of medicines and medical supplies provided by the Germans; I imagine the health of prisoners of war was not one of their priorities. He was the only coloured person in the camp and came in for a lot of banter mainly of a mild racial nature, which did not appear to upset him.

When anyone reported sick, Dr Rana had just three options: the first to pronounce him fit for work, deducing he was malingering (quite a number were and were just chancing their arm), or he could treat them with aspirin and put them on light duty for a few days, or thirdly he could send them to hospital, as he did with severe cases of beriberi. There was no sickbay or 'lazarett' as the Germans called a sick room in this camp. Light work consisted of work inside the camp, cleaning and sweeping the paths, cleaning the ablutions or most likely doing chores in the cookhouse. Work in the cookhouse was the favourite because it was warm and one could scrounge extra scraps of food. I remember doing a spell of spud bashing. Later it was decided that the potatoes would not be peeled as the skins contained vitamin B and this helped to prevent beriberi. A little episode sticks in my mind. A man went sick with sore feet; the doctor examined him and put him on light work for a few days and gave him two aspirins. The man, exasperated, exclaimed, 'What do I do with these bloody pills, put one in each boot?' The poor doctor just did not have anything else to prescribe. No doubt it was very lonely for him being the only officer in the camp and the only Indian.

The food at Teltow camp was pretty poor. We had a daily ration of bread, a bowl of so-called stew and a few potatoes issued at midday or after we got back from work. The stew was more a soup than stew, made with vegetables (mainly cabbage and turnip) some rice and a very small amount of meat – one was lucky to get even two or three very small pieces. The potatoes were usually served in their skins but were so overcooked that the skins were burst and looked very unappetising. The skins containing vitamin B were no doubt good for us.

The meal was brought round to the door of the room in containers on a little handcart and dished out by the kitchen staff. Not surprisingly, they could be rather selective in dishing out the ladles of stew, digging deep if they liked you and just skimming the liquid from the surface if they did not. There was always some bickering and bantering about the quality of the stew and the quantity dished out, and naturally there was some reference to the fat cooks which did not go down well with them and anyone who was heard to grumble got a smaller ladle of food.

We had a ration of margarine as well, amounting to about 3 or 4oz a week, called '*kunstbutter*': 'kunst' in this sense meaning 'artificial' or 'ersatz', in fact we thought it quite tasty. The only margarine I had known at home had been Stork which I had thought rather disgusting, and which my mother only used for cooking. There was a weekly ration of sugar which lasted about two days, especially as it was given loose and we also had about two tablespoons of jam, once a week. Then rather spasmodically we had small tins of either meat or fish (often sardines). The contents, I suppose, were about 3oz; no doubt these appeared as and when available.

Bread formed the bulk of our ration. It was dark brown, made from rye flour and came in rectangular loaves which seemed about the size of our two pound loaf, so probably weighed a kilo. It was not the type of bread we were used to in England which was usually white – even wholemeal bread was not very popular then. I had heard of brown Hovis loaves but not eaten one. It took a while to get used to this heavy rye bread and throughout POW life we dreamed of white bread. The amount of the bread ration varied considerably; at the very best, it was half a loaf per man per day but as the war went on, it decreased and for the last few months it was down to one eighth of a loaf. At that same time the quality deteriorated, becoming even coarser and quite gritty. We speculated that it was being bulked up with sand or some other inorganic substance.

The correct number of loaves was issued to the room; the problem then was to decide how to divide it up between the men. Four or five of us were given a loaf, which we had to divide up into equal pieces, a quite impossible task to achieve exactly, so no one wanted the task and responsibility of cutting the loaf. At first there was quarrelling about the slightly differing sizes of the individual pieces, but soon we worked out an agreeable system: we took it in turns to cut the loaf and to choose a piece, with the one who cut the loaf always having the last piece. The bread issue was made when we returned to camp after work and it was each man's choice as to when to eat his ration; some would scoff it all straight away, but most were sensible enough to eat half of it in the evening and save the remainder for a rather dry breakfast before going out to work in the morning.

More often than not there was nothing to put on it, so we tried toasting it to make it more palatable. The obvious way was to open the top of the stove and using a crude toasting fork made from scraps of wire, lower it gingerly into the stove. There was always the danger of the bread falling off the fork – almost impossible to rescue – so it became fuel instead of food, which we could not afford to let happen. The other method of toasting was by pressing the slice against the outside of the round stove. As the bread was quite moist it would stick to the stove, eventually dropping off and the other side was then toasted in the same way. The result was charred rather than toasted bread, but we found it did improve the edibility slightly. Sardines on toast or bread made a tasty change to dry bread. On one occasion, I remember a cockney voice piping up, 'Say chaps, could anyone force another sardine?' He showed us half-starved men one left in his tin, but did not give us a chance to answer before devouring it himself. There was always a lot of humour and banter amongst the men in our room (and no doubt in all the others) and, despite the intense cold, crowded conditions and poor food, morale amongst the prisoners remained very high. The odd Jonah was soon pounced on; we always believed in our ultimate victory over the Germans.

The only drink the Germans gave us was ersatz coffee, probably made from toasting some variety of grain rather than acorns as widely rumoured. It was not a pleasant drink – many men preferred water – but it was hot and we needed hot drinks. A few of us had some tea – I am not sure of the source. When Red Cross parcels came later, we had constant supplies of tea and coffee. Our problem then was how to boil water. The only receptacles were our dixies, the small enamelled bowls the Germans issued for our food, or empty tins, but none of these could boil water if put on the top of the stove. In due course a method was devised by using an army water bottle. This was flask shaped but covered with some khaki-coloured material. We stripped the bottle down to the bare blue metal, a small hole was made at the top by the stopper and a piece of wire threaded through it so it could be lowered right onto the fire below where it boiled quite quickly. We had to be careful not to let it boil over and put the fire out.

Later on, when we had empty tins from food sent in Red Cross parcels, one ingenious 'inventor' devised a machine or 'contraption' to boil water. A tin had a little perforated platform fixed inside it; below this, a fan made of strips of tin was fixed and operated by a protruding wire handle, then burning matches were placed on the perforated platform and the container with water was placed over the machine. By turning the fan rapidly, the embers of the matches glowed and gave off heat enough to boil the water, the burned matches acting rather like charcoal. The amazing thing was that it worked: its inventor claimed he could boil a cup of water using just three matches purchased in the canteen.

There was very little organised social life at the Teltow camp as we had very little surplus energy after work to do anything but rest. There was not even any football. Usually, whatever condition the men were in, they could not resist trying to set up a game of their beloved soccer but at first we did not have a football and nowhere to play. Then again during that first winter it was too bloody cold for outdoor games and often the ground was covered with snow. Because of the poor food and the heavy manual work we were generally content, after work, to stay in the room. Our time would be spent in conversation or we chattered in groups. Often the talk would be about food and the things we missed: HP sauce, Heinz tomato ketchup, Colman's mustard, Branston pickle and other proprietary brands, and all the dishes our mothers used to make – and, of course, cakes and white bread.

From time to time there were sing-songs, mainly of old army songs. We had no music, no gramophones, no musical instruments and naturally no wireless. There were very few books and just the odd Bible. I still had my New Testament which I had bought in Egypt (the one bound in olivewood) and I had a number of photographs to look at, including those ones taken at Moascar camp and in Athens, and a few from home including some polyphotos of Stella. They had all been examined by the Germans, I think at Luckenwalde, and each photo, the New Testament and my army pay book were stamped *Geprüft*, indicating I could keep them, which I have done for some sixty years; most of them also have the Stalag IIID stamp.

There was no padre at the Teltow camp. In fact, it was not until the fourth camp in the Berlin area that I came across a padre. The RSM gave no lead in arranging any religious services, but one man did: Jimmy Ellis. Jimmy arranged Sunday services in the recreation room which he conducted himself and did sterling work, even though it was only the relatively few faithful who attended, maybe up to thirty out of the whole camp, including me. Jimmy also spoke fluent German and acted as an interpreter throughout the time I knew him, that is until we left the Berlin area much later. It is interesting that the Germans never provided interpreters: it was always us who found the *dolmetscher* or interpreter for any translating that needed to be done. The only English-speaking German I came across was the commandant at the last camp we were in, in the Berlin area at Wuhlheide.

The work in this camp, as in almost all the working camps I was in, was for the German railways, the only exceptions being an agricultural working party from Stalag IVB and the camp at Mühlberg. The usual working hours at the working site were from eight in the morning until around half past four in the afternoon, except in midwinter when it was dark earlier in the afternoon. At Teltow the guards came knocking on the doors at half six in the morning with their shouts of, '*Raus, raus, aufstehen, aufstehen*', words which became very familiar throughout our POW lives. We would wearily climb out of bed and make for the ablution block to wash and shave in cold water: it certainly woke us up.

Shaving was somewhat difficult because the only soap was gritty German ersatz soap which hardly lathered. Razor blades were often in short supply; occasionally we could buy '*rasierklingen*' (razor blades) in the canteen. Not everyone wanted to wash and shave and some gentle persuasion had to be used on the reluctant ones. It was felt necessary that everyone should make the effort to wash and be cleanly shaved. Amazingly, we could buy cut-throat razors in the canteen – apparently not considered offensive weapons – and in time I became very proficient with mine. Then we ate our break-fast – provided we had saved some bread from our daily ration. Some men went out to work without having eaten anything at all.

We were then called out on parade and sorted out into various working parties; often it was still semi-dark. We were counted and marched out with our guards, two to each party, to the waiting lorries to be transported to the work sites. We travelled in the back of open lorries, whilst, naturally, the guards got in the cab with the driver. There was a shortage of petroleum and diesel fuels, which were reserved for the armed forces and essential services. These lorries were interesting because they were powered from woodchip-burning boilers. The cylindrical boilers were placed in the back of the lorry on the left-hand side immediately behind the cab. They became quite warm and proved to be an incentive to be first on the lorry rather than eagerness to get to work. As can be expected, the bigger, stronger men pushed their way on first to have the best positions – I rarely got near the warmth. We were crammed on the lorry, standing room only, so we swayed against each other during the uncomfortable ride to the work site.

The work entailed building embankments for railway lines. We were issued with shovels and allocated two or three to a skip or bogey. The skip was on four wheels, triangular in section with sloping sides and a tipping mechanism operated by a lever and mounted on a narrow-gauge railway line; the tipping mechanism allowed the skip to be emptied on either side. Our work was to fill the skip and then push it up the slope to the top of the ever-growing embankment and tip out the contents; others then levelled it, consolidating the soil. The material for building the embankment was a kind of sandy loam and quite easy to shovel.

There were about ten skips working on our section of line and all the skips had to be filled before the whole string of them could be pushed up the slope and be emptied. We were never in a hurry to fill them, so there was constant shouting by the foreman or ganger as he walked up and down the line. He was sometimes assisted by the guards, although some guards were quite uninterested and could not care less whether we worked or not. The rate of progress of the work depended on the slowest to fill their skip because we could not push them up the slope for emptying until they were all filled. We were in a bit of a quandary because, on the one hand, the shovelling helped to keep us warm in the very cold weather but on the other, we all intended to do as little work as possible for the German war effort. So as soon as the ganger or guard had passed by exhorting us to work, we would stop and lean on our shovels and have a chat until we were 'rudely' shouted at again.

Their shout was always '*Raus, raus*', whether to get out of bed, get on parade, get on the lorry or get some work done. We were always exhorted to work; the Germans seemed to be bred to work. We told them that we were certain that when a German baby began to talk his first word was not 'mummy' but '*arbeit*' (work), but our jokes were rarely appreciated. There were posters everywhere stating '*Arbeit Macht Frei*' (work makes you free); it certainly did not make us free. We turned leaning on shovels into an art form – nowadays we would have been awarded a Turner Prize for it!

And so each working day ground along until the lorries reappeared around 4.30 p.m. to return us to camp. One incident remains firmly in my mind. It was a bitterly cold day and we were loading the last skips before finishing work for the day; the lorries were already waiting. One last skip was being filled very slowly. 'Dodger' Green (also from Burton-on-Trent) stood leaning on his shovel, deaf to all the shouting and exhortations of the guard. Both the guards and the rest of us were eager to get back to camp and out of the shivering cold. Dodger stood his ground despite the pleas of the guard who accused him of selfishness. Dodger replied, 'I'd rather freeze to death than put myself out working for you bloody Germans,' then added, 'If you're in such a hurry to fill the skip, do it your bloody self!' and handed the guard his shovel. The guard accepted it and set about filling the skip, he was that eager to return to camp and some warmth. Dodger was one of those awkward men who would rather talk and argue than do anything, and was our greatest expert in the art of doing nothing. He was a likeable man and a real character. No one ever forgot that the 'square heads' were the enemy and every opportunity must be taken to avoid helping them. It is interesting to note that the stories published about POW camps, especially the Oflags (officer's camps), refer to the German guards as 'goons' or sometimes 'krauts'. Those names were never used in our camps – I did not come across them until after the war. To us they were called 'square heads' or more often than not, 'square-headed bastards'. We did occasionally call them 'huns'.

The weather became very harsh but the railway foremen insisted we continue working until the ground was so frozen we could not dent it with pickaxes, let alone shovel the soil, so we had a couple of idle weeks in camp until the weather improved. In the very cold weather it became dangerous to touch any metal with the bare hands, as they would freeze to the metal and pull the skin off. The Germans provided us with '*handschuhen*' (gloves), mostly mittens with no separate fingers and made of some very coarse material, not at all warm and rather uncomfortable for working. The only thing in their favour was that they prevented freeze burns, but even they, if they got slightly damp, would sometimes stick to metal. They did not wear well either and as the Germans were reluctant to replace worn ones, we had to try to repair them. Later, once we began to receive personal parcels from home, we were thankful to get woollen gloves knitted by mothers, sisters and grannies.

Another task we were sometimes given was to move rails from the delivery point to their positions on the embankment. These rails were between 20 and 25ft long, and very heavy. It took eight men to lift one and carry it up the slope to its position. They were lifted by a tool called a 'stange', which was like a giant pincer with handles about three feet long, the end of which was bent at right angles. Each of the four pairs of men, standing either side of the rail and spaced along its length, used a stange. The pincer end gripped the rail which was lifted using the part of the handle bent at right angles. The rail could just about be lifted as the men staggered to put it in its place ready to be fixed to the sleepers which were already in position. The fixing of the rails was carried out by other prisoners, mostly French. The Germans said they could not trust British prisoners to do this task as they suspected we would find some way of sabotaging the process. I was lucky in this work to be paired with big Charlie Whitaker who was strong enough to lift the rail himself whilst I was particularly weak; he became a close 'mucker' for a long time.

Footwear was, during the first year or so, a very serious problem. As our army boots wore out we were issued with prison boots. These had wooden soles with uppers of a coarse canvas type material and had to be tied up with tapes in lieu of laces. They were uncomfortable and difficult to get used to as they had no flexibility, so we tended to shuffle along in them. The Germans also issued us with backless slippers called '*pantoffeln*' also with wooden soles which we wore in the evenings in our rooms.

When, after a year or so, Red Cross supplies slowly began to arrive, we were issued with British army battledress uniforms, boots, warm greatcoats, shirts, socks and underwear, but that was not until we had moved onto our second camp at Staaken. Even then, articles arrived haphazardly so it was some time before we were well kitted out. Surprisingly many of us had managed to hold on to our army sidecaps complete with regimental cap badges.

At Teltow, perhaps the biggest clothing problem was socks. Our own socks soon wore out and needed to be replaced. The German replacements were not socks, but what they called foot cloths: largish squares of roughish

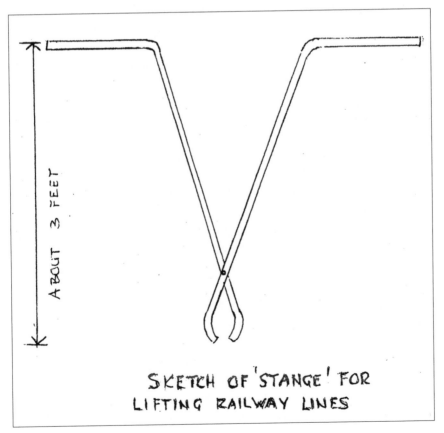

SKETCH OF 'STANGE' FOR LIFTING RAILWAY LINES

off-white cloth which we had to wrap round our feet and then tie round the ankle with pieces of tape. They were neither warm nor comfortable, and soon developed holes but were just about better than nothing. We must have looked a pretty ragged lot, which pleased the Germans who liked to see us degraded, downtrodden and visibly the underdogs. We did our best to keep clean and tidy but there was no real incentive to act like soldiers. This was to change dramatically later on and give concern to our captors.

We were paid for our work. I suppose this was a provision of the, then unknown to us, Geneva Convention. We were paid in 'camp marks', all paper money in various denominations, about the same size as Monopoly money. It was said to be equivalent to real German marks. These paper notes could only be spent in the camp canteen and were not accepted in the outside world – not that there was any opportunity of shopping outside the camp. We had reason, later on, to believe that the Germans themselves could exchange them for real marks. Presumably the money taken in the canteen had to be used for the purchase of stock and so at some stage must have been negotiable for German marks. I do not recall how much we were paid; we did not pay very much attention to the amount. Once a month, I think, the Germans called a pay parade. We queued up to receive and sign for our pay; days off work were carefully deducted, the notes counted out, all with the due solemnity and precision of the Germans, not unlike a British army pay parade.

There was the small canteen where we could buy a limited range of goods, many useless. The few essentials available included matches, razor blades and the gritty, green soap. When soap came from the Red Cross or in personal parcels we stopped buying canteen soap. There were no sweets or food for sale except for '*senf*', German mustard, not strong like our beloved Colman's, but rather milder like French mustard; this we did buy to put on our very dry bread. We could also buy paper and pencils but little else was of use to us. Over time we accumulated sizeable amounts of camp marks, used mainly for gambling. There was always someone running 'a book' on something or other. Various card games including whist, bridge and poker were played, although in the early POW days, packs of cards were at a premium, but a few of the men had brought cards with them. No one really took the wages very seriously: it was just play money.

We were allowed to write home on letter cards of white, rather glossy, paper. On one side was printed Kreigsgefangenen (POW) post with lines

PASSED
P.W. 507

10.1.45—16

An MISS STELLA JEAN SPARKS

1, RYE HILL.

Empfangsort: LONGBRIDGE DEVERILL,

Straße: WARMINSTER

Kreis: WILTSHIRE

Land: ENGLAND

Landesteil (Provinz usw.)

Gebührenfrei

Deutschland (Allemagne)

Lager-Bezeichnung: STALAG IV D CAMP. SCH 484.

Gefangenennummer: 114807

Vor- und Zuname: ALFR. SYDNEY LITHERLAND.

Absender:

NOTICE

Parcels containing written communications for the receiver and objects, which are prohibited or by the way in which they are packed, are intended to be withheld from the control (means of all kinds for facilitating escape) **will not be delivered any more.**

Prohibited objects are:

Money of all kinds and currencies.

Civil clothing for prisoners of war (interned civil persons excluded) and underclothing, which might be worn as outward civil clothing (pullovers are allowed).

Badges (brassards) for sanitary personnel sent to persons not entitled to wear them.

Weapons and tools to be used as weapons, large clasp-knives and scissors.

Ammunition and explosives.

Tools which are suitable for facilitating escape and for committing acts of sabotage.

Copying apparatuses, carbon paper, and tracing paper.

Compasses, haversacks (rucksacks), maps, cameras, binoculars, magnifying glasses.

Electric torches, lighters, match-boxes, matches, wicks, candles.

Spirit, alcohol, and alcoholic drinks.

Solidified methylated spirits, objects which easily catch fire, radiators.

Telephones and apparatuses for transmitting and receiving and component parts for those.

Medicals of any kind and form, vaseline tubes, ammonia muriate (solid or dissolved).

Fruit juice of any kind, chemicals, acids.

Books and printed matter of doubtful or indecent character, newspapers, books with maps attached to them.

Cigarette-paper, and cigar-holders made of paper.

Blank paper of any kind, notebooks, writing paper, postcards.

Potatoes.

NB. Books are to be sent separately (one at a time) or in Red Cross parcels.

Parcels are to be made up solidly and wrapped tightly to avoid losses or theft.

englisch

The printed letter we were given to send home, listing all the articles we were not allowed to send. This is the one I sent my mother.

for the address and on the back lines for the name of the sender, camp and stalag numbers (see page 141). I still have a number of them which I had sent to Stella. The letter cards were rather like our own blue airletter forms but white, fastened by tucking a flap into a slit in the back rather than gummed. The writing area was also lined. We wrote in pencil as pen and ink were prohibited. The issue was one a fortnight with occasionally an extra issue of a postcard. So we were able to write home to give limited news of ourselves: all our letters were censored by the Germans and presumably on arrival in England by our own censors. Our early letters were mainly requests to our families to send us warm clothing such as jerseys, socks, gloves, balaclava helmets and items such as soap and cigarettes or pipe tobacco. I have a faint recollection that we could buy pipes in the canteen. We also asked for gramophone records and books. I am not clear how we obtained gramophones – perhaps the Red Cross provided them. These personal parcels began to arrive towards the end of our time at Teltow and were a tremendous boost to our morale as well as to our comfort and warmth.

One day we were issued with a printed lettercard to be addressed and sent to our next of kin – I still have the one I sent home – containing a long list of the items which were prohibited from inclusion in personal parcels, including explosives, guns, ammunition, petrol and inflammable liquids, baseball bats, darts, money and a whole host of other things which in any case would not and could not possibly be sent. Perhaps the most extraordinary item on the prohibited list was '*kartoffeln*' – potatoes. We looked at the letter and immediately decided it was not to be taken at all seriously. Rather than sending them home, we decided to address them to various celebrities both famous and, to us, infamous, including Hitler, Goering, Goebbels and Himmler, and to President Roosevelt, Winston Churchill, King George VI, Charlie Chaplin, Gracie Fields and Vera Lynn, to mention but a few. Off went the letters and, surprise, surprise!, the German censors were not at all amused. Presumably they destroyed them before issuing a second set with very strict instruction to address them to our next of kin, with the warning that failure to do so would result in the withdrawal of all rights to have any more letter cards. We duly complied, but we felt we had made a point.

At the time I gave little thought as to how long it took for our letters to reach home. Looking at one of those I still have, I see it was written to Stella, dated by me 13 June 1943 and has a Marlborough, Wiltshire, post office date stamp of 19 June 1943, whilst another dated by me 16 July 1944 had an English post office date stamp of 28 July 1944 – relatively fast in the circumstances. I do not know the route they took but assume they went via Switzerland, our protecting power and intermediary. Considering they went though censors' offices at both ends, it seemed there was very little delay.

There were a small number of prisoners who never seemed to have anyone to write to, nor did they receive any letters, so their letter cards went spare and it seemed a pity to waste them. One of my fellow prisoners was George (Paddy) Baxter who also came from Burton-on-Trent, so he was a 'townie' of mine. I felt very sorry for him, as he always looked sadly on when we received and read our letters from home. I asked Stella to write to him, which she very kindly did and I persuaded him to write back to her; he did so for a short while. On one of the letter cards he wrote his story. He had run away from home at the age of fourteen, completely lost touch with his family as he travelled around, eventually joining the army at eighteen and had almost completed his 'seven' (in those days soldiers signed up for seven years). However, Paddy was not keen on writing letters and in due course handed his letter cards for me to use. Because we were restricted to one letter each I would write them but put his name on the back as sender. This was helpful, as I could now write regularly to both my mother and Stella.

Thus began our communication with our families and loved ones. The letters I received were overwhelmingly from Stella and my mother with a very occasional letter from my sisters. I do not recall my two brothers ever writing to me.

Then, slowly, personal parcels began to arrive. Mine were exclusively from my mother and family. They were very important for us as they brought us warm pullovers, balaclavas, gloves, scarves and socks. We also received tins of cigarettes, pipe tobacco and tablets of soap. Later, at my request, I was sent some technical books to allow me to continue studying. I cannot say that conditions were very conducive for study, but I did some reading and some of it probably sank in over the years.

When a personal parcel arrived, which was about every three or four months, we were called to the RSM's room where they were opened by a German guard, usually a feldwebel (sergeant), in the presence of the man of confidence, usually the RSM. The parcel's contents were examined to see if there were any contraband articles – never happened in any of my camps – before being handed over. I must say that the Germans were always quite strict and correct in their procedure when dealing with these parcels. As far as I am aware, nothing was ever stolen by them: they strictly abided by the Geneva Convention in this respect. It may have been different in other camps, but I suspect overall the Germans were correct in their handling of our parcels. Sometime later we met up with POWs who had been prisoners of the Italians and had been transferred to Germany after the fall of Mussolini. They told us the Italian guards would open tins of cigarettes, tear the paper off each cigarette, ostensibly looking for any messages concealed in them, but really just being bloody-minded. They also told us they thought the Italians stole parcels including Red Cross food parcels.

News would soon spread around the camp that a load of parcels had arrived, so we got rather irritated when they took their time in notifying the recipients. I was always sure there would be 'one for me', as were others, and there was considerable disappointment if there was not. There were some poor men who never received any personal parcels, so we always made a point of sharing our cigarettes and tobacco with them.

For many, the most welcome items were the tins of cigarettes and pipe tobacco. The majority were habitual smokers – we never thought of it as a drug habit – and it was certainly a smoother of tensions, a sort of sedative and important in POW camps where something was really needed to relieve tensions and boredom. The cigarettes were in round sealed tins of fifty, the usual brands being Players or Woodbines; the pipe tobacco, also in round sealed tins, was usually St Bruno or Craven A. Later on when we started bartering with the guards – strictly illegal for them and us – cigarettes became the most important currency (together, somewhat later, with coffee). It was then that non-smokers had an advantage.

Throughout POW life, before we got supplies from our personal parcels and from the Red Cross, the Germans supplied a cigarette ration, I think about twenty a week. These cigarettes were manufactured in eastern occupied Europe, we thought Poland or Czechoslovakia, but they could have been from the Balkans. I remember two of the varieties were Dravas and Junaks. They were made with strong dark brown tobacco not at all like Golden Virginia tobacco and had quite a pungent smell, but not as bad as the French Gauloise. One brand – I am pretty sure the Junak – was unusual in that half the cigarette was a hollow tube made of thin card, the end which went in the mouth; the other half contained the tobacco wrapped in normal cigarette paper. They needed quite a strong suck to get going: one way of making tobacco go further. Very occasionally, Gauloises were obtained by trading with French POWs. Later, when we started bargaining with the Germans, usually for extra bread and later still eggs, we found the guards very keen to get hold of our Virginia cigarettes. It did occur to me that this gave them an added incentive not to break up our cigarettes.

We were intrigued at the ban on darts and baseball bats when we could freely receive cricket bats and stumps. I have a faint recollection that when we did receive various items of sports equipment later on, most of it was sent by the YMCA; in fact the YMCA was one of many charities that sent goods out to POWs.

Early in 1942 a few men in the camp began to suffer with swollen legs. The swelling started at the ankles, gradually working to the thighs. Those who developed this complaint reported sick and Dr Rana fairly soon diagnosed the complaint as beriberi. Beriberi is an illness prevalent in the Indian sub-continent. One of the symptoms is a severe swelling or oedema in the legs which can lead to paralysis. Its name derives from the Sinhalese

Box of 100 Junak cigarettes made in occupied Poland.

word beri meaning literally 'I cannot', referring to the weakness and lassitude engendered by it. It was said the oedema could rise up to and beyond the genitals, which could swell to an enormous size and, we heard, that if it reached the kidneys the result would be certain death: I do not know if that is true. I suppose up to twenty men in the camp had the disease over a period of several months. Dr Rana had no vitamin pills to give us. I say 'us' because I was one of those who got beriberi: all he could do was advise us to eat cooked potato peelings as a source of vitamin B1 and hope it would help. If the swellings persisted and moved up past the knees, he would ask the German commandant – who usually agreed – to admit the patient to hospital for treatment.

I developed the symptoms, reported sick and was put on light work for a few days so that Dr Rana could monitor progress. The disease continued to develop so I was sent off to hospital somewhere on the outskirts of Berlin. It was a military hospital which had a section set aside for the treatment of POWs, divided into subsections by nationality. I was put in a section exclusively for British and Commonwealth POWs.

The building was old, rather stark with plain unadorned walls and very high ceilings. The walls were painted darkish green to dado height. The walls above and ceilings were greyish-white, typical of any military hospitals of that time. For patients arriving from the cold, crowded camps, the hospital ward was a considerable improvement: not only was it more spacious but also warmer. Even so, some of the beds were two-tiered, the upper bunk being in general allocated to those well on the way to recovery. The doctors and male nurses/orderlies on our ward were French; unfortunately there were no female nurses. A German doctor appeared to do a weekly inspection and confirm with the French doctor those who were fit enough to be discharged and those who needed further treatment.

On arrival, I was taken to the ablutions, seated on a chair while an orderly shaved off all my hair. I was then given a shower followed by disinfection by an orderly with a bucket of disinfectant and a lavatory brush who dabbed it under the armpits and around the genitals (as at Luckenwalde); no doubt this was to try to keep the hospital free of lice. My clothes were taken away for storage and I was given a hospital gown made of coarse material with prison-like vertical stripes. As I left the room, I looked in a mirror and saw a stranger and I turned round to see who was behind me. There was no one – I was looking at myself.

We had three meals a day: porridge for breakfast, a stew at lunch time and again in the evening, plus the bread ration and, of course, the ersatz coffee. There was therefore some incentive to try to stay in hospital for as long as possible. The prisoner-patients who were getting better and allowed to walk around would be sent to the cookhouse to collect the food for each meal and wheel it on trolleys to the wards and then serve it out to the other patients. In due course, when I was convalescing, I was given this job. We served food to three wards. In true army fashion, we managed to give our ward slightly larger portions than the other two – considered acceptable practice as the servers from the other wards did exactly the same – no one complained and all were reasonably well fed. In our ward the bunk beds were along the walls and the single beds in the middle of the room. We were generally looked after by one of the French male nurses called La Floche from Brittany.

The treatment for beriberi entailed a daily injection of vitamin B, which was administered by La Floche. We lay on our stomachs while he slapped our bare bottoms and then threw the needle in like a dart, screwing the syringe in to give the injection: it was quite a painless and efficient method. He also took our temperatures daily. The method of doing so was quite new to us and at first somewhat disturbing, because he stuck the thermometer up our bums; we learned this was normal practice on the Continent.

There was, at first, some difficulty in communicating with La Floche, as he spoke little or no English and our schoolboy French proved very inadequate. One day he spoke in Breton, his home language, and was immediately answered by one of our men, a Welshman who realised that Welsh was very similar to Breton. From then on, all communication with La Floche was conducted in Welsh/Breton, and very useful it was. There were a large number of Welsh prisoners scattered around the camps in the Berlin area – the 1st Battalion of the Welch Regiment had served in Crete. In one camp I remember two brothers who always conversed in Welsh; both of them had great difficulty in speaking English.

My treatment worked well and I was soon up and about. As I recovered I was allowed to wander around our section of the hospital and was able to catch glimpses of the main German hospital. There I saw German Luftwaffe patients walking around an enclosed garden. I was amazed and shocked at what I saw. They were being treated for horrible facial injuries, mostly burns, with skin grafts. It was a while before I understood what I was seeing. The skin for the grafts came from the underside of the arms from which it had been cut but not detached. The arm was held close to the face supported by a light wooden frame and the piece of skin placed on the face and bandaged. The whole thing looked quite ghastly, so uncomfortable and no doubt very painful. I could not help but feel very sorry for these poor airmen, yet they appeared to be very cheerful as they walked around the garden chatting away to each other. I do not know how successful their skin grafts were. Undoubtedly this was pioneering skin-grafting much like that going on for our injured and burned airmen at the Queen Victoria Hospital at East Grinstead in West Sussex – the famous 'guinea pigs', treated by Dr Archibald McIndoe, one of the first plastic surgeons.

During my stay I came across a fellow prisoner who was not from our camp, but who was seriously ill and, unusually for a POW, had been put in isolation. He was a tall, handsome man from the Coldstream Guards, a regular soldier. Arthur Tilston (from my camp and also in hospital) and I would go each day to see him.

We took him books and when we arrived he would pick up his book to read. I soon discovered that sometimes he was holding the book upside down; when we pointed this out he admitted that he could not read. I was quite flabbergasted that here was a regular soldier in an elite guards regiment who could not read. It was the first time in my life I had met an adult who was illiterate. I had believed, wrongly, that all adults could read and write because there was universal education in England with school inspectors to see that everyone went to school. So we went every day to read to him and write his letters for him. His condition deteriorated, almost visibly, every day. He was being attended by some German doctors who seemed exceedingly concerned at his condition. This we found quite unusual, because prisoners were usually expected to get by with whatever treatment they were given without any real interest being shown by the Germans.

He then told us that one day at his camp some German doctors had arrived and given all the prisoners an inoculation by injection. They were not told what it was for, but it was apparently a new and experimental vaccine. They were using the prisoners as guinea pigs – contrary to the Geneva Convention. After the injection he had suddenly been taken ill and rushed off to hospital by the Germans concerned that it was a reaction to the injection. They became very worried: if he were to die, his death would be reported to the Swiss protecting power and then investigated, with possible serious consequences for them.

As his condition worsened, he was visited daily by the German doctors. I remember one day, whilst we were with him, a whole delegation of them, obviously of very senior rank, came to see him. They said his diet should be improved and that he could have anything he wanted. Shortly after that, baskets of fruit arrived and all sorts of other goodies, things like peaches, oranges, bananas and so on, which we had not seen since being taken prisoner. The poor man just could not eat them as he was too ill and insisted we take them. I must confess that we did and shared them with the others in our ward.

One day the German doctors were accompanied by a young French doctor, a POW himself, working in the hospital. He examined the patient, questioned him about his army career and where he had served and then said he had an idea what his ailment was, but it would be necessary to carry out a number of tests and it would take several days to get the results. The German doctors agreed to the tests. We were very concerned because he was sinking very fast and starting to have periods of semi-consciousness. The diagnosis came: Malta fever. As soon as treatment for this started he showed distinct signs of improvement. He gradually got better and in time made a full recovery, much to the immense relief of the German doctors. The illness had had nothing whatsoever to do with the experimental inoculation. Malta fever is a type of glandular fever which can be contracted from drinking goat's milk or eating goat's cheese. Our friend had served in the East African Campaign in Abyssinia (now Ethiopia) where our forces had defeated the Italians and freed the country from occupation. Whilst there, he had often eaten goat's cheese which must have been the source of his illness. This episode gave an insight into the Germans' reaction to a situation in which they had knowingly breached the Geneva Convention by using POWs for medical experiment.

Clearly life in hospital was much easier and more comfortable than in the working camp so we tried to draw out our convalescence for as long as possible. The German doctor on his weekly visit never examined anyone, just looked at the charts hanging at the end of the bed, asked the French doctor for his opinion, which in general he appeared to accept and made his decision as to who was fit to be discharged. In due course, when I was fully recovered, he ordered my discharge. I happened to have been allocated the bunk over Arthur Tilston. Arthur was still quite weak; I think he was suffering from a type of anaemia and needed to stay in hospital and wanted me to stay with him. So after the German doctor had ordered my discharge and passed on, we swapped our charts. On their way back, we drew the doctors' attention to the chart (really Arthur's) now hanging at the end of my bunk which showed that I was not fit for discharge: there must have been a mistake. They agreed I should stay another week at least. In this way I wangled another week in hospital; the French doctor did not seem to mind. This additional week gave my recovery an extra much needed boost. I spent my time lazing and reading, helping with the collection of food from the kitchen and distributing it to the wards. I also had the satisfaction of depriving the enemy of a week of my work, such as it was, but the principle was important. We decided the deception would not work a second time, so at the next weekly inspection I was discharged, thankful that the beriberi had been cured.

At Teltow camp we were still infested with lice and still spent hours squashing them in the seams of our clothes. We did reduce their numbers quite a lot, but they still persisted. However, not everyone was concerned about cleanliness. In one of the other rooms the boys noticed that one of the men rarely went to the ablutions in the mornings to wash and he rarely went for the weekly shower. We had hot showers once a week, each hut taking its turn on the day appointed for its showers. The man in question happened to be a sergeant who had opted, when we were at Luckenwalde, to come to a working camp simply by removing his three stripes. The others in his room became so disgusted with him that they manhandled him to the bathhouse. We saw them passing our room so went to watch. He was forcibly stripped, pushed under the cold shower and then scrubbed vigorously whilst he tried unsuccessfully to resist. There was a large audience to see the show: he was humiliated, but he learned his lesson and kept clean afterwards.

Another man who wore a balaclava announced he would not remove it until the spring and kept it on all the time, even sleeping in it and so inevitably his beard grew through it. He trimmed his beard outside the balaclava. When the weather became warmer and he decided to take it off, he had to cut it off bit by bit − a very slow and quite painful process. His face was in quite a mess with sores underneath that took a couple of weeks or so to heal.

We worked six full days a week with Sunday free for rest. Early on Sundays we did our laundry as well as the poor soap would allow, and hoped to get it dry in time to wear on Monday by draping it around the room or on improvised washing lines outside in the better weather. It was not until some time later we had changes of shirts and underwear to ease the problem. Quite often we would have to don our clothing semi-dry and let it dry on us, which was not very comfortable.

The rest of the time on Sundays we lazed around and read if we had any books. I always went to the religious service in the recreation room conducted by Jimmy Ellis. I found it helpful to have this organised session of prayer and contemplation. Jimmy was assisted by Harry Price who also spoke good German. I was in the same camps as them until we left the Berlin area and were separated at the transit camp of Stalag IVB.

9

Staaken

I n mid-1942 the Germans decide to move us from Teltow, even though the work on constructing the embankments was nowhere near completion. We were ordered to pack up our belongings, rather more now than when we had arrived, lined up on parade and then marched away to the railway siding. We were loaded into the usual cattle trucks and travelled to north-west Berlin where we disembarked at a station yard near Staaken station. Staaken station was, and still is, on the *Ringbahn*, the circular rail system running around the outer suburbs of Berlin. Staaken is not far from Spandau, where Rudolph Hess was incarcerated. I revisited the site of our camp in the 1980s and found it had been converted to a children's playground and was separated from Staaken railway station by the Berlin Wall – the station at that time being in East Germany.

The site of our new camp was immediately adjacent to the railway line and was a considerable improvement on Teltow, being more spacious and with more facilities. Nor was it so isolated from the German public as Teltow had been. The entrance was from the main road and almost immediately opposite that to Staaken railway station.

Passing through the main gates you entered quite a spacious forecourt with the German staff's barrack on the left. This was where the working parties were counted before departing for work and where we were counted on our return and searched for smuggled contraband, but this became just a cursory frisk.

From this area a smaller pair of gates led into the prison camp proper. Inside, the barrack buildings in which we lived were arranged on either side of a quite large, central, grassed area. There were concrete paths all round giving access to each block. There were two barrack blocks on each side, whilst on the right-hand side opposite the German barrack and tucked away in the corner was a small block containing the lazarett which had a ward with about ten beds, a dispensary, doctor's surgery, stores and the doctor's living quarters: something we had not had at Teltow.

Across the far end of the grassed area was a large building containing an assembly hall with a stage, various storerooms and the ablutions. It was here that the Red Cross parcels were stored and where we went to receive them. This assembly block was raised up about 4 or 5ft above the general level and approached by steps.

Another new feature was the punishment block. This was the end part of the furthest 'residential' barrack on the left-hand side, blocked off from the remainder of the building and surrounded by a barbed wire-fence with its own separate entrance. Prisoners were sent for punishment for such misdemeanours as threatening guards, refusing to work, etc. and also for attempting to escape or having been recaptured after escape.

Behind the assembly hall was a large gravelled parade ground, mainly used as a football pitch, albeit a little small. I do not recall it ever being used for parades. It was here that we received our first footballs, courtesy of the Red Cross, and so were able to play football. One of the other uses of the parade ground was for pack drill. Prisoners sentenced to spells in the punishment block for attempted escape were made to run around the perimeter of the parade ground carrying a heavy pack on their backs, under the supervision of a guard who might or might not treat them leniently, depending on which guard it happened to be and what mood he was in. Luckily it was well out of sight of the German barrack and only rarely did the commandant go to supervise the punishment.

I remember the commandant, Hauptmann Konig, at Staaken very well. He was a typical Prussian with a clipped moustache, tall and upright, fierce in expression and bearing, with a commanding voice, and obviously a regular soldier of the pre-Nazi time. He seemed quite old to us, although probably around 50; a proud man and a strict disciplinarian. Nevertheless we found out, in due course, that he had a weakness and were able to exploit it. He was very hard on malingerers (men who pretended to be sick) who managed to be given a few days in the lazarett. He would visit the sick ward daily and root out those he considered were fit enough for work.

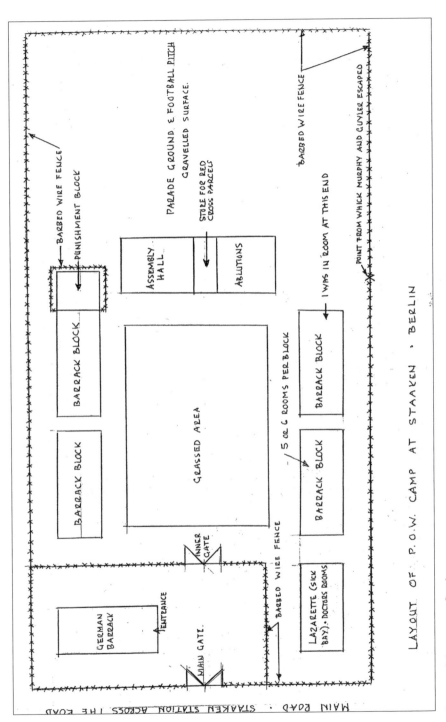

LAYOUT OF P.O.W. CAMP AT STAAKEN · BERLIN

Layout of the camp at Staaken.

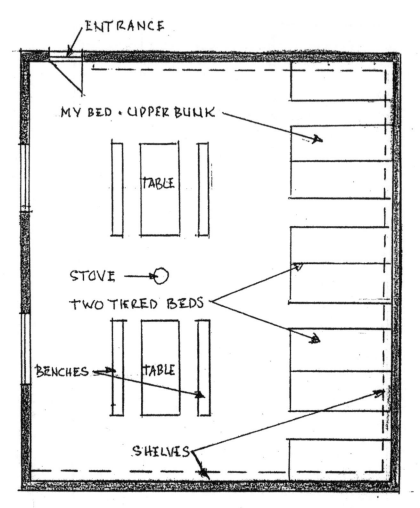

LAYOUT OF BARRACK ROOM
AT STAAKEN CAMP - BERLIN.

One day when he was inspecting the sick ward, he came across a man who clearly had a high fever. Dr Rana told him on enquiry that the man had malaria. Hauptmann Konig fled the ward. He was, apparently, very frightened of malaria (and any other tropical diseases) and certainly thought it was highly contagious. Thereafter, he would refuse to enter the sick ward if it contained a malaria patient. Naturally the doctor and his assistants cottoned on to this quickly and from then on always contrived to say there was a malaria patient, this keeping Konig at bay.

I was allocated to a room in the block furthest from the road on the right-hand side. The room was much bigger than the one at Teltow. The beds were bunks and placed along the back wall for sixteen men. The living space in front of the beds was about 10 to 12ft wide. There was a central round tortoise stove, which had a vertical round metal chimney or flue, for heating the room. On each side of the stove was a table with benches on each side. Another useful addition was a shelf running all round three sides of the room above the upper bunks, wide enough to take a Red Cross parcel box.

We used these empty boxes in which to store our worldly possessions apart from any packs or kitbags which went under the beds as there were no cupboards. The cardboard Red Cross boxes were approximately 15in long by 9 or 10in wide and 8in deep; the lids were the same size and depth, fitting completely over the box. Thus from one Red Cross box we had two open storage units. The lids of the Red Cross parcels from England were marked with the Red Cross insignia in red but also the insignia of the Order of St John's Society, with its Maltese Cross, in black.

Our room had two windows on the side facing the central square. As at Teltow, the buildings were made of wood. They had horizontal boarding outside, dark brown in colour, having been treated with a preservative. The roofs were also boarded and covered with roofing felt. Inside the walls were lined with plywood or hardboard and painted white. I could lie on my upper bed in relative comfort and look out onto the 'front lawn'. The weather also helped as it was now late spring when we arrived at Staaken; it was rather like moving from a no-star to a one-star hotel!

At Staaken we received our first Red Cross food parcels, and thereafter we received them almost continuously until near the end of the war. The aim of the Red Cross was to provide POWs in Germany with one food parcel each week. No doubt conditions for providing them were different in other countries especially in the Far East. From time to time there were gaps but, by and large, we were given a Red Cross food parcel each week.

This is an appropriate place to write about the food parcels and their importance to us. For a start, our health improved dramatically. From being half-starved and weak, we became quite fit and healthy and this had a marked effect on our morale. I am absolutely certain that the Red Cross food parcels saved the lives of hundreds, perhaps thousands, of POWs scattered in camps all over Germany and some of its occupied territories. I can only speak from my own experience in Stalags IIID, IVB and IVD,

In these three Stalags the receipt and distribution of the parcels to the prisoners was regular and reasonably smooth. As far as I was able to observe the German military authorities did not interfere with their distribution nor have I any evidence of them ever confiscating any parcels or parts of their contents. As the war progressed and food became short in Germany, there must have been some real temptation for them to take the parcels, but in my experience they played absolutely by the rules of the Geneva Convention in respect of parcels to British and Commonwealth POWs. There must have been a considerable organisation within the German military for dealing with the transport, storage and distribution of the parcels – an unwanted burden on their own war efforts – and I must admit they handled it well.

Later I came across American POWs who also received their own parcels without hindrance. The Russian prisoners were treated abominably. I doubt if they ever received any parcels from home. I understand that Russia was not a signatory to the Geneva Convention and so had no protecting power. French and Belgian prisoners were treated quite well and leniently. Often they were not in camps but lived and worked in the civilian community. Surprisingly there were camps for Italian 'guest workers' which were little better than prison camps, such was the German's attitude to their 'valiant' allies. Sometime later in the war we were in a small camp adjacent to one with Dutch POWs and later still to one with Danish POWs, who also appeared to be treated quite well.

We valued the food contents as much for their vitamin content which we called vitamins B, R, C, and S (i.e. British Red Cross Society vitamins) – a rather apt accolade for the society. Later on, we also received food parcels from New Zealand and Canada. The New Zealand parcels were packed in cardboard boxes identical in size to the British ones. The Canadian parcels used a flatter wider box made of corrugated paper, stronger than the British ones but containing the same amount. The parcels were packed in bulk in plywood boxes which were cube shaped and measured about three feet in each dimension.

The parcels contained a variety of foods mostly in tins, including meat loaf, meat stews, sausages, bacon, corned beef, fish (mainly pilchards and sardines), meat paste, butter, sugar, dried egg, condensed sweetened milk, cheese, Ambrosia creamed rice (a great favourite), jam, marmalade, tea and bars of chocolate, and lastly a tablet of toilet soap. The Canadian parcels had coffee instead of tea, which became a very important commodity for trading with the Germans. They also had quite large tins of dried milk called Klim (milk spelt backwards) and 'spam'-type pork meat loaf. The New Zealand parcels had similar contents to the British ones but also contained tins of corned mutton, lamb stews, and packets of dried peas. Many of the tins had brightly coloured paper labels around them depicting the contents, which could be removed – a feature that proved useful.

Cigarettes and pipe tobacco were sent separately by the Red Cross, other charitable organisations or from our families and friends by way of personal parcels. As my sister Betty's husband smoked Craven A, that was the type I received from her and, I recollect, my mother also sent me a pipe. I still have a note sent by my mother telling me that my youngest sister Ruth had sent me 500 cigarettes. My godmother Jennie Bakewell also sent cigarettes, as did other friends.

The Germans, not only the guards but the civilians with whom we worked, soon got to know we had good cigarettes made of Virginia tobacco, bars of chocolate and later real coffee. All of these items became increasingly scarce in Germany, mainly because of the Allied blockade of their shipping routes. Naturally we were keen to trade any surplus or unliked items for extra bread, eggs, and on one occasion at least, for liquor in the form of schnapps. Bartering was, of course, strictly forbidden to the German guards and I am sure was also forbidden to civilians; nevertheless it always went on surreptitiously.

We heard on the grapevine that complaints about our bartering with our guards and with some civilians on the work site had been made by some German civilians and the matter was brought to the attention of Hauptmann Konig. I am certain he was not involved: he was much too strict in obeying the rules. However, these complaints indicated to us that the Germans authorities were not eager to admit that we poor prisoners had cigarettes, chocolate and various foods which their glorious Third Reich could not supply to their own people. Because of the complaints, the commandant decided he must put a stop to bartering.

At Staaken we were never issued with a whole Red Cross parcel to take away and use as and when we wished. We had to line up at the parcel store on the days allocated for the issue of parcels. The parcels were issued by one or two prisoners who worked in the camp store, always supervised by one or two German guards. We were given a parcel – our name and POW number were marked on it – and it was then opened and we were allowed to select three or four items of food. It was then closed and put away. During the week the store was opened several more times when we could choose further items. The whole process was rather cumbersome. Later, in all the other camps we were in, we were issued with the complete parcel. The system at Staaken was devised by Hauptmann Konig on the assumption that if we only had what we immediately required we would be less likely to barter, but it did not really work and, in any case, there was little he could do to stop the trade in cigarettes.

When he received more complaints that bartering was still going on, he decided more drastic action should be taken. He ordered that all tins of food must be opened in the Red Cross store, and we were to be given the contents only and the tins discarded and thrown away. This he felt would prevent tins of food with their bright labels depicting the contents being seen by the people of Berlin. Thus one day we went to receive our parcels only to be told by the two guards on duty that we had to open them and empty the contents into containers. This presented practical problems because most men only had one round enamelled bowl, issued by the Germans and a mug for coffee.

We were handed tin-openers and told to open the tins we had selected. We refused and told the guards that if they required the tins to be opened, they must do it themselves, and this they very reluctantly did. They emptied the contents into the bowl we had brought with us. The guards became fed up very soon with the whole idea and grumbled about this extra chore. I clearly remember one man, Charles Lusted I think (always one to make a point) who selected a tin of Ambrosia creamed rice, a tin of pilchards and a tin of beef stew but he only presented one bowl. The guards opened the tins and indicated that he should not put them all in one bowl, but did so as he had only the one container. He then took this concoction to show our man of confidence, an RSM from a Scottish regiment (not the one from Teltow, who had disappeared elsewhere), and demanded he go with him to see the commandant to ask for more containers to be supplied. His request fell on deaf ears and the system continued for a couple of weeks. The guards got more and more disgruntled and gradually it was discontinued.

From this episode we gathered that what concerned the German authorities most about the trading was that it revealed to Berliners that we, their POWs, were better off for food than they were. We decided this was an opportunity for some propaganda. As we were not allowed then to take the tins away with us, we just removed all their colourful labels and the chocolate wrappers and saved them. We also saved empty cigarette tins. These labels showed things which were unobtainable in Berlin and which the residents sorely missed.

It so happened that some of the working parties from the camp were taken to work by train on the *Ringbahn*, catching the train at Staaken station. Prisoners of war were only allowed to travel in the last carriage of the trains, but there would often be a few civilians and guest workers in it as well. Our men took the various labels with them and scattered them out of the windows onto the platform at each stop. We felt sure this was useful propaganda serving to undermine, even if only a little, the morale of German civilians. It must have succeeded because some weeks later the commandant, after receiving more complaints, ordered all labels to be removed from tins of food and chocolate bars and destroyed. The guards complied in a half-hearted fashion, reluctant because it affected their own chances of bartering. In due course most of them bartered with us and the various restrictions gradually faded away – market forces prevailed.

One of the most cherished articles in the Red Cross parcels was the bar of toilet soap, which we carefully guarded as it was used not only for our ablutions but also for washing clothes. We also received sticks of shaving soap (shaving brushes could be purchased in the canteen).

The Canadian Red Cross boxes did not have removable lids so were not so useful for storage, but being disposable were used for fuel. The plywood sides of the crates and the wooden strips supporting them were very useful indeed. From these we were able to make a variety of pieces of furniture including small storage cupboards, small tables, stools and – most ambitious of all – armchairs, whilst all the waste bits were used as fuel. Of course there was a temptation in very cold weather to burn the lot, but luckily after the first bitterly cold winter at Teltow the following winters were milder. At first the Germans were reluctant to give us the crates, the guards themselves would have liked them, but our confidence man insisted they were our property and the guards had to give way.

The tins of Klim, powdered milk, were opened with a key which removed a metal strip around the lid so that the lid could be replaced, so the empty tins were used for storage and cooking.

The coffee contained in the Canadian parcels was not popular with the hardened tea-drinkers. Many men had never tasted real coffee, only the horrible German ersatz. Naturally, they were willing to trade it. Tea was at a premium and some men were prepared to give cigarettes, chocolate and tins of food in exchange for a packet of tea. Thus coffee became a very important item of barter. We soon found out that the Germans were great coffee drinkers and that the real bean coffee (*bohnen kaffee*) was very scarce – almost unobtainable for the ordinary people in the Third Reich. Soon coffee became the most important and valuable item of barter we had.

Empty tins were not only used for storage but 'manufactured' into useful items: with handles attached they were mugs, or made into a contraption for boiling water using a fan (the Klim tin was the best for this); with wires attached, they could be lowered into the stove to boil water (see page 134).

There was another type of food parcel from the British Red Cross: the 'milk parcel', made up of light, largely milky, foods for men who were in hospital or convalescing and needed a light diet. They contained more milk products including tins of semolina, tapioca and extra creamed rice, also jellies and tinned consommé. These parcels were in general reserved for hospitals and camp lazaretts. Later on, in the smaller camps, a few were provided and kept as a reserve to be used as and when needed, at the discretion of the man of confidence.

Our food parcels became the central and most essential feature of POW life – literally life-savers. They must have been even more important for the men in working camps than for the officers and NCOs in non-working camps. Our men, who were often doing very heavy manual work, really needed the extra nourishment to keep them fit enough. Any disruption to the expected weekly issue of our food parcels was the cause of considerable unrest and the Germans took all the blame.

We did not give very much thought to the logistical problems in getting the parcels from their places of origin in Canada, New Zealand and the United Kingdom to individual prisoners in their camps all over Germany and occupied Europe. We did not think, at the time, of the hundreds of willing hands who volunteered to pack the parcels or how they were transported, often under very difficult conditions, to Germany. Distribution was undoubtedly affected as the war progressed by the disruption in rail transport caused by Allied bombing. And no doubt the Germans gave priority to the distribution and transport of their own war materials. To achieve the relatively constant and smooth delivery of food parcels one must recognise the efforts of the Germans and their rigid compliance with the rules of the Geneva Convention. Of course it was a two-way process as they were also, presumably, sending parcels to their prisoners in Allied hands, although food parcels were not as important for their prisoners, especially those sent to Canada where food was plentiful.

During 1942 and early 1943, when the Germans were still in the ascendancy, there were very heavy Allied losses of shipping especially in the Atlantic from the activities of German U-boats and surface raiders. The Germans, in their newspapers, which we sometimes got hold of or were shown and in the camp newspapers they provided, gave lists of the tonnage of Allied shipping sunk together with their assessment of the available tonnage of our merchant fleet and our ability to construct new ships. We studied these figures over the weeks, deducing from them that the Germans had sunk much more shipping than we ever had and were still sinking ships much faster than they were being replaced. We soon decided this was all propaganda aimed at their own people, but in the case of the camp newspapers, was designed to undermine our morale. So we asked the guards, 'How is it that, when the Allies have no shipping, crates of food parcels are crossing the Atlantic from Canada, also coming from New Zealand and arriving safely in the camp?' This clearly puzzled the guards who had no answer. We told them the plywood crates of parcels were strung together with ropes and floated across the Atlantic. This nonplussed them even more – they had no sense of humour or of the ridiculous.

As the camp at Staaken had about twice as many men than Teltow, I came across many new faces, as well as a few I had known previously. In my room the men were about half from the previous camp and half new to me. Amongst the fresh faces were Danny McCormick, a short, vibrant, very talkative Irishman; a very tall Canadian (whose name escapes me) but I remember that he wore a tam-o'-shanter, was a pseudo-Scot and a bit of a Bible basher who lapsed occasionally; Charlie Whitaker, a large, former rugby league player from Yorkshire; Chalky White and Steve Donaghue. The latter three were my close companions for the rest of the war. Charlie, Chalky and Steve became my muckers. We shared our resources and stuck together until our eventual freedom. Sometime later, two more Irishmen, Murphy and Guyler, joined the room. Here at Staaken I met an Australian from the outback Andy Murnin, a rather simple-minded man, rough and ready but kindly in his own way. Despite his huge frame and rough appearance, he was really a timid, lonely man. As he did not get on with the men in his room, he would come to visit our little group for 'afternoon tea' and we made him welcome. In due course, he persuaded the Germans to let him move in with us, where he was much happier.

Andy reported sick to Dr Rana, saying he had broken his arm. The doctor examined him but could find no sign of a break, told him so and asked him when and how did he think he'd broken it, to which Andy replied it was about five years ago. The doctor sent him packing. Andy was annoyed at not getting away with it, and shouted, 'You bloody black-enamelled bastard.' This naturally upset the doctor and was overheard by the guard who sat in on the sick parade. The insult was explained to the guard who reported Andy to the commandant and Andy, quite rightly, was sent to the punishment block for a few days.

Dr Rana only stayed a few months at Staaken before he was moved elsewhere. His replacement was a New Zealand doctor (whose name I have also forgotten). When men went sick he soon discovered that almost all were infested with lice. He was most concerned and decided to examine everyone in the camp and found that well over ninety per cent were infested. He announced his intention of ridding the camp of this pest. He addressed the camp and said that each day as working parties returned, they would be marched to his clinic and be examined for lice. He recruited two or three men to be his orderlies and assist in the examinations. In due course the whole camp was examined and he noted a quick improvement but he continued the daily checks. Until now we had been resigned to having lice whilst we were POWs, but with the incentive from the doctor we made efforts daily to rid ourselves of them. There were a few men who made no effort. The doctor tackled them by 'naming and shaming': he listed the names of everyone still with lice on the notice board. His mission succeeded and within a few weeks lice in the camp were a thing of the past: we owed him a big thank you. I did not find any evidence of lice in any of the camps I was in subsequently, except for the final camp at Falkenberg where we noticed that some of the guards were infested, so we gave them a wide berth.

In our camp at Teltow, our man of confidence, unelected by us, had been an RSM from the Black Watch; we never questioned his role mainly because we then had no knowledge of the procedures. At Staaken, we gathered from the grapevine that under the conditions of the Geneva Convention, the detaining power (the Germans) could not remove our man of confidence from office or from the camp without the consent of the prisoners. At Staaken we had a man of confidence who was also an RSM from a Scottish regiment, I think the Highland Light Infantry. He was a shortish man, very dapper and smart, but more importantly very popular as we thought he did an excellent job in fighting our corner. He irritated the commandant, Hauptmann Konig, because he was a strong character and became a thorn in Konig's side with his constant representations on our behalf.

One day we returned from work to discover that our popular man of confidence had been taken away from the camp and sent to a non-working camp. This had been done secretly by the commandant without any prior consultation with the prisoners. We were all flabbergasted and infuriated, and demanded his immediate return, telling the commandant he had broken the Geneva Convention. He answered that the man of confidence had gone at his own request – which we knew to be untrue – and completely ignored our demands for his return.

By overwhelming numbers we decided we would go on strike and refuse to return to work until our man was brought back to the camp to resume his post. The next morning we all paraded outside our barrack blocks for the morning *Appell*, were counted and all declared present and correct. The working parties were called out but to the amazement of the guards no one moved. The hauptmann was summoned. He ranted and raved at us and threatened, (as it was all in German we did not understand exactly what he threatened), but still we all stood fast. We just stood there outside our barrack rooms in the lines of four on the footpaths either side of the grassed central area and waited and waited. Meanwhile our guards almost pleaded with us to go to work as they did not want any trouble. Hauptmann Konig stormed off to his office ordering us to remain on parade.

We were there well over an hour when suddenly there was tremendous activity at the camp entrance as several military vehicles drew up and about a platoon of German soldiers jumped down, armed with machine guns. The camp gates were thrown open and these heavily armed soldiers came into the camp at the run. In the centre of the gateway was a wooden block where the two halves of the gates met; the first couple of the German soldiers tripped over the block and went sprawling on the ground much to the amusement of us all and we all spontaneously burst out laughing, Hauptmann Konig who had again taken up his stance in the middle of the lawn was even more furious at our laughter. The machine gunners then took up positions in front of us lying on the ground with their guns covering us. Our own guards were ordered to take up positions behind us to prevent anyone breaking ranks and going back into the barrack rooms. They were terrified because they were also in the line of fire.

Hauptmann Konig shouted at us, 'Either agree immediately to go to work or be shot.' From our knowledge of him we decided that he was not bluffing and would certainly have ordered the machine gunners to open fire had we refused his order. He kept repeating the order and after a few minutes of rapid consultations amongst the assembled ranks, we capitulated very reluctantly. The platoon of machine gunners got up and marched off to wherever they came from, to the immense relief of the guards.

Our man of confidence was not returned and another was appointed in his place. On reflection we decided it had been a worthwhile stand against our Prussian commandant. The Germans had lost a whole morning's work – not that that amounted to very much. More importantly, they had been put to a considerable amount of trouble in bringing in soldiers from some Berlin garrison to quell a strike in a POW camp. We had made it abundantly clear that we expected them to abide by the rules of the Geneva Convention and I have a feeling that Hauptmann Konig was probably impressed by our little strike. There were no punishments or recriminations afterwards. Indeed, from that point on, we had very few problems with the commandant. On one occasion, he even sided with us against a German railways' works foreman.

In the evenings we often had sing-songs and a certain amount of entertainment. As a result of the daily diet of cabbage soup provided by the Germans, we all tended to suffer from a great excess of wind. One day one of the wags decided to find out if the gas would ignite, so took his trousers down to expose his bare bum whilst someone else stood by with a box of matches and lit the fart which burned with a blue flame. Thus started the 'blue flame competition' to decide who could produce the longest flame. Only a few of the men took part (I was not one of them), but not only did it produce some interesting blue flames but also created much hilarity. The Bible-bashing Canadian took part, to my surprise. I cannot recall whether anyone's bum got burned. Then one of the men – I have an idea it was Danny McCormick – said he could fart 'God Save the King' and then others claimed to be able to fart other tunes. This caused a great deal of laughter and certainly was entertainment of a rather unusual kind.

Then someone suggested there should be a competition to see who had the longest, largest penis, although the word used was 'cock'. Very few entered this competition, which was easily won by Danny McCormick who, despite being one of the shortest men in the room, certainly had the longest weapon. That was as far as it ever went.

During my years as a prisoner I never encountered any cases of homosexuality or even of masturbation; if anything like that did go on, it was certainly well hidden from the rest of us. Perhaps homosexuality was less likely in working camps than in non-working ones because the men had little energy left after a day's hard labour. At one stage, later on, at Staaken I was sent with a small working party to a timber yard where we spent our time stacking planks of timber. One of those on the working party was Danny McCormick, who would wander off amongst the timber stacks where he claimed he had found some young boys and had sexual relations with them. We just did not believe him and put his claims down to bravado, fantasy or just frustration.

The only other interesting part of that short-term working party was meeting Bulgarians for the first time, so-called guest workers, although they were treated only slightly better than we were. My lasting impression of them is of small swarthy men in dull, ill-fitting, dark clothing with flat black caps, reminding me of pictures I had seen of miners in England and Wales. They were not at all friendly and hardly ever tried to communicate with us.

The work for the majority of us at Staaken was again for the German railways, but this time we were employed on a building site where a large complex of buildings was being erected, presumably for railway workshops and warehouses. We were, as usual, employed as labourers on a variety of operations, attached in smallish groups to various civilian construction workers, with each group under the control of a ganger or sub-foreman, and the whole of the workforce under the control of the general foreman who oversaw the whole project.

After the morning *Appell* we were assembled in parties of about thirty, in the usual columns of four, allocated two guards and marched to the gate where the party would again be counted. The march to the building site took us about twenty minutes. On arrival, we again lined up whilst the general foreman selected men for different small working parties or gangs and a ganger was assigned to each group.

After the first few days, having got to know our ganger, we automatically went to him and off to work without waiting to be detailed, and so the various gangs became established and the early morning process of allocation to gangs became quite casual. The guards did not accompany us on our working groups, but generally patrolled around the site or, more usually, congregated together in or around the German workers' rest hut.

Arthur Tilston and four or five others and I were assigned to a ganger who was known to all, including the Germans, as 'Langsam', the German word for 'slow', because he was not only slow-moving but also rather slow-witted. The rest of the German workers treated him as a figure of fun and were generally unkind to him.

Some lucky men got cushy jobs such as working in the tool store where they helped with the storage and issue of tools to the workmen and each morning quickly went to their post in case anyone else was detailed for the job. However, after a few days we all accepted our own gangs.

The one man who, in our opinion, had the cushiest job was Jimmy Bunnel, a sapper like me. Jimmy was given the task of preparing the ersatz coffee for the German workmen ready for their morning, lunchtime and afternoon breaks. This was made in a large copper supported by a brickwork structure with a fire hole under it in the open air just outside the Germans' rest hut. It was just like the coppers we had had in kitchens at home at that time – there was one in the scullery of my childhood home.

Jimmy had to fill the copper with water, light the fire and spoon in the ersatz coffee grains when the water was boiling, then serve the coffee to the German workers during their breaks. We were not given any. It was a nice easy job with plenty of free time and Jimmy soon got rather bored. One day it occurred to him that the boiling water would be useful for washing his socks in: you can imagine the state of our socks, pretty dirty and smelly. So he washed his own and the socks of a few friends in the water before making the German's coffee in the same water. He said he did this daily because he was intent on having clean socks. The ersatz coffee itself had, to us, a rather awful taste and the socks probably did not make a lot of difference; maybe they even improved it! The Germans gladly drank their sock-flavoured coffee and never complained about the taste. However, Jimmy and the rest of us got a lot of amusement and pleasure watching them drink it. Our socks certainly did get pretty dirty, smelly and sticky and occasionally we were forced to wash them. One of the tests to decide whether or not they were ready for washing was to throw them up to the ceiling; if they stuck, they were ready for washing!

My small group, including Arthur Tilston and his close friend Jack Butterfield, working with old Langsam, were given odd jobs and fairly light ones, such as clearing up after other gangs, carting rubbish away, filling in excavation holes with soil and dismantling scaffolding. I do not think the general foreman could trust Langsam to supervise any important work. We would do a little work, then tell him we needed to go to the toilet or we would just give him the slip. When he realised we had disappeared, he would come shuffling after us, very worried that the foreman would catch him without his gang.

Near the storerooms and the outdoor copper stood two wooden buildings, both toilet blocks for the prisoners; each had ten or twelve seats all in a row, sitting over a trench dug out beneath, another typical long-drop lavatory. Of course there was no partitioning between the seats, a real friendly meeting place. These earth closets soon became rather smelly, unsavoury places, despite the daily dusting of the trench with lime. This was unacceptable for those just going into the buildings to have a smoke and a chat and avoid work. So early on it was agreed that only one of the toilet buildings would be used as a loo; the other was to be kept solely as a meeting place where we could go for a conversation whilst avoiding work. Thus some time during the day we would slip away, one by one, from Langsam and assemble in the 'recreation room'. He soon knew exactly where we had gone and would come creeping up to the door, peer over the space above the door and implore us to return to work, but quite often we persuaded him to join us instead. This he reluctantly did, but he was always on tenterhooks in case he was caught out by the foreman who was quite strict in monitoring the gangs, but I think he considered ours as a minor one and paid scant attention to us, so generally we managed a number of unofficial breaks during the day.

In the early days of our work on the site, the framework for the building was still being erected: a series of vertical steel stanchions supporting horizontal steel beams. The stanchions were set in massive blocks of concrete about three feet below the surface of the ground. Once the concrete blocks were fully set, the holes around them had to be filled in with soil and consolidated: this was one of our tasks. We were issued with wheelbarrows and shovels. We were not the only ones on this work. We had to take the soil from a heap about a hundred feet away, fill the wheelbarrow, push it to the hole and tip it in. I found this work very hard.

We had noticed that the contractors had already stockpiled many of the materials for the construction of the buildings, including massive stacks of bricks, hundreds of bags of cement and prefabricated reinforced concrete slabs. When we asked about the slabs we were told they were for the flat roof of the building and that there were special heavy metal clips to fix them in place. The clips were stored in boxes next to the slabs. It seemed that the Germans paid little attention to these stacks of materials until they were actually needed. So we decided it would be a good idea to dispose of the clips and surreptitiously spirited them away when all the Germans and other workers had gone for their coffee break. We dumped them in the excavations and quickly covered them with soil and consolidated it before anyone returned to work. The Germans did not notice and they were not missed until the time came to fix the roof slabs. They had to order replacements which delayed the work by several weeks.

Having had that success, one day when all the others had departed for their lunch break, we dumped our wheelbarrows in one of the excavations and covered them with soil, then went off on our break. When we came back to work, we expressed complete surprise in finding our wheelbarrows and most of the shovels had disappeared, so we had another long break until replacements were found; the foreman never discovered where the wheelbarrows and shovels had gone. This was part of our regular attempts to create minor problems for the Germans; as the supermarket advertisement says, 'Every little helps'. Amongst the other workers at the site were some Czechs, more guest workers, who amazed us by working very hard, even having competitions between themselves to see how many barrow loads of soil they could wheel from the dump to the excavations in a day. As far as I recall, they managed around ten times our number. We never understood why they were so dedicated to working for the Germans; perhaps they were put under pressure by the foreman and feared the consequences of slacking.

There were a large number of German civilian workers on the site: steel erectors, bricklayers, carpenters, general labourers and so on. Many of them were quite well disposed to us, even friendly, though this may have been connected to the bartering which had quickly begun. When occasionally we found ourselves alone with one of them, he would look very carefully to check that he was out of earshot of any other Germans and then confide to us that he was a Communist and opposed to the Nazi regime. Quite a few of them told us they were Communists; I learned later that Berlin had been a stronghold of the German Communists before the rise of the Nazis. They said they had to be very careful of their fellow German workers, because if they were caught criticising the Nazi party they would soon be whisked off to prison. They had to be particularly careful as there were Gestapo agents and informers planted throughout the workforce. They said they could not trust anyone unless they were well known and close to them. There was certainly a great fear of the Gestapo: it was a regime which encouraged fear and distrust.

One day an argument started between two German workers, which soon developed into a fight. Out of the blue, one of the other workmen stepped forward, drew out a revolver, confronted the men and marched them off. We had thought of him before just as an insignificant, nondescript, sullen little labourer. Clearly he was a Gestapo agent and having blown his cover was immediately moved from the site; we never saw him again. This was my only firsthand experience of the dreaded Gestapo.

One of our small working groups was assigned at first to a foreman/ganger who gave them some task work – which they soon completed – whilst the ganger went off to do other work elsewhere. Thereafter, each morning this gang, on arrival at the site, fell out immediately saying to the general foreman that they were on X's gang. They were waved away to go to work in a gang which did not exist anymore. Somehow the men had managed to tunnel into the huge stacks of bricks on the site which were well out of the way of the general work activities and had created inside a hidden den to which they repaired each morning. They spent the day lazing around and playing cards. They never did any work, nor were they ever found out.

At one stage my gang were assigned to dismantle scaffolding on one side of the building where the brickwork had been completed. There were about five tiers and we would climb to the top, ostensibly to start taking it down. Langsam himself never came up with us as he was scared of heights. At the top there were guard boards which screened us from below. It was now lovely midsummer weather, so instead of working we settled down to sunbathe. We had several days of leisure in the sun before the general foreman discovered there was little or no progress being made in dismantling the scaffolding and we had to do some work.

At some point someone told the general foreman that I was an architect. He seemed quite interested in this and told me in a friendly way that I should not be doing heavy work. He arranged for me to be transferred to work with a gang of bricklayers. As two men were needed, Arthur Tilston joined me.

The steel stanchions had to be encased in brickwork and six bricklayers, working in pairs, carried out this task. We had to paint the stanchions with a cement slurry before they were bricked up. It was easy to keep up with them as a couple of minutes daubing gave the bricklayers at least a quarter of an hour's work. It was certainly the lightest of work and we had plenty of time to laze about and chatter.

Each of the three pairs of bricklayers had a labourer working for them, whose task was to supply them with bricks, mortar and water. The bricks were carried in a sort of hod which was L-shaped and strapped onto his back. The mortar was a ready-made dry mixture of sand and cement and was carried in a cylindrical shaped hod tapering slightly from bottom to top; there was a similarly shaped hod for carrying water, and these also were strapped onto the labourer's back. He certainly had to struggle up the ladders to deliver the materials. His was really heavy work because the bricklayers were working some three stages high and moving upwards and there were no hoists or lifts to carry the materials. Each pair of bricklayers had a smallish wooden trough about 2ft 6in long, 18in wide and 8in deep, with sloping ends at which were two carrying handles. They also had small, short-handled spades with square blades. A hod full of dry mortar was put into the trough, the water added and the two men, one working from each end, would very rapidly mix the mortar. I found it was a quick and efficient way to mix mortar freshly, as required. The trough was light enough for the men to move along even when full, and it held just enough mortar to use before it began to set.

It soon became apparent that there was some rivalry between the pairs of bricklayers to see who could lay the most bricks in a day; they were hard workers and took a lot of pride in their work, which they seemed to enjoy thoroughly: they really were skilled workers. I did not get any impression of it being regarded as 'war effort' and I am sure they were not Nazi party members. On one occasion, the general foreman who had become quite friendly with his 'architect prisoner' asked Arthur and me if we would like to try our hand at bricklaying. This we did for two or three days but we did not show much aptitude and were soon put onto other work.

It became evident that there was a shortage of bricklayers. The time came to start constructing manholes for the drainage system and the Germans enquired if there were any bricklayers amongst the prisoners. There were a number of them and some of them volunteered to work on the manholes. At the time we were very disgusted with them for offering to provide skilled work for the Germans and they were given a rough time by the rest of us. The German bricklayer foreman gave them their instructions, watched them work and carefully supervised the construction of the first manhole. He was completely satisfied, complimenting them on the excellence of their work. Having passed this test, they were allowed to continue building all the others manholes for the drainage system with little or no supervision. At the same time we continued to regard them as scabs, almost traitors. But when all was completed and the system was tested, it was found that the liquid drained the wrong way. Our 'traitorous' bricklayers had deliberately set out from the start to build the manholes to the wrong levels and ensure the system would not work. Naturally the Germans were absolutely furious saying they had been given precise measurements, but our men responded that it was not their fault, as they took the measurements to be in yards, feet and inches in which they always worked: the metric system was unknown to them. The Germans appeared to accept this explanation and did not realise the faulty work was quite deliberate. There was not much they could do but put their own bricklayers to rebuild all the manholes. And so our men changed from scabs to heroes!

Building supplies for the works were brought to the site by rail or lorry. The prisoners had to help with the unloading during which they would look for the chance to put sand in the axles, brake systems and fuel tanks of the engines or lorries; these were minor things but we felt they all helped in a small way to hinder the enemy. Such was the spirit of the prisoners in all the camps I was in that we never ever forgot who was the enemy. No wonder the Germans had a very poor regard for British workmen! They themselves were completely obsessed with work and there were slogans everywhere calling on people to work hard for their beloved Führer and the glorious Third Reich.

As part of our light work, Arthur and I were set to whitewashing the walls of some of the completed rooms, more or less unsupervised, although Langsam occasionally put in an appearance. Later Arthur and I were given brooms and told to sweep the floor of one of the large storage rooms which was littered with all sorts of small debris. We did a few brush strokes then paused, lent on our broom handles and had a chat, then swept a little more and had another break and conversed again; I have no idea what we talked about. Our intention was to make such a cushy job last as long as possible. In fact it is surprisingly quite difficult to do nothing, but we persisted. Occasionally we shovelled some of the rubbish into a bucket and took it out of the room to dump elsewhere. The days ticked by and slowly we cleared a little of the floor. Then after two weeks had passed and we had swept about half of the floor the foreman arrived and rather angrily removed us from the task. It put me in mind of Lewis Carroll's 'The Walrus and the Carpenter' and the seven maids with seven brooms sweeping on eternally. With only two of us it would have taken even longer.

Some gangs of prisoners were given task work: that is, they were allocated a specific task for the day and when it was completed they were finished for the day and could sit around and relax until it was time to return to camp. The task work enabled the Germans to get more work done than if the men worked at our usual slow pace all day. If the men agreed to task work, then they expected the Germans to keep to the agreement.

One day one of our gangs had completed their day's task work and were waiting for everyone else to finish work before going back to camp. The head foreman came along, saw they were hanging about doing nothing, and ordered them to move some steel girders. The men were most indignant and refused to comply with his order as they had completed their allocation of work and suggested he got German workmen to do it. There was an immediate uproar with the foreman screaming and shouting and exhorting the guards to force the men to work. By this time, most of us had also finished work and as the guards were eager to start off back to camp, we all supported them in their refusal to do extra. The foreman got angrier and angrier, accused us of mutiny, and then telephoned and complained to the commandant.

The commandant decided to send some extra guards to help the foreman enforce his instructions. When they arrived, our men explained the situation and said it was a matter of principle: the Germans had broken an agreement and they still refused to do the work. All the rest of us backed them to the hilt. Stalemate was reached. The commandant ordered us to be marched back to camp where he would deal with the revolt. We were marched back with a larger escort than usual, rather apprehensive as to what would happen to us. Knowing Hauptmann Konig, we fully expected some severe punishment for refusing to work.

Back in camp we were all kept on parade until the hauptmann came out and demanded an explanation of our refusal to work, before, he said, deciding on the punishment. Through our man of confidence, the reason for refusal was explained. Hauptman Konig considered for a while and then announced that he agreed with us: the foreman had broken an undertaking and was entirely in the wrong. There would be no punishment and he would personally reprimand the foreman. This ended a very tense situation with a moral victory for us. We developed some belated respect for the commandant.

The building work at the railway factory was gradually nearing completion and we foresaw that we would soon be moving on to other work. A small gang of us were given the task of erecting a row of telegraph poles from the road leading to the building. I, as 'architect', was entrusted with the task of spacing them out, lining them up and ensuring they were vertical in the holes which had been dug for them. In the process, we discovered that the line of poles followed the line of the main drains and that some of the drain pipes were exposed in the holes dug for the telegraph poles. The opportunity was too good to miss: as the holes were being filled in, the drainage pipes just happened to get smashed with the tools used for tamping the fill. Of course we never knew the outcome of this little act of sabotage; certainly there would have been severe problems with the drains and the Germans would have found it very difficult problem to locate the source of the problem as the pipes were smashed not in just one but in several places along the line.

One day on returning from work, we found a group of about twenty unexpected new prisoners. They were sent in twos and threes to rooms which had spare beds or room for extra beds and two were allocated to our room. It transpired that they were Irish.

You will recall that the Irish were separated out from the rest of us in Salonika and had been sent to an exclusively Irish camp near Berlin. Some of them we knew from Crete. They told us their story.

To begin with, the Germans treated them very well as they hoped that many could be persuaded to return to Ireland to work for the Germans in carrying out acts of espionage and sabotage against the British. The Irish Republic was neutral in the Second World War and some Irish were pro-German ('my enemy's enemy' etc.). But the Irish prisoners were not all from the Republic, some came from Northern Ireland and those from the Republic were, of course, volunteers and all had been fighting in the British army. The Germans had virtually no success in turning any of them – rather the reverse: the Irish caused so much trouble the Germans decided to disband the camp. Convinced of the great antipathy between the English and the Irish, the Germans hit on the brilliant idea of sending a few of the Irish to each English camp to cause friction. The Germans were completely nonplussed when we welcomed them warmly. Even though almost all the prisoners in the Berlin working camps, including the Irish, were from Crete, our commandant and the camp staff somehow did not make the connection. I remember guards asking, 'When you talk together which language do you use: English or Irish?'

Two Irish citizens were allocated to our room and extra beds were brought in for them. They introduced themselves as Murphy and Guyler: I do not think we ever knew their Christian names; they were always addressed by their surnames. They told us that after segregation at Salonika, they travelled much as we did by train to Berlin where they were installed in a camp near a railway marshalling yard. German officers promised them that if they would agree to change sides and work for the Germans, they would be taken to good civilian accommodation, given good food, drink and clothing, they would have considerable freedom to move about and female company would be available. Then they would be repatriated to the Irish Republic to begin their work against the English. Whilst they made up their minds, they would be treated better than other prisoners with better food and accommodation, and given only light work. When they decided to change to the German side they had only to inform the commandant and he would arrange for their course of training in espionage. Murphy and Guyler told us not a single man had fallen for this propaganda and none had changed sides. They said the camp was somewhat better than Staaken and the food marginally better.

The work they were assigned was in a warehouse close to the railway marshalling yard and consisted of packing food for the German soldiers on the Russian Front and then loading it into railway trucks. One of the items they packed was tinned food which had to be put in wooden boxes and then the lids nailed on. They decided to pierce the upper row of tins with a nail before putting the lid on in the expectation that the contents would 'go off' before reaching the German soldiers.

Another task was to fill sacks with sugar, flour and dried beans, peas and lentils. When a sack was full they urinated on the contents before sewing them up, 'just to add a little flavour' they said. In their enthusiasm to under-mine the troops on the Eastern Front they decided to send them messages in the boxes of tinned food telling them it was time to give up and surren-der as they were clearly losing the war. Unfortunately these messages were found by the soldiers unloading the food supplies at the front who reported this to their officers and the messages were traced back to the Irish camp in Berlin. So the Germans decided they had had enough of the Irish and disbanded the camp.

Murphy and Guyler told us they had worked on loading railway trucks for a number of locations and had observed the pattern of freight trains leaving the marshalling yard in Berlin. Amongst the regular departures, always from the same siding, were trains going to Belgrade in Yugoslavia. They said it would be quite easy to slip onto one of these trains and escape to Belgrade. All the men in our room agreed to help in any way we could. One of the first requirements was civilian clothing, preferably workmen's. Unlike the stories we later heard about officers' camps, we had no tailors nor any escape organisation: we had to steal items gradually from the work sites.

The German workmen changed into their working clothes each morn-ing on arrival at the site, so it was relatively easy to 'half inch' (steal) various items belonging to men who were off work or who were just careless. These then had to be smuggled back into the camp past the guards searching us on our return each day. However, by this time the search had become a rather casual frisk, so it was not too difficult to accomplish. The real problem was concealing the clothes in our room, which was searched, unannounced, about every two weeks. As it was mid-summer, the stove was not being used, so we carefully dismantled the tubular metal chimney and thoroughly cleaned it of all soot and grime. Then we packed the civilian clothes inside and reassembled the chimney, correctly assuming that the guards would not think of dismantling the chimney during the searches. The escapees would need some hard rations to take with them so we all agreed to donate items, especially bars of chocolate, but in order not to raise any suspicions of hoarding by them we all kept the articles individually until the time of departure.

Guyler and Murphy decided the actual escape had to be under cover of darkness and therefore from the camp and not from the working party. The only way out was by evading the patrolling guards and the searchlights and cutting their way out through the perimeter wire fence. The door to the room was not locked at night as we were allowed to go to the toilet block. The timing of the perambulations of the guards patrolling the perimeter of the fence at night was carefully studied, as was the movement of the searchlights. The most difficult task would be to cut through the wire fence as wire cutters were needed. Our men working in the tool store at the work site said there were rarely used wire cutters there and set about 'acquiring' them (we sappers never stole anything, just acquired it). Having done so, the next problem was to get them safely into the camp. The man detailed to carry them retired to the 'rest room' and strapped them, with a little help and persuasion from the others, to his inside leg in the hope they would not be detected in the search at the camp; he was placed in one of the inner ranks to hide any 'lameness' he might display. We all kept a good lookout so as to be able to distract the guards if they showed any interest in him. At the camp the guards casually frisked everyone and our man kept his legs tightly together and passed muster.

Now they had the wire cutters, Murphy and Guyler decided to go that very night. After lights out, they put on their civilian clothes, hiding their uniforms in the chimney and then replacing it in position; we handed them the hard rations, they said their farewells and quietly departed. Half an hour later they returned saying, 'The bloody wire cutters were bloody useless': they were not strong enough to cut the wire. They clearly needed a much stronger pair. They took off the civilian clothes, dismantled the chimney, hid them and retrieved their own clothes, the items of food were handed back and we all went to sleep.

The next day the wire cutters were returned without problem as there was no search going out of camp. Our store workers were able to acquire a much heavier pair about 18in long. The same man (I think John Denham) was detailed to carry them, again strapped to his inside thigh. The discomfort was much greater and he had great difficulty in marching along. I know because I was marching beside him! Luckily the guard was as casual as before and he again got into camp with the cutters.

That night we repeated all the preparations as soon as lights went out. We handed them the hard rations and quietly wished them well and off they went. They did not return so we assumed that they had got away. Next morning this was confirmed when the patrolling guard discovered the hole in the fence, big enough, he said, to drive a horse and cart through. An alert was sounded and we were all summoned for an *Appell* and counted several times, after which it was concluded that two men were missing. In due course the escapees were traced to our room. The commandant was naturally furious. I believe the guards on patrol that night were disciplined, petty restrictions were imposed on the camp: no football for a month, lights out earlier, extra *Appells* and parades, more frequent searches of our rooms, all irritations for us, but it was a case of bolting the door after the Irish colts had gone. As always, after a while the restrictions were gradually eased.

About two to three weeks later Murphy and Guyler arrived back at the camp under armed guard. They said they had had no difficulty in cutting their way out of the camp, nor of getting clear under cover of darkness. They had made their way to the marshalling yard and soon located a freight train labelled for Belgrade. They had found an open truck covered by a tarpaulin, climbed up and hidden underneath. The train in due course set off, taking about four days to get to Belgrade. On arrival there, they crept out of the truck and had started to make their way out of the freight depot when they were most unfortunately spotted, arrested by the local police and handed over to the Germans for interrogation. Luckily, although in civilian clothes, they were able to produce their *Kriegsgefangene* (POW) identity discs and were, a few days later, sent back to Staaken under armed guard and handed back to the camp authorities; so ended the escape attempt. They were hauled before the commandant who sentenced them to fourteen days' solitary confinement in the punishment block and to pack drill.

The punishment block at Staaken was the end half of one of the barrack blocks (opposite ours) with a barbed-wire fence around it and a separate locked and bolted gate. The prisoners were locked in separate cells. Periodically a guard went in to check on them and give them their food, which was bread and water. During the day they were taken out to the parade ground at the back of the camp to do their pack drill, which the hauptmann himself enjoyed watching. Sometimes they were also put on gardening work in the camp, so their confinement was not completely solitary. The main punishment was the diet of bread and water. The men in the 'cooler' soon discovered there was a trapdoor in the ceiling which gave access to the roof space above. Another trapdoor gave access to the adjoining barrack room so it was possible to communicate between the two by crawling along the inside of the roof. We used this route to supply those in solitary confinement with food, hot drinks, books and other comforts; it was easy enough to avoid guards because in true German fashion they kept to a rigid routine, always inspecting at the same times of the day. Thus anyone in solitary confinement on bread and water was provided with adequate food, a sort of 'manna from above'. The Germans never found out.

Only on one occasion did we find Hauptmann Konig in a relaxed mood. Our Scottish RSM man of confidence received a parcel from home, opened, as usual, in the presence of the hauptmann. It contained a set of bagpipes. Hauptmann Konig was quite astounded and exclaimed, 'Dudelsack!' He said he could play them and asked the RSM if he could try them. He came out of the barrack and strode around the forecourt playing the dudelsack, really enjoying himself like a child with a new toy. We decided he was human after all – but only just, and very occasionally.

As the work at the railway factory came to a close, we were moved back to our previous type of work for the railways: building embankments for future railway lines, filling bogeys with sandy soil, pushing them along a mini line of rails, up a slope and tipping them to gradually create the embankment. It was endless, tedious, repetitive work all day long. We reverted to our normal work pattern, leaning on our shovels as the guards and gangers chivvied men further along the line.

Two incidents have firmly remained in my memory. One of the guards was very keen that we should always try to be clean and smart, especially clean shaven. Charles Lusted was almost always up too late to shave before being called out on parade to go to work. On this particular day, when we arrived at the work site, the guard reprimanded him for not shaving ('designer stubble' was unheard of then). Charles explained that he just had not had time to shave before leaving camp but he was prepared to do so now. He opened the small haversack he had with him, took out his razor, soap, shaving brush and a mirror, poured some water into his tin mug and started lathering his face. There was nowhere to put the mirror, so he handed it to the guard and asked him to hold it so that he could see to shave. The guard meekly complied and was scolded by Charles when he did not keep it straight, or hold it still. Everyone was in fits of laughter. Incidents like these did wonders in keeping our morale up.

The second incident involved Docherty, one of the Liverpool Irish. He was one of the 1003 Docks Operating Company from Liverpool – a really rough crowd, mostly Irish, who gave the Germans considerable trouble and were real thorns in their side. They were as near to being mutinous as any prisoners dared. As a group, the Germans soon identified them and indeed referred to them as that '*ein tausend und drei kompanie*'. No other regiment or company was ever individually identified in this way by our captors. Docherty was a big, strong, rough man who had no problem with any of the work, no matter how heavy it was. One day, quite out of the blue, he announced loudly whilst we were out on a working party that he was completely fed up with the work and prison camp. He said simply, 'I am leaving now.' He was dressed in British army battledress and wore a beret on which he had sewn a large Union Jack; he also carried a small British army haversack. His method of escape was the easiest possible. He made no preparations at all. Seeing a bicycle belonging to one of the guards leaning against a nearby fence, he just walked up to it, got on and cycled away. He was out of sight before the guard realised what was happening. All he did was stare down the road after him and later, very reluctantly, had to report his disappearance to the commandant. This time the guard was reprimanded and no doubt punished for letting a prisoner escape right before his eyes. For once we were lucky. Because it was the guard's fault, there were only a few short-lived restrictions on the camp, extra searches and check parades.

Where he went and what he did we never knew, but he was at liberty for four or five days before being recaptured and brought back to camp under armed guard. I do not know how he managed to last so long as he had no food or drink with him, no German marks, no knowledge of Berlin or Germany, nor did he speak any German. He was duly sentenced to fourteen days' solitary confinement on bread and water, augmented, of course, by extra food through the trapdoor in the ceiling.

He was also given pack drill and had to do gardening under the close supervision of a guard. That was the theory: in practice, it was Docherty who was boss. He asked the guard for cigarettes, which were forbidden whilst in solitary confinement and when the guard refused, Docherty grabbed his rifle and threatened to beat him up. He got his cigarettes. The guard was absolutely terrified of him. From time to time Docherty threatened him with his spade, threatened to take his rifle and shoot him, made him make tea for him; he even made the guard light his cigarettes. The guards were so pleased when Docherty finished his spell in the cooler. One wondered how he got away with it without getting himself shot or locked up for the duration. He was without a doubt the hardest man I came across in any POW camp and, I suppose, the most stupid. He was always a thorn in the Germans' side, and that we appreciated and applauded.

Not long afterwards we were informed that we were being moved from Staaken to another working camp. I am uncertain of the date of our move.

10

Lichtenfelde

Our new location was somewhere in one of the southern suburbs of Berlin. The camp itself had been newly constructed and we were its first occupants. The accommodation which housed around twenty men to a room was similar to the other camps with the usual two-tiered bunks, tables, benches, stove. The main improvement was that the assembly hall had a large stage. It was a somewhat larger camp than Staaken, and here I met a number of new faces, some of whom were with me for the rest of my time in Germany. The regime in this camp was more relaxed; I do not know whether this was because the Germans still felt they were winning the war and were able to ease up on the treatment of British prisoners or just because this particular commandant was more humane. He certainly was a quite decent man and treated us well, the best commandant so far.

We had not been there very long when he announced there would be a weekly ration of beer, a most welcome addition to our fare: we certainly had not expected to have beer. The beer turned out to be dark brown and rather sweet and, I think, low in alcohol. It was called *Malzbier*, but it was not ale or bitter beer. Some of the men disdained it, but never refused to accept their ration which was given out straight from a wooden barrel. After some debate, we decided it might be improved by some extra fermentation. We got hold of suitable containers – even a small barrel – which were half or three-quarters filled with the beer and then dried fruit such as raisins and prunes, which we received in Red Cross parcels, were added and the mixture left to ferment until a much stronger and, to us, a more palatable liquor was produced. This began an appetite for alcoholic drinks.

Although we had talked and dreamed of them, we had never thought we would ever get them in a prison camp. Some men began to get addicted and if none of our own fortified beer was available, they sought to get hold of raw alcohol to enhance the beer. Alcohol and methylated spirits could be acquired from the doctor's dispensary, and a few even tried to get industrial alcohol or things containing alcohol from the work site. Luckily this involved only a small number of men as the use of industrial alcohol could be very dangerous.

It was at this camp that our first real attempts were made to put on concerts in the assembly hall. They were very amateurish, quite entertaining and there was lots of laughter, more often than not at the mistakes and blunders of the actors. One of the great characters of this camp was a man named Sykes. He put on a show which included a trapeze which he rigged up and which most unfortunately collapsed in the middle of the performance to the great amusement of the audience. On one occasion he got hold of a live duck for one of his sketches, but on stage he could not control the duck and it shat all over his costume. He was very good at getting things comically wrong and he certainly succeeded in entertaining us.

Sykes, a strange man, made friends with a Spaniard named Blasco. I never found out quite how a Spaniard came to be in a camp of British prisoners. Blasco hardly spoke any English and Sykes spoke no Spanish, but they seemed inseparable and could be seen walking round and round inside the perimeter fence for hours on end with hardly any communication between them. Sykes, a light infantry soldier I think, also had a passion for badges and flashes, and claimed to have been awarded many for a whole variety of army skills which he said he was allowed to wear on his sleeves. Most of them were homemade but he did have one or two genuine ones. He sewed them all down both sleeves right down to the cuffs, also put some on his epaulettes, so that both arms were completely covered. We thought he was quite mad and even the German guards were fascinated. The commandant was present when he received a personal parcel and thereafter called him 'feldmarschall' (field marshal).

Our work at Lichtenfelde was the usual monotonous one of building railway embankments. We had one particularly obnoxious guard, a fierce, bad-tempered little man, very anti-British, having, it was rumoured, lost his house in an RAF bombing raid. He was continually marching up and down the lines of skips ranting and raving and threatening any slackers with the butt of his rifle. On one occasion, Charlie Whitaker and I were throwing shovels of soil up into the skip when some soil went right over the skip – not unusual, especially when it was windy – just as he was passing on the other side. He accused me of deliberately throwing soil at him and raised his rifle either to shoot or hit me with the butt. Luckily another guard saw what was happening and restrained him, preventing a nasty incident. He was also unpopular with the other guards; I think he had become somewhat mentally disturbed.

Some time later a group of men were working and chatting together when this guard shouted, from a distance, to one of them, Sammy Spencer, to move to another gang. Sammy did not want to move as he was with his usual muckers; the guard persisted. Sammy refused to move and made a threatening gesture with his shovel; he was standing about twenty yards from the guard. The guard raised his rifle and shot him: Sammy died almost immediately. The guard insisted he had shot in self-defence as Sammy had attacked him with his shovel, which was untrue.

This was the only deliberate shooting of a British prisoner I encountered during my four years in the prison camps. Everyone at the site was in shock and all work was immediately suspended. We were marched back to camp and Sammy's body was removed to a mortuary. There was considerable hatred of the guard amongst us and great consternation amongst the other guards. The man of confidence demanded that the Swiss protecting power be contacted. He prepared a report on the killing, which included full details of the guard, his regiment, army number and rank. The report got through and the Swiss representative, in due course, visited the camp. This Swiss visit was the only one I witnessed during my time as a POW.

The immediate reaction by the Germans was to remove the guard at once from the camp as he would have been in danger from some of our wilder elements. After the war, the incident was, I was informed, reported to the War Crimes Tribunal, the man was arrested and brought to trial, tried and executed. I heard this from Charlie Whitaker who was called to give evidence at the trial. This was a sad time for us all. I was amongst those allowed to go to Sammy's funeral. He was buried in a local cemetery in an impressive and moving ceremony. A military service was conducted at the graveside; one of our buglers sounded 'The Last Post' as the coffin draped in the Union Jack was lowered into his grave. All of us who attended were deeply moved.

It was around this time – I suppose early to mid-1943 – that we began to witness Allied raids on and over Berlin. These were all at night. There were air-raid shelters at this camp unlike either Teltow or Staaken. These were somewhat like glorified Anderson shelters: a deep trench dug out and roofed over with corrugated iron covered with a layer of soil and grassed over. There were steps down to a door at one end and inside were benches along each side for us to sit on. The German air-raid warning system was twofold: first a fore-alarm was sounded which indicated that aircraft were approaching, then the full alarm, a much louder longer blast, to indicate aircraft were overhead. Usually we were alerted to be ready to go to the shelters when the fore-alarm sounded, but we only went into the shelters at the sounding of the full alarm.

Naturally we became very excited when the Allied planes came over – it was the first sign or sight of action by our own forces since we had been taken prisoner and a huge boost to our morale. We stayed outside the shelters as long as possible to watch the development of the raids. As soon as our planes were over Berlin, the sky was illuminated by the criss-crossing beams of the German searchlights, a fascinating sight. Sometimes we could see the planes caught in the searchlights and watch the tracer bullets from the German anti-aircraft guns. Then we saw flares dropped by the pathfinders over the targets, the whole spectacle like some huge firework display. For us it was exciting and exhilarating, so uplifting to know our gallant airmen were fairly close and inflicting damage on the enemy. We knew now that the war was going our way because our planes could penetrate Germany and fly as far as Berlin to carry out bombing raids. We stood outside the shelters and cheered them on. More rarely we picked out German night fighters firing their tracer bullets, to shouts of, 'Crash, you bastard.'

A few of our planes were shot down. We saw them spiralling down to the ground and said a prayer for the crew, thankful when we saw a parachute open and float down and knew that someone had been able to bale out. What impressed us was the formations of planes which never deviated from their course even when one was shot down. After a raid, the Germans would claim a large number of enemy planes had been shot down, but from our own observations we considered their claims greatly exaggerated, although we had no way of assessing losses on the long journey to and from England.

All the targets appeared to be in the northern parts of Berlin, well away from our camp. As we watched these fascinating raids, we felt there was no danger to us at this distance, but it turned out there was danger from shrapnel. Tragedy struck us again. One night as an air battle raged, one of my fellow prisoners, Don Herring – a very likeable Scotsman from one of the Highland regiments – was standing just outside the door to the shelter when he was hit by shrapnel and died immediately. As with Sammy Spencer, he was accorded a military funeral with a Union Jack-draped coffin and 'The Last Post' sounded by our bugler. Even after this sad incident, we still tended to stay at the door of the shelter during raids to see as much as possible. As far as I remember, the air raids were at first spasmodic but gradually became more regular. When the raids were over, the 'all-clear' sounded, the same very long continuous blast as in England, and we could return to beds to get some sleep before the monotony of work the next day.

I broke my spectacles and reported this to the sick room. The staff asked the Germans about replacements and they agreed to get a pair for me. For some reason unknown to me the commandant decided that I was to be put on light work until the new spectacles arrived, which meant I did not have to go out to work and was given light duties in the camp – very much more enjoyable than filling bogeys!

Somewhere not far away from us, there must have been a camp for political prisoners and, probably, Jews. One day we saw two men in blue-striped pyjama-like prison clothes running across the open space opposite our camp, about two hundred yards away and being chased by armed guards who were shouting and gesticulating. When the guards got close enough they stopped, raised their rifles and shot at the two prisoners who fell to the ground, presumably dead.

I had heard before the war of the repression of political prisoners and the persecution of Jews, but had not seen any evidence in Germany until this incident. We had seen some indication of discrimination against the Jews from the signs on seats on railway stations, on shops and pavement seats saying '*Für Juden Verboten*' (forbidden for Jews). We had also seen people in the streets wearing large yellow Stars of David. Years later I was to see similar signs in various places in South African towns: 'For whites only'. At this date we had heard only vague references to concentration camps and I did not learn of the extermination camps until after the war. Whatever our government might have known about the extermination camps, I can say quite categorically that we in the ranks of the army did not, at this time, know about them. Later on, we were to see more political prisoners and slave labourers and experience a concentration camp at first hand.

Life at Lichtenwalde continued in its slow and monotonous way until one night the full air-raid alarm sounded. We were in the shelter when suddenly there was an enormous blast close by. There had been a direct hit on one barrack and considerable damage to some of the buildings from the blast making the camp uninhabitable. Although it was the middle of the night, the German staff reacted with remarkable speed. We were ordered to collect as much of our worldly goods and chattels as could be salvaged from the wreckage; luckily I was able to get most of my things as our hut had escaped most of the blast. We all assembled in the forecourt of the camp in the dark. The commandant must have been in communication with his District Command to report on the raid and to ask for instructions, because after about an hour we were told to fall in and were marched off into the darkness carrying all our possessions. We were not told where we were going, just marched away up the road for several miles. After a couple of hours or so on the road, we arrived at another camp for British POWs, at a suburb of Berlin known as Marienfelde.

11

Marienfelde, No. 520, Stalag IIID

The POW camp at Marienfelde, our fourth in Berlin, at which we had suddenly and unexpectedly arrived, was already almost fully occupied. We – two hundred or more men – had been together for over two years and had become a fairly homogenous group. Now, out of the darkness of the night, we were thrown into another camp of a similar size, whose occupants were, by and large, strangers to us. Some men did meet up with a few colleagues they had known previously, but most were from regiments unknown to me.

I met for the first time a number of New Zealanders, men from the Middle East commandos – the so-called 'Layforce' who had passed by us during the retreat on Crete – and men from the 1st Battalion of the Welch Regiment. As time went on, many of them became quite close friends.

However, my little group of four men, my muckers, still Charlie Whitaker, Steve Donaghue, Chalky White and myself who had been together since Staaken, remained intact. I do not recall how we originally came together – probably over sharing a loaf of bread – but we remained together right until the end of the war and our eventual dispersal at Naumburg-Saale. Two other close friends, Arthur Tilston, who had been in hospital with me, and his close friend Jack Butterfield, were also still with us.

The camp administration at Marienfelde had been alerted to our arrival and had made rapid arrangements to accommodate the extra two hundred or so men. They had emptied rooms for us and doubled their men into other rooms. There was some natural resentment by the men who had been dispossessed. Of course we were all rather overcrowded, but on the whole we were generally welcomed and helped.

The room we were allocated had extra beds installed and we crowded in, grabbing beds and depositing our haversacks, Red Cross boxes, kitbags and so on. After some chaos and the usual bickering it was time to try to get a little sleep. As soon as the lights were put out men started complaining of being bitten and soon everyone on the top bunks was getting bitten. We managed to get the lights switched on again and there were hundreds of bed bugs dropping from the ceiling. This was another first for me as I had never seen a bed bug. We tried to squash them, but not only were there too many of them to make any impact on the numbers but a squashed bug gave off the most awful stink and made red stains on our clothing. They got onto the beds, into the palliasses and onto us. So after being bombed out of our camp by our own RAF we were now being viciously 'bombed' and attacked by these German auxiliaries! We did not know that this particular room had been unused. Thinking about it, I could hardly imagine that the men already there could have lived in and tolerated the conditions. The next day we had to vacate the room temporarily so that it could be thoroughly fumigated.

The new camp turned out to be quite different from all our previous ones, not in its buildings which were of much the same construction, but in the facilities and organisation. The camp had two doctors, a dentist (Captain Neale) and a Roman Catholic padre (Father Scarborough). This was the first time we had had a dentist and a padre. With the two doctors and the padre our medical and spiritual needs were well catered for. The padre was treated rather lightly and with amusement by many of the irreligious men, they called him 'Father F*** 'em All'. Father Scarborough was thought to be a little mean.

Naturally, no sooner had we settled in and had a day's rest than we were sent out to '*arbeit*'. Surprise, surprise, it was building railway embankments for the Third Reich!

At this site, for the first time, there were other POWs working on the same embankments, divided into separate gangs of French, Belgian and now for the first time, American prisoners. By contrast with the British prisoners, they managed to fill and tip twenty or more loads a day. The German foreman was disgusted with our tally of around six and insisted we raise it to at least ten, still only about half that completed by the other nationalities. He made all sorts of derogatory remarks about the laziness of British workmen which pleased us immensely. We negotiated with him and agreed to do ten loads a day but only on condition that having finished the '*Aufgabe*' (task) of ten loads, we would be allowed to return to camp and rather reluctantly he agreed.

On the first day of task work, we arrived at the work site at about eight in the morning, got down to work straightaway and worked diligently, finishing the task before eleven o'clock and in accordance with the agreement were marched back to camp. We were delighted and so were our guards. It left the rest of the day free to do what we liked. Most importantly, for the sports-minded, it allowed them to play football or rugby. I was one of those who played rugby. There was a reasonable playing field on the other side of the road outside the camp, complete with goal posts and it was set aside for our use. The rugby players managed to acquire some poles, which we tied to the football goal posts as vertical extensions to make rugby goal posts. By this time the camp had received footballs and rugby balls either from the Red Cross or from other charitable organisations.

However, a week or so after we had made the agreement to do task work the German foreman said he was not satisfied; we were only working a half-day or even less and this he could not and would not accept. The other nationalities of prisoners were disgruntled and complained that our short working day was unfair to them who had to labour all day and grumbled about our preferential treatment. Obviously they did not know anything about our collective bargaining. The foreman then announced that the task had been increased to fifteen skips per day. We could have done this quite easily and been back in camp in the early afternoon. On principle, however, we politely declined to accept the increased task and opted to revert to working all day. He could not really object to our offer to work the whole day as all the other POWs did so. So we returned to working all day and the number of skips we loaded per day fell back to five or six, which naturally pleased the foreman even less. After a week of slow work, he capitulated and allowed us to resume the task of ten loads a day. He was getting twice as much work as he normally would from us and we worked for rather less than half a day. Clearly he could not use force to make us work harder, no matter how hard he tried. We felt we had won a great victory which did much to raise the morale of the camp.

It was here at the work site from Marienfelde camp that we first encountered American POWs. We assumed they had been captured either in the Western Desert or during the invasion of Italy and after the fall of Mussolini. We did not have much opportunity to talk to them, but I clearly recall that they just could not fathom how we managed to work such short hours. I remember one of them shouting in his southern drawl, 'Say, pal, what is the secret of your success?' We told them, but they made no attempt to emulate us, continuing to work all day and to do much more work than we did. They appeared to have no idea of how to deal with the Germans, and seemed to lack the cohesive camaraderie which helped us so much.

Thus we created for ourselves considerable free time during the working week. Some used this time to laze and doze or read and, possibly, study. For many it was an opportunity to play some sport. Thanks to the extra foods we received from the various Red Cross organisations which augmented the basic rations provided by the Germans, we were reasonably well fed and physically fit. We had enough energy to play energetically, especially as we were only doing a half a day's work.

We had a number of New Zealanders, some of the 1st Battalion of the Welch Regiment, one Australian Rugby League International and among some of the Middle East commandos a number of English county players, including, I recall, two from Somerset and one from Northumberland. To help organise the games we had our dentist Captain Neale, who was also a keen player. All these men ensured a good standard of rugby. I remember a Maori soldier who spoke the most impeccable King's English without any Kiwi twang.

We lacked football or rugby boots. A few men had written home to ask for them to be sent out in personal parcels, but only a very small number received them: probably they were difficult to obtain in wartime Britain. For the rest it meant playing in army boots. We had to improvise to get them suitable for playing football and rugby by removing the heels from any old boots we had, cutting them into strips or bars and nailing them across the soles of the boots – this proved successful.

We played rugby matches once or twice a week, the other days being reserved for soccer. Mixed sides were selected and we had some most enjoyable games. One rugby player I remember well was 'Biffer' Llewellyn from the Welch Regiment, a stockily built bull of a man with a lovely lilting Welsh voice: Biffer was a popular man. I became friendly with him and he gave me the best possible Welsh accolade by saying I was one of his 'townies'. With his build he was a forward, a prop, and played the game fiercely like a bull terrier. On one occasion he broke away from a scrum, or rather bulldozed his way out, charged down the field with the ball under his arm and scored a try under the posts. Everyone cheered him on amidst great laughter, because he had run the wrong way and scored under his own posts! When we left Berlin, Biffer was sent to a different camp. However, we heard on the grapevine that he had been in a spot of bother. He and his colleagues were working in a factory in which was a vat of water standing about 3ft 6in high. Biffer, with his short fuse, had got annoyed with the foreman, lifted him up and dumped him in the vat. Result: Biffer went to the cooler to cool off for a week.

Through our rugby I became friendly with some of the New Zealanders. I still have a photograph taken at this camp (see over) which includes three of them and signed on the back with their best wishes: Lindsay Nicholls, Bruce Watt and Arthur James, together with Captain Neale, the dentist. The New Zealanders were marvellous friends.

At first I played second row forward with Captain Neale; at the time we did not have the luxury of skull-caps, although later on we made some rudimentary ones. As a result of playing without them, there was much rubbing of ears against the bums of the front row and both Captain Neale and I both developed cauliflower ears. We both went to see the doctors who told us that cauliflower ears could be drained so that the ears would then look normal again. As there were two doctors, they decided that one would operate on Captain Neale's ear and the other on mine in a sort of contest to determine who could get the best result. They duly operated on both of us: the result was that mine was declared the best and so I was very chuffed. However, a few days later I began to have severe earache, so off I went to see 'my' doctor who told me the wound had gone septic. Not to worry, he said, he had a small supply from the Germans of a new drug called sulphonamide which would soon clear it up. I duly took the first of the tablets, and found to my horror the next morning that my urine was bright red. I thought I must be bleeding internally and that the Germans were experimenting on us with the new drug. I reported to the doctor who told me it was nothing to worry about, the colour of the urine was because the drug was manufactured from a dye and this side-effect would soon wear off, as it did.

Back row, fourth from left: Arthur James, and end right: Lindsay Nicholls; front row: fourth (pale coat): Captain Neale, and end right: Bruce Watt.

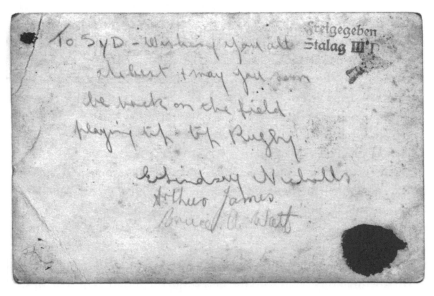

'To Syd – wishing you all the best. May you soon be back on the field playing tip-top Rugby. E. Lindsay Nicholls, Arthur James, Bruce Watt.'

Two more photographs from Marienfelde. In the top one, I am standing fourth from the right in the second row down. Unfortunately I have not written anyone else's name on the backs of the photographs.

My infected ear had been bound with a bandage going right round my head which made sleeping difficult. However, the sulphonamide was working and a few days later the ear was getting back to normal. Then, quite suddenly, our two doctors were whisked away from the camp and replaced with an elderly doctor; he, I supposed, was a regular army doctor. He was informed of my problem and said he would make a routine examination of the ear to check on progress, he prodded the ear with an orange stick with a bit of cotton-wool on it. Afterwards I began to get severe pains again and reported back to him. He re-examined the ear and discovered that he had inadvertently perforated my eardrum whilst probing with the orange stick. He said he could not deal with this problem, so he consulted the commandant. The commandant discussed the matter with a German army doctor who immediately advised I should be sent to see an ENT specialist. This was arranged and accompanied by a guard I was sent off on the *Ringbahn* to visit the specialist.

I had an interesting train journey sitting as usual in the rear compartment. I welcomed this diversion from being penned up for months on end in the camp. I have no idea which part of Berlin we went to, but it was about an hour's journey from the station near the camp. The specialist, a civilian doctor, examined the ear and confirmed I had a perforated eardrum and was quite certain that it would heal with the correct treatment. I was to put a few drops of alcohol in the ear two or three times a day; he would check on it again in a couple of weeks and I was given a bottle of alcohol. I like to think I was the only British POW to be prescribed alcohol! It worked and on the next visit the specialist said it was almost completely healed. I should add that he treated me purely professionally, like any of his other patients. I was soon able to resume playing rugby, this time with the improvised skull-cap but not again in the second row; I played as flanker thereafter.

On one of the working parties, we were transported to work by lorry travelling down some fairly narrow roads lined with cherry trees, full of fruit. As we passed by the men leaned out and pulled off branches full of cherries, the first fresh fruit we had had in Germany. When we had been very hungry earlier, we had worked close to fields of mangolds and sugar beet, and had tried eating them raw but with disastrous results: they stuck in the throat and almost choked us. I have since heard stories about horses being choked after eating raw sugar beet.

On our way back to camp from work, we had to cross a railway level-crossing with gates which lowered when a train was approaching. One day our party with our two guards arrived to find the crossing closed and the barrier down, so we had to wait some minutes for the train to arrive and pass by. Near the crossing were one or two horse chestnut trees replete with conkers, many of them lying on the ground. Naturally some men picked up conkers, pierced them and threaded them on string and started to play. This intrigued and fascinated the two guards and the civilians who also were waiting to cross: it was obviously something quite new to them and they gathered round to enjoy this strange sport of the British prisoners. Then up strode a very young SS leutnant who was not at all amused and ordered the civilians to move away, ticked off the guards furiously and began berating everyone for fraternising with POWs, making derogatory remarks about us. This incensed one of our party who stepped forward and hit the young SS officer with a right hook, knocking him to the floor.

Our immediate reaction was one of horror at such stupidity. We began to imagine the consequences which would most surely ensue. We knew the pride and arrogance of the SS and were certain this officer would not take this insult 'lying down'. However, much to our great surprise, the civilians applauded our boxer; the young officer got to his feet, dusted himself down and slunk off, jeered at by the German civilians. It was a most extraordinary episode. The man who hit the German officer was a Scot, I think from the Highland Light Infantry, and had been a former army boxing champion. The train eventually passed by and we continued our way back to camp. We all dreaded and awaited the expected repercussions, as we had no doubt that the officer would report being assaulted by a British POW, which we knew was a very serious offence. Time passed without us hearing anything more; perhaps the young officer was too ashamed to report the incident. We felt we had had a narrow escape.

Until, later, in Stalag IVB when we managed to get access to wireless news – 'wireless' not 'radio' in those days – our only news came from the Germans, some from the guards and civilian workers, but in the main we had to rely on newspapers. There were three types of newspaper, first the German ones, second the newspaper *The Camp*, produced in English for us by the Germans and third, newspapers produced by the prisoners themselves. Only occasionally were we able to get hold of recent German newspapers, either the *Volkischer Beobachter* or the *Frankfurter Allgemeine Zeitung* but then we had the problem of understanding the contents. It was here that Jimmy Ellis and Harry Price came in useful, being able to translate for us. In this way we got to know something of what the German press was saying, even if it was days late and naturally biased. We felt that so much of it was propaganda for the consumption by the German public. Our principal use for these German papers was to cut them up into small squares for use as 'bum fodder'.

The Camp was a little smaller than the present tabloids in size. The front pages were dedicated to world news and news of the war, always slanted to the German point of view, and it was here that we picked up the very exaggerated figures of Allied shipping and aircraft losses. We treated this news with a pinch of salt and tried to read between the lines. There were some articles on England, the arts, the theatre, poems, a crossword puzzle, chess problems and short stories on the inner pages.

The back page was devoted to German lessons which started right from the beginning and went on by weekly stages to more advanced lessons. I was one of a very small number who assiduously studied them and built up a reasonable, if largely theoretical, knowledge of German. I made little or no attempt to speak the language as I have never been very good at speaking foreign languages. Indeed, when later as a man of confidence I had to deal with the commandants, I found it useful to know what they were saying without them knowing that I understood most of their conversation. Because of my inability to speak German I was allowed to have an interpreter (*dolmetscher*) who did all the translating for me, but sometimes when left alone with the Germans, waiting for my interpreter to arrive, they would say things I was not meant to hear, most of which I could translate myself. Although I found it difficult to speak in German, I had less difficulty in understanding what was being said. The German lessons in *The Camp* also included the old German Gothic script, which I also learned.

Then there were our own camp newspapers, the first one, I recall, being produced at Camp 520, Marienfelde. I still have a few pages of a copy but missing the title page. I am fairly sure it was called *Contact*. In this surviving copy there are a variety of articles; one page is devoted to an inter-camp boxing tournament between Camp 520 (our camp) and Camp 517 held at Camp 520 before a crowd of 500, the contests including featherweight, lightweight, welterweight and light-heavyweight bouts. Another page is on 'highways and byways' in the British Isles; another is devoted to music with a song entitled 'Miss, You', words written by Charlie and Harry Tobias and musical score, which is printed, by Henry M. Tobias. There are short stories, crossword and other puzzles, poems and cartoons.

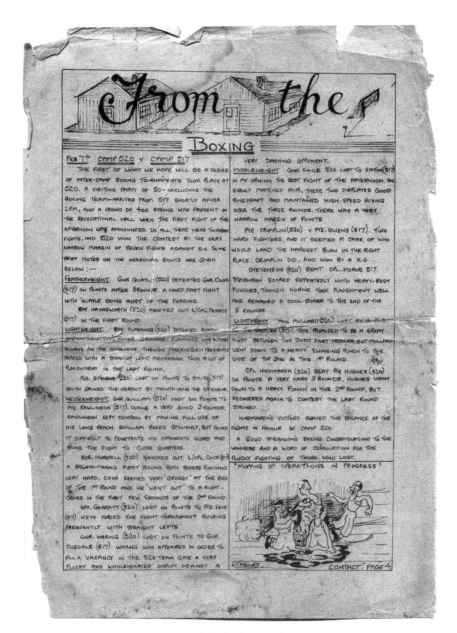

From the

BOXING

FEB 7TH CAMP 520 v CAMP 517

THE FIRST OF WHAT WE HOPE WILL BE A SERIES OF INTER-CAMP BOXING TOURNAMENTS TOOK PLACE AT 520. A VISITING PARTY OF 50 - INCLUDING THE BOXING TEAM - ARRIVED FROM 517 SHORTLY AFTER 1 P.M., AND A CROWD OF 400 STRONG WAS PRESENT IN THE RECREATIONAL HALL WHEN THE FIRST FIGHT OF THE AFTERNOON WAS ANNOUNCED. IN ALL, THERE WERE THIRTEEN FIGHTS, AND 520 WON THE CONTEST BY THE VERY NARROW MARGIN OF SEVEN FIGHTS AGAINST SIX. SOME BRIEF NOTES ON THE INDIVIDUAL BOUTS ARE GIVEN BELOW :—

FEATHERWEIGHT. GNR. QUAYLE (520) DEFEATED GNR. COOK (517) ON POINTS AFTER 3 ROUNDS. A HARD, FAST FIGHT WITH QUAYLE DOING MOST OF THE FORCING.

SPR. HAWKSWORTH (520) KNOCKED OUT L/CPL. PEARCE (517) IN THE FIRST ROUND.

LIGHTWEIGHT. BDR. CUMMINGS (520) DEFEATED ROMAN MACKINTOSH (517) AFTER 3 ROUNDS. CUMMINGS WAS ALMOST ALWAYS ON THE OFFENSIVE, THOUGH MACKINTOSH FREQUENTLY PARRIED WITH A STRAIGHT LEFT. MACKINTOSH TOOK A LOT OF PUNISHMENT IN THE LAST ROUND.

FUS. STEVENS (520) LOST ON POINTS TO SMITH (517). SMITH GAINED THE VERDICT BY MAINTAINING THE OFFENSIVE.

WELTERWEIGHT. GNR. QUILLIAM (520) LOST ON POINTS TO PTE. RAWLINSON (517). DURING A VERY GOOD 3 ROUNDS, RAWLINSON KEPT CONTROL BY MAKING FULL USE OF HIS LONG REACH. QUILLIAM BOXED STYLISHLY, BUT FOUND IT DIFFICULT TO PENETRATE HIS OPPONENTS GUARD AND BRING THE FIGHT TO CLOSE QUARTERS.

BDR. HORSFALL (520) KNOCKED OUT L/CPL. COOK (517) A BREATH-TAKING FIRST ROUND. BOTH BOXERS PUNCHING VERY HARD, COOK SEEMED VERY "GROGGY" AT THE END OF THE 1ST ROUND AND HE "WENT OUT" TO A RIGHT-CROSS IN THE FIRST FEW SECONDS OF THE 2ND ROUND.

SPR. GARRATT (520) LOST ON POINTS TO PTE. KEYS (517). KEYS FORCED THE FIGHT THROUGHOUT SCORING FREQUENTLY WITH STRAIGHT LEFTS.

GNR. WARING (520) LOST ON POINTS TO GNR. DUGDALE (517). WARING WHO APPEARED IN ORDER TO FILL A VACANCY IN THE 520 TEAM GAVE A VERY PLUCKY AND WHOLEHEARTED DISPLAY AGAINST A VERY DASHING OPPONENT.

MIDDLEWEIGHT GNR. FAYLE 520 LOST TO EATON (517) IN MY OPINION THE BEST FIGHT OF THE AFTERNOON. AN EVENLY MATCHED PAIR, THESE TWO DISPLAYED GOOD RINGCRAFT AND MAINTAINED HIGH-SPEED BOXING OVER THE THREE ROUNDS. THERE WAS A VERY NARROW MARGIN OF POINTS

PTE. CRUMPLIN (520) V PTE. OWENS (517). TWO HARD FIGHTERS, AND IT SEEMED A CASE OF WHO WOULD LAND THE HARDEST BLOW IN THE RIGHT PLACE. CRUMPLIN DID, AND WON BY A K.O.

STEVENSON (520) BEAT CPL. HORNE 517. STEVENSON SCORED REPEATEDLY WITH HEAVY-BODY PUNCHES, THOUGH HORNE TOOK PUNISHMENT WELL AND REMAINED A COOL BOXER TO THE END OF THE 8 ROUNDS.

LIGHT-HEAVY. MNR. MULLARD (520) LOST BY A K.O. TO SADDLER (517). THIS PROMISED TO BE A GREAT FIGHT BETWEEN TWO GOOD FAST HEAVIES, BUT MULLARD WENT DOWN TO A HEAVY SWINGING PUNCH TO THE SIDE OF THE JAW IN THE 1ST ROUND.

CPL. HINDMARSH (520) BEAT PTE HUGHES (520) ON POINTS. A VERY HARD 3 ROUNDS. HUGHES WENT DOWN TO A HEAVY PUNCH IN THE 2ND ROUND, BUT RECOVERED AGAIN TO CONTEST THE LAST ROUND STRONGLY.

HINDMARSH'S VICTORY SWAYED THE BALANCE OF THE FIGHTS IN FAVOUR OF CAMP 520.

A GOOD AFTERNOON'S BOXING. CONGRATULATIONS TO THE WINNERS AND A WORD OF CONSOLATION FOR THE PLUCKY FIGHTING OF THOSE WHO LOST.

"MOPPING UP OPERATIONS IN PROGRESS"

"CONTACT" PAGE 4

Contact, 7 February, with the account of the boxing match.

$\underline{\text{SOLVE}}$ $\underline{\text{THIS}}$

"Life"

THE PROBLEM OF THE BILLIARD BALLS

IN THE LAND OF NOWHERE THERE IS AN EXTRAORDINARY BRIDGE WHICH IS TWO MILES LONG AND CROSSES A ROCKY RAVINE ONE MILE DEEP. THE BRIDGE IS EXTRAORDINARY BECAUSE IT CAN SUPPORT A WEIGHT OF ONLY 200 LBS, ALTHOUGH THIS WEIGHT MAY BE DISTRIBUTED IN ANY WAY ALONG ITS SURFACE.

TO THIS STRANGE BRIDGE THERE COMES A YOUNG MAN WHO IS LIGHT OF HEART, SURE OF HAND, STRONG OF WILL, AND KEEN OF MIND. HE BEARS THREE BILLIARD BALLS, EACH OF WHICH WEIGHS TWO POUNDS. HEEDING THE DANGER SIGN AT THE APPROACH TO THE BRIDGE, HE STEPS ON A SCALE PROVIDED BY THE GOVERNMENT OF NOWHERE. TO HIS CONSTERNATION, HE FINDS THAT HE WEIGHS 195 LBS. THE BALLS, OF COURSE, TOTAL SIX EXTRA POUNDS.

THE YOUNG MAN, HOWEVER, IS RESTRAINED ONLY FOR A MOMENT. WHILE ALL THE OFFICIALS OF NOWHERE ARE TRANSFIXED BY SHOCK, HE BLITHELY PROCEEDS TO APPARENT DESTRUCTION AS HE MAKES FOR THE BRIDGE, CARRYING HIS SPHERICAL CARGO WITH HIM.

HOW THAT BRIGHT YOUNG MAN GOT ACROSS SAFE AND SOUND, BILLIARDS BALLS AND ALL, IS NOW A LEGEND IN THE LAND OF NOWHERE. THE QUESTION IS, HOW DID HE DO IT?

[EXTRACTED FROM "THE POCKET ENTERTAINER"]
$\underline{\text{ANSWER ON PAGE 7.}}$

In brief!

A P.O.W. FRIEND, A SHORT TIME AGO RECEIVED A LETTER FROM HIS MOTHER-IN-LAW. THE LETTER RAN:-

DEAR REGINALD,

JUST A FEW LINES HOPING YOU ARE KEEPING WELL.

SINCERELY, MRS ——

BENEATH WAS A LARGE EXPANSE OF WHITE PAPER. MY FRIEND WAS NOT OFFENDED. "IT'S THE FIRST TIME SHE'S CALLED MY 'REGINALD' HE CONFIDED.

"OFT TIME I SIT AND DREAM OF THINGS WE
USED' TO DO
THE LITTLE JOYS, THE PLEASURES, THAT BELONGED
TO JUST WE TWO
I THINK OF THE HOURS SPENT UNDISTURBED
WHICH WERE ALL OUR OWN
BUT MOST OF ALL I THINK OF YOU, AS I SIT
HERE ALL ALONE
I LONG FOR YOUR SMILE, THE TOUCH OF YOUR
HAND, THE KISS THAT THRILLED ME THROUGH,
I LONG TO TAKE YOU IN MY ARMS THE WAY
I LOVED TO DO.
I THINK OF THOSE THINGS WITH A PAIN IN MY
HEART & A LONELINESS IN MY SOUL,
WITH AN EMPTINESS DEEP INSIDE ME, A
FEELING I CANNOT CONTROL
AND THEN I THINK OF THE FUTURE, THE
WONDERFUL THINGS TO DO
AND A NEW LIGHT SHINES THROUGH MY
DARKNESS A NEW HOPE RISES AT ME
I TURN MYSELF RESOLUTELY - FROM ALL THE
PAIN OF THE PAST.
AND MY HEART LOOKS FORWARD TO THAT
GREAT DAY WHEN YOU WILL BE HOME AT LAST
SO WHENEVER YOU FEEL THAT EMPTINESS
DEAR, AND YOU FEEL LIFE CANNOT BE BORNE
JUST REMEMBER, DARLING, THE DARKEST HOUR
IS JUST BEFORE THE DAWN."

(RECEIVED IN A LETTER FROM HOME)

THE LAND-GIRL MILKS HER FIRST COW

ME.

CONTACT PAGE 3

Reverse of the previous page.

SOCCER — CAN £ BUY SUCCESS ?

BY T. SHARPE (520)

MONEY IS CERTAINLY NOT ALWAYS THE KEY TO SUCCESS, FOR SUCH IS THE GLORIOUS UNCERTAINTY OF FOOTBALL. SOME CLUBS HAVE REACHED DIZZY HEIGHTS WITH THE AID OF MONEY, OTHERS HAVE ACHIEVED AS MUCH WITHOUT.

ABOUT 10 YEARS BEFORE THE WAR, ARSENAL — THEN QUITE A MODERATE KIND OF TEAM — BOUGHT TWO INSIDE FORWARDS — ALEX JAMES FROM PRESTON FOR THE SUM IN THE REGION OF £9,000, AND DAVID JACK FROM BOLTON FOR THE OFFICIAL RECORD SUM OF OVER £10,000. THIS MADE THE NUCLEUS OF A TEAM WHICH HAD A PHENOMENAL RUN OF SUCCESSES. OTHER EXPENSIVE "CAPTURES" FOLLOWED LATER. — COPPING, LEFT-HALF, FROM LEEDS; CRAYSTON, RIGHT-HALF, FROM BRADFORD; DRAKE THE SOUTHAMPTON CENTRE-FORWARD & BASTIN, WINGER FROM EXETER. (THE LATTER'S TRANSFER FEE WAS COMPARITIVELY LOW) ALL THESE MEN PLAYED FOR ENGLAND.

SO MUCH FOR THEIR SUCCESSES. WHAT OF THEIR FAILURES? PROBABLY THEIR BIGGEST DISAPPOINTMENTS WERE JAMES DUNNE, INTERNATIONAL CENTRE-FORWARD FROM SHEFFIELD UNITED AND DR MARSHALL, THE GLASGOW RANGERS INSIDE-RIGHT. OTHERS WHO DID NOT STAY LONG AT HIGHBURY WERE — COLEMAN, CENTRE-FORWARD FROM GRIMSBY; MILNE A WINGER FROM BLACKBURN, AND DAVIDSON, INSIDE-RIGHT FROM ST. JOHNSTONE.

A SEASON OR TWO PRIOR TO THE WAR THE ARSENAL WERE REPUTED TO HAVE PAID £14,000 TO THE WOLVES FOR BRYN JONES, THE WELSH INTER-NATIONAL. HIS PERFORMANCES DID NOT REACH THE HIGH STANDARD OF SUCCESS EXPECTED.

MANY OTHER CASES OF APPARENTLY UNNECESSARY EXPENDITURE MIGHT BE QUOTED. THE CLASSIC EXAMPLE WAS PERHAPS THE BRILLIANT CHELSEA FORWARD LINE WHICH FAILED TO LIVE UP TO REPUTATION AND BECAME A MUSIC-HALL JOKE. (ALEX JACKSON, ALEX CHEYNE, HUGHIE GALLACHER, ANDY WILSON, JACK CRAWFORD.)

IF MONEY ALWAYS COMMANDED SUCCESS, MUCH OF THE CHANCE ELEMENT WOULD DROP OUT OF BIG GAMES. THE FATE OF WALSALL WOULD HAVE BEEN SEALED, WHEN THEY TOOK THE FIELD AGAINST THE ARSENAL IN THAT MEMORABLE CUP-TIE.

GIVE HIM A CHANCE !

THE CONFIDENCE MAN AND HIS WILLING BAND OF HELPERS RETURNED FROM STALAG WITH A LORRY-LOAD OF RED CROSS FOOD SUPPLIES. IT HAD BEEN A VERY WET MORNING AND THE MEN WERE ALL SOAKED WITH THE HEAVY RAIN. AS HOWEVER, THERE HAD BEEN SOME TEMPORARY SHORTAGE OF SUPPLIES IN THE CAMP, THE CONFIDENCE MAN GOT TO WORK IMMEDIATELY AND, WITHIN AN HOUR, THE TABLES IN ALL THE BARRACK-ROOMS WERE LOADED WITH TINS AND PACKETS. IT WAS A TRIUMPH OF ORGAN-ISATION.

LATER IN THE DAY, THE QUESTION WAS OVERHEARD. "DID ANY CHEESE ARRIVE TODAY?" ON BEING ANSWERED IN THE AFFIRMATIVE, THE INQUIRER CONTINUED — "WELL, WHY DIDN'T THE CONFID-ENCE MAN GET IT ISSUED?"

In Memoriam

I SEE HIM — 'TIS BUT MY MEMORY'S EYE
SMILING, SMILING AS THE YEARS PASSED BY
I SEE HIM SITTING IN HIS FAVOURITE CHAIR
HE WILL BE NO MORE THERE.

HE WILL BE THERE NO MORE — ONE FATEFUL DAY
A LETTER TOLD ME THAT HE HAD PASSED AWAY
HOW CAN A LETTER'S HURRIED LINE,
EXPRESS THE LOSS IN HEART AND MIND.?

MY JOYS ARE LESS WHEN I ARRIVE BACK THERE
FOR I'M FACE TO FACE WITH HIS EMPTY CHAIR
DEEP IN MY HEART WILL HIS MEMORY LIVE
THIS VERSE IS MY TRIBUTE — ALL I CAN GIVE.

IN MEMORY OF MY DEAR FATHER WHO PASSED AWAY ON THE 13TH DEC. 1942.   ALFRED. JOHN. DRIVER (520)

THE BILLIARD BALLS PROBLEM SOLUTION

HE JUGGLED THE BALLS EN ROUTE. ONE BALL WAS ALWAYS IN MID-AIR. THE BRIDGE HAD TO SUPPORT ONLY 199 POUNDS.

"CONTACT." PAGE 7.

Contact, p. 7. See solution to the Billiard Balls Problem.

L.J. Cordwell's cartoon strip. The left-hand column is what soldier Len writes and the right-hand column is how girlfriend Brenda interprets it.

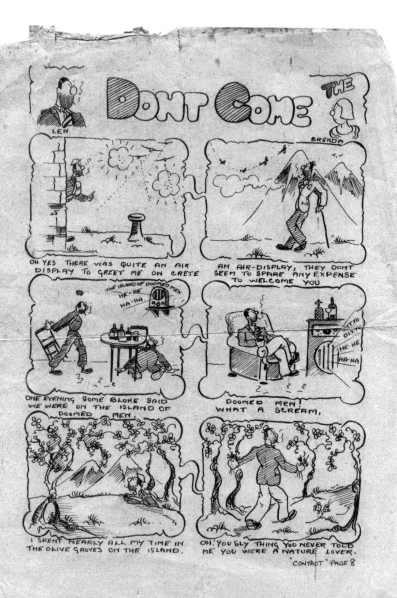

"CONTACT" PAGE 8

We derived great amusement from the cartoons by L.J. Cordwell, *Kriegsgefangener* No. 11838. His cartoons are in two columns; the one on the left depicts scenes of a soldier's progress through the war as experienced by him and written about to his wife/girlfriend in censored letters; the right-hand column depicts the same sequence of events as interpreted by his wife/girlfriend.

This particular newspaper was edited by one Joseph M. Kennedy, *Kriegsgefangener* No. 11224 and approved by Hauptmann Haenchen the commandant. It was from this paper I found out the name of our commandant. I still have a copy of another of our own newspapers called *The Courier* and issued from the headquarters of Stalag IVD at Torgau on the River Elbe – Torgau is the town where the American and Russian troops first met up.

The numbering of the Stalags is rather confusing. Stalag IVB was the large, mainly transit, camp at Mühlberg on the Elbe and Stalag IVD controlled a series of small working camps in the area around Mühlberg, but also covering a wide area to the east of the River Elbe.

The Courier was edited by Ernest Wray, a sergeant attached to the headquarters of Stalag IVD at Torgau. In this there is a short story on the title page, inside an editorial, newsflashes from home, a quiz and a page devoted to sport including items gleaned from home as well as from the various camps in the district. Another page is entitled 'Kommando corner' with news from the working camps, which in German were called *Kommandos*. There is an article entitled 'The voice of the man of confidence': RSM Parslow, senior man of confidence for the whole of Stalag IVD, based at Torgau. There is also a 'Courier appreciation fund' listed. This was a collection from the various working camps to be forwarded, I understood, to the Red Cross in appreciation for their help. In this issue of *The Courier* dated July 1944, the fund stood at almost 120,000 German marks. It is also interesting in listing the names and Stalag numbers of the camps who contributed to the fund and gave the number of men in each camp. Other pages have short stories, jokes, cartoons, a crossword puzzle, a poem and an article on the House of Commons and the Speaker of the House. Another page gives details of the 'Stalag circulating library'; the books available included new American novels published by the Council on Books in Wartime, a non-profit organisation of American Publishers, also books together with syllabuses for a number of professional and technical institutions which were sent out by the YMCA.

We were from time to time, when attached to Stalag IVD, sent books from Torgau. There were also obituaries of prisoners who had died, with a note that letters of condolence had been sent to the next of kin together with a donation to the family of 4,000 German marks. In this issue the RSM gave a note of encouragement. He said although there was some delay in receiving letters and personal parcels, we should not be discouraged because the reason was obvious – a clear reference to the successful D-Day landings in Normandy.

In one of the camps we were all provided with copies, in English, of Hitler's book *Mein Kampf* (My Struggle). Very few took any notice of it, being, for them, a very dull book. However, I did persevere with it and read it from cover to cover, which gave me an insight into the rise of the Third Reich, in particular Hitler's anti-semitism with all the terrible consequences which followed. One thing which surprised me was his quite favourable opinion of England. Generally newspapers were not kept as they were too valuable as loo paper and this was also the fate of many of the copies of *Mein Kampf*, including mine.

Some prisoners kept diaries or records of POW life but they were few and far between. I do recall seeing one which was quite beautiful. I think this must have been either at Wuhlheide or in the transit camp at Mühlberg. It was kept in a large well-bound hardbacked journal and was written in the most elegant Gothic script, with illustrated chapter headings and the most exquisite illustrations, rather like the books produced by monks in medieval times. As a work of art I hope it has survived: it ought to be in the Imperial War Museum, a priceless treasure and record.

Whilst I was at Marienfelde, the Germans put up posters on our camp notice board informing us all about the Katyn Massacre. A mass grave had been found in the Katyn Woods in Poland in which were found the bodies of a large number of Polish army officers who had been brutally murdered and buried in these woods. The Allies, in particular Russia, had announced that this crime had been committed by the German army during their occupation of Poland when that country was divided between Germany and the Soviet Union in 1939. The Germans were very clearly upset and annoyed by this allegation, claiming they had proof that the massacre had in fact been carried out by the Russians. The coloured posters put up on the notice board showed photographs of the mass grave and included an invitation to British POWs to be taken to Katyn to visit the site and be able

THE COURIER

Headquarters
Stalag IVD
Torgau-
Elbe
Editor:
Ernest
Wray

NUMBER 4   **JULY 1944**

NO REASON, NO PURPOSE

A Short Story by C. R. BAILEY (Arb. Kdo. D. 601)

"Twenty-four today ! Nothing auspicious has happened : much like any other day. Not even any presents. Eric would have presented a little gift to mark the occasion. He was so good and kind. But now no more kindness, no more goodness from dear Eric — just a memory remains. Heart-rending memory. (Everybody had said how tragic to be cut away from life so young.) Like a slender buttercup before a scythe. Killed in a car accident. How horrible ! Why ! — no reason, no purpose. Insane? And now I'm alone : alone to face a life full of hardships, difficulties and the greater misfortunes, such as that which had carried Eric away for ever. Nobody to care, nobody to love. Life had been so full of promise, a great adventure to enjoy together side by side, each in each, in love. But now — emptiness. Next spring would come with warm sunshine and fresh flowers, yet no marriage, no bliss."

Catherine sighed and moved towards the open bedroom window to breathe the freshness of the late summer evening. For the past six months, almost every evening, had she framed herself in the same open window to stare vacantly, as if transfixed by a vision. It always seemed as if she were holding sweet communion with some unseen being hidden away in the foliage of the sycamore tree which stood opposite, just inside a field. Once, sometimes twice, each evening she would move away from the window to change her attire, to don a new dress or a fresh suit and then return to her original position looking straight into the middle of the tree with a glittering eye as if seeking some approval, some admiration. She would always make subtle adjustments, however, in front of the large wardrobe mirror before presenting herself to the sycamore leaves — the smoothing of a slight crease below her bosom, the tightening of a belt or the straightening of a pleated skirt. Perfectly, presentable. Supporting her small, round breasts on her slim arms; folded on the window-sill, she had often been seen to move her lips as if in conversation, to smile strangely. People knew she hadn't any intimate friends to admit to her bedroom and her aunt with whom she lived was old and kept herself entirely aloof. Consequently, some said she was a pervert, a sex-pervert. Others said she was just crazy.

Old man Jakeley thought her a slut, a common strumpet who liked to parade her not unattractive body before all who may pass the window. Nevertheless, he spied upon her from a vantage point at the foot of the sycamore, but concealed from Catherine herself by a low hedge. In this latter he had cut a small opening through which to peep with his gluttonous eyes. He had been doing this for many weeks, unbeknown to Catherine, of course. Jakeley was of doubtful character. He had never been married, mainly because he had shunned the company of women due to his being most sensitive of a gross deformity. An untriendly star had ordained him with a withered arm and a hunched back. Always horribly aware of his physical awkwardness, he cursed fate, the stars and even his parents. His incapacity had caused him, throughout, to be neglectful of himself. A permanent leer had been cultivated upon his untidy features, revealing three dirty brown teeth. And he slobbered tobacco-stained saliva. Like dirty sump oil leaking. Once only had he made physical contact with a woman — a half-wit from a neighbouring village. She had bitten him viciously. He had never forgotten.

Leering now lustfully, he feasted his eyes upon Catherine in the act of changing into a

> *The Editor regrets to state that, although a number of stories have been received in response to the... Possible, the illustrations destined for this issue are not yet to hand. In the event of their arrival, they will be incorporated in a later edition*

pale blue evening dress : a shaft of sunlight played upon the bare flesh below the armpit as she struggled with the dress around her head. She was adding garments but Jakeley's imagination was taking them away, one by one. He was drawing her nearer and nearer, running his rough hands over her velvet skin. He could even now feel a tingling sensation in his fingertips. His blood gushed up into a mad race around his body. His mind menaced her, his thoughts crazily crushed her, mentally, he violated her. The brown spittle oozed from the sides of his mouth.

Catherine's mind was transported back to the last evening she had worn the lovely pale-blue frock. Eric had announced their betrothal at a house-party given in her honour. There were many congratulations, much toasting with some heady wine. Rapturous and blissful moments in the conservatory afterwards, with Eric whispering his admiration. The pale evening sun kissed her breast and her heart warmed again towards her absent lover. She felt his soft warm kisses, his caressing hand. Her body trembled and thrilled as it echoed to the ecstatic experience in the conservatory, as if a net of gossamer were brushing her nakedness. The dress fitted her perfectly : she smoothed it out, rearranged her hair before the friendly wardrobe as if prompted by her unseen betrothed. Framing herself again in the window she observed a darkening sky. Ominous black clouds were fast approaching with disturbing rumbles of thunder. Her mind was saddened. Why, oh why had Eric driven her home so recklessly after the party ? He was so gay and happy. Recklessly happy.

Reckless happiness had killed him. There had been a crash like thunder. Her consciousness was blackened as if by a heavy dark cloud. She awoke in hospital to learn that Eric would never awake. Why, oh why ?

Jakeley licked his lips. His eyes gleamed. Go on ! lean over a bit more more and show yer breasts, you whore! Change yer frock again. Parade yerself, suits me. I'm used to the performance, but its good. Gosh ! how I'd like to climb up that ivy and in through the window."

Catherine looked into the depths of the tree. It seemed gloomy and sad somehow — as if it were waiting to be beheaded. "What a strange thought ! Must dismiss this constant spectre of tragedy." Thought association. Eric, happiness and ecstasy — but always the finality of the sudden, eternal severing.

A blinding flash, with a simultaneous crack as from a gigantic whip — the sycamore was split in two. The shock moved Catherine to the floor into a trembling heap. Two hours later Jakeley was picked up dead from the base of the lightning-struck sycamore.

Catherine passed through a sickening, nightmarish darkness. Early the following morning Eric's child appeared — stillborn. Dead before it should have been born.

LAUNCELOT SAYS...

THE LAGGARD - DROWSE SLIPSHOD 12

The third in my series but no less important for that, this car is the first to introduce curved wheels for corners and to be run on a mixture of three parts petrol and one part dessicated bismuth to reduce wind resistance. It is fitted with the new non-fuliginous sump dredger and with retractable head-lights for long-sighted drivers. A further new adjustment is a fifth wheel, centrally fixed beneath the chassis which, upon application of the sneeshing ganglion, lowers itself and spins the car round for a quick turn.

The car has super-ejectory sniggle-nipples and a sphygmomanometer is fitted on the dash-board for faint-hearted drivers. This model runs so smoothly that you need a stethoscope to hear it ticking over. A special recently patented acicular generator brings the electricity back to the battery after use.

Laggard-Drowse guarantee you absolute satisfaction. It is impossible to be pinched for speeding, though a charge of furious loitering is quite possible.

Next Month : — The Swifton Suddon Six.

The Courier, No. 4, dated July 1944. It was printed on both sides.

to see for themselves that the Germans were innocent of the crime and to see the proof of Russian culpability. At the time we assumed this was just more German propaganda and although tempted with the offer as a way to get away from the camp for a 'swan', no one from our camp went. I suppose the same offer was made to other camps and I do not know if anyone went. Of course we know now this was one atrocity that the Germans did not commit.

As time went on, the bombing of Berlin intensified; there was rarely a night without the sounding of the alarms. We watched all the raids and spent every night in the air-raid shelters. As always, we were fascinated by the 'firework' displays in the sky and continued to cheer and applaud as the planes made for their targets and dropped their bombs. There was considerable noise from the anti-aircraft guns and the sound of bombs exploding not far away. The bombers flew in tight formation until over the target marked by flares from the pathfinders, then peeled off to start the homeward journey.

Very occasionally we saw one shot down, but most casualties seemed to be caused by night fighters rather than anti-aircraft fire. We also saw German night fighters shot down. During these raids we began to see strips of silvery paper, rather like aluminium foil, floating down and from time to time some of them fell in our camp. We learned these were a sort of decoy to confuse the German radar system. At the time few of us knew of the existence of radar detection. I certainly had never heard of it and it was not until the end of the war we found out what it was. We became accustomed to the nightly raids and disturbed sleep. At this point in the war we saw no sign of daytime raids and only the RAF, as yet no American planes.

Suddenly, with no warning, we were told to collect all our belongings and prepare to move. As usual we were not told where we were going. We were then entrained and transported to a new camp further away from Berlin.

12

Wuhlheide, No. SCH 184, Stalag IIID

Without a map of Berlin and the surrounding areas, I could not be sure of the exact location of our new camp called Wuhlheide: I understood it to be near Potsdam to the south-west of Berlin. What I do know is that the camp was within a short walk of the Karlshorst horse-racing track. It was well away from the bombing and we gathered that the reason for the move was to house us in a safer location. Perhaps there was some pressure from the protecting power to move the camps out of danger, but at the time we doubted the Germans were particularly concerned about our safety.

Wuhlheide camp, my fifth in Germany, was considerably larger than any of the others: I think there were around seven hundred men in the camp. The grounds also were very much larger with a grassed area large enough for a small cricket ground. We also had a very big assembly hall complete with stage and dressing rooms. The accommodation was also better. Each barrack block had a central corridor with rooms leading off on each side; the rooms were smaller, with just ten or twelve men to a room, making them much quieter and more congenial; easier to organise, especially for the cleaning rosters.

We tended to form small groups with our own muckers. The groups were usually four to six men, probably because these were the numbers which seemed to work best, originating from sharing out our loaves of bread. It must be difficult for anyone who has not had a similar experience to imagine the importance placed on one's ration of bread and the efforts involved to share it fairly. With the regular supply of Red Cross food parcels, we would pool most of the tinned foods, tea and coffee but individually kept such items as chocolate, sweets and tablets of soap. This made sense in helping to build up a good community spirit within the group. I was with the same group from Lichtenfelde for all the time we were in the Berlin area.

In our room at Wuhlheide were the six muckers plus three New Zealand friends, former Middle East commandos Johnnie (known as 'Mary') Manson, Ray Overs and Ken Griffin. The other three were 'Blondie' Naylor, a young Welshman called Barry and 'Dodger' Green. H. Corbett Green was a 'townie' of mine in that he came from Burton-on-Trent. Our room was in the end block of the camp, the furthest away from the camp entrance and facing the 'cricket ground'; the room itself was the end one next to the entrance door. There were six double bunks, a table and benches, the usual tortoise stove, one window and, quite surprisingly, an electric plug; all in all, the most comfortable room I had had with the most amenable companions. The only drawback to our room was that it was a long way from the ablution block – especially at night.

As in all camps, we cleaned our own rooms with brushes and dust-pans provided by the Germans. We drew up a roster but when it came to Dodger's turn, he always queried the roster and argued that it was not his turn, on and on, until someone else did it. We accepted he would never do any cleaning and tolerated his attitude with good humour. He was the POW at Teltow on a bitterly cold working party who insisted that he would rather freeze to death than work for the Germans.

Ray Overs' surname interested me because at school I remembered (because we were given tinned peaches for tea) playing cricket against Cotton College (a Roman Catholic College in north-east Staffordshire) who had had a bowler called Overs. I wondered if there was any connection and by coincidence this was the very same Ray Overs.

The commandant at this camp had the rank of major and was a very different sort of German from those we had encountered previously. Unfortunately I cannot recall his name. To us he appeared a gentleman; he spoke excellent English and told us he had worked as a businessman in London for a number of years. He was certainly well disposed towards us and made considerable efforts to run a happy camp. I heard later on the grapevine he had been implicated in the conspiracy to assassinate Hitler, was arrested and later executed. He had given the clear impression of not being a committed member of the Nazi party.

Here at Wuhlheide we had a new man of confidence, an RSM, whose name again I do not recall, but I do remember him as a good and efficient leader of the camp. He insisted we were soldiers first and POWs second and therefore we must always be well disciplined, obedient and, most importantly, clean and smart in turnout, especially when out of the camp. At his behest, our battledress had to be clean, our trousers pressed, our boots highly polished and we must wear our side caps with, if possible, our cap badges, also polished. There was no excuse for us not being smart because by this time, mid-1943, we had all been issued with complete British army uniforms, battledress, side caps, greatcoats and army boots.

The man of confidence made frequent inspections and soon had the whole camp smartened up to the standards expected in the British army. So, after the rather ragged dress and shuffle of the first years of POW life, we now marched off to work each day as smart soldiers in almost immaculate uniforms, highly polished boots and shining badges. Indeed we were very much smarter than the guards who accompanied us. As a result the commandant, one day, called everyone on parade and announced that he had received a complaint from the Gauleiter (literally district leader) of Berlin District, the Nazi boss, that the British POWs were much too smart and marched through the streets as if we were occupying troops and not prisoners. This, the Gauleiter stated, would not be tolerated. He said our British uniforms must be exchanged for the tattered clothing which we had had during our early days as prisoners. The commandant refused to comply, arguing that we were British prisoners of war clothed as British soldiers in accordance with the Geneva Convention on the treatment of prisoners of war and our uniforms had been issued through the protecting power appointed by the International Red Cross and agreed with by the German government. The commandant even complimented us on our appearance and general demeanour. Perhaps this incident alerted the authorities to his anti-Nazi feelings and contributed to his eventual downfall. Thanks to our man of confidence and our commandant, we were beginning to feel proud: morale took an enormous boost.

It was now summer and having a space large enough for a cricket ground, games were organised. We had cricket equipment sent out by the YMCA and the Red Cross which included bats, pads, gloves, cricket balls, stumps and bails. It seemed amazing that we were allowed to have cricket bats and stumps when baseball bats were prohibited as being potentially offensive weapons: obviously the Germans had little or no knowledge of cricket. Our games were organised by the two padres, each picking a side. The two padres were Father Scarborough, the Roman Catholic, and the Reverend Thomas, a Welsh Anglican priest, often referred to as 'dai pulpit and prayer book'. The memories of any church services they held in the assembly hall have completely faded, but not so the cricket matches. As captains of the respective teams they had selected, they first set up the stumps but not without constant disagreements and arguments about the length of the pitch, each one accusing the other of trying to vary the length to suit his own bowlers, causing considerable amusement for the rest of us. The ground was not very good for a cricket wicket being rather rough and uneven, making much of the batting really hit and miss; nevertheless, we had some very enjoyable matches relieving the boredom of prison camp life.

As summer faded into autumn and winter our attention turned to the winter sports of football and rugby. Our commandant had arranged for us to use some nearby playing fields owned by the Dresdner Bank which were not being used by the bank staff during the war. This was excellent news because the grounds were properly grassed, still well maintained, constantly mown and were in first-class condition, quite unlike the rough, hard, scruffy pitches we had had at the previous camps. The playing fields just happened to adjoin the Karlshorst racecourse which was still being used as a steeplechase course on most weekends. The commandant arranged that those men who were deemed not fit enough to go out on the working parties but were capable of some light work to do their work at the racetrack, generally repairing fences, raking over the ground around the fences after races and other cleaning work in and around the stables. They mixed with the stable boys and the jockeys and obtained details of the race cards for the forthcoming races and were given some tips on the form of the horses.

At weekends we were allowed to go to the playing fields – under half a mile away – for our games of football and rugby. A notice on the camp notice board informed us of a forthcoming game and directed anyone – spectators as well as players – who wished to go to assemble at the gate at a specified time to be taken by the guards to the ground. Surprisingly large numbers of prisoners would assemble on each occasion, requiring several guards to control the crowd. We were carefully counted before being marched to the playing fields. On arrival, the players would get ready for their match and a few spectators would stay with them; however, the majority would slowly drift over to the boundary with the racecourse, to watch the afternoon's racing. As can be expected, some of the men had been regular race-goers at home and some enterprising ones, making use of the information from the 'light workers', set up as bookies and took bets on the races, everyone using the camp marks for money. The German guards did not seem to mind us watching the races or betting, although I do not recall any of the guards placing bets with our bookies!

Not everyone went to the races; some of us were keen on playing and we had many very enjoyable games. I only played rugby. The playing fields had several pitches so there was space enough for rugby and football matches to take place at the same time. The Germans only provided football goal posts, so, again, we had to get poles to extend the uprights to allow for rugby conversions. We had a number of very good rugby players so the standard of play was very high, certainly as high as any club rugby back home. In addition to the English, Welsh and New Zealand players I have already mentioned, we now had a few South Africans including Vic Els and Ernie Erasmus and more Welsh players, including Peter Davies (I think that was his name) who was a first-class three-quarter and had been tipped to play for Wales. We had some good, enjoyable games, including an international match between England and the rest of the world. It was in this match that I obtained my international cap! My recollection is that the rest of the world won: the New Zealanders were certainly the best players.

As well as the few POW spectators we also had, most unexpectedly, some German civilians: some men but more were young women. It was clear they had never seen rugby played before and were fascinated by the game and vocal in their appreciation especially of the scrums and rucks. Some of them became regular spectators. Most of the girls were quite attractive and it was good to see them close to, but we did not have any conversation or real contact with them, more's the pity! Nevertheless, we considered it a bit of a propaganda coup to attract, week after week, German civilians to come and watch British and Commonwealth prisoners of war playing rugby and thoroughly enjoying the games and cheering the line-outs and scrums. We hoped they talked about their entertainment with their families and friends.

Somehow a man on one of the working parties had come into contact with a German girl, got to know her and in due course they fell in love and it became a serious affair. The girl persuaded him to go and live with her, so one day he deserted from the working party and went to live with her in a flat. Of course there were repercussions for the guard who had allowed the escape, but I do not recall any punishment measures or even petty restrictions for the rest of the camp. He lived with the girl for about two or three weeks until it became apparent to him that it just would not work. The girl simply could not support both of them with just one ration book and a small wage. In addition, he had to spend every day cooped up in the small flat to avoid being seen. Although still in love, they decided it could not continue. He decided to return to the camp and presented himself at the gate and asked to be admitted, telling the guard that he was the prisoner who had escaped, but now wished to return to the camp. The guard just did not believe him, thought he was some displaced person or guest worker trying to get into the camp, and turned him away, indicating that the camp was solely for British prisoners and he could not let just any riff-raff in. Our man persisted and eventually persuaded the guard to call the man of confidence who confirmed his story. He was given a spell in the cooler and resumed his prison life. There was no pack drill at this camp, so he was spared that.

Following the call by the man of confidence for us to smarten ourselves up, there grew a desire to have collars and ties. At that time collars and ties were not permitted for non-commissioned officers in the British army. We decided as we were not under the direct control of any British officers, we could make our own decision to wear ties in order to enhance our turn-out, especially when going through the streets in the Berlin area. The army shirts were collarless, awful in appearance, always much too long. To me the collarless shirt was a form of class discrimination. The answer was easy: cut off the long tails of the shirts and use the material to make collars and ties – the result can be seen in photographs taken at Naumburg-Saale after we were freed. I became the tailor for our room. We were able to buy needles and thread and scissors in the canteen, and after some experimentation, I became quite an expert in making collars and ties for my friends. I also made various coloured flashes to sew on the arms of our battledress tunics. This also raised our morale.

Somehow I managed to acquire a small electric hot plate; I think I must have got it from another prisoner in exchange for, probably, cigarettes or maybe a pullover. I managed to connect it to the electrical system and it proved a godsend for heating up food and doing a little cooking of a very simple kind. I had to be careful to hide it from the prying eyes of the guards. By very good fortune I managed to keep it safe until it was eventually lost when my last camp was bombed.

The summer of 1943 was very hot both by day and night, so we took our palliasses outside in rows on the grass and slept under the stars: this was quite a novelty which we thoroughly enjoyed. Surprisingly at Wuhlheide we were not really disturbed by air raids, just the occasional fore-alarm. The sky was clear and the moonlight was bright enough to light up the long trek to the ablutions.

The work at this camp was the same as previously: carting soil in bogeys to build embankments for railways. We kept up our system of task work and having filled the quota of ten skip loads, returned to camp with plenty of time for leisure activities.

Our commandant was very keen for us to use the facilities of the recreation/assembly hall and put on a theatrical production. After some discussion we decided not to arrange the usual variety show but aim for something more serious. The commandant suggested Shakespeare and after more discussion we chose *Henry V*, with the twofold intention of raising our morale whilst annoying any Germans who attended. In fact, they enjoyed it! Copies of the play were obtained through the Red Cross and rehearsals commenced. The major problem was costumes as we had only very limited access to suitable materials. The man of confidence was aiming at a high standard of production so he decided to ask the commandant if it would be possible to hire costumes, saying we had sufficient money, albeit in camp marks, to pay for the hire. The commandant listened sympathetically, but he doubted if any of the theatrical outfitters in Berlin would agree to hire costumes to prisoners of war. However, he said there was no harm in trying. He suggested we approach one firm he knew about in Berlin. Thus three of us were chosen to visit a theatrical outfitter whose shop was situated in north-east Berlin, very close to the Stettiner Bahnhof. The chosen three were Jimmy Ellis, Harry Price and myself; both Jimmy and Harry spoke fluent German and I understood quite a lot, but perhaps the main reason I was selected was that at the time I was helping with camp administration. Before setting out we discussed our tactics and approach in persuading the outfitter to loan us costumes. We armed ourselves with packets of coffee, bars of chocolate, bars of soap and cigarettes which we thought would be good bargaining aids and a guard was assigned to accompany us.

We set off on the *Ringbahn*, travelling in the rear coach, as always. This carriage was not restricted to POWs and guest workers: some German civilians also travelled in it and naturally had priority in seating, and generally prisoners had to stand. On this particular day there were a number of civilians, including some children. We had to stand, the guard keeping a watchful eye on us whilst he chatted to civilians and answered their questions about us. During the journey, as had been planned, Jimmy produced a large block of chocolate and speaking in German he offered some to Harry who declined, explaining (also in German) that he had eaten too much chocolate and was fed up with it. Jimmy then offered some to me and I also declined it, for the same reason. Jimmy then announced that he also was tired of chocolate and quite deliberately threw the bar on the floor and kicked it under the seat. All this was observed closely by the civilians, especially the children. They had been clearly interested in us as British prisoners of war, but then were much more interested in the discarded bar of chocolate and kept glancing at it. Chocolate was virtually unavailable in wartime Germany as their supplies were cut off by our blockade of their ports. So their mouths must have been watering as they eyed the precious bar under the seat. Eventually we arrived at Stettiner Bahnhof and as we got off the train, we were able to glance back and see an almighty scramble for our bar of chocolate. We were very amused and satisfied with this consciously staged incident. We had lost one rather precious bar of chocolate but had achieved a useful bit of propaganda. We could imagine them talking to their families and friends about those British POWs who had so much chocolate they could afford to throw it away!

The guard got directions to the theatrical outfitters. We walked into the shop and the guard told the girl receptionist (with Jimmy and Harry chipping in), that we wished to hire costumes for a Shakespearan play to be put on in our POW camp. She went off and returned a few minutes later with the irate manager, furious that his premises had been sullied by British prisoners. He ranted on about how POWs were a drain on German resources and should all be shot. He ordered us off the premises, turned on his heel and stormed off back to his inner sanctuary. The poor guard who had taken the brunt of his outburst, sighed and said, 'That's that, we must return to the camp, I told you it was a stupid idea.' Jimmy said he should wait for a minute or two and then produced a packet of coffee from his coat pocket and asked the receptionist to take it to the manager and asked him if he was interested in a supply of *'Bohnen'* coffee. Reluctantly she agreed and went off to see him. We waited a few minutes then back came the manager with half a smile on his face, saying he had perhaps been rather too hasty in turning us away. Would we please come through to his office?

We outlined our requirements and explained that we could only pay in camp marks. He replied that he had the costumes and could hire them, but the camp marks would have to be converted into real marks: here there might be some difficulty as the bank might want to know how a theatrical outfitter had obtained camp marks. He added that there were ways and means, but he would have to charge us double the normal hire. This did not worry us as we had so much of this useless money it might just as well be used to hire costumes, so we agreed and made a deal. The manager added that he had a good selection of costumes readily available as there was little call for them because of the war but he would need to have his supply of coffee – for him the essence of the deal. We returned to the camp and reported to the man of confidence, who was delighted. The costumes were sent to the camp, the commandant handled the payment on our behalf, and the play was a great success.

Life at Wuhlheide continued smoothly but was generally dull and monotonous. We continued to receive our weekly Red Cross food parcels and our personal parcels came from time to time. We had letter cards to write home every fortnight, occasional additional postcards, and we received letters from home regularly. The guards told us the war would go on for another year before they eventually won; they thought the idea of staying that much longer in camp would dampen our spirits and lower our morale. We were beginning to pick up bits of news and knew the tide had turned in our favour. We retorted to the guards that we did not mind the wait because we knew Churchill was planning on a ten-year war, so it was of no consequence to us how long it lasted; we were well prepared to sit back and wait. The poor guards could not understand our nonchalance. Of course our long imprisonment was irksome, but our morale was high; we knew the Allies were winning the war and it was just a matter of time.

During our work we sometimes had to walk along the railway tracks and so came in close contact with political prisoners. They were also working on the track, wore striped pyjama-like clothes and were very emaciated, clearly not properly fed. Some were clearly Jews as they wore the yellow Star of David badge, but there were others also who had fallen foul of the Nazis. Their guards tried to prevent them having any contact with us, continually threatening and bullying them. From time to time we were able to slip them a little food.

Occasionally we also came across Italian 'guest workers', supposedly the gallant allies of the Germans, but who were kept in camps not much better than ours, although they did not have guards and were able to come and go as they wished and were even provided with brothels. This was before the fall of Mussolini. Afterwards they were probably treated as prisoners of war. There were also slave labourers from other occupied counties; we met ones from France, Belgium, Poland and Bulgaria, housed in barrack-like camps similar to ours, but in reality their conditions were worse. They were treated as third-class citizens and of course had no status with the International Red Cross as they were not prisoners of war: it is certain many did not survive the war.

In the autumn of 1943 the air raids on Berlin and the surrounding areas increased so much that the Germans decided to move our camp away from Berlin, possibly under pressure from the Swiss protecting power. We were just ordered to get ready once again. The date must have been some time in October 1943. As before, we were moved by cattle truck, forty men to a truck, but this time the commandant bade us farewell and wished us well. Our destination was a village called Mühlberg and the new camp was in Stalag IVB in the Leipzig district. We had left Stalag IIID and Berlin behind.

Mühlberg, Stalag IVB

ühlberg is a small town on the east bank of the River Elbe approximately 40 miles due east of Leipzig and about 15 miles south of Torgau, on the west bank. I never discovered why it was designated Stalag IVB because the working camps in the area were part of Stalag IVD, which had its headquarters in Torgau.

Stalag IVB featured in a book and a film called *Jenny's War* (by Jack Stoneley, Hamlyn/Panther, 1980), the story of a British woman who had married a German who became a Luftwaffe officer. She also had a son who had joined the RAF who was shot down and became a POW in the camp at Mühlberg. She lived in Mühlberg town but got into trouble with the German authorities and was forced to hide. She was smuggled into this camp where she was hidden for the duration of the war. I never came across her during my time at the camp nor did I hear any talk of a woman in the camp; she may have been there during my short time there. The book gives the number of prisoners in the camp as 15,000: I think this may be an exaggeration, but does indicate the huge size of the camp.

This vast camp housed British, French, Belgian and Russian prisoners and perhaps other nationalities as well; it was designated a *Stammlager*, which we understood meant a transit camp. The camp processed newly arrived prisoners before dispatching them to working camps; it also housed some non-working prisoners who were there more permanently. The British prisoners included some RAF as well as army men, mostly WOs and sergeants. The Russian prisoners were completely segregated from the rest by extra barbed wire around their compound, whilst guards

The entrance to Stalag IVB at Mühlberg.

permanently patrolled the perimeter of their sector with guard dogs. We could only peep into their compound whose conditions were very primitive. The other nationalities, although living in their own sections of the camp, were not physically separated and all mixed relatively freely together.

Inside the main entrance was a large administrative area with offices, guardroom, German barracks, workshops, stores and a disinfection section with a shower block. On arrival, all prisoners came into this area and were immediately marched to the disinfection centre where they were showered, deloused and their clothes disinfected. So when we arrived we were marched straight to the delousing buildings. We protested that as prisoners of long standing we had already gone through this process, were quite clean and it was all unnecessary. This cut no ice; we were ordered to strip naked and our clothes and baggage were taken away to be fumigated. After showering we were disinfected by a guard with a bucket of disinfectant and a lavatory brush which he dabbed, as on former occasions, under each armpit and around the genitals. It was a rather degrading experience. We were not provided with towels and had to wait to dry off before collecting our fumigated clothes, other belongings and being allowed to dress.

We were then taken to the administration block to be photographed holding a card in front of us with our POW number on it, then were finger-printed and registered. Why we had to go through the process again I do not know, as we had been registered over two years before at Luckenwalde. I suppose it was the system which had no flexibility and could not be varied. Perhaps it was because most of the British prisoners already in the camp were new to Germany and had not, like us, been transferred from else-where in Germany. When the Italians surrendered to the advancing Allied troops, the Germans transferred many of the Allied prisoners previously held by the Italians to Germany. Some British prisoners escaped when the Italians collapsed; those escapees who were recaptured by the Germans, together with any captured in the ensuing battles, were sent to Germany and many of them landed up at Stalag IVB.

Not long before Christmas a new batch of prisoners arrived to be processed and were quickly sent out on working parties. Some 'resident' prisoners thought it unfair that new prisoners should not be given a break and allowed to spend Christmas in this camp before being sent to working camps. They decided to halt the registration process by stealing the camera and a plan was devised to raid the administrative office after it had closed for the day. It was successful and the camera was spirited away into the prisoners' compound, never to be seen again. This created a tremendous hoo-haa in the administration system and it did halt registration for about a week before a replacement camera was obtained; no more prisoners were sent out to work before Christmas so the objective was achieved. The camera was never recovered nor were the thieves ever identified.

Once registered, we again formed up and were marched into the prison-ers' compound expecting to be taken to one of the normal barrack blocks, but instead we were marched right past them to be put into isolation in a quarantine area away from the rest of the camp. Guards were posted on the gate to prevent our communicating with the rest of the camp. We protested loudly that there was no need for us to go into isolation and quarantine as we were prisoners transferred from Berlin and had already been prisoners for over two years. The Germans paid no attention to our protests, appar-ently believing that we had been recently captured in Italy.

The barrack rooms were the typical wooden ones with the customary two-tier bunks. There were no facilities for boiling water to make tea or coffee or to heat up our food from the Red Cross parcels we had brought with us. We were just given the usual camp rations of a piece of bread and a watery potato/cabbage/turnip soup brought to the compound by other prisoners from outside under strict guard. We quite politely requested hot boiling water to make our tea and coffee and the Germans demanded to know how we had managed to get tea and coffee; they just could not or would not accept that we had been prisoners for some time and had brought these supplies with us from our previous camp. We were particularly incensed at this treatment after the very reasonable regime we had had at the Wuhlheide camp.

We felt these guards were particularly dumb. We never called them 'goons'; rarely 'huns'. One of our favourite expressions was 'square-headed bastards' which translated into German is '*quadrat kopf*'. They would ask, 'Was ist das square head?' to which we answered, that you take a square solid block of wood and that is a German guard's head. They were quite bewildered and never took exception to the description – perhaps they really were blockheads.

We were very frustrated at the Germans' refusal to provide us with hot water for tea or give us fuel for a fire. In desperation we decided to take down the wooden shutters from outside the barrack room windows and break them up to make fires for boiling water and heating food. This we did and, as expected, the Germans reacted furiously. We were called out on parade, the commandant arrived and read the riot act (in German so not widely understood), accusing us of wilfully destroying German property and threatening all sorts of punishments.

Then out stepped a New Zealander, I think a sergeant. He was a natural leader, in civilian life a school master who spoke fluent German. He demanded that the Germans abide by the provisions of the Geneva Convention on the treatment of prisoners of war. The commandant replied he had never heard of any Geneva Convention. Our new leader persisted and quoted from it, demanding the commandant produce a copy. After a protracted argument, the commandant sent a guard off to his office who returned with a copy in French which the commandant claimed he did not understand. Our New Zealander said he also spoke fluent French and proceeded to translate the document into German. The Germans then left but did nothing to meet our requests, so we continued to burn the shutters for fires until there were hardly any left. The next day the guards called us all out on parade again. The commandant accompanied by other officers got up on a box to address the ex-Wuhlheide prisoners, threatening us again with dire punishment for continuing to destroy German property. We hissed and booed him, surrounded his box so he could not make himself heard until he stormed off in a rage: perhaps he was afraid of being lynched. We returned to the barrack room, burned more shutters to brew more tea and awaited further developments.

Soon after dawn next morning there was a lot of commotion at the gate to the compound. A large number of armed guards marched in. We were ordered to gather all our belongings together and form up outside in four ranks. There was a tremendous amount of shouting and '*raus*'-ing by the guards. Within a matter of minutes we were all lined up, then the order was given to march and we marched out of the quarantine compound, out through the main camp and out of Stalag IVB. At a rough estimate there was one guard to every three or four prisoners. As usual we had no idea of our destination. As we marched the guards constantly chivvied us, screaming at us to move along and using their rifle butts on anyone who dawdled. About every hour we had a short halt for a '*pinkelpause*'. We were given no food and the only drink was what we had managed to put in our water bottles. I have no idea how many miles we covered but suppose it must have been at least twenty. I know that I got very exhausted and would have dropped by the wayside if it had not been for my friends helping me along; in particular I remember Blondie Naylor carrying one of my bags for me.

We were eventually halted outside a very bleak-looking camp, thankful to stop after a most gruelling forced march with constant harassment from hostile guards. The camp was called Jacobsthal (Jacob's Ladder) and we learned it was a concentration camp. Recent research leads me to believe that this camp may have been the one at Zeithain, close to Jacobsthal station, about 4 miles from Riesa and 15 miles from Mühlberg. It was notorious for its brutality to Russian POWs and Jews: thousands had already died in the camp in 1941 and 1942 in the most appalling conditions.

We had no idea what lay ahead for us at this place and were very apprehensive. The guards who had marched us there handed us over to the commandant of the camp with a letter from the commandant of Stalag IVB and then disappeared. The commandant of Jacobsthal, an army officer, read the letter and through our interpreter informed us of the contents, which in essence stated, 'Herewith about three hundred British prisoners of war who were captured on Crete and who have not yet surrendered, sent to you for punishment.' We felt this was certainly an accolade and momentarily felt quite proud of this achievement. We never found out why the commandant at Stalag IVB had chosen a concentration camp for our punishment; certainly it was an admission he knew of the existence of these camps. This was clearly in breach of the Geneva Convention. In his book, *The Colditz Myth*, Professor S.P. Mackenzie states the men sent to Jacobsthal were mostly RAF sergeants for refusing to salute and for complaining about food. That is not correct: I was on that march to Jacobsthal and incarcerated in Jacobsthal. We were all from the quarantine area of Stalag IVB and were all POWs who had been captured on Crete, and all had been transferred there from Wuhlheide camp near Berlin.

The commandant at Jacobsthal seemed very puzzled at our arrival, clearly unexpected. He said this was not the place for military prisoners of war. He questioned us about our circumstances and why we had been sent there. We related our story from capture on Crete to our problems at Mühlberg and the forced march to Jacobsthal. He considered all this for a while and then asked for the name of the commandant at Wuhlheide. By a lucky coincidence he said he knew him well and would seek confirmation of our story from him before deciding what to do with us. He returned about half an hour later, with our story not only confirmed but we had been warmly commended. He was clearly appalled at the treatment given us at IVB, was extremely sorry but he had no option, in the circumstances, but to keep us in the camp for about three weeks. The orders he had received from Stalag IVB were for us to be punished, but now knowing the real situation he would just put us in a barrack for the three weeks with no physical punishment. The conditions, he said, were unsuitable for us but he would do his best to see that we were reasonably treated. We heaved a huge sigh of relief, very glad to be rid of the vicious guards who had brought us there.

Before entering the compound allocated to us we were body-searched and all our kit inspected. The new German guards set up a row of trestle tables on which we placed our kitbags and packs etc. in batches. We lined up in a queue and awaited our turn. When mine came, I put my kitbag and Red Cross box on the table. The guards on our side of the table frisked us and then we emptied out our possessions for examination by the guards on the other side of the table. I was worried because my little electric hotplate was in my kitbag and I did not want it discovered and confiscated. The guards seemed to be searching everything but, as usual in searches, there was a certain amount of confusion. I thought quickly: if I could confuse the man searching my things I might get away with my hotplate not being found. So, as he delved into the kitbag, I presented him with a roll of drawings (I had been doing some sketching, including designs for an ideal house) saying I thought he should check them in case there were maps or other prohibited drawings in the roll. I kept on at him until he left off searching the kitbag and looked at the innocuous drawings, lost interest, told me to put my things back in the kitbag and dismissed me, so I succeeded in keeping my precious hotplate – not that it was to be of any use in this horrible place.

After everyone had been searched we were marched to our new home. The compound allocated to us was quite large and very bleak, bare earth with hardly a blade of grass anywhere, which sloped quite steeply down from the back down to the front. There was just one very large barrack block sited centrally in the compound towards the lower end of the slope. At the top was the toilet block, a timber building containing a row of wooden seats over an open trench, the usual 'long drop' toilets. There was no running water in the compound; the only source was a well situated in front of the barrack block for all of our ablutions as well as drinking water. Looking at this arrangement, it occurred to me the Germans might have deliberately sited the toilet building above the level of the well so there would be contamination of the water in the well by leakage of sewage. It was the sort of thing they were capable of doing at this type of camp.

The barrack block itself was one huge barn-like structure. The sleeping accommodation was arranged all around the walls and in blocks in the centre. It was entirely different from what we had become accustomed to as there were no individual beds, but a series of continuous shelves in three tiers. There were no palliasses or mattresses; we just crowded and huddled together on the shelves with only our greatcoats to keep us warm, although a few of the men had a thin blanket they had acquired somehow or other. It was November 1943 so the weather was becoming very cold. The whole three hundred or so were crowded into this one huge barn of a barrack, literally packed like sardines with very little space for each man, the only redeeming feature being that being so crowded, we warmed each other. The only source of heating was a large, rough, brick-built stove in the front of the room; here there was a space about 20 feet wide running across the width of the hut containing a few crude tables and benches. This was the only indoor area for socialising and quite insufficient for all of us at once, so the rest of us just had to lie on the shelves. The brick stove was supposed to heat the whole room – it did not – and be used for cooking, but the fuel provided – a few coal briquettes – was hardly sufficient to last much more than an hour each day. We were able, just about, to heat up the small number of tins of food we had with us; even then we had to queue up and not everyone got a turn. There was not enough heat to boil water to make tea. We had not brought much Red Cross food with us and what we had did not last long, so we were reduced to eating the very thin meagre soup supplied by the camp and the small bread ration, whilst the only hot drink was ersatz coffee twice a day. The light inside the barrack was poor, the windows insufficient to give enough light by day and at night there were just a few scattered naked light bulbs.

True to the commandant's word, there was no physical punishment of any kind nor were we sent out to work; our only duties were to keep the barrack and the compound clean and tidy. Not having to exert ourselves helped to keep us in reasonably good health and preserved our energy despite the minimal rations. However, by the time we left, we were beginning to feel real pangs of hunger. I hate to imagine what would have happened had we stayed in this camp for a long period.

The main irritants were the innumerable *Appells*; we must have had about six or seven every day when we stood outside in the cold for an hour or so each time waiting to be counted. The first parade was about six in the morning. For this we were roused by a bugler playing 'Reveille' and at the last parade at night he played 'The Last Post'. This was because we just happened to have a bugler with a bugle in our midst. It was the only occasion during the whole of my time as a POW we had a bugler. The only other time I heard a bugle was at the funerals of Sammy Spencer and Don Herring. At 'bleak house' this bugle was a welcome addition in the general monotony of our existence there.

Those of us who had books were able to read a little if lucky enough to be under one of the light bulbs, otherwise the light was insufficient. During the long evenings we had sing-songs, generally old army songs, patriotic songs and one German song, 'Lili Marlene'. We had picked up 'Lili Marlene' from the Germans and we sang it in German, which pleased the guards. I sensed they felt they were somehow influencing and, perhaps, converting us, when the only reason we sang it was because it had such a catchy tune and nostalgic air, conjuring images of a beautiful young girl leaning by a lamp post waiting for one of us. It is a song which has stood the test of time and is still well known some seventy years later.

We were in an isolated part of Jacobsthal camp; the main part was along the ridge at the top of the hill and housed political prisoners and other people considered to be enemies of the Third Reich, or those from the 'wrong' ethnic groups such as Jews, gypsies and coloured people. We occasionally caught glimpses of groups of gaunt emaciated men wandering aimlessly and listlessly around in their striped pyjamas. We did not see any women. If we approached the dividing fence to try to communicate with them, we were quickly moved away by the constantly patrolling guards. I did not witness any actual brutality towards them, but we could hear the raucous shouting of their guards and were in no doubt of the severity of their regime. What we did witness every morning was a procession along the ridge carrying corpses for burial or disposal. We gathered there were mass graves although we did not actually see them.

Jacobsthal was our only experience of a concentration camp but it enabled us, albeit marginally, to experience the cramped, overcrowded conditions of these camps. We had heard rumours of the existence of concentration camps, occasionally seen the prisoners in their striped pyjama suits, but had had no positive proof of their existence. Now we had firsthand knowledge, even if of only a minor one. We were disgusted and saddened at this degradation of fellow human beings and frustrated we were unable to do anything about their plight. On the other hand it strengthened our prayers that the Nazis must not be allowed to win the war. We also noticed many of the guards at the camp were not Germans but were largely from Eastern Europe, particularly Romania. We ascertained this by observation and talking to our guards, noting these foreign guards did not wear German uniforms. We also got the impression they were even more brutal than the Germans. The guards in our compound were all from the German army; we had no direct dealing with the others.

Since the war I have read and learned a lot about concentration camps. Most of the focus is on the big concentration and extermination camps mainly in Germany and Poland. There must have been a number of small concentration camps like this one, which did not attract the same attention as the larger and more notorious ones. It is possible that Germans who never moved out of the towns and cities or lived in remote areas might have been unaware of them, but everyone living in the country and those who travelled around the country could not help but notice the gangs of political prisoners and slave labourers moving about and working, especially on the railways. The claim that many Germans did not know of their existence just does not hold up. They knew of – and must have talked with their families and friends about – the existence of concentration camps, even if they did not know details of the atrocities which were perpetrated in them. I accept that amongst those Germans who knew about them were those who were opposed, but were too scared, especially of the Gestapo, to express any contrary opinions. Most of the civilians I met were absolutely terrified of the Gestapo, and did not trust anyone including their close neighbours and or even, sometimes, members of their own families.

The three weeks crawled by until we were marched back to Stalag IVB at Mühlberg. This time the march was not forced and there were fewer guards who were not so menacing. When we entered the camp we were cheered by many of the other prisoners. We learned our stand had had repercussions and as a result the Germans had been forced to act more correctly and in accordance with the Geneva Convention. We were returned to the quarantine compound where we stayed for about another three weeks or so. We were visited there by the chief man of confidence WO1 J. Meyers and his deputy RSM Gibson. If my memory is correct WO1 Meyers was a New Zealander. He told us the conditions in the quarantine section of the camp would be improved; we would be provided with buckets of very hot water for making tea and we would be issued with Red Cross food parcels. When the parcels eventually arrived we had our first decent food for over a month. We did not receive any of the back parcels we had missed. Meyers and Gibson told us our so-called 'mutiny' had had a profound effect on the German regime at the camp, following which the conditions for everyone had improved tremendously.

Early in December the chief man of confidence again visited our quarantine compound. This time he announced he had been told to provide about twenty men to go out on a short-term working party for a job expected to last about a month and this might include Christmas. He soon obtained his twenty volunteers, including me. We sought some assurances about the type of accommodation we would have, about food and cigarettes, and he promised he would arrange for Red Cross parcels and cigarettes to be sent out to us each week. We especially wanted them to allow us to have decent food over Christmas and have some sort of a celebration. With his assurances we gathered together our worldly possessions and got ready to leave. Amongst those in the party were Charlie Whitaker, Chalky White, Steve Donaghue, Ken Griffin, Johnny Manson, Ray Overs, Reg Starling and Lofty Pierce. Our leader was Cook. I do not remember his Christian name as he was always referred to as Cookie.

We marched to the gate, were counted and our names confirmed, then a couple of guards joined us, and we climbed on board a waiting lorry and set off on our new little adventure. After a couple of hours we arrived at our destination: a farm somewhere in the vicinity of Magdeburg. Only then did we discover this was a very different type of working party. The work, we were told, would consist of sorting potatoes, bagging them and loading the bags onto freight trains. And so the working party became known as the *kartoffel kommando* (*kartoffel* being German for potato).

The farmer directed us to our living and sleeping quarters: a room attached to a barn; there were no beds or palliasses, just very thick layers of straw strewn on the floor. We were surprised and rather appalled. However, despite the very cold winter weather we were surprisingly warm at night snuggled down in the deep straw. The one drawback was that the straw was very dusty and bits of straw and dust got everywhere: in our hair, inside our clothes and in our pockets. No latrines were provided: we were expected to go out into the adjoining fields to perform our natural functions. We had to use a pump with a trough in the farmyard for our ablutions, a rather spartan existence but we knew it was only for a short period. Luckily, despite the extreme cold, the pump was not frozen. There was some advantage being in a small group as we already knew each other reasonably well and we were not subject to the wearying check parades and other camp restrictions, so we had some degree of respite from the usual camp discipline.

The potatoes to be sorted were placed on trestle tables with chutes along the sides, under which hung hessian sacks. The idea was to pick out all the bad potatoes, discard them and push the good ones via the chute into the sacks. When full, the sacks were dragged away for someone to sew up the top and replaced by empty sacks. The work was not hard but our hands got very cold; our gloves were inadequate to keep out the midwinter cold. It was rather stupid of the Germans to select British prisoners for this type of work because we made certain there were a few bad potatoes placed in the top of each sack, in the hope that they would rot the remainder.

Occasionally we would have to load the sacks onto railway trucks which I found particularly hard. There were two men to a large sack; we caught hold of the four corners of the sack, lifted and swung it up into the railway truck, the floor of which was between four and five feet above ground level. I found this almost impossible: I just did not have the strength in my arms. Luckily I was paired with my mucker Charlie Whitaker who was immensely strong and could easily lift and throw the sack into the truck on his own, often almost lifting me off the ground as well.

We were not the only workers at the farm sorting and loading potatoes. There was a gang of young Russian women, an example of the forced slave labour the Germans employed throughout the Third Reich. Presumably they came from areas of western Russia then occupied by the Germans. They were rough peasant women all muffled up in long coarse coats tied up at the waist and most of them were wearing fur hats with flaps to cover their ears; even after deprivation of female company for so long we were in no way sexually attracted to them. In fact we had very little to do with them, just acknowledging them as they arrived to work at their separate tables. However, Lofty Pierce (the same man who had tried to be interpreter for the Chinese sailors at the camp on Crete) claimed he had managed to have sex with one of them in the open behind a hedge. I have no idea how he could have managed it in that bitter cold with both of the participants tightly wrapped up in overcoats. We were sure it was a figment of his imagination: an attempt at a bit of bravado.

After we had finished at one farm we moved on to another, about three or four altogether. By now we were back on German rations as the few items from our Red Cross parcels had been consumed in the first few days. The food we were given was quite abundant, consisting mainly (as might be expected) of thick potato soups, boiled potatoes in their skins and bread, with ersatz coffee to drink.

The Red Cross parcels promised by the man of confidence at Mühlberg did not arrive. We asked the guards to make enquiries when they contacted the camp, which they were required to do periodically; they said they had raised the matter but still nothing was sent out to us. We were naturally very annoyed and angry: it seemed we were out of sight, out of mind. We spent a rather sombre Christmas without any of the goodies we would have had from the parcels. The farmer and guards made no attempt to make it a festive occasion; it was my quietest Christmas ever. Even more serious for the smokers was the shortage of cigarettes. They ran out of English cigarettes and tobacco, and even the Dravas and Junaks issued by the Germans. I had smoked a little when first cigarettes arrived from the Red Cross and in personal parcels and I had occasionally smoked a pipe but I was never a committed or addicted smoker. I preferred to keep my cigarettes and tobacco for bartering for extra bread.

Some two weeks into the *kartoffel kommando*, tobacco began to become scarce and then ran out completely. The smokers became quite frantic, even trying to smoke straw wrapped in newspaper; they turned out their pockets to search for fragments of tobacco, and moaned and groaned like drug addicts wanting a fix. Unknown to them I had hoarded some tobacco. One evening I announced that I had found some cigarettes and tobacco in my kitbag, which I said I had forgotten all about, and then produced some Junak cigarettes and a tin of Craven A pipe tobacco, sent by my mother. I did not give it to them all at once, but rationed it over several days. Nevertheless, I became an instant hero for saving their sanity and Ken Griffin christened me 'Lord Junak'; this was taken up by them all and I did not dissent. Thereafter, for the rest of my time as a POW, I was, I think quite affectionately, called 'Lord Junak' or more generally just 'Junak', and amongst some of them just 'Lord'.

About the middle of January 1944 our work on the farms came to an end and a lorry duly arrived to take us back to Stalag IVB. Once counted and checked in, we were once again dumped in the quarantine compound for a couple of weeks.

Cookie was immediately asked to find out what had happened to the Red Cross parcels we had been promised and to demand we be given the current week's parcel and all the ones we had missed. Our only contact with the outside camp was with the prisoners who brought the buckets of hot water from the cookhouse for our tea-making, so Cookie sent messages with them to the man of confidence; they brought messages back to say we would soon be getting some parcels. Two or three days elapsed with no sign of any parcels; we were all getting restless and annoyed. The men were losing confidence in Cookie whose problem was that he was not allowed out of the compound to see anyone.

I thought if only I could get out of the compound and seek out Meyers or Gibson, the men of confidence, then matters would get sorted. The problem was how to get out of the gate and past the guards. Our hot water from the cookhouse came in wooden pails brought by prisoners working in the main camp cookhouse; they were allowed into the compound where they deposited the buckets and then later returned to collect the empties. I suddenly thought of a way to try and get out of the compound and talked it over with, I think, Arthur Tilston. So Arthur and I picked up the empty buckets and went to the gate. We told the guard we had collected the empty buckets and were returning them to the cookhouse; he accepted our explanation and opened the gate and let us through. We had to find the cookhouse where we dumped the buckets and asked directions to Meyers' quarters. We found his room and confronted him in his den.

I told him who we were and in no uncertain terms said he had let us down, that he had promised faithfully to send parcels out to us whilst we were on the *kartoffel kommando*, that he had broken his solemn promise; we emphasised that we had been without Red Cross parcels over Christmas. Furthermore, I said, we had already been back at Mühlberg several days and still there was no sign of any parcels; it was just not good enough. He was quite taken aback, but immediately apologised saying he had tried to get parcels to us but there had been logistical problems and he had not been able to get transport to send them to us. I said that might have been true but he knew we were back in the quarantine compound and had done nothing at all to provide us with parcels. He replied he would arrange to issue a parcel to each of us straight away. I said this was just not good enough either: we had missed four issues of parcels whilst away on the farms and were entitled to them and demanded we receive them at once. He concurred reluctantly but suggested it would be unwise for the men to have so many parcels at one time. We acquiesced and agreed we would immediately be issued with two parcels per man and afterwards two more each week until we had received our full entitlement and I am pleased to say he kept his word. He then arranged for us to get back into our compound where we broke the news to the men. Any doubts were dispelled when about an hour later handcarts arrived at the compound loaded with parcels, two for each man. We had not had so much food at one go for a long time, certainly not in a prison camp. We set about having a belated Christmas party in great style. RSM Meyers kept his word and over the next weeks we received all the food parcels due to us.

The men were angry with Cookie because he had failed to get the parcels and there was a lot of criticism of his leadership. A meeting of all the *kartoffel kommando* men was convened. It was proposed that Cook must give up the leadership and he was voted out. As I was the one who had been successful in getting the parcels, I was asked to take over as leader of the group and I agreed. This was my first leadership, a sort of mini man of confidence. Cookie accepted the decision with good grace. I firmly believe that the actions earlier of the prisoners from Crete and this parcel episode gained us some prestige in this huge camp and helped to improve the conditions for the whole camp. Having completed our two weeks in quarantine we were moved back into the main camp. I still have no idea of the reason for the quarantine – they certainly did not do it with the Russians – it may have been something to do with the fear of tropical infections as most of the Allied prisoners came from North Africa and Italy and the Germans were afraid of tropical diseases.

The Belgian prisoners who shared our main compound were not particularly popular or trusted. The Russians were treated abominably by the guards. They were overcrowded and very poorly fed, having no protecting power to look out for them; they never received parcels from home. I was told on one occasion when there was a disturbance in the compound, the

The main street at Stalag IVB.

Germans sent their Alsation dogs in to break it up. The Russians were said to have torn the dogs to pieces, skinned and ate them and then threw the skins and bones out to the guards. There was also talk of cannibalism of bodies when men died, but I have no proof of these stories.

Our compound was well planned and laid out with plenty of space between the barrack blocks; the roads and paths were concreted and there were large grassed areas and a few spindly trees. The individual blocks were large, each holding sixty men or possibly more, quite spacious with high roofs, no ceilings, rather barn-like in design and as always made of timber treated with dark brown preservative. There were the usual two-tiered bunk beds along each of the long walls complete with straw palliasses and thin blankets. There were tables with benches and some wooden stools; heating was provided by the familiar round cast-iron tortoise stoves, either two or three of them to each room. The blocks were all numbered for ease of finding one's way around the camp and for each there was a room leader, usually a senior NCO, sergeant or above. He had the privilege of having a room, or cubicle, of his own which served as an office and his living quarters. The majority of our prisoners were army but there were some RAF men, pilots and aircrews from planes which had been shot down including, unusually, a few officers. The chief man of confidence, WO1 Meyers, was RAF and his number two, RSM Gibson I think was also RAF. As far as I could judge they did a good job administering the inside of the camp, doing whatever they could for the men, trying to keep up morale and maintaining discipline.

We had the usual *Appells*, three times a day – early morning, midday and evening – carried out block by block in sequence. We lined up in front of our blocks in columns of four to be counted, often recounted, especially if someone was absent through illness or for some reason confined to the room, in which case the guard would go inside to ensure he really was there: all this was taken very solemnly by the Germans. Occasionally when a man was absent and somewhere else in the camp which created a space in the back row, a man already counted would bend down and creep along to fill the empty space before the guard got there – it always worked. It was the duty of the room leader to report to the Germans how many men were in the room and how many absent through sickness, either in the room or in the lazarett. By and large the check parades went quite smoothly but there would be some moaning if it was cold and the Germans were late in arriving to do the check. We settled down to dull camp life whilst waiting to be sent out on working parties.

The main irritation we encountered was from a German senior NCO with the rank of oberfeldwebel. He was in charge of discipline within the camp, a typical sergeant major not so very different from those in our regular army. This one was particularly strict and petty and was very much disliked. What irked most of us was his insistence that we salute him if we met him. If a prisoner refused, he was immediately arrested and put in the punishment block for a couple of days in, supposedly, solitary confinement. We did our best to avoid him, dodging round a corner at any sign of him, so that we would not have to salute him.

Over time he sent so many to the punishment block that it became overcrowded and could not take any more, so he had to institute a waiting list so men had to wait some time for their turn to go in the overcrowded 'solitary' confinement block; it was almost comical. The punishment block was within the German administrative compound, but the rear wall of it abutted against the fence of our compound. The entrance was on the other side, but on our side there were, high up, openings with bars across for light and ventilation, right up against our fence. The men soon found it was possible with the aid of a long stick to pass food, chocolate and cigarettes through the openings to the inmates and even books, thus the solitary confinement on bread and water became a bit of a farce.

In fact we were incorrect in refusing to salute their senior NCOs. The German system was that other ranks saluted all officers and senior NCOs, whereas in the British army we only saluted commissioned officers and this was the basis for our unwillingness to salute their senior NCOs. However, the Geneva Convention on prisoners of war apparently requires them to abide by the military rules and regulations of the detaining power. We stubborn British POWs preferred to stick to our own code of practice, whatever the Geneva Convention laid down, so in a way it became tit for tat, with the overcrowded punishment block rather defeating the German objective of making us comply with their army regulations, much to this particular oberfeldwebel's annoyance.

Amongst the inmates of Stalag IVB with whom I became friendly was a Mr Herbert (?) Barker. He was a true Christian, a civilian worker for the YMCA, a non-combatant, so not really a prisoner of war at all. I think he was captured in Italy. He came from Herne Hill in London. The Germans had offered to repatriate him but he refused, saying he would rather stay to give help and advice to the prisoners. He did a tremendous amount of good social work in the camp and would help anyone who had personal problems; for this he was highly respected. He had very few possessions and really felt the cold as he had no warm clothes. Sometime – I think it must have been in January 1944 – I received a personal parcel from home containing two nice warm pullovers and a Bible amongst other things. Knowing his need for a pullover, I decided to give him one as a late Christmas present. I went to see him and said, 'Here, Mr Barker, is a belated Christmas present. You really do need it to keep you warm.' He replied, 'How wonderfully kind of you, I know just the man who really needs a pullover and I am sure he will be most grateful.' I have never forgotten that gesture; he was so utterly unselfish, so dedicated to helping others, I feel proud to have known him. He told me he was in the rag trade in London. I corresponded with him for a while after the war, but lost touch when I went off to Africa.

The Bible from my mother was a rather large handsome one. I already had a small one and the olive-bound New Testament I had bought in Cairo. I knew that the Welsh padre only had an old tattered one and so I presented him with the new one with which he was thrilled.

At Mühlberg Stalag IVB the Red Cross food parcels were distributed block by block and the issue was spread over the week. When our turn came, the room leader would usually detail four men to collect them from the Red Cross storeroom in the German compound. We used handcarts kept at the store to transport them. Quite frequently I was selected to collect the parcels. We announced our mission to the guard on the gate who would check us through – in fact the guards paid little attention to who or how many went in and out between the two compounds – it was just part of the camp routine.

On one occasion we had collected the parcels and were making our way back when a large crowd of Russian prisoners arrived and were being herded, rather than marched, towards the delousing centre. I am not even sure that the Germans bothered to register Russian prisoners. The accompanying guards halted them and went into the centre to make the arrangements. At this stage they had probably not even been counted. We stopped to have a look at these new prisoners, one of whom was a young blond man about my age, in appearance quite like some of our men; certainly not what we expected a Russian to look like. He spoke a few words of English and seemed to understand our intentions. On the spur of the moment we made a decision to try to help him. We handed him a British greatcoat and side cap, told him to put them on quickly and come with us, so he joined our party pushing the handcart which we trundled to the gate, and the guard opened it and let us through without noticing the extra man. We informed the room leader so that arrangements could be made to conceal his presence from the Germans.

Thus we had obtained an extra man in the barrack room. Of course, he was very much better off with us than he would have been in the Russian compound where he most probably would not have survived. He was of value to the camp because he was 'an extra' to replace any escapee, a ready-made replacement. When it came to check parades, he just stayed hidden away in the room – the Germans never checked for extra men, only for missing ones. If the German guard came into the room to check sick men, our extra man just hid under a bed. He was not discovered whilst I was there. Undoubtedly he was better fed than he would have been in the Russian compound; he got the normal German ration plus other food we gave him from the Red Cross parcels we got for him. I have often wondered what his eventual fate was because later on the camp was liberated by the Russians. I hope by then he was sufficiently anglicised to pass as a British soldier.

One day a group of renegade British POWs arrived in the German compound. They were from a tiny number who had volunteered to join the British Free Corps. There had apparently been German propaganda in some POW camps to try to persuade British prisoners that the greatest threat to Europe and Britain was Russia, and it would be wise for the British to join with the Germans to help them in defeating the Russians. Thus they had set up this British Free Corps for any prisoner to join and help defeat the Russians. This delegation had come to the camp to give a lecture and get some recruits – they hoped. This was the first and only occasion I came across them. The chief man of confidence was informed of their arrival. He called a meeting to tell us about the visit and the proposal to address the camp. We responded in no uncertain terms that we would have nothing to do with these traitors; that we utterly despised them and would not listen to them. So when the commandant asked him if we were willing to let them into our compound to give their lecture, the chief man of confidence was able to tell him that we were willing to let them in but could not guarantee they would ever get out again alive. Presumably the commandant conveyed the message to them and they departed from the camp empty-handed. I understand there was a contingent of the British Free Corps sent to the Russian Front – I do not imagine they were very numerous.

One day we heard a commotion going on in the German administrative compound, and rumours as always began to fly around. We gathered that the Germans had just recaptured a very dangerous POW who had been brought into the camp with an escort of several guards. We soon learned that he was a New Zealander who, in escaping from another camp, had beaten and severely injured a German guard. He had been brought to Stalag IVB to be court-martialled and had been lucky not to have been shot during recapture 'whilst resisting arrest'. We were told the court martial was likely to sentence him to death.

He was incarcerated in solitary confinement in the punishment block with extra guards on duty. A plan was devised and executed to get him out of the punishment block. I know nothing of the details or even who planned it but I do know he disappeared from his cell. When the Germans discovered he had again escaped there was a tremendous hue and cry and a widespread search was started with special squads of heavily armed soldiers with Alsation dogs. They combed the precincts of the camp and gradually spread the search wider and wider. All their efforts were wasted as he was never caught and after about a week the search was called off. It had been a tremendous use of valuable resources of men and equipment all to no avail.

He had indeed 'escaped' – into the prisoners' compound and been 'lost' amongst the thousands of other prisoners. In fact he was in our barrack room. Special care had to be taken to ensure he was never seen by the guards during check parades or when they occasionally carried out a search. The Germans never considered the possibility he might still be in the camp; to them a prisoner, especially a dangerous one, escaped *from* his camp not *into* it. I know no details of his previous escape; to me he was a very pleasant, quiet New Zealander. He was looked after well and fed by the room leader. He was still there when I left to go to a working camp and I saw him occasionally, when visiting from the working camp, until we were later moved on to Falkenberg. I hope he stayed safely hidden and survived the war; his was a remarkable story.

There were often attempts to escape, although none were successful whilst I was there. For instance, a man decided to escape in the tanker which came periodically to empty the septic tank. This was one of the few camps which had a water-borne toilet system. The vehicle which came to empty the septic tank was a typical metal tanker, like a fuel tanker, with a large covered opening on the top, mounted on a chassis and drawn by a horse. The work was contracted out to a civilian who employed a French prisoner to carry it out – there were some French prisoners living in the community and housed where they worked. The septic tank needed to be emptied quite frequently. The escapee had bribed the man with cigarettes and coffee to clean out the tank before coming to the camp. When he arrived, our man climbed in and the lid was closed, and after waiting the normal time it took to fill the tank, they proceeded to leave the camp. There was no supervision by guards inside the camp as it had become a routine operation and a rather smelly one. This time the guard at the outer gate just happened to tap the side of the tank with his rifle and hearing it ring hollow, he became suspicious and ordered it back into the camp to be properly filled, sending another guard to ensure it was done. We never knew if there had been a tip-off, but the escapee had to climb out quickly to avoid being really 'in the shit'.

From time to time the straw in the palliasses was changed and the old straw carted away in lorries. Naturally an attempt to escape by hiding under the straw was made. However, the guards at the gate usually prodded the straw with the hay forks to see if anyone was under it. Whilst I was there a couple of escapees were caught this way. I doubt if anyone managed – it was just too obvious.

Once when I was on a party collecting Red Cross parcels from the store in the outer compound, and we were pushing the loaded handcart back towards the gate of our compound, a file of RAF prisoners was marched in towards the delousing centre. One of them was carrying a cardboard box; he sidled up to me and put the box in my hands which I put in an empty plywood crate from a Canadian shipment of parcels amongst the other parcels on the cart. He asked me for the number of the block I was in and said, 'Take care of my parcel, I'll come and collect it later.' He duly arrived to collect his parcel and said thanks for taking care of his wireless and so it was smuggled into the camp. In fact there were a number of wireless sets in the camp.

It was from this period that we began to get the BBC versions of the progress of the war. The Germans realised there were wireless sets about and from time to time carried out extensive searches to try to find them but they had very little success. One of the sets was well hidden away in our hut. The room leader and, I think, no more than two others, tuned in at night and later relayed the news to the men in the room. This did a lot to raise our spirits because we now learned the Germans were being defeated on all fronts, although the Second Front in Europe had not yet been opened. We also got some fairly up-to-date news from recently captured airmen. The Germans seemed to have an inkling there was a wireless in our room and one day about a dozen German soldiers arrived unexpectedly, announcing their intention of finding the wireless they knew was hidden in our hut. They really pulled the place apart, searching every palliasse, every pack, every kitbag, every Red Cross parcel box and under the beds, but still they found no sign of it. One of us was sitting on a stool by the stove and was ordered to stand up and the guards demanded, 'Where is the wireless?' He nonchalantly picked up the stool and replied, 'It's in here,' for which cheek the guard took a swipe at him. He then quietly resumed his seat. After an exhaustive search they finally gave up and went away. In fact the wireless was screwed to the bottom of that stool, invisible from view; he had quietly bluffed them and so the wireless was safe. There were lots of these spot searches in other blocks looking for wirelesses, although I never heard of any being found. We kept fairly up to date with war news from the Allied side and were able to compare it with the news given by the Germans, forming our own judgement and knowing that the war was going better for us all the time.

One day the chief man of confidence came to our room and announced that a hundred men were required to go and work from a camp situated about four miles from Stalag IVB. He asked me if I would take charge of this camp as man of confidence, subject to the approval, in due course, of the men who 'volunteered' to make up the hundred. I suppose he selected me because of his previous dealings with me over the *kartoffel kommando*. He told me that as the camp we were going to was not too far away, the arrangement was for us to continue to draw our Red Cross parcels from his camp Stalag IVB and we would be able to continue to use the medical facilities, which included several British doctors and a German doctor, as the new camp was too small to warrant its own doctor. There were plenty of men wishing to go on this venture, including most of the people who had been on the *kartoffel kommando*. We had no idea what type of work we would be given at the new camp. Many of the men were work-shy and anxious to stay in a non-working camp.

When the hundred men had been selected, their names and numbers were taken and recorded. Our preparations to leave Stalag IVB were almost completed when I was approached by two young RAF officers. They said they wished to escape, told me they had been briefed on routes for escape and were equipped with maps and compasses and other aids, which were, of course, disguised or well hidden, but they felt their only hope of success was from a working camp. They asked if it would be possible to get on our working party. The problem for me was that the hundred men had already been selected and their names and POW numbers (we all had identity discs with our numbers on them) registered with the Germans. After thinking about it, I told them the only possibility would be for them to change identities with two of the men on the list and hope the Germans would not check too closely. I asked for volunteers to change places with the two officers. Several came forward and I selected two men who then

One of the watchtowers at Mühlberg IVB.

Luftpost

10. März 1944

BEI TAG UND NACHT, VOM WESTEN UND SÜDEN

Systematische Zerschlagung
der deutschen Luftabwehr

46 000 : 1 700

In der Zeit vom 21. Januar bis 1. März warf die englisch-amerikanische Luftwaffe 36 000 Tonnen Bomben auf Industrieziele in Deutschland und weitere 10 000 Tonnen auf Industrieziele im deutschbesetzten Europa.

Im gleichen Zeitraum warf die deutsche Luftwaffe in insgesamt 16 Streuangriffen 1 700 Tonnen Bomben auf England, einschliesslich der Angriffe auf London. In 16 Angriffen warf die deutsche Luftwaffe also ungefähr zwei Drittel der 2 500 Tonnen Bomben, die die R.A.F. in einer einzigen Nacht, nämlich der Nacht vom 15. auf den 16. Februar, in einer halben Stunde auf Berlin abwarf.

Die deutsche Produktion an Jagdmaschinen ist auf ein Drittel ihres Höchststandes herunter. Das ist das vorläufige Ergebnis der neuen Phase des englisch-amerikanischen Luftkrieges gegen die deutsche Rüstungsindustrie.

In den achtzehn Tagen vom 20. Februar bis zum 9. März wurden die Produktionsstätten der deutschen Jagdwaffe in Deutschland systematisch angegriffen und zerschlagen. Daneben wurden weitere Grossangriffe auf Industrieziele in deutschbesetzten Europa geflogen.

Die Angriffe erfolgten in fast ununterbrochener Aufeinanderfolge vom Westen und vom Süden, bei Tage und bei Nacht. Die deutsche Jagdwaffe erlitt bei ihren Versuchen, die vernichtende Wirkung dieser Angriffe wenigstens abzuschwächen, schwerste Verluste. Die Hinopferung der deutschen Jagdwaffe war umsonst. Die kleine Auswahl von Zielaufnahmen, die wir auf dieser und der nächsten Seite veröffentlichen, beweist eindeutig, wie die Produktionsstätten der deutschen Jagdwaffe zerschlagen wurden.

Vor einem dreiviertel Jahr, am 25. Juni 1943, tröstete Dr. Goebbels: „Im übrigen sind die Verluste, die der Feind bei seinen Tages- und Nachtangriffen erlitten hat, so hoch, dass er bald vor der Frage stehen wird, ob sie ihm in diesem Sinn und mit diesem Risiko noch lohnen."

Die Antwort war die weitere Steigerung der alliierten Luftoffensive, war der Beginn des systematischen Zerschlagens der deutschen Luftabwehr.

Jetzt, am 3. März 1944, tröstet Dr. Goebbels wieder: „Zwingen wir dem Feind zudem in steigendem Masse Verluste über Verluste auf, dann kommt der Augenblick, in dem diese niederträchtige Art der Kriegsführung sich für ihn nicht mehr lohnt."

Die Antwort hat Premierminister Churchill am 22. Februar vorweggenommen: „Die Luftoffensive wird Ausmasse annehmen, die alles Bisherige weit hinter sich lassen, und von denen man bisher nicht zu träumen wagte."

Volltreffer auf die Messerschmitt-Werke in Regensburg, 25. Febr.

Bevor die neuen Bomben fielen:
Diese Zerstörungen und die Bombenkrater im Schnee wurden 3 Tage vorher bei einem Angriff vom Süden her verursacht.

Nach dem neuen Angriff:
Der neue Angriff vom Westen her setzt die Zerstörung fort: Das gesamte Fabrikgelände ist mit Einschlägen übersät.

Südfront verschlingt Reserven

Kesselrings Reserven in Italien, die zum Einsatz gegen mögliche alliierte Angriffe auf Südfrankreich, Nord- und Mittelitalien oder den Balkan bereitgehalten wurden, sind von 18 Divisionen im Januar auf 6 zusammengeschmolzen. Denn statt 7 Divisionen wie bei Salerno stehen jetzt, nach der englisch-amerikanischen Landung bei Nettuno, nicht weniger als 19 Divisionen in der vordersten Kampflinie. 9 Divisionen halten die alte Südfront und weitere 10 Divisionen sind jetzt als 14. Armee unter Generaloberst von Mackensen am Landekopf von Nettuno gebunden, nämlich die:

Panzergrenadierdivision „Hermann Göring". 26. Panzerdivision. 3. Panzergrenadierdivision. 90. Panzergrenadierdivision. 65. Infanteriedivision. 362. Infanteriedivision. 715. Schnelle Division (vorher in Südfrankreich). 114. Leichte Division (vorher auf dem Balkan). 4. Fallschirmjägerdivision. SS-Brigade „Reichsführer SS".

Diese Verbände haben bei ihren bisherigen drei Versuchen, den alliierten Landekopf einzudrücken, rund 24 000 Mann an Toten, Verwundeten und Gefangenen verloren. Der alliierte Landekopf blieb unversehrt.

Churchill bemerkte über diese neue strategische Entwicklung in Italien am 22. Februar:

„Hitler ist anscheinend entschlossen, Rom mit demselben Starrsinn zu verteidigen, den er bei Stalingrad, in Tunis und kürzlich wieder am Dnjeprbogen gezeigt hat. Dieser Entschluss Hitlers, rund eine halbe Million deutscher Soldaten in Süditalien einzusetzen und aus Italien eine grosse Ablenkungsfront zu machen, ist den Alliierten aus gesamtstrategischen Gründen nicht unwillkommen. Die Abnützungsschlacht in Italien beschäftigt Truppen, die in anderen, grösseren Operationen fehlen werden, und bildet ein wirksames Vorspiel zu diesen Operationen."

G. 12

proceeded to exchange identities and details. As we would be visiting Stalag IVB at regular intervals, it would be possible to let each couple have their correct mail. When all was ready we were marched out and assembled outside the German administrative office; a roll-call was made, the RAF officers answered to their new identities, and all were declared present and correct. No check was made against the photographs the Germans held. Guards were now assigned to the party, the gates were opened and out we marched to cover, on foot, the four miles to our new camp, carrying all our kitbags and other possessions. Our stay in Stalag IVB, the largest camp I had been in, was over: it was now back to small and better.

14

Liebenwerda
Camp L125, Stalag IVD

Camp LI25, our destination, was a small camp situated about half a mile out of the small town of Mühlberg on the River Elbe. I have no idea why it was officially called Liebenwerda when it was at Mühlberg or why it was numbered Stalag IVD when the 'big' camp nearby was Stalag IVB.

This new camp had just one barrack block which was divided into two rooms for living and sleeping. There was an entrance porch and a store-room in between the two barrack rooms. The block was the usual timber building with a roof covered with roofing felt, and walls treated with a creosote-type preservative giving it a dirty brown appearance. The left-hand room was the largest, with two-tiered bunk beds housing about sixty men; the right-hand room was somewhat smaller and had beds for forty men. The storeroom in between was used for the storage of Red Cross parcels. The entrance porch/hall was quite spacious and was used mainly as a place to put the toilet buckets at night – we were locked in at night and had to use buckets to pee in. In the far corner of the compound was the toilet and ablution block. The whole of the small compound was surrounded by a tall barbed-wire fence, without a watchtower or any searchlights. In front of the barrack block stood an unused well. The Germans had their barrack block outside our compound, on the left-hand side, facing the camp from the access road. This was also a single-storeyed timber building with a central entrance leading to a central corridor with rooms leading off either side, the first room on the left being the guard room. The block had the luxury of internal toilets and ablutions. Outside the compound to the left was a field which we were allowed to use and we converted into a football pitch. The Germans erected goal posts for us and the only game we played was soccer. The days of my prison-camp rugby were over as we did not have enough rugby players to field teams. The road from the camp led to the small town of Mühlberg and on to the River Elbe.

We were met at the gates by our new commandant and his guards; we were handed over to them and the guards who had brought us departed back to the 'big' camp. We were marched inside the camp, formed up for our first check parade and reviewed by the new commandant. He was a lieutenant – I am pretty certain he had not reached the dizzy heights of hauptmann – a short, stocky, blustering, man, with a very fiery temper and a wall-eye. He was immediately christened 'Wall-eye' and known by that name throughout his time with us. Having formed us up in the usual four ranks and delivered his opening address, strutting backwards and forwards like the little Napoleon he was, he told us we were to behave ourselves, obey all his orders and those of his guards. Above all, we were not under any circumstances to attempt to escape from the camp; if we did then everyone in the camp would be punished severely. If anyone was foolish enough and determined to escape he must do it from the working party; then the guard only would be held responsible and be punished. It seemed sensible advice but was given mainly to protect his own back.

He then asked who was to be the camp leader and I indicated I was. He then asked the men if this was acceptable; they all agreed and from then on I was officially recognised as the man of confidence. He then informed me I would not have to go out to work but would stay in the camp to deal with the administration, which was very little. He added I could also appoint a medical orderly who would also stay in the camp to look after anyone who was sick and confined to camp. There were no army medical orderlies amongst the men but naturally several men immediately volunteered; after all it would be a 'cushy' number. After questioning them, I selected Peter (Pete) Yeomans, who seemed intelligent and a quick learner. Pete became a good colleague and companion.

Then the commandant said I must appoint a camp cook as our camp was too small to have its own cookhouse. He said there were a few other non-British POW working camps in the area, so a central cookhouse had been set up in Mühlberg to which we could send one cook. Naturally there

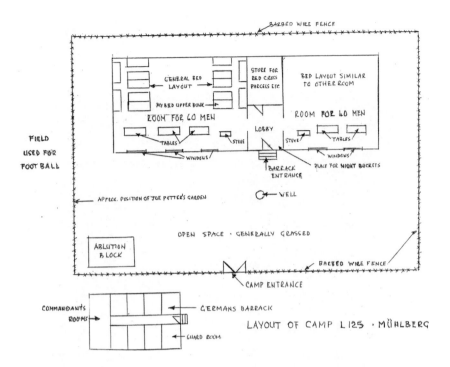

were plenty of volunteers and it was difficult for me to ascertain who had been genuine army cooks. Eventually I selected a strong character, whom I felt would hold his own with the men from the other camps. He was a bit of a bragger and a loudmouth but I was convinced he would be able to look after our interests. His name was Harry Layden, a regular soldier and Yorkshireman. He served us very well, was a tremendous character and also happened to be a very good footballer. Then I was told I was allowed to have a *dolmetscher* – an interpreter. Unfortunately neither Jimmy Ellis nor Harry Price were with me, so after some discussion I selected Blondie Stead, probably because he was the only one who claimed to speak fluent German. Later on I found out that one of the South Africans also spoke good German. Blondie usually went out with the working party, only staying in the camp when needed by the commandant to do some translation. I still have a photograph of him standing by me at the well in front of the barrack building, wearing an American air force jacket and a white fur hat.

We soon discovered the type of work at L125 was entirely different from any we had previously done and quite a new venture for the men. The work site was a boat yard on the eastern bank of the River Elbe

Blondie Stead and me at Liebenwerda.

and the work consisted of dismantling the superstructure of barges. The barges had been requisitioned, i.e. stolen, by the Germans, mainly from France. They were destined to be used on canals, rivers and waterways in Eastern Europe, especially, we were told, on the Danube and its tributaries. Apparently the superstructure on the barges was too high to go under some of the bridges on the waterways on which they were to be used and so it had to be removed. The operation was carried out by a civilian firm run by a man called Herr Leper. He was a large, corpulent, rather flabby man, pompous and quite unpleasant; in essence he was a bully. He was very unpopular, not only with our men but also with the guards and the German civilian workers at the site.

It was clear most of the barges had been seized without notice, some of them even had unfinished meals on the cabin tables and all the equipment and some personal belongings of the previous owners were still on board including such items as crockery, cutlery, cooking utensils, mirrors, cushions and bed linen. The men were quite content working in these pleasant surroundings, especially when spring and summer arrived and it grew hot, as they were able to bathe in the River Elbe during the lunch break. This was a great improvement on the monotonous work of building railway embankments. I still have a few 'mini' photographs taken on one of the barges.

Life soon settled down to a new routine, for me a much more congenial one, as I did not have to get up to go out to work. The guards, usually two of them, would unlock the barrack about 6.30 a.m., come in and with cries of '*Raus*' and '*aufstehen*' go between the beds to get the men out of their bunks. They were a reasonably friendly group of guards and it certainly was the first time we got to know the guards as individuals and, in due course, by name. Several of them were Germans who came from Czechoslovakia or Poland, known as Sudeten Germans. They were not very popular with the 'real' Germans and for this reason they were the ones who became most friendly with the prisoners. I remember one tall Polish German who would push his way between the beds to '*raus*' the men, whilst those in the top bunks would bang on his steel helmet which he took in good humour as part of the daily routine.

The first duty in the morning was for the men to take out the 'pee' buckets and empty them – not a task anyone relished. I instituted a roster for this duty in order that everyone participated in this unsavoury duty. One of the problems was that often the buckets were full to overflowing, and the floor had to be mopped if they spilled, another distasteful task. The buckets had to be carried down to the toilet block to be emptied and it was difficult to avoid spillages on the way.

The men on the working party then went off to the ablution block to wash and shave. It was expected throughout our POW life that everyone should wash and shave every day. Then they would eat a little bread and something for breakfast before going out on parade to be counted and marched off to work.

Whilst they were preparing to go to work, Pete Yeomans and I would lie on our top bunks chatting away to them, waiting until they had departed before leisurely getting up. There were always greetings from the boys:

Working on the barges.

'Good morning, Lord,' or 'Good morning, Junak,' to me and, 'Good morning, Doc,' to Pete; we felt rather privileged. Soon after they had departed for work a guard would arrive to escort Harry Layden to the central cookhouse in Mühlberg. After the room was quiet we got up, went out to wash, shave and dress, after which we prepared our breakfast.

We had soon discovered that we could barter for fresh eggs: a pleasant change from the tinned powdered egg which came in the Red Cross parcels and from which we had made a sort of scrambled egg which was not particularly appetising. This was the first time in prison camp we had fresh eggs which could be boiled or fried. In the Red Cross parcels we received rather fatty bacon, packed in tins in a roll with greaseproof paper between the slices. The barrack room had a cooker, a cast-iron one with hot plates for cooking, a great improvement on anything we had had previously. We were also able to supplement the ration of briquettes with pieces of timber the men reclaimed from the barges. Pete and I were now able to cook a breakfast of fried eggs, bacon and fried bread.

We always tried to time our breakfast to coincide with the morning visit of the commandant. The Germans were getting very short of food, whilst we were better off than ever for food, thanks to our regular weekly Red Cross food parcels. We were now able to vary our diet by bartering for fresh eggs and extra, often white, bread. The commandant would allow us to finish our breakfast before he made his inspection of the barracks. We then made some real coffee and got out our tins of cigarettes. We politely offered the commandant and the gefreiter (lance corporal) who accompanied him, a mug of coffee and a cigarette. The idea was to entice him into accepting cigarettes and/or coffee in the hope he would want more and eventually barter with us. At first he rather haughtily refused saying that as a German he certainly would not accept anything from a prisoner of war. He reminded us that bartering with prisoners of war was strictly prohibited and anyone caught would be severely punished. Bearing in mind the very strict hierarchy in the German army, we thought the higher the rank we could get bartering with us, the better. Once a German soldier bartered, we could always threaten to report him to a superior if he treated us badly – a type of blackmail that worked.

We persisted with our daily offers of coffee and cigarettes and it was not long before the commandant first accepted a cigarette and then a cup of coffee and before a month was out, he was willing to barter for cigarettes and coffee. This meant two things: first he could not now stop his guards from bartering and secondly, we had a lever against him. If he was told to put restrictions on us, we could persuade him to go easy. For example, later, after the mass escape of RAF prisoners from the camp at Sagan, Hitler had personally ordered the execution of fifty of the escapees and had additionally commanded the regimes at all British POW camps to be tightened, made harsher and that anyone attempting to escape was to be shot. We were informed by the Germans of the Sagan killings and shown the orders sent out to every camp about the new restrictions to be placed on us.

We were absolutely traumatised by the news of the murder of our airmen, especially as we found out Sagan was not too far from Mühlberg. The commandant and camp guards were also disturbed by the news, but had been given strict orders to clamp down on us. We did hear stories of prisoners in other camps being shackled and mistreated, and although we could not confirm these stories, we believed them to be true. When he talked about the new restrictions we told him we would have to reveal his bartering to his superiors. So he decided to pay lip-service to the new regulations and as a result we were hardly affected.

I learned on the grapevine that the restrictions were eased fairly quickly at other camps. I cannot remember any senior German officers visiting our camp during this period so we were very lucky; perhaps we were too small for them to bother too much with us. Given the way the war was going for the Germans by now, some of the commandants of POW camps may have had an eye to their own future prospects, despite the orders from above; many of them must have realised they were facing defeat and probable imprisonment themselves.

The time came for the two RAF officers to make their escape. They made their preparations and we chipped in with some hard rations, chocolate, dried fruit, tinned cheese, corned beef and so on. They took the commandant's advice to escape from a working party and one day they disappeared at the shipyard.

On return to the camp the poor guard had to report to the commandant that he had lost two prisoners. The commandant (then still old Wall-eye) was furious, but relieved they had escaped from the working party and not the camp. He vented his fury on the guard who was severely reprimanded, possibly had some other punishment, I do not know, but he remained at the camp.

We had a few restrictions for a while: extra check parades, football was cancelled for two weeks and so on, but it was soon back to normal. The Germans of course knew nothing of the change of identities, so their search for them was low key. The two RAF officers helped by the maps they had concealed, compasses hidden in buttons and the escape routes with which they had been briefed, made their way westwards across Germany and France where they safely reached the Atlantic coast. They were about to make contact with a safe house when they were stopped by a Vichy policeman, arrested and handed over to the locally based Germans – it was the end to an almost successful escape. They revealed their true identities – they still had their RAF identity discs – and disclosed they had been in Stalag IVB, the big camp at Mühlberg. Some three weeks or so after their escape they were returned to Stalag IVB. There, at first, the Germans did not accept them as RAF officers because on checking they found they already had the two officers they claimed to be, safely in the camp. There was utter confusion until they had to disclose that there had been a change of identity with the two soldiers. Then they and the two soldiers were given the usual two weeks' solitary confinement, after which the two soldiers were returned to our camp. I do not know what happened to the two RAF officers, but we got some satisfaction at having been able to facilitate their escape.

The few of us left daily in the camp – Pete Yeomans, myself and anyone off sick – had a relatively leisurely time. We did some tidying up in the room and around the camp. I now had some architectural books so was able to do some studying. I also continued with my tailoring business of making collars and ties from shirt tails, becoming quite skilled.

I was able to get sheets of cartridge/drawing paper, I think from the canteen at Stalag IVB, so I started some pencil portraits from photographs; I clearly remember doing one pencil portrait of Stella's sister Heather who was in the Wrens. When some of the men saw this portrait I was asked to do drawings of their wives or sweethearts. Then one day when the commandant saw me drawing, he asked if I would do one of his son and I agreed. Anything which kept a good relationship with him benefited the camp. He came back with a photograph of a young German naval officer; I duly did the portrait with which he was very pleased. He then told us that his son's ship had been sunk, he had been captured and had been sent to a camp in Canada. I told him how lucky it was for his son: no more action amongst the dangers of the Atlantic, good food, much better than the Germans gave us and he was well away from any bombing and air raids. Also being an officer he would be in a non-working camp. At this the commandant was most upset; he said he was horrified that his son would be idle: it was very bad for him not to have work. The portrait helped thaw relations and the commandant and guards became relatively friendly. Except for the fanatical Nazis, it was becoming clear the changing fortunes in the war subtly changed German attitudes to us.

Now that we had a better stove we could do some simple cooking although rather limited in scope. Those of us left in the camp prepared things for our muckers on their return from work. On one occasion I decided to make a cake as a surprise. We never had any cake from the Germans or in our food parcels. I did not have any flour so the base was made from crushed biscuits mixed with dried powdered egg, dried powdered milk, dried fruit and water. The cake tin was a small green enamelled dish, with handles, one I rather treasured as I had had it a long time. The mixture was put in the tin and as the stove had no oven, the cake was cooked amongst the embers beneath the fire. It appeared to cook quite well and browned nicely on top, but when I took it out, just before the men got back, I discovered it had sunk in the middle and was not set inside. So I told them I had made them a fruit pudding; it tasted good and was deemed a great success.

Although the work on the barges was less strenuous than at previous camps, the men began to complain it was too much for them. I think there may have been a couple of reasons: first, they disliked Herr Leper and secondly, our cook, Harry Layden, mentioned the prisoners in other camps were given extra rations for doing heavy work. He had noticed extra food was being prepared and issued from the central cookhouse. This was mentioned to the commandant by the guards, none of whom liked Herr Leper. The commandant thought it was a good idea and so he decided that Herr Leper must arrange to provide the workers with extra meat. He instructed Herr Leper to deliver the meat to the central cookhouse, to be cooked there by Harry and then brought to the camp together with our normal food rations. Our food came to the camp on a handcart each day about the time the men returned from work.

The extra meat was in a large piece which Harry roasted, and it was delivered, still piping hot, to the camp in a large roasting tin. Harry then proceeded to carve the joint and hand it round to the men; the only problem was that it was horse meat. A number of men would not eat it – they could not have been very hungry. In fact, I found it quite edible, with a rather sweet taste and was very tender. The 'dripping' from it was excellent, as good as any I have ever tasted. But some of my muckers including Charlie Whitaker and Steve Donaghue would not eat any of it. I thought I would try to get them to eat some, so I got Harry to mince some cooked meat for me, which I seasoned, covered with mashed potato, put in the little green dish and baked it on the embers under the stove until it browned quite nicely. When Charlie and the others came in from work I told them I had made a cottage pie for them. They ate it all and said how much they had enjoyed it. I told them then it had been made with horse meat. They were outraged and threatened to murder me! However, it did overcome their prejudice against horse meat which they ate thereafter.

At Camp L125 we had a good supply of Red Cross parcels which we had to collect once a fortnight from the 'big' camp Stalag IVB. Our commandant arranged for the hire of a horse and cart for their transport. The party which went to collect them consisted of the driver, a guard, myself, Pete Yeomans and sometimes Blondie Stead or Harry Layden. We looked forward to this fortnightly outing as a break in the monotony of the camp. At Stalag IVB we were able to meet other people, exchange views and obtain the latest news from their 'wireless service'. Pete Yeomans was always intrigued, sitting behind the horse, to watch its backside when it defecated, because in doing so, the anal muscles came out and then slowly retracted. Pete said this looked very much like a red rosette. Thereafter the day of the journey to collect Red Cross parcels was known as Red Rosette Day.

Harry Layden, working at the central cookhouse in Mühlberg, had some limited contact with local people in the town and occasionally managed to visit the local grocery shop. There he found he could barter for a few things we could not get in the camp, including, I particularly remember, saccharine tablets and a brown sauce in bottles, rather like Daddy's sauce; although not as good as HP sauce, it was acceptable nevertheless. One day when Harry joined us on Red Rosette Day, he took a bottle of sauce to Stalag IVB and found there was a huge demand for it and was asked to get as much as he could. This was an opportunity not to be missed! He could get hold of almost any amount, so he bought several cases and we decided to take them up to the big camp and sell them for cigarettes, coffee or chocolate and at a big profit. We could then barter the items with the Germans for things we wanted, especially eggs and white bread. However, we had the problem of smuggling the bottles into Stalag IVB. When we arrived at that camp there was always a cursory search as we went in, so we had to be very careful. We usually put the bottles in a sack disguised as food for the horse and luckily we were never caught. We also found there was a good market for saccharine. The bottles of sauce and saccharine were traded with the prisoners who ran the Red Cross parcel store, mostly senior NCOs, who 'bought' all we could smuggle into the camp, in exchange for cigarettes and coffee, etc. I, for one, was pleased to make a profit out of these senior NCOs as I well remembered the way they had cheated us out of our food gifts from the Cretan girls in the camp on Crete. Pete and I could now have brown sauce with our bacon and eggs. The saccharine came in very useful as there was usually a shortage of sugar in the camp. Some men even crushed tablets to make saccharine sandwiches with their dry rye bread.

Sometimes we needed to make other trips to Stalag IVB, for instance to take sick men to see the doctors in that camp. If we did not combine it with Red Rosette journeys we had to go on foot. In the big camp there was a large clinic complete with a lazarett and at least two English army doctors. One of our men, Fred Howlett, developed eczema which gradually spread until it covered most of his body. Fred was a quiet, reliable and most likeable man, in civilian life an officer in his local fire brigade. He was very sensitive about his complaint and so embarrassed he would not wash with the other men but crept away on his own. I noticed this and tackled him about it, insisting he must see the doctor at Stalag IVB.

We walked up to the big camp accompanied by a guard and after a wait saw a doctor, a colonel in the British Army Medical Corps, elderly – to us – and most certainly a regular army officer. He rather casually examined Fred, said it was just a rash caused by being dirty through not washing properly. He then prescribed soap and provided him with a bar of Lifebuoy soap. I was dissatisfied with his diagnosis and casual treatment of what I was sure was a rather serious illness but could not argue with the doctor. Fred tried the soap regularly but there was no improvement; in fact the rash got worse. Again we went back to this doctor who insisted the problem was only one of personal hygiene and told us not to waste his time. At last he called in the other British doctor, who had a casual look at Fred and he agreed with his superior. Still there was no improvement and more embarrassment for Fred.

I think it was the fourth time I took him that I got really annoyed as the old colonel still insisted it was only a hygiene problem. He was very rude to me and to Fred. I confronted him, expressing my dissatisfaction with his treatment and added I had no option but to ask the German doctor in the camp. At this, 'Colonel Blimp' became furious and red in the face, said how dare I question an officer's competence and be so insolent and disrespectful and that I must face the consequences of my insubordination. He took my name, the name of my regiment, my rank and army number and announced he would see I was court-martialled after the war. I am still waiting!

Nevertheless I still insisted on Fred being seen by the German doctor and asked our guard to arrange it. The German doctor gave him a thorough examination and said he it was clear that Fred was suffering from an acute type of eczema which he could not treat himself and would need to refer him to a skin specialist. He told me he would make all the arrangements and inform our commandant in due course. When the appointment came through, Fred, I and a guard set off by train to Torgau to see the skin specialist, a civilian doctor who confirmed it was a very severe form of eczema. He said he would do his best to cure him but we must realise there was a shortage of suitable medicines in Germany for the treatment of this type of illness. He added he would continue what treatment he had available for four or five weeks and if the treatment did not work, he would recommend Fred be repatriated on medical grounds. I was very relieved that I had persisted and that we had found such a sympathetic German doctor. The treatment continued with weekly visits to the specialist and Fred's condition gradually improved until, thankfully, it cleared up completely. I felt my stand on Fred's behalf had been vindicated. I assume the German doctor reported the outcome to the British colonel because on subsequent visits to the clinic it was never mentioned by him.

Most of us looked forward to the arrival of letters from home – there were a few prisoners who never received any mail and did not write to anyone. Pete Yeomans, 'Doc', was a married man with two children, whose framed photograph hung on the wall by his bunk on which he would fondly gaze from time to time. He even made a little curtain to pull across the photograph. When the mail arrived without a letter from them, he would ritually close the curtain on his family and would not look at them again until one came. The receipt of letters from home was very important for us, not only helping us to keep in touch with our families, wives and fiancées, reassuring us that they were alive and well, but also providing a tremendous support during the very long and generally monotonous years, buoying up our spirits and really keeping up our morale.

In addition to the regular Red Cross parcels, I was also issued a small number of 'milk parcels' intended for men with stomach problems or who were convalescing after an illness. I rarely had to make use of them. Occasionally we managed to get the odd extraordinary food parcel, over and above our requirements. As time went on, we accumulated about twenty or so of these surplus parcels and I had to decide what to do with them. I called a meeting of the whole camp to discuss the matter as there were not enough to share out equally. The decision made by the majority was that we should have a raffle for them. We decided there would be top prizes of three parcels, other prizes of two parcels and the rest single parcels. Tickets were prepared, one for each man with his name written on it. The whole camp was assembled so all could witness that the draw was completely open and fair. Different men were selected to draw out each winning ticket. The first ticket was drawn and very much to my embarrassment it was mine but as it was absolutely clear there had been no cheating, my good luck was accepted by all. Winners shared, as I did, the parcels with their muckers. Overall the raffle was a big success and was a fair way of disposing of the extra parcels.

The New Zealand Red Cross food parcels contained packets of dried peas which needed to be soaked overnight in boiling water, with a tablet of bicarbonate of soda added, before cooking, but we had no soda. We tried boiling them for hours but they never ever softened. One of the men in the camp was Joe Potter from Devon and not the brightest bulb. He was teased constantly but took it all in good part and did not complain. But he did get very frustrated when, after boiling his dried peas for a day or two, they were still as hard as bullets. 'What am I to do with them?' Joe pleaded. Some bright spark said with his tongue in his cheek, 'Look, Joe, the best thing you can do with them is to make a little garden and plant them.' No one thought he would take this seriously, but he did. Out he went and cleared a patch by the perimeter fence, made a small bed and duly planted his peas. He watered the bed each day and to everyone's amazement except Joe's, they germinated. He carefully tended them every day, training them to climb up the fence; they flowered and began to produce pea pods. Joe was over the moon; he waited anxiously for the little pods to swell. He became very excited and wanted to pick them but we advised him to wait until they were really ready. One night we told him that he could pick them the next morning. He got up early the next morning and went out but sadly he was too late: a goat had managed to get its head through the fence and had eaten all the pea pods. The goat had certainly known they were ready. Poor Joe was so upset. Damn those New Zealand dried peas!

The working days at the camp were Monday to Saturday inclusive, from about 7.30 a.m. to 5.00 p.m. with a lunchtime break. Sunday was a rest day, and the day on which the men did their laundry, in the hope their clothes would dry before Monday morning. That had been a real problem in earlier camps when we had no spare underclothes. However, by now most of us had extra changes of clothing. Sunday was the day when we played football on the ground just outside the camp. In midsummer the men were also able play in the light evenings.

There were complaints that having to do their laundry spoilt the rest day and interfered with the sport. Someone suggested the camp should organise a laundry service. I said I would mention it to the commandant, which I did with my tongue in my cheek, telling him the men felt they should be provided with a laundry service as they felt too tired to do their laundry on their only rest day. He said he would think about it and the next time I saw him he said he had decided it was a good idea and a service would be provided, but only if it was paid for by Herr Leper. I suspect his decision may have had more to do with his dislike for Herr Leper than his desire to do us a good turn. He said he would have to inform Herr Leper of his decision and then he would make the necessary arrangements.

The commandant told us he had found a lady in a neighbouring village who was prepared to do the laundry. She was a widow with a young daughter and needed the money. We could take the dirty laundry once a week and collect the clean clothes when we took the next lot of dirty laundry. We would have to walk to the village (about 2 miles away) taking the laundry on a handcart, accompanied by a guard. Thus we started a series of weekly outings. The laundry party comprised Pete Yeomans, Blondie Stead, myself and one guard. It is possible we were the only working prisoner-of-war camp in Germany to have a laundry service! The German widow turned out to be very pleasant, and very happy to do our washing.

Once we got to know her, we would stay for an hour or so, part of which was spent teaching her young daughter some English, as the mother was keen for her to learn. Our weekly visit became friendly and inevitably we decided to take some chocolate for the young girl and some real coffee for the mother. Could one say this was weakness towards the enemy? I rather think not. The point of the exercise was to get the men's laundry done to save them the trouble of having to do it on Sundays and, for this, it was a great success. Our laundress became embarrassed when we took her tablets of toilet soap, which was by then almost unobtainable in Germany, in addition to all the things we gave her for her young daughter. We hoped she told her neighbours of these little kindnesses by the British POWs and let them realise the British were not against the ordinary German people. She asked if there was anything she could do for us in return. It so happened she had a dog, a German Shepherd that had recently had puppies. Pete Yeomans suggested we ask her for a puppy and she gladly agreed to give us one. We asked the commandant (Wall-eye's successor) who said he had no objection provided we fed and looked after her.

When she was weaned we took her back to camp in Pete's charge and he named her Bess. He looked after her with great affection; there was sufficient food to spare to feed her, and Harry Layden bought bones and titbits from the cookhouse. She was a quiet, lovable dog and became a great favourite with the whole camp. Only once did we have a problem. She became ill and we worried that she might have distemper. We had no access to any veterinary medicines. Luckily the problem was solved by one of the newer guards. He offered to take her to a vet, which he did, all at his own expense. Bess soon recovered and had no more illnesses.

This guard was an older man, I suppose in his mid-fifties, who had recently been called up for military service and allocated duties as a guard at our camp. He was almost openly anti-Nazi and certainly did not hide his views from us. When the men played football in the early evenings some local boys would come to watch and try to scrounge some chocolate from us and on some occasions they were lucky. One day this guard was patrolling outside the fence during a football match when he spotted a couple of boys. He called them over saying he could get them chocolate, took hold of them by the scruff of the neck, boxed their ears and told them to get back to their Hitler Youth Group and not bother 'his' prisoners. It appeared quite a number of the boys would much rather come and watch our football matches and perhaps get some sweets or chocolate than attend the Hitler Youth sessions. This we felt was another small propaganda coup.

This elderly guard was friendly and good to us; on several occasions he came along with some cake, a luxury for us, which he said his wife had baked for us. Two of the other guards called Jeskowitz and Schmidt were almost as friendly and helpful, and not just because they were trading with us. All three were guards here and later at Falkenberg.

On one of our laundry outings we were accompanied by a new guard. We looked him over and decided he seemed somewhat gullible, being new to the job, and would not really know the procedures. We duly delivered the dirty clothes, picked up the clean laundry and stayed for our usual chat with the laundress, taught the girl a little more English and eventually set out on the return journey. When we came to the local *Bierhaus* (pub) we stopped and parked the cart outside the entrance. When the guard asked what we were doing, we replied that we always stopped there and the guard usually took us in for a drink. We were, of course, just trying it on, but very surprisingly the guard said in that case he would do the same and so we went in and enjoyed a tankard of sweet *Malzbier* and he paid. We could not believe our luck and tried to make sure he was given the guard duty for future laundry outings – another little unexpected pleasure to look forward to each week.

On our visits to the big camp we were able to barter on the black market there for American air force jackets, flying boots and fur hats (I am not absolutely sure the hats were American) from American pilots who had been shot down and were, or had been, in transit in the camp. The jackets were well tailored and of a much finer cloth than our battledress so they were much in demand by some of our more fastidious men. These American prisoners were not yet properly 'in the system', so were short of cigarettes and 'candy' and were easily persuaded to barter uniforms for them. Several of our men got jackets including Blondie Stead, Harry Layden and Pete Yeomans. I never bothered.

The Germans made a great celebration of *Ostern* (Easter). Easter 1944 was a memorable one for the prisoners in Camp L125. The Germans, civilian adults in Mühlberg town and all our guards, were issued with a special ration of schnapps, one bottle per person. Naturally with our barter system going well, a fair number of bottles found their way into our hands and into the camp. This was the only occasion that bottles of liquor came into any of the camps I was in. Easter Sunday was a rest day so the men soon started celebrating.

In the early evening one of the guards came across and said the commandant, old Wall-eye, requested Blondie (as interpreter) and me to go and have an Easter drink with him and some of the guards as Easter was a time for goodwill and friendship. I sent a curt message back to him saying I did not drink with the enemy. The guard returned saying we were ordered by the commandant to go to the German barrack. We had no option but to obey, were escorted across and into their mess room. There was the commandant and two or three guards, including one named Kampfe, a gefreite (lance corporal). We were ordered to have a drink with them, as it was, Wall-eye said, a time to forget the war for a day and celebrate Easter; he could see nothing wrong in our joining in. We somewhat reluctantly accepted a drink of schnapps. They had also prepared some small snacks. So we had a few glasses of schnapps, I suppose not realising its potency.

Afterwards the commandant prepared coffee which, of course, he had obtained from us. He carefully explained the method of making it, quite a ritual. Coffee was placed in a jug, one desert spoon per person, and a pinch of salt added; this, he said, was most important to bring out the flavour of the coffee. Then absolutely boiling water was added and the pot left to brew for exactly three minutes. Then the side of the pot was tapped with a spoon; this, he explained, would make the coffee grounds sink to the bottom and now the coffee was ready to drink. The coffee was very good and ever since then I have always put a pinch of salt in coffee when brewing it.

At the same time as we were drinking with the Germans, the men in the barrack were also drinking hard to celebrate the occasion. I am not certain Easter came into it very much. The time came for us to stagger back to our barrack and the Germans somehow remembered they had to carry out the nightly check parade to make certain we were all present. Gefreiter Kampfe and another guard were sent to carry out the check. Reluctantly the men gathered to be counted inside the rooms as was customary at night, forty in one room and sixty in the other. Gefreiter Kampfe said we would start counting in the larger room. He walked, or rather staggered, along the ranks counting as he went; the men were noisy and raucous with drink. The actual number to be accounted for was fifty-eight as Blondie and I were with him. On the first count he made it ninety, he was that inebriated. He asked how many it should be, I told him fifty-eight, so he said he must recount; he staggered along once more and this time he counted a hundred and twenty, to a great deal of hilarity from the men. So he drew himself together, as best as he could, and asked me how many were in the whole camp. I said one hundred. He replied that as there are more than a hundred in this room there is no need to count the other room – we'd got more than enough! He attempted to salute and stumbled his way out of the barrack quite satisfied with the count and we were locked in for the night. I tried to settle down but there was still some drinking going on, a great deal of noise and drunken chatter. It turned out to be a most disturbed night; the sudden intake of large quantities of strong liquor after years of abstinence took its toll: many of the men were bilious and I have to admit I was one of those who was very sick. The next morning there were many thick heads and much cleaning up to do. The floors had to be washed and some of the blankets and clothing had also to be washed and hung out to dry. It was a most remarkable and memorable, once-in-a-lifetime, Easter.

Herr Leper complained to old Wall-eye that the prisoners had been stealing a variety of goods from his barges. He demanded an immediate search of the camp and for all the goods found to be confiscated and returned to him and the culprits punished. He was quite correct of course, the men had acquired – we did not like the word 'stolen'– a great variety of things from the barges. However, we felt we were fully justified as all the barges had been confiscated – that is stolen – by the Germans from the French and Belgian owners and, we were sure, without any compensation being paid. In a sense, as allies of the French and Belgians we were only recovering their goods. The men had supplied me with white sheets and pillow cases – a real luxury – it was the first time I had had any sheets in a prison camp, or, indeed, in the British army. The other useful items were cutlery and crockery; we could now eat our meals with knives and forks off china plates instead of from tin bowls with spoons which had greatly improved our standard of living. We also got mirrors and other useful items. We knew the German guards were also helping themselves to anything they wanted and had supplied some items to the commandant. We knew not only because the men had witnessed the guards stealing them, but also because we had seen stolen mirrors and clocks in the German barracks, together with crockery and other things.

Early on a nice sunny day the commandant suddenly ordered us all out of the barrack rooms onto the area in front of the building. He then sent in all the guards to carry out a thorough search of the camp, instructing them that they must remove any item which they thought had been taken from the barges. At first the men tried to hide all the various items but we then were told to take all our possessions out and completely empty the rooms. We soon realised what it was all about. We sat around outside in the sunshine surrounded by all our belongings.

The commandant addressed us, outlining the complaints he had received from Herr Leper, called us thieves and stated every stolen item must be returned to Herr Leper. Then, he, the commandant, would consider how we were to be punished. He divided his guards into two groups, one to search inside the building and the other systematically to search us and our belongings.

As soon as their search started, I approached the commandant, with Blondie to interpret, and told him that it was all very well to search us for stolen goods, but what about the many stolen items now in their German barrack and in his own possession? I said if our goods had to be returned to Herr Leper, I would make certain Herr Leper was informed of the items he and the guards had. We would also have to report him and his guards to his superior officers when they next visited the camp. I also reminded him of the trouble he would be in for bartering with us. It did not take long for this to sink in. He thought for a while and told us he appreciated the position but, in the circumstances, he was bound to make a gesture to Herr Leper. He suggested therefore we should give up a token amount of goods and he would then inform Herr Leper, despite a thorough search, that it was all he could find and the missing items must have been taken by the civilian workers. I agreed this was a way out and we handed over a few items of crockery, mostly chipped, and some cutlery. Herr Leper was not satisfied but there was nothing he could do about it. After some three or four hours out in the sun we were allowed to return our possessions to the barrack rooms; I was relieved to be able to keep my bed linen and china plates.

In the evenings there was much social activity in the barrack room before lights out at either 9.30 p.m. or 10.00 p.m. There were games of dominoes and cribbage, various other card games amongst which poker was very popular and there was one four of bridge. The men habitually kept to their own choice of game; I usually played cribbage. Others read or just chattered in groups; we were all reasonably contented in a most congenial atmosphere. I sometimes read my architectural texts in the evenings but the humming, vibrant atmosphere was not conducive to serious study. Others took the opportunity to write their letters and postcards to their families and sweethearts.

One night our relative peace and quiet was shattered when old Wall-eye accompanied by Gefreiter Kampfe burst in. He started shouting and raving and it took a minute or so for us to realise what had upset him. Apparently it concerned a pair of *pantoffeln* – these were the wooden-soled slippers or mules with which we were issued and which we usually wore in the barrack in the evenings, although by now quite a few of us had received proper slippers from home. When our boots needed repair they were sent away and we would be issued a pair of *pantoffeln* as temporary footwear whilst waiting for their return. These were kept in a store in the German barrack. The commandant had discovered that someone had committed the serious offence of not returning the slippers when his boots had been repaired and he was demanding they be instantly given up. I shouted out his order in English several times but there was, amongst all the usual noise, no response from anyone. By now the commandant was getting really angry. He drew out his revolver, cocked it and proceeded to fire a couple of shots through the roof shouting that if the slippers were not returned he would shoot the man concerned. The shots certainly focused everyone's attention, including the culprit, Ken Griffin, who hastily got up from the bridge table, collected the slippers from under his bunk and handed them over. The commandant accepted them with ill grace and he and Kampfe departed having managed to upset our evening. Naturally Ken, one of the Middle East commandos and a county rugby player, was properly blamed and blasted but soon everything quietened down once more. Ken, one of the bridge four, must have been playing a hand, his concentration making him completely oblivious to anything else, except a gunshot. I had always considered bridge a dangerous game and this proved it! Our greater concern was that with his wonky eye, there was no way of knowing which way old Wall-eye was aiming or where the bullets would go, certain that they would not go in the direction he appeared to be looking.

Inevitably our main interest as POWs was food. At Camp L125, not only were we getting regular weekly Red Cross food parcels but also the rations given by the Germans were better cooked and presented than in previous camps, thanks to the efforts of our cook, Corporal Harry Layden. At this camp we were all well fed; it was certainly the best period for food during the whole four years of prison life. Food was always a principal topic and we talked about all the things we missed and what we would like for our first meal when we eventually got home.

Many of the men never really liked the German dark brown rye bread; they all yearned for some decent white bread. This was, of course, long before the merits of wholemeal bread and the importance of fibre were discovered and promoted. Thus every effort was made to try to get hold of white bread. The Germans were able to buy it in lieu of rye bread, but it was rationed so they had to use ration coupons when buying it. The civilians working with our men on the barges were willing to barter white bread for cigarettes, chocolate or coffee. So it became a feature of the evening march back to camp for men to have loaves of white bread under their arms while the guards turned a blind eye.

The route back to camp was partly through Mühlberg town and when some civilians saw them with the bread they complained to the commandant. They said that we prisoners, who were already well fed, were now getting white bread which was theirs; they were short of food and we were taking their rightful food. They were angry, outraged and demanded the commandant put a stop to our getting extra bread. The commandant had to take action, especially because some of the complaints came from Nazi Party members. He informed me that he, reluctantly, would have to stop the practice. He issued orders to the guards to search all the men as they left the barges to come back to camp and again as they entered the camp. The searches were thoroughly carried out and no more bread came into the camp. The commandant was very pleased with himself and I congratulated him on the effectiveness of the searches and said how clever he was to have defeated our white bread racket.

On our side we had given much thought about how we could get over this impasse and obtain this extra bread. Harry Layden suggested, as he had access to the village bakery, it might be possible to get some directly from the bakery through his contacts at the central cookhouse. He pointed out, however, he could only get bread from the baker in exchange for ration coupons. We thought this over and decided on a solution. I called a meeting of the whole camp and informed them that in future, if they wanted the extra bread, they should get the bread coupons from the civilians at the work site. The bread coupons would then be given to me; I would record their names and the number of coupons they had purchased in a notebook. The coupons would then be given to Harry Layden. Harry would arrange to buy the bread and send it to the camp with the daily rations. The civilians readily agreed to exchange their coupons for our cigarettes and other things and the baker was willing to supply the bread as long as he got the coupons.

Having bought the bread, we had the problem of getting it into the camp and distributing it to the men who had bought coupons. Our rations were brought daily to the camp from the central cookhouse on a handcart with two men pushing it and accompanied by a guard. The hot food came in containers and the bread ration was always in sacks. From now on Harry put the extra bread in a separate sack and sent it along with the other rations. The Germans never took any interest at all in our rations, only looking at the hot food if we made a complaint about the quality of the so-called stew; they never ever checked the sacks of bread. In this way, the extra bread arrived in the camp most days. I took charge of it, consulted my notebook and issued it to the men who had given me coupons. We just had to be careful there were no guards about when it was distributed. The system worked smoothly; the commandant and his guards never found out we had hoodwinked them once again. Wall-eye was happy to have been complimented on his prowess in apparently stopping this trade.

One would expect a certain amount of petty thieving amongst a large group of men, especially amongst POWs who were deprived of so many things. I can remember just one isolated case in our camp L125. From time to time there was a shortage of tea, particularly when we had a run of Canadian parcels which contained coffee instead of tea, and then tea might be at a premium. There was a complaint from someone in the other, smaller, room that tea was going missing from his store of food which he kept in a Red Cross box. A careful watch was set up and in due course the culprit was caught red-handed. I then had to decide what action to take against him: clearly we did not want to get the Germans involved in what was our domestic problem. Neither did I want a kangaroo court. I discussed suitable punishment with those involved and finally it was determined to 'send him to Coventry'. So no one at all spoke to him for a month, then it was all forgotten. He certainly learned his lesson and did not repeat the offence.

After our lights had been turned out from the German barrack, we would settle down for what we hoped would be a peaceful night. However, it was not always undisturbed. One particular man would sometimes start talking loudly in his sleep. What was surprising was if someone spoke to him, he would answer quite normally, but would have no recollection of anything when he awoke. Quite near my bunk was a man who occasionally had a nightmare and would start shouting in Welsh before subsiding again into sleep. He was one of two brothers from the Welch Regiment whose English was pretty basic. As may be expected, there was much flatulence and farting, to which we had grown accustomed and slept through.

Then there was the case of Reg Starling who was a sleepwalker. One night he got up and walked to the outside door and started hammering on it and shouting he was going to kill one of the guards who had upset him, mentioning his name. We had to get up and deal with him. We believed one must not deliberately awaken a sleepwalker as it could endanger him in some way, so we decided the best way to deal with him was to light a cigarette and hand it to him. Reg would take the cigarette, start to smoke and quite naturally wake up, not knowing what had happened, and go off quietly to sleep. We had to be careful the guards did not hear his threats.

Sometime in the summer of 1944 we had a change of commandant and old Wall-eye departed. Despite his occasional outburst, he had been a reasonable commandant and we had been able to manipulate him. The new commandant was a much younger man whom I found much easier to deal with. He was rather carefree and a very keen footballer. He claimed to have been goalkeeper for Hamburg Football Club. I think he may have been wounded on the Eastern Front and so transferred to light duties, although there was no outward sign of any disability. The whole atmosphere in the camp became more relaxed under the new regime. It did not take very long before we had him bartering with us; he was a smoker and that gained us some leverage over him.

He suggested we arrange a football match against a team from the big camp at Mühlberg Stalag IVB, which would make a pleasant change from always having to pick sides amongst ourselves. We made all the arrangements during one of our visits to that camp to collect Red Cross parcels. The match was fixed for Sunday 18 June 1944 and took place at our camp. My recollection of the occasion is aided by the report of the match which appeared in the Stalag IVD newspaper, *The Courier*. The match apparently ended in a draw. It was watched by the rest of the camp who were not playing and also by a number of young German boys who hung about the camp. The German boys who should have been at Hitler Youth events often borrowed a football from us to play impromptu games on our football pitch.

After the match we managed to put on a cold buffet lunch most ably prepared by Harry Hunt, a caterer by profession from Bexhill-on-Sea. Harry Layden was able to get a few extra items of food from the cookhouse and the commandant provided some food and I think the visitors also contributed. There were speeches by WO1 Meyers, the chief man of confidence in Stalag IVB, his deputy RSM Gibson and myself. As often happened, my name was wrongly printed as Lance Corporal Nitherland. It was a gala day for us, the first time we had played a football match against another camp, yet from *The Courier* it seems there were other inter-camp matches, probably more easily arranged because the camps were closer together.

We became aware of the D-Day invasion of Normandy and Western Europe from snippets of news from the guards and got confirmation when visiting the big camp. There was also news of the rapid advances of the Soviet Red Army into Poland. Now we were optimistic the war would be over by the end of 1944.

It was now midsummer and we were lucky for the first time in Germany to get fresh fruit: strawberries and cherries by barter from the guards and from the civilians working on the boats in Herr Leper's shipyard.

Jeskowitz, mentioned earlier as one of the three most friendly guards, was a little man, a Sudeten German from Czechoslavakia. Being a little runt of a man and not a 'true' German, he was disliked and despised by most of the other guards who were forever taking the mickey out of him. Because of this, he was very lonely and became friendlier with the prisoners than with his own colleagues. To some extent, I suppose, we shielded him from their taunts.

He tried his utmost to make friends with me, even took to calling me 'Syddy' which was a bit embarrassing and gave me a photograph of himself in uniform which, unfortunately, has not survived. I clearly remember one Sunday morning, taking care to avoid the other guards, he came into our barrack carrying a covered plate which he presented to me: strawberries with cream. He said it was in appreciation of my kindness to him. An unusual gesture but it showed the humanity of one of the guards. There were a few others who treated us kindly, but he was the only one who did so partly as a reaction to his own treatment by his fellow guards.

Before we came to Camp L125 at Mühlberg there had been two brothers called Simnor from Liverpool with broad Scouse accents. Their unit was the Royal Horse Artillery. The elder one was Bob; I forget the name of the younger brother. Bob was a strong robust character whilst the younger one was very shy and timid who relied heavily on protection from his elder brother. When the selection was made for the Mühlberg camp, the younger Simnor came with us and Bob was left behind and later sent to a camp at Bitterfeld. Just before we left Stalag IVB they had received a personal parcel whose origin rather puzzled them because it was not from home nor any recognised charity. The parcel contained, amongst other items, two shirts. Naturally they took one each and as the brothers separated, so were the shirts. Sometime later when the younger Simnor at last washed his shirt he was amazed to see lines appear on it which turned out to be half of a map of Germany with routes marked on it. We presumed the other half must be on the other shirt with his brother Bob at Bitterfeld. The shirt was carefully hidden away.

After a while, young Simnor became very depressed without the support of his brother, so I put in a request on his behalf for him to be transferred to Bitterfeld and rather surprisingly this was agreed. After some delay, arrangements were made for him to go to Bitterfeld and I was allowed to accompany him. We set off with an accompanying guard by train. Not only was the train journey a welcome change from the camp, but it enabled me to meet men in another camp and to renew a few acquaintances and exchange news.

The men at this camp were housed in a large room on the upper floor of the factory in which they worked. In a sense it was not a camp because it was in town and the windows looked out onto the streets. They had very little opportunity for outdoor recreation, as they were in a very much more restricted environment than ours. In comparison we were very lucky indeed. They worked in the factory below, but lived, ate and slept in the upper room. From the German point of view, this was secure accommodation where they could easily be locked in for the night. However, the Germans had overlooked a trapdoor in the floor and the men discovered they could get out through it and into the street below. A few of the more adventurous went out at night for a stroll.

Nearby was a camp of Italian 'guest workers' – forced labour and very much despised by the arrogant Germans. They were not locked in and could freely go about the town. One amenity provided for them was the use of a brothel in the town, which had possibly been set up especially for them. Some of the Italians worked in the factory and the British prisoners got to hear about the brothel, so naturally two or three of the braver, or perhaps randier, of them decided to try their luck. They armed themselves with cigarettes, coffee and chocolates to pay for what they hoped they would enjoy. They had obtained directions to the brothel from the Italians, made their way out through the trapdoor and out onto the street. Unfortunately they got the wrong building and walked into the local police station. They were promptly arrested and marched back to the factory. The main consequence was the sealing of the trapdoor – there were no more walks around the town.

Back to our camp at Mühlberg, where we had noticed two women from the village arriving in the evenings at the German barracks. We gathered they were mother and daughter from the local community and were obviously prostitutes coming to service the guards. The rumours around our camp were that the daughter was for Kampfe and for the younger guards, whilst Jeskowitz and the older guards had to be content with the – to us – old woman. We were certain the commandant did not participate because he had his wife staying with him; neither did a young guard named Albert, who had recently come to the camp. Albert was about nineteen or twenty years old and engaged to a girl who often came to visit him. He was very friendly towards us.

Certainly there appeared to be quite an amount of sexual activity in the evenings in the German barracks. This seemed to arouse the libido of two of our men, Blondie Stead and Harry Layden. Somehow, I think it must have been when he went occasionally with the escort to the central cookhouse, Blondie met a young local schoolmistress, or she may have been one of the group of Germans who came regularly to watch our football matches. He became more than friendly with her but the difficulty was to meet her in private. He gradually managed to cultivate a friendship with the young guard Albert and provided him with cigarettes and chocolate and in due course persuaded him, when he was on duty in the evening, to let him out of the camp to meet the teacher. Where they went for their love sessions I do not know, but Blondie had certainly made a conquest and achieved an outlet for his sexual needs. Their liaison and the almost nightly visits were never discovered by the commandant.

All this was common knowledge throughout the camp and clearly irritated Harry Layden who was also a bit of a randy man. He announced to us all he had met a girl through his work at the central cookhouse. She had agreed to come to the camp at night, before lights out, to see him, but as he had not been able to persuade Albert to let him out of the camp, they had had to meet with the barbed wire between them. Notwithstanding this, he had been able to have intercourse with her through the barbed wire. If this were true, it must have been a tricky and prickly operation; we all regarded it as a bit of bravado and did not believe his claim. Blondie Stead was a bit of a dandy and liked to be smartly dressed. He strutted about the camp wearing the fine worsted American airman's jacket he had acquired, with its pleated patch pockets, and a collar and tie which I had tailored for him. He wore American airman's boots and topped this with a white fur hat. The hat, I think, came indirectly from a Russian prisoner (see photo on p. 250).

At this stage, the late summer of 1944, Camp L125 ran very smoothly. I would say it was the pleasantest period of my POW life. On just one occasion was there a murmur of discontent at my stewardship of the camp as man of confidence. This was led by a rather disgruntled Welshman named Hughes who claimed I was not doing the job satisfactorily. He was known as a bit of a moaner, so I decided to confront him. I called a meeting of the whole camp. We assembled on the grass in front of the barrack. I asked Hughes to state the complaints he had about my administration of the camp. I explained I was rather fed up with the complaints he was spreading around and if they thought I was not doing my work satisfactorily, I was willing to step down. I answered his complaints, asking if anyone else had complaints against me, which no one did, but there were shouts of support. I then asked for a vote of confidence, which was given overwhelmingly, so I continued in office. Hughes took it well and agreed to co-operate with me thereafter, thus ending the one challenge to my leadership.

In the autumn of 1944 the work at the boat yard was just about completed and the commandant informed us we would shortly be leaving Mühlberg to go to another camp. Immediately preparations for the move began. Then tragedy struck. On the morning of their last day at work, being a fine sunny day, some of the boys decided that they would have a last swim in the River Elbe. The river had some very strong currents and this time some of them got into difficulties. Sadly three of them disappeared, swept away by the currents and were drowned. The rest of the men were immediately sent back to camp. The civilians at the boat yard and local police who had been called, set up a search for the missing men and they recovered the three bodies in the evening. Of the three, I only remember two. One was Taffy Maddocks, a small Welshman, and one was the other Scouse. About two weeks earlier he had received a letter telling him that his wife had gone off with another man. He was terribly upset and depressed at the news, and we had spent hours trying to comfort him in his distress. Sadly, I have lost all recollection of the third man.

I had hoped the move, scheduled for the following day, would be postponed to allow us to attend the funerals of the three men, but the commandant said his orders from the district administration of prisoner-of-war camps at Torgau were that the move must go ahead. I wanted to attend the funerals, but the commandant said I must go with the men to help to organise the new camp. Instead, Blondie Stead could stay behind, especially as he spoke German, to identify the bodies and attend the funerals. The families were informed by RSM Parslow, the chief man of confidence at Torgau who also attended the funerals. We made a collection of camp marks which was sent to the office in Torgau to be sent to the next of kin. This was a very sad ending to our time in what had been, and remained, the best of all our POW camps.

During the few days Blondie Stead stayed on at Mühlberg, he was allowed to stay in the German barrack rather than be alone in our empty barrack room. When he eventually arrived at the new camp at Falkenberg, he reported on what had happened.

Taffy Maddocks and 'Doc' Peter Yeomans at Liebenwerda.

He had identified the three bodies and had attended the funerals with RSM Parslow, which he said had been solemnly carried out at the local cemetery with the coffins draped in Union Jacks. He also related his exploits in the German barrack. The guard Albert had accompanied us to our new camp at Falkenberg, but had left his fiancée behind staying at the Mühlberg camp. Blondie informed us that he always fancied the girl and had lost no time in making advances to her which, he said, she seemed to reciprocate, so in the middle of the night he had crept to her room, seduced her and had intercourse. Some time later we heard on the guard's grapevine that Albert had been forced to bring his marriage forward because his girlfriend was pregnant; the timing fitted in with Blondie's seduction. Whose baby?

15

Falkenberg, No. SCH 184, Stalag IVD

We were transported to the new camp by lorry. Naturally Bess the Alsatian, now fully grown, came with us. We found the new camp was sited within the railway marshalling yards of Falkenberg, on the edge of its fenced compound. Falkenberg is a town some miles north of Mühlberg and almost due east of Torgau, the latter on the west bank of the River Elbe. Falkenberg was a very important railway junction of main lines running from north to south and from east to west.

There was a single barrack for us, constructed, as usual, of dark, creosoted timber with a felt-covered pitched roof, but the layout was completely different from that at Mühlberg. Here the entrance was central at one end of the building with rooms on either side of a corridor. At the far end of the corridor, a door led to the commandant's rooms, which also had a separate entrance from outside.

The first two rooms, one on each side as one entered the block, were respectively the guards' quarters on the left and a storeroom-cum-guard-room on the right. The latter was where the Red Cross parcels were stored as well as the German food supplies. Then a door in the corridor led to our rooms; most were small, containing five two-tiered bunks which had the usual slatted supports for the hessian palliasses, supporting ten men to a room. There was a window on the outside wall complete with the usual outside shutters, which at nights were closed and barred by the guards. At the end of the corridor were two larger rooms with accommodation for

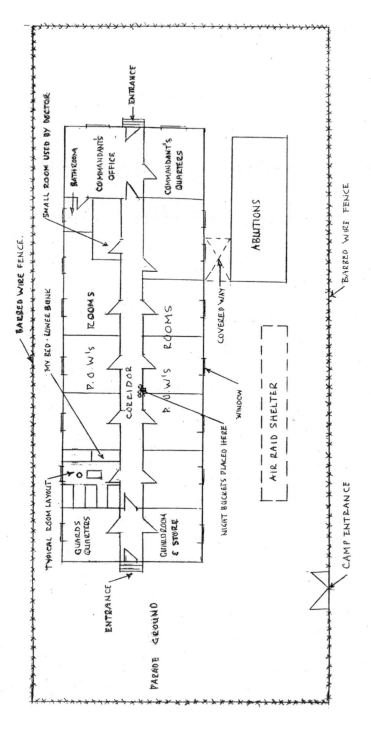

LAYOUT OF CAMP SCH 184 STALAG IVD · FALKENBERG

about sixteen men each. There was also a small room, almost a cupboard, right at the end on the left which later was allocated to a doctor who was with us for the last few weeks at the camp. The commandant's quarters at the end of the corridor comprised a large office-cum-living room, off which, on one side, was his bathroom and on the other his bedroom.

This was the only camp in which the commandant, guards and prisoners were all under one roof. As usual the whole compound was surrounded by a high barbed-wire fence. Outside the entrance to the barrack block was a large gravelled area used for the check parades and where the men assembled to be counted before going to work. If one faced the entrance to the building the main gate to the compound was on the right-hand side. On the left-hand side the fence was only about six feet away from the building. On the right there was much more space because here was an air-raid shelter – the usual Anderson style with an entrance at one end and inside wooden benches on each side – and beyond the shelters was the ablution block with a covered passageway separating it from the main building.

There were rows of wash hand basins and rows of showers, all with cold water. We had to heat shaving water on the stoves in the rooms – that is, for those who bothered; by now most of us were quite used to shaving with cold water. However the toilets adjoining were the *pièce de résistance*: instead of the usual rows of wooden boxes with seats cut out to enable us to sit in relative comfort, there was just a horizontal pole supported at intervals running the length of the latrine trench on which we had to perch to perform our functions; it was certainly not designed for long stays. The trench below, completely open to view, was not a pretty sight. To disinfect the contents of the trench and eliminate the smell, quicklime was daily sprinkled over the surface. I had to set up a roster for this work as no one really wanted to volunteer. The only advantage of the pole seat was it was difficult to foul, unlike the box seats which sometimes had to be scrubbed clean.

Inside the rooms we had the usual table and benches and a round tortoise stove with its round metal chimney. There was, unusually, an electrical point to which I was able to connect my small hotplate. Cooking of rations continued to be from a central cookhouse serving several camps. Harry Layden was again appointed as the cook as he looked after our interests very well.

My bed was in the first room on the left. The fence was quite close on this side and there were some trees nearby in which I could hear woodpeckers pecking away; my only recollection of birdlife during my years in the camps.

It reminded me of one of Stella's and my favourite songs, 'The Woody Woodpecker Song'.

The commandant at SCH 184 Falkenberg was Hauptmann Zimmermann – '*zimmermann*' in German means carpenter. He was an older man, tall, thin, and rather gaunt, not unlike Neville Chamberlain. His attitude was paternalistic and he was very dedicated to his allocated task of looking after his flock of prisoners. He was slow in his movements, rather pedantic, very meticulous and pernickety. Nevertheless I could not help liking the man.

He tried so hard to do his best for us, but his slowness irritated the men and me and he was a poor disciplinarian. For example, when personal parcels arrived, he insisted on handing them out himself; this took place in the storeroom near the entrance. Sometimes he did not get round to it until a day after the parcels arrived which annoyed us. He insisted I be present when he gave them out: he said it was to ensure fairness. When he was ready, he would summon me and the recipients, who accompanied by a guard, made our way to the storeroom. Even then sometimes we had to wait until he was ready. He would greet us, then sit down, slowly take a parcel and open the wrapping, then have a look at the contents before handing it over. This was not always immediate because quite often he would close his eyes and nod off, keeping us waiting and frustrated. When he did this we and the guards quietly sniggered at this dozing man. Then he would awake with a start and always apologised before proceeding methodically once more to open the next parcel, remarking on the contents and adding how happy he was the men were getting parcels from home.

One constant problem in the camps was a shortage of razor blades. These could be bought in the camp canteens, but at Mühlberg and Falkenberg there was no canteen; a few items were available from the German quarters but not '*rasierklingen*' (razor blades). They became difficult to obtain and those we did get blunted quickly. Some men, including me, had purchased cut-throat razors and learned to use them successfully, sharpening them by stropping; strops had also been available in the earlier camps. Trying to keep ordinary razor blades sharp was a real problem. They could be honed a little using the palm of the hand as a strop. Then we received a small box-like contraption which turned out to be a razor-blade sharpener. It arrived in a parcel from one of the charities and I am fairly sure it was Swiss made. The blade to be sharpened was placed in position and by pushing a lever backwards and forwards the blade was automatically stropped on both edges; the lever worked a mechanism which flipped the blade over at each movement. It was very ingenious and worked very efficiently, extending the life of blades for a long time. We only had the one, so it was passed around the rooms.

For the Germans being a coffee-drinking people, one of the essential items of equipment in every camp was a coffee grinder. This was in the form of a wooden box with a removable wooden drawer to catch the ground coffee, the grinder operated by a handle protruding from the top and turned round and round by hand. The lid was removable to put the coffee beans in and the ground coffee dropped into the drawer. Sure enough there was one in the guards' room. I am sure they were available in the earlier camps but we had no access to or need for one. We received packets of coffee in the Red Cross food parcels from Canada, but as most of us were tea drinkers we bartered much of the coffee with the Germans.

At Falkenberg the Germans complained that the Canadian coffee was too coarse and they preferred finer ground coffee. We decided to oblige them by grinding it to a finer texture, so we arranged to borrow the coffee grinder from them on a more or less permanent basis as they had no coffee of their own to grind. The grinder came into general use, being passed round from room to room. But the coffee from Canada was not the only coffee we had as the Germans continued to issue us with ersatz coffee which we hardly ever used. It was not long before someone hit on the idea of also grinding some ersatz coffee and blending it with the '*bohnen kaffee*', the real bean coffee, before bartering with the Germans.

At first a little ersatz was added, but when the Germans did not seem to notice, a little more was added until it became standard practice to mix the two, half and half. We would sit at the table in our room with a newspaper laid out on it with two heaps of coffee one real Canadian and the other ersatz, grinding the coffee into two separate heaps before blending fifty/fifty and re-packing in the Canadian packets. From time to time a guard would wander through the barrack to see what was going on. He would smell the coffee, say how good it smelt, say it was good to grind it finer and wander off again. No guard ever remarked on the two separate heaps or cotton on to the fact that we were blending the real coffee with ersatz coffee. The going rate for a packet (about 4oz) of coffee was either two loaves of bread or a dozen eggs. Bread, especially white bread, and eggs were the chief items we bartered for: I do not think there were many other items of food available at this time. Now by blending the coffees half and half, we had doubled the purchasing power of the coffee, and were able to get more food. The system worked very well; the Germans never discovered what was going on and were satisfied with the quality of the ground coffee. Thus assured, we then diluted the real coffee still more: one third real to two-thirds ersatz which we felt was the most we could get away with. One or two men thought it would be a good idea just to fill the packet with ersatz coffee and just sprinkle a little real coffee on top to give the aroma when the packet was opened. However, we decided this was pushing it too far and would jeopardise the whole operation.

We also continued to barter with cigarettes and chocolate. Some of the guards were eager to get chocolate for their children as it was almost unobtainable in Germany. I recall one guard who was transferred away from our camp but would come back to the camp fence in the evening, whistle to attract attention, and barter through the barbed-wire fence, so eager was he to get chocolate. This went on until he was seen by a patrolling guard and chased away and warned not to come back. He was told in no uncertain terms that this black market was only for those guards actually working at the camp.

Sometime in the early part of the winter of 1944 a camp of identical size less than a quarter of a mile distant was occupied by some American POWs. We were close enough to have a fairly clear view of the camp and their activities. From their clothes we deduced they had been captured in a warmer place because they were in khaki drill uniform which had become very ragged. They looked dishevelled and appeared to be in a rather pitiful state. I asked old Zimmermann for permission to send them some cigarettes and 'candy' to which he readily agreed. We sent over some cigarettes and chocolate and for this they were most grateful as they seemed to have nothing. I had no idea what arrangements were made by the American government for their POWs in Germany.

It soon transpired they had a scheme similar to ours through the International Red Cross because a few weeks later they began to receive their Camel and Lucky Strike cigarettes and Hershey bars. I was appalled at the state of their thin tattered uniforms, most unsuitable for the cold German winter. I asked Hauptmann Zimmermann if he would contact RSM Parslow at Torgau and ask if would be possible to provide them with

British battledress: shirts, boots and so on. He did so and RSM Parslow made arrangements for them to be kitted out in British uniforms. They were extremely grateful and sent over messages of profuse thanks for our help.

A little further away again from the American camp was another small camp of similar size for Dutch POWs. We were surprised and amazed a short while afterwards to find Dutch prisoners wearing almost new British battledress uniforms while some of the Americans wore old Dutch uniforms. It transpired some of the Americans were so addicted to cigarettes and desperate to get hold of them they had exchanged the new British uniforms that we had supplied for cigarettes and uniforms from the Dutch POWs. We felt not a little disgusted with them.

Each morning, as soon as we were awakened by the guards, the men who were going out to work got out of bed and staggered out to the toilets and ablutions, washed, shaved and ate a snack washed down by a mug of tea before being called out on parade to be detailed to their working parties. It was an accepted rule that everyone shaved every day. Not so the American prisoners. We watched them as they staggered out of the barrack just two or three minutes before setting out to work. It seemed few bothered to wash, let alone shave, before going to work. Their camp appeared disorganised to us, with little self-discipline: a complete shambles in fact.

The American camp leader soon became acutely aware of the difference between our well-organised and disciplined camp and their poorly run one. He persuaded their commandant to send a note to Hauptmann Zimmermann to enquire if it would be possible to send someone from our camp over to help them and advise them on how to organise their camp. Old Zimmermann was delighted at the glowing tribute to his camp which reflected well on him, so he readily agreed. Thus I, Blondie Stead and Pete Yeomans paid a number of visits to the camp to explain how we managed to have a smooth-running and disciplined camp, stressing that the main ingredient was comradeship with everyone pulling together and pooling resources, above all creating discipline and insisting on self-discipline in the men. Our advice did seem to help and we saw some improvement, but they never seemed to be able to reach our standard. I think the problem stemmed from the laxness of discipline in the American army in general, or so it appeared to me.

I vividly recall one incident which I thought was shameful and disgusting. Our little delegation had gone over to their camp soon after their men had arrived back from the day's work. On entering the building we saw one of the American prisoners, just back from work, on his hands and knees scrubbing the floor of the guards' room. We asked why was he doing this extra work having already completed his day's work. Was he being punished for some misdemeanour? 'No,' replied their man of confidence, 'It's because he's a Jew'. We were flabbergasted and horrified that he had received no protection or support from his fellow prisoners who had made no complaint to the Germans about this treatment: he was just a Jew – so bad luck. It was something which would never have happened in any of the camps I was in; we would have protested, even mutinied, until it stopped and be damned to the consequences. We could not understand why the Americans had done nothing to protect this poor man.

On one occasion we were getting rather short of tea because we had been getting a run of Canadian parcels which only contained coffee. One of the men, Benny, was desperate to get hold of some tea – he just could not do without it. Benny was a rather skinny man with dark hair and moustache, a grocer in civilian life and he certainly looked the part. He said he would do anything to get hold of a packet of tea. Harry Layden asked if he would be prepared to drop his trousers for him and allow Harry to roger him. Yes, he said, he was even prepared to do that. So in one of the two larger rooms at the end of the corridor, Benny duly dropped his trousers and bared his bottom. Harry brought along a small block of margarine – a bit of a waste we thought – and proceeded to grease Benny's arse. He then took out his erect penis and rubbed it with margarine and asked if Benny was ready for action, who replied in the affirmative and bent right over in readiness – all the spectators were roaring with laughter and anticipation. Then Harry just put his weapon away and said, 'Benny here is your packet of tea, you do not have to earn it in this way.' Benny was so relieved. It caused a great deal of amusement for those gathered around as we knew Benny was safe.

One morning not long after the men had left for work, Hauptmann Zimmermann appeared and told me he had been ordered to have the barrack rooms thoroughly cleaned and disinfected because, he said, of the widespread infestation in POW camps of lice, bed bugs and other creepy-crawlies. We felt outraged that he was implying we were a dirty camp; we prided ourselves on being particularly clean, having been absolutely free of lice since Staaken and if there had been any bed bugs, we would have surely noticed by then. Even Bess did not have any fleas. He said the orders were that we must take all palliasses and blankets out into the sun, all beds had to be taken outside and scrubbed with disinfectant and floors were to be swept and then scrubbed with disinfectant.

I protested that it was totally unnecessary as we were all absolutely clean. He said he was sorry but it was an order and we must obey. When I still refused he began to get really agitated and began to threaten in his weak sort of way. I got so annoyed I told him to go to hell and I had decided to resign immediately and he would have to find another man of confidence to carry out his stupid orders. I stalked off to my room and left him to it. He fumed and spluttered and then also retired to his room. A quarter of an hour or so later he came to my room and said he had come to apologise for losing his temper. He agreed our barrack was very clean and the order did not really apply to us but was intended for other camps which were not so clean. However, he had to be seen to be obeying orders so would we please just take out the palliasses, blankets and bed linen into the sun to air them which he felt would be sufficient. If anyone came to inspect from headquarters, we were to give them the impression we had taken all the beds out and scrubbed them. I agreed. He then asked me to withdraw my resignation and continue as confidence man because he liked working with me. In light of his change of mind, I told him that I was prepared to carry on in the post. This was the first – but not the only time – that a commandant apologised to me.

In fact the order was, in our opinion, misplaced: it should have applied to the German guards' barrack room which was much dirtier and untidier than ours. We had seen lice crawling on the guards' heads, collars and necks. I assume that they had became infested with lice, as we had been on Crete, because of the deteriorating conditions in health caused by worsening food supplies which had led to cuts in their rations. It was clear that at this stage of the war we were much better fed, thanks to the Red Cross parcels, than were our German guards.

As in our earlier camps, with the exception of the *kartoffel kommando* and the work on barges at Mühlberg, the work at Falkenberg was for the German railways. However, not all the men were filling skips for building embankments; some were employed on a variety of jobs in and around the marshalling yard. There were freight trains coming in and out all the time and some would lie in sidings for days at a time. The men were always on the lookout for anything useful they could 'half-inch', especially anything edible.

Amongst the workers in the marshalling yards were some French prisoners or forced labourers who lived not in camps but were billeted in the town and had considerable freedom of movement. One day a Frenchman found a freight tanker in a siding and discovered it contained wine. After announcing this and locating the 'tap' on the tank there was a stampede to partake of the wine by the prisoners, guards and civilian workers. The guard on the camp gate opened it and let the camp staff out to partake in this bonanza. The tap was opened and we all crowded round with any receptacle we could quickly get hold of to fill with wine; I saw guards take off their tin helmets to fill with wine. It was not a very good vintage, a *vin ordinaire*; nevertheless the tanker was soon completely emptied and the contents enjoyed by many people. We wondered what happened when it arrived at its destination empty!

There was another episode with liquor which also involved a French guest worker. Whilst working in the marshalling yard he was approached by a German civilian who told him he was distilling alcohol illicitly and asked if the Frenchman would be prepared to sell it to passengers on trains which stopped for short periods in the marshalling area at Falkenberg, for which he would be well paid, and so the Frenchman agreed. One of the first trains to stop happened to be a troop train; the soldiers on it were eager to buy the liquor and he sold them several bottles. We heard, later, that on drinking the alcohol they were taken violently ill and that several of them died. The source of the alcohol was traced to the marshalling yards and the Frenchman was promptly arrested and gave up the name of his German supplier. The German culprit was arrested and disappeared. What surprised us was that the Frenchman was let off with a caution and freed to carry on working. The liquor the man had distilled was a lethal wood alcohol. We were glad to hear of a few more dead German soldiers but not the manner of their deaths. Luckily none of us had been tempted to buy the liquor.

One of our guards at camp SCH 184 Falkenberg was named Schmidt. He had fought on the Russian front and had been wounded in the leg and walked with a distinct limp. Having been declared unfit for active service, he was sent to do guard duty at our camp. Schmidt became concerned on Sundays we were confined to camp without any recreation. Schmidt had been a keen footballer, so he got permission from Hauptmann Zimmermann to arrange football matches against other small POW camps in the neighbourhood. We were delighted and Schmidt arranged matches against two or three separate camps. We did not have a football pitch at our camp so any matches had to be away fixtures. Thereafter, each Sunday, Schmidt gave up almost the whole of his day to accompany the players as they marched to these other camps and back again. A number of spectators were also allowed to go with them. Poor Schmidt had to limp along on his injured leg.

He was a good German, a very good one. He was the most considerate of all the guards I came across during my four years in the bag. It had soon become abundantly clear to us that the best of the guards were those who had seen action on one of the fighting fronts. There seemed to be an inherent camaraderie between fighting men on all sides, men who had undergone the rigours of the front line.

Christmas 1944 arrived. Hauptmann Zimmermann said it was a time for Christians to celebrate and we must do our best to have a festive time despite the war. He obtained a Christmas tree and set it up at the end of the corridor near the door to his quarters, decorating it all by himself with baubles and fairy lights. The reaction of the men was mixed; some appreciated his efforts whilst a few rather mocked him for trying to play Father Christmas. On Christmas Eve he asked us all to gather round the tree to sing carols, especially the German favourite '*Stille Nacht*' (Silent Night) and other carols we seemed to have in common. Despite the misgivings of some of the men who thought it all rather childish, his efforts were appreciated and he succeeded in raising our spirits. In his strange way he was a good man, kindly, and let us run the camp much as we wished. He was certainly a devout Christian, which seemed to be rather against the grain of Germans in those days.

Whether his superiors at the Torgau headquarters decided he ran too lax a regime at the camp, or whether a posting came up elsewhere, I do not know, but early in the New Year of 1945, quite unexpectedly, he announced that he was being transferred elsewhere. I believe he was genuinely sorry to leave us.

The new commandant was an entirely different kettle of fish: much younger, smarter and very arrogant. As soon as he had assumed his command he summoned Blondie Stead as interpreter and me to his room. By now I had a reasonable knowledge of German and could understand almost everything they said.

My darling Stella. Here is my Christmas Day letter to the one I value most in the whole world. It is now 10·15 pm and I am writing this on my bed. I meant to write this afternoon, but I felt so full of Pudding that I had to lie down and rest. We received some Canadian Parcels for Christmas, as the Christmas ones hadn't arrived. However I made a Steamed Pudding and we all busied ourselves making cakes of all sorts and sizes and with varying success. My cake was about 10 lbs and was very successful, no doughy lumps in the middle of it. Our rooms were very nicely decorated with coloured streamers lanterns, cartoons, even tinsel round Stella's portrait. We had a very nice Christmas Card from the Y.M.C.A. This Stella must be our last Christmas apart, let us hope and pray that we shall be together again long before next Christmas,

perhaps we shall be married by next Christmas. Nowadays there is so much tension in the air that it is almost nerve racking, it is a trying time to be in charge of a camp. Lots of love to all at home to Marion and all the others. Every bit of my love to you Stella my darling. May God bless you always and bring me safely to you soon. Sydney.

When we entered the room, the new commandant told us to stand to attention and salute him. He then harangued us in a most aggressive tone of voice, announcing he had been sent to bring some order and strict discipline because under the previous commandant the men had become slack, ill-disciplined and out of control. He informed us that recently he had been commandant of a Russian POW camp, where, he said, he had had no hesitation in shooting a number of prisoners as an example to the rest and he thus maintained the strictest discipline. He said he would not hesitate to do the same at this camp if he felt it necessary. For him, he said, there was no distinction between Russian and British prisoners: we were all an unnecessary burden on the Third Reich.

This certainly set the alarm bells ringing. We tried to explain this was an entirely different camp; we were British POWs and naturally were disciplined soldiers unlike the unruly Russians. We further told him that, unlike the wretched Russian soliders, we were protected by the Geneva Convention which had been signed by both the German and British governments and we expected him to abide by the Convention. He shouted that this was completely irrelevant: to him, all prisoners were just prisoners – just scum with no rights. If he had his way, all prisoners would be shot as they were a drain on German food supplies which should be reserved only for the German people.

He then proceeded to lay down the law on the discipline he required in the camp. Whenever he entered a room, all were to immediately stand to attention and salute him; he would then require the senior man in the room to report to him on the number of men living in the room, the number present, the number working and the number sick. If correct, he would then inspect the room to make certain it was being kept clean. He then dismissed us, requiring us to salute again as we left.

We reported back to the men and warned them to be extremely careful, to expect trouble and avoid anything which might give the commandant an excuse to use his revolver and shoot someone. The following morning after the men had gone off to work, he called Blondie and me to his room: he was ready to carry out his inspection of the camp and we were to accompany him. We entered one of the larger rooms in which four or five men were present. They drew to attention and saluted the commandant. I pointed at random to one as the senior man. The commandant then proceeded to put his questions: 'How many men live in the room? How many are now present? How many men are sick?' The senior man replied with no hesitation to the three questions, 'Sixteen destroyers', 'Five cruisers' and 'Two battleships'. The commandant replied, '*Bestimmt*' (agreed). He saluted and went on to the next room, quite happy his orders were being carried out. We had great difficulty in suppressing our mirth – he never realised we were taking the piss. The rest of the inspection went in a similar fashion without a hitch.

During the next night the fore-alarm sounded, as it did most nights, warning us there were enemy planes approaching but not necessarily targeting Falkenberg. If they came closer overhead, the full alarm would sound. We ignored this fore-alarm as we had always done previously. We usually only went out to the shelters on the rare occasions when the full alarm sounded. Had we got up and gone out at every fore-alarm we would never have an undisturbed night. But on this occasion, the door burst opened suddenly and in rushed the guards, steel helmets on, carrying their rifles shouting, '*Aus, Aus,*' ('out, out'), ordering us to get up and go to the air-raid shelters. As the lights went on there was an instant chorus of, 'Fuck off,' and other appropriate obscenities. 'We need our sleep, we have to work tomorrow, and so have you, so just bugger off.' The guards were quite per-plexed, said they agreed with us, but the new commandant had given the order and they had to obey him, whatever they felt themselves. No one moved at all, we just continued to tell them to go away. After a while they departed to report our refusal to comply to the commandant. We settled down again to sleep, but a few minutes later in stormed the commandant in a great fury and ordered Blondie Stead and me out of bed.

He said it was his duty to protect the lives of the prisoners in his charge; therefore we must get up and go to the air-raid shelters. This was quite a change from his attitude the previous day when he had said he would like to shoot all prisoners. I tried, through Blondie, to explain that this being a fore-alarm, we did not go to the shelters because if we did, we would be in the shelters every night and the men needed a good night's sleep as they had to work hard in the daytime. He was not prepared to listen to us but said as the men would not obey his guards, they would no doubt obey me as camp leader. He then ordered me to get them out of bed and out to the shelters. Everyone else was still in bed, most of them sitting up or turning towards us to see what was going on. I addressed them, 'The commandant orders you to get up and go to the shelters. This is a tricky situation as far as I am concerned. For myself I am going back to bed, but this is a time when each of you must decide for yourself whether to get up and go out to the shelters or stay in bed; it is your own individual responsibility. If anyone wishes to obey the commandant, so be it. I intend to go back to bed.'

Not a single man got out of bed. The commandant turned to me, 'You have deliberately disobeyed my order. You are under arrest and will be court-martialled tomorrow,' and ordered a guard to hold me. It was a scary moment. He then turned to Blondie and said, 'You will now order the men to get out of bed and go to the shelters.' Blondie repeated what I had said and that he also intended to return to bed. Once again no one budged and Blondie was also placed under arrest to await his court martial. The commandant complained that no one would obey his orders and the guards were useless. He, surprisingly, then asked how was he to get the men to the shelters? I suggested he would have to get them out himself. Then he took out his revolver, cocked it, and strode off down the corridor with Blondie, me and a guard trailing behind. He went into the large room on the right-hand side, near his own room. In one of the lower bunks, just inside the door was Reg Holst, an Afrikaaner and a policeman before joining up. As he spoke Afrikaans, he could also understand and speak some German.

The commandant went up to him and poked his revolver in his face shouting, '*Raus, raus, auf, auf*'. Reg sat up slowly, looked the commandant in the eye and calmly said, in German, 'You are a German officer. I have always understood that German officers were gentlemen. You threaten me, an unarmed man, half asleep, with a revolver: this is not the act of a real officer. I can tell you that if I also had a loaded revolver you would not be within a hundred yards of me; you would be absolutely shit scared,' and lay down again. This really flummoxed the commandant who did not know what to do next. He stood back and then quickly turned on his heel, walked out of the room and went back to his own room. There were immediate huge sighs of relief from everyone, including the guards who now also departed for their room and locked the door. The situation had been very tense. Blondie and I had taken a big, possibly stupid, calculated risk. On the spur of the moment we had challenged the authority of a bullying commandant which might have gone very badly with extreme consequences for Blondie and myself. Would he shoot someone as an example? We were still unsure. For the moment the tension was gone; he had taken no immediate action so we all went back to bed and slept. We were still very apprehensive the next morning, wondering what the commandant would do next: were Blondie and I really going to be court-martialled?

Next morning the men got up, washed and dressed, had a snack, went out on parade and departed for work as normal. There was no sign of the commandant or of anything unusual. Soon after they had gone, a guard was sent to summon Blondie and me to the commandant's office. We entered his office, saluted as required, and waited, having no idea what to expect and rather fearing the worst. He looked up and rather quietly said, 'You were quite right when you said British prisoners are very different to Russian ones. You have shown guts and courage which the Russians never did. I must admire the stand you took last night; I now hope we can work together in a friendly way to make this a good camp.' We were flabbergasted, very relieved and pleased. It could all have gone so badly wrong but we had gambled and won. After that, the commandant became most friendly and co-operated with us in every way, becoming one of the best I ever had to deal with. I regret I cannot recall his name. At the end of our incarceration when we met up with the Americans, we handed him over and gave him a good reference.

At this camp, as in others, we occasionally had inspections by an officer from the district headquarters of the German prisoner-of-war administration located, in this case, at Torgau. It appeared the district was sub-divided into sub-districts with a major in charge of each sub-division. In our sub-district, the major was a smart, well turned-out, upright man, rather arrogant, a bit of a dandy with his immaculate riding breeches and highly polished boots. When he arrived at our camp he asked the commandant to call an *Appell*, had us counted, talked briefly to the commandant and was on his way, almost as if it was beneath his dignity to inspect a prison camp. He never went inside to inspect the conditions in the barrack block.

However, one day he spotted Bess sitting outside and was told she was our dog. Immediately he said it was absolutely forbidden for POWs to have dogs and that he was going to confiscate her, taking her away with him. It is quite conceivable that prisoners were not allowed to have dogs although we had not seen any such regulation. Our impression was that he had taken a liking to Bess, who was a very nice dog, and wanted her for himself. Everyone was upset, most especially Pete Yeomans, who had taken responsibility for looking after her.

About two or three weeks later we had a surprise visit to the camp by the officer commanding the district of Stalag IVD. He was a large man, I suppose in his fifties, with a lovely, red, boozy complexion; he gave the impression of being a genial, jolly sort of man. He was an oberst (colonel) and was accompanied by the galloping major, our *bête noire*. We took one look at him and decided he was the sort of person who might conceivably help us out over the theft of our Bess.

First we needed to isolate him from the major, so we got Blondie to talk to the major whilst I asked the oberst to come outside to look at the loos, where we said there were problems of hygiene to be addressed. Having got him on his own, I asked him if he had any objection to our having a pet dog in the camp, and went on to tell him how Bess had been given to us whilst we were at the camp at Mühlberg and that we brought her up from a puppy, only to find she had now been taken from us. I said she was no trouble at all, we fed her from our own resources, that she was useful as a good ratter (not that we had never seen any rats). I added that, from the German point of view, she was an asset because if anyone tried to escape she would most certainly bark and give the game away. I told him the whole camp was very fond of her and distressed that she had been taken away. He thought it over and then said he personally had no objection but would have to consult with the major who was, he said, in charge of day-to-day matters in this part of the district.

When the major and the rest of the party caught up with us he told the major about our request to have Bess back, saying, 'I personally have no objection but it is up to you.' This obviously put the major in a quandary because in the German army a mere major would not dare to go against the wishes of an oberst. Looking somewhat peeved, he said, 'No, Herr Oberst, I have no objection to the camp having a dog.' This was another little victory over our captors. The next day, with much reluctance, the major returned Bess to our care. She stayed with us until eventually we marched to freedom, when we managed to find a good home for her with a German civilian family. There was, to us, an amusing sequel. The major came again on one of his periodic visits to inspect the camp. As the parade was called to attention, Bess came wandering out of the barrack, walked over and licked his highly polished boots all over and wandered off again. All this was much to his annoyance, but to the immense amusement and cheers of the men. The major departed in a foul temper and it was the last we ever saw of him.

Very occasionally I, as man of confidence, was required to visit Torgau, on the west bank of the River Elbe, to see RSM Parslow in Stalag IVD, the district headquarters where Red Cross parcels, personal parcels and supplies of British uniforms were stored before being distributed to the camps. It was also where the POW newspaper for the district, *The Courier*, was compiled and printed. Our incoming mail and outgoing letter cards and postcards also went through this office.

Towards the middle of February 1945, quite unexpectedly, a doctor arrived at our camp. He was a New Zealander; sadly his name has gone from my memory, but I am fairly sure his Christian name was Hamish. When he arrived he was in a complete state of shock and, we discovered, with very good reason. He had been locked in a train in the vicinity of Dresden station during the bombing of Dresden on 13 and 14 February 1945. It had been a terrifying experience for him and he was so lucky to have survived the massive air raids which destroyed so much of Dresden. We took care of him but it took several weeks for him to recover from his terrible experience. We never found out why he had been sent to our small working camp of about a hundred men which did not warrant a doctor. Maybe things were getting so chaotic for the Germans they just offloaded him when the train reached Falkenberg, not knowing what else to do with him. I do not remember what he was doing on a train at Dresden at that time.

We soon heard from the Germans about the very heavy raids on Dresden and of the inhumanity of them. Their version, as told to us, was that there was first pattern bombing of the city centre and as the people fled to the suburbs, the bombers then bombed the suburbs killing an immense number of people, especially civilians, and that the bombing had gone on continuously for twenty-four hours, with the Americans bombing by day and the British by night. From the reports we had from the Germans there were a large number of refugees in Dresden at the time of the raids. A number of the guards had family relations or friends in Dresden and knew of people who had been killed or injured and thereafter those guards were not well disposed towards us.

I clearly remember one occasion when Blondie Stead and I were being escorted by our guard from the station to the District Offices when along the road from the opposite direction came a file of political prisoners in their striped clothes. As they approached us, we were amazed to see at the head of the column two girls in British battledress who smiled and waved as they passed. There was nothing we could do to intervene or find out more about them. Who were these British girls being marched towards the station at Torgau? The date most probably was March 1945. It has remained a mystery. Why were these cheerful girls with the political prisoners? Were they captured British agents or SOE (Special Operations Executives)? If so, why were they in British uniform? Were they, as seemed probable, being taken to a concentration camp there to await some awful treatment and possibly death? Somewhere there probably is some record of them and their fate. At the time I felt so helpless at not being able to intervene and a sense of guilt in not being able to help. The incident has continued to puzzle and worry me ever since.

Around this time we also began to see streams of refugees coming from the east, passing through Falkenberg on their journey westwards. This vividly reminded me of the Greeks I had seen fleeing from the Germans in 1941 as they advanced south through Greece, harassed all the way by Messerschmitts and Stukas. Now it was the Germans' turn to flee ahead of the Russian army, but I did not see them strafed by the Russian air force. I do not remember ever seeing any Russian planes. It was the same sad, human disaster with all its upheaval and suffering, but at the time we felt they were getting their comeuppance. I felt sorrow at the plight of ordinary innocent people fleeing for their lives, carrying what they could with them, by whatever means of transport they could find: handcarts, wheelbarrows, prams, some had vehicles or horses, and here in Germany, there were also overcrowded refugee trains often with people clinging to the outside, all caught up in the catastrophe.

We put Dr Hamish in the small cubbyhole next to the commandant's room. He was completely on his own, one officer in a camp of ordinary soldiers. I became quite friendly with him. Amongst his valued possessions was a backgammon set; he taught me to play and from then on I played backgammon with him almost every evening, becoming quite proficient. The doctor stayed with us for a while, then some time in early April he was transferred to an Oflag (officers' camp).

As in the previous camp, the most distasteful feature was the latrine bucket for use during the night. In this camp there were, I recall, three of them put about midway along the central corridor just before we were locked in for the night. The three buckets were for about a hundred men and by the morning they were usually full and overflowing. I had to prepare a roster – everyone had to take their turn, including me – to empty them without spilling. A disgusting arrangement but we put up with it and shrugged it off as there was not any alternative.

Now in early 1945 we began to get news of the rapid advances of the American and British Forces from the west and the Russian advances from the east, the Germans being gradually trapped between the approaching armies. At Falkenberg we had no wireless news, so had to rely on other sources. The German newspapers began to admit to losses and talked of strategic withdrawals to new positions and regrouping of their armies ready for new offensives. For sometime now our most reliable source of news came from leaflets dropped by Allied aircraft during their sorties over Germany. We had been picking these up since late 1942. By the middle of 1944 the Allied air forces had complete freedom of the skies over Germany. It was rare to see any Luftwaffe planes. I do recall on one occasion seeing a couple of German aeroplanes flying very low as they went past; they were unusual because they had no propellers and the guards said they were a new experimental plane. Perhaps they were the German prototype jet-propelled planes.

It was, of course, strictly forbidden to collect the news pamphlets dropped by our planes, and anyone, especially German, found in possession of one could be severely punished. The guards were as anxious as we were to read the leaflets as they were beginning to doubt the veracity of their own news media. So we collected them and passed copies on to the guards. These gave us detailed information on the battles on all fronts together with maps and photographs. One which I had until quite recently was issued by SHAEF (Supreme Headquarters Allied Expeditionary Forces) and headed '*Es Geht Zu Ende*' (the end is coming). Sadly someone borrowed and did not return it; however, I still have copies of two others. I remember the euphoria in the German newspapers about the capture of Stalingrad. General Von Paulus was promoted to field marshal and given the highest German military award – the Knight's Cross with diamonds and oak leaves – only to read in one of the leaflets a few days later of his capture by the Russians and his interview on Russian wireless. We got the impression the leaflets from the air were truthful and were eagerly, although clandestinely, read by the civilian population.

Some time, I think in January or February 1945, the Germans sent round a notice to inform us that the camp marks we had received for working could be handed in and would be exchanged and transferred to our own army accounts through the Swiss protecting power. Most of us had accumulated sizeable amounts of this 'Monopoly money', which we considered

Nr. 347, Donnerstag, 29. März 1945

NACHRICHTEN FÜR DIE TRUPPE

Ob. West verliert die Front-Übersicht

Die Lage wird hoffnungslos—Ruhr überflügelt—USA-Panzer stossen in verteidigungslosen Raum

JEDE Hoffnung, den Zusammenbruch im Westen noch irgendwo durch die Errichtung einer festen Verteidigungslinie aufzuhalten, ist jetzt geschwunden. Nach den letzten Meldungen hat im Nordabschnitt jeder geordnete Widerstand aufgehört. Panzerverbände der Alliierten rollen auf breiter Front durch die Norddeutsche Tiefebene auf Münster vor. Im Mittelabschnitt und im Süden gibt es keine zusammenhängende Front mehr und USA-Panzer rasen durch unverteidigtes Gebiet tief nach Bayern und Kurhessen hinein.

Die Durchbruchsoffensive im Norden hat die deutschen Abwehrstellungen im ganzen Raum zwischen dem Ruhrgebiet und der holländischen Grenze überrannt. Hamborn ist gefallen. Weiter nördlich haben überlegene Kräfte der Alliierten die 116. Panzer-Division aus Dorsten geworfen. Alliierte Panzerkolonnen stossen auf breiter Front gegen den Dortmund-Ems-Kanal vor und werden dicht vor Recklinghausen gemeldet.

Gross-Berlin wird durch NSV geräumt

Die ersten Marschblocks von Flüchtlingen, meist Frauen und Kinder, wurden gestern vor den Berliner NSV-Stellen zur neuangeordneten Evakuierung zusammengestellt und zogen dann beladen mit ihren Habseligkeiten los auf den Weg ins Reichsinnere.

Zwei Gründe haben die Behörden veranlasst, jetzt die Evakuierung Gross-Berlins durch die NSV vorzunehmen.

1. Der bevorstehende Grossangriff der Sowjets auf den Raum Berlin.

2. Die Unmöglichkeit, die Millionen Menschen in der Reichshauptstadt weiter mit Lebensmitteln zu versorgen.

Überall dasselbe Bild

Auch aus den Grosstädten des mitteldeutschen Industriegebietes beginnt die Bevölkerung abzuwandern, nachdem sie durch die Zeitungen von der Neuordnung der Lebensmittelverteilung unterrichtet wurden und sehen, dass die Mangelgebiete ihrem Schicksal überlassen werden.

Viele versuchen, dem Beispiel der Hoheitsträgerfamilien zu folgen, die sich bereits nach Schleswig oder Bayern abgesetzt haben, um wie sie verschiedentlich bemerken, nicht in der Steckrübenwüste Mitteldeutschland zu verhungern.

Jabos bahnen einen Weg

Gleichzeitig rollen andere Panzerverbände nach Münster vor. Weiter nördlich sind die Alliierten in Rhade, Borken und Bocholt eingebrochen.

Am deutschen äussersten rechten Flügel kämpfen die zusammengeschmolzenen Verbände der 6. und 8. Fallschirmjäger-Division mit kanadischen Truppen, die in Emmerich eingedrungen sind und gegen die holländische Grenze vorstossen.

Die Verbindung zwischen den einzelnen deutschen Verbänden hat fast überall aufgehört. Wo deutsche Truppen noch in einzelnen Stützpunkten Widerstand leisten, bahnen Tausende von Jabos und raketenfeuernden Jägern den Panzern einen Weg. Flammenwerfer räuchern die Bunker aus.

Auf die deutschen Kampfgräben geht ein vernichtendes Trommelfeuer aus Hunderten von Sturmgeschützen nieder. Betäubt von dem Vernichtungs-Bombardement hissen immer mehr deutsche Einheiten weisse Fahnen auf ihren Stützpunkten und lassen sich gefangen nehmen.

Mitten in der allgemeinen Massenflucht vor dem totalen Vernichtungskrieg im Westen, die jetzt Millionen Menschen mit sich reisst und immer weiter ins Innere des Reichs übergreift, liegen heute als einzige ruhige Inseln das Sauerland und das Gebiet von Oberhessen ostwärts Giessen.

Marschkolonnen, die auf dem Rückzug von den blitzartig vorstossenden Panzerspitzen eingeholt werden, Panzer, Geschütze und Vortrauben werden den Alliierten überlassen. Englische Lufttandetruppen verfolgen die flüchtenden deutschen Truppen in Hunderten von erbeuteten deutschen Lkw.

Über die Kampflage im Mittelabschnitt und im Süden ist jetzt auch im Hauptquartier des Ob.-West jeder genaue Überblick verloren gegangen.

Nach den letzten Meldungen sind amerikanische Panzer in ihrem Vormarsch auf bayerischem Gebiet weit über die Autobahn Würzburg-Fulda vorgestossen. Andere Panzerkeile dringen direkt gegen Würzburg und Fulda.

(Fortsetzung Seite 4)

Alles flieht in die Schutzzonen

Diese beiden ruhigen Inseln sind zwei von den sieben bombensicheren Zufluchtszonen, die laut Informationen eines neutralen Gewährsmannes in Berlin demnächst von General Eisenhower anerkannt werden.

Als erste dieser sieben Zufluchtszonen werden das

Sauerland und Oberhessen durch die blitzartigen Vorstoss der alliierten Panzerspitzen bald überflügelt sein und Hunderttausende von Flüchtlingen, die nur den Todeszonen um Ruhrgebiet, Frankfurt und Mannheim-Ludwigshafen rechtzeitig in diese Zufluchtsgebiete gekommen waren, bleiben jetzt dort.

Neue Flüchtlingstrecks treffen noch immer in letzter Stunde ein, während weiter im Innern des Reichs Hunderttausende bei Tag und Nacht in die übrigen Zufluchtsgebiete ziehen, um dort die letzten Kriegstage sicher zu überleben.

Die sieben bombenfreien Zufluchtszonen sind:

1. Das Sauerland zwischen Kreuzthal, Menden, Scherfede, und Marburg. Dazu das gesamte Gebiet des früheren Fürstentums Waldeck.

2. Der gesamte Landkreis Northeim im Gau Südhannover-Braunschweig.

3. Das gesamte Gebiet des früheren Fürstentums Schwarzburg-Sondershausen.

4. Ganz Oberhessen ostwärts Giessen.

5. Das Grabfeld und die Hassberge in dem Dreieck Meiningen-Coburg-Bad Kissingen.

6. Der gesamte Landkreis Bamberg.

7. Der gesamte Landkreis Ansbach in Bayern.

Was das Reich einbüsste

21 371 000 Bewohner des Reichs sind durch alliierte Besetzung vom übrigen Reich abgetrennt worden.

Jede graue Figur bedeutet 250 000 Mann

1 171 483 Wehrmachtsangehörige haben sich seit Beginn der alliierten Invasion gefangen gegeben. Das sind soviel wie 113 kampfstarke Divisionen.

Nur noch 160 Panzer sind im Westen kampffähig von den 1 180, die zu Beginn der Rundstedt-Offensive verfügbar waren.

17 von den 46 Gaue sind bisher von ihren Gau...

BERLIN

590 KM

375 KM

Gemünden

Donau

In der Zange

as pretty useless and valueless. Most of the men were very suspicious of this offer, feeling there must be a catch in it somewhere and refused to take part in another German swindle. Everyone was issued with a form to complete on which we were asked to fill in our name, regimental number, our unit and home address. Most men threw them away or used them for that other purpose. However, Pete Yeomans, I and a handful of others decided we had nothing to lose as we would be left with a horde of useless camp marks at the end of the war anyway. Even if they were to be convertible then, they would not be worth much and most probably would have to be thrown away. So we decided to have a go. We collected as many camp marks as we could, filled in the form and handed it over to the commandant for onward transmission, never really expecting to hear anything more and forgot all about it. Several months later, quite unexpectedly, a letter filtered down to me from the army paymaster general to inform me my army account had been credited with a sum of round about £100, being the proceeds of the transfer of the camp marks. £100 was a sizeable sum in those days; I presume Pete and the few others who had handed in their camp marks also received their money. I only wish I had collected more marks as there were plenty on offer. The doubters just jettisoned their camp marks at the end of the war. For once we few were right in deciding to trust the German authorities.

By late February 1945 some of the leaflets dropped by the American and British air forces were advising prisoners of war not to escape but stay put in their camps and await liberation. Escaping, they explained, might confuse the advancing units and could lead to unnecessary casualties amongst escapees. We decided to accept the advice.

By March 1945 the Allies had advanced on all fronts and conditions in Germany were becoming chaotic: the transport system was erratic affecting the distribution of our Red Cross parcels, food supplies were disrupted and shortages occurring which particularly affected our guards who were getting very hungry and discontented.

Not far from us was a '*Mädchenlager*', a training camp for Hitler Youth girls. We had seen them marching around and they had naturally aroused some interest amongst the men who would wolf-whistle after them. The Hitler Youth camps were given priority with food supplies. We had spotted at one end of their building complex, fairly isolated from the main buildings, a storeroom for vegetables and had seen sacks of potatoes, carrots, turnips and so on being put in there. Our thoughts went to acquiring some of their vegetables for ourselves and for our half-starved guards. We made a plan to raid the store and discussed it with the guards. They agreed to let us out and back in again, provided they themselves were not involved and compromised. A dark night was fixed and a party of six of us slipped quietly out of the camp and silently made our way to the *Mädchenlager* without being spotted. We found the storeroom unlocked and helped ourselves to as many sacks as we could carry. We got safely back to our camp, the guard let us back in and the spoils were divided with the guards. The commandant knew what was going on and turned a blind eye.

On another occasion, Lofty Pierce, who had a light job in the marshalling yards and kept an eye on what came in and out, reported that he had seen a truck containing sacks of dried peas, lentils and carrots in one of the sidings. By now the German guards were beginning to get desperate for food, so we mentioned to the commandant that there was a source of vegetables waiting to be tapped and suggested another raid. He agreed on the same terms. Four or five of us including Lofty as guide (but not me this time), were duly let out. Lofty led them to the railway truck, which they carefully forced open and took a sack each, then started back. Unfortunately they were spotted by the German railway police who patrolled the marshalling yard at night and who, of course, gave chase to the robbers. Luckily our men were far enough ahead to reach the camp and be let in by the guard. They quickly deposited the sacks in the guard room and slipped into bed.

Shortly afterwards the German railway police started banging loudly on the camp gate, shouting they had seen some British prisoners with sacks stolen from a truck and that they knew they were British because they had seen their uniforms. The guard said he knew nothing about it and would have to fetch the commandant. Out came the commandant demanding to know what was going on and the police repeated their story. The commandant said this was nonsense; the men had earlier been counted and locked in the barrack for the night; the camp gate was locked, so it could not possibly be prisoners from his camp. The police insisted, so the commandant with reluctance agreed to call an *Appell* to check everyone was present and correct. In front of the police the barrack door was unlocked and we were all called out on parade, counted and found to be all present. The railway police were clearly very puzzled but had to accept that the raiders could not possibly have come from our camp. They still insisted the culprits were British prisoners but could not prove they were from our camp and had to leave disconsolate. After they were safely out of the way, the spoils were divided between the guards and ourselves before returning to bed with the mission accomplished.

At the beginning of March we heard from the guards that they had heard a prison camp near Wittenberg had been evacuated in a great hurry and some Red Cross food parcels had been left behind. We were told it had been a convalescent camp – we had no idea such camps existed and I still do not know if that was correct. There was some scepticism about the rumour, but as we were now getting low on food parcels I thought it would be a good idea to go and investigate. I discussed the idea with the commandant who agreed it was worth a try but thought the difficulty would be getting some sort of transport to carry the parcels. He said he would do his best to arrange something and eventually located an old man who had a horse and cart which he was prepared to hire out to us. Pete Yeomans, Blondie Stead, I and a guard set out with the old man and the poor old horse, and made our way slowly towards Wittenberg. This was to be our very last Red Rosette journey. Travel was very slow and we took several hours to reach our destination. The camp was deserted apart from a caretaker guard. Sure enough, there was a store of Red Cross food parcels which turned out to be milk parcels intended for convalescents. So that part of the rumour turned out to be true. We loaded the cart to the brim with parcels; I calculated there were enough for two parcels per man. When we arrived back eventually we were greeted like heroes. However, I was not a hero for long.

The situation in Germany was getting more difficult every day and I felt we might not get any more Red Cross food parcels through Stalag IVD. I was convinced we should ration and eke out the parcels we now had. There was a possibility we might have to evacuate the camp away from the advancing Russians and would need to take food with us on any forced march. I decided to issue one parcel to each man and keep the second one in reserve for the expected emergency. By now we had run out of our usual parcels and these were the only ones we had. Pete Yeomans and my muckers agreed with me but when I announced it with my reasons to the men, there were murmurings of discontent. I called a meeting of the whole camp and explained why I believed we should ration our supplies. However, the mood was against me, surprisingly led by Blondie Stead. The men shouted these were their parcels and they wanted both parcels at once.

I tried to reason but was shouted down on the grounds I had no right to keep their parcels. This was a bit rich: if it had not been for me, there would not have been any at all! I took a vote of confidence and was heavily defeated. I immediately resigned as man of confidence and Blondie Stead was elected in my place. Blondie immediately issued all the parcels. There were no more left in store and we never received any more. This was a mistake as most of the men set about consuming their parcels without any concern for the morrow. The more prudent, including my muckers, saved most of the tins of food and they came in very useful sooner than we thought. When the time of shortages came, those who had eaten all theirs began to pester the rest of us to help them out.

As I was no longer camp leader, I was required to go out and join the working parties. At this late stage of the war the nature of the work had changed. Because of the bombing which was now mainly aimed at disrupting the railway network, the German priority was to keep the railways running. There was much repair work to be done daily. We had to fill in bomb craters. One of the main centres of rail communications was at Leipzig. The station there was huge with, we were informed, the largest number of platforms of any station in Europe. Our working parties were sent out by train each day to Leipzig to fill in bomb craters, in and around the station. We travelled in normal passenger coaches, not in the usual horse/cattle trucks. We would spend the whole day working there and were given a bowl of soup at midday. This soup was in addition to the food issued at our camp. During this time we saw a lot of forced labour working on the repair of railway lines: emaciated men in their blue-striped prison clothes, presumably from nearby concentration camps; they were very thin and gaunt and the majority appeared to be Jews. Occasionally we were able to pass them a little food but had to be very careful, because if their guards saw us they would chase us off and beat the poor prisoners for accepting food. We understood from our own guards that the guards of these political prisoners were Romanians and were a brutal lot, forever shouting at and hitting the prisoners. It was very upsetting for us to watch.

I now understand this type of work was contrary to the provisions of the Geneva Convention because we were being deliberately exposed to the dangers of air raids. At the time we thought little about our rights and were ignorant of these niceties and even if we had known, there was little we could have done about it.

As usual we worked in our normal British POW fashion, spending most of our time leaning on the shovels and peering into the bomb crater. One morning as we were doing this, the fore-alarm sounded followed very shortly after by the full alarm. Schmidt, our guard, immediately ordered us to get away from the station as quickly and as far as possible. The Americans were making many daylight bombing raids on railway stations and their approaches: Leipzig was a prime target. The ever-thoughtful Schmidt added we were not to wait for him as his lameness prevented him from keeping up with us. Some quickly threw their shovels into the crater and covered them completely with some soil. After the 'all-clear', when the men returned they complained to the ganger that during the raid someone had stolen the shovels, so there was another break from work for an hour or so while the Germans went off to find some more.

We soon left Schmidt far behind and all scattered in different directions down the side streets with no thought of trying to keep altogether. I was with Charlie Whitaker, Steve Donaghue and Chalky White.

As we made our way down one of the side streets we saw a column of British prisoners with a couple of guards coming towards us. They said they were returning to their camp in a nearby school building after a shift at a factory where they worked and invited us to visit. On the spur of the moment we agreed and joined on at the end of the column. The brick-built former school was right in the city centre in a very vulnerable position. We marched into the camp with the column; no one counted the returning shift.

We found a few men we knew who brewed up some tea and we talked about our respective camps, the progress of the war and so on. After a while we realised we ought to be getting back to Leipzig station to rejoin our own working party before they went back to Falkenberg. Off we went to the camp gate and told the guard we needed to return to our working party at the station. He looked at us in disbelief and would not let us out of the gate. We began to panic a little, not knowing what to do, when a few minutes later another working party came out and lined up ready to go out to work on their shift. After they had been counted and the gate opened, we quietly tagged on behind and with some relief got out of the camp. We asked the men to distract their two guards to give us an opportunity to slip away, and so eventually made our way back to the station.

One day in 1999 I was waiting for a train at Bexhill Station and sat down next to a man of about my age. We started a conversation and, in due course, he mentioned that he had been a POW. He had been captured by the Italians in the Western Desert, had been put on a ship to Italy which had been torpedoed by the Royal Navy and sunk. He had managed to get off and spent some hours in the water before been picked up by another Italian ship and taken to a POW camp in Italy, remaining there until the Italians had surrendered. He had been released only to be recaptured by the Germans and sent, believe it or not, to a small camp in Leipzig. I told him about my experience and of visiting a small camp in Leipzig, but just then my train came and we parted. Unfortunately I did not ask for his name and address which was rather remiss of me. I still wonder if he had been in the camp we had inadvertently visited.

We eventually got back to our bomb crater some two hours after the air raid was over and the 'all-clear' had been sounded; we had been away much longer than anyone else. The foreman was very angry and deprived us of our watery midday soup as punishment.

The time limped into April. On our return to camp in the evenings, our routine was first to prepare our evening meal, partly with the food supplied from the central cookhouse and partly from our own food parcels. One evening in the midst of getting our meal the full alarm sounded, so we dropped everything and rushed out to the shelters. Half a dozen American fighter-bombers flew over, strafing the marshalling yards and dropping a few light bombs. After they had gone and we were back in the barracks, I thought about the raid and said to Blondie that if it was following the usual pattern, then it had been a softening-up raid and we should expect a big raid the next morning. I thought it would be wise to be away from the camp at the crack of dawn. He agreed and we went to the commandant to explain how we read the situation. His immediate reaction was that he could not possibly allow us to leave the camp and go out to the woods, which were about a mile from the camp. It was his duty to ensure we all went to work in the morning and certainly the railway authorities would not permit us to stay away from work. Furthermore, if he did agree, he would probably be in big trouble.

We explained how we felt things had changed and that this was, in effect, a matter of life and death. If he and his guards wished to live then they would be well advised to get away from the camp at dawn the next morning. He, I am sure, knew the war was coming to an end soon with the defeat of his country. After we had argued our case for some considerable time he finally, somewhat reluctantly and with some apprehension, agreed we would get up at crack of dawn and move away from the camp. The men were then informed of the decision and told to get together all their remaining food and anything else they needed and were able to carry, ready to leave at daybreak next morning.

Just before dawn – it must have been 18 or 19 April 1945 – we got up, washed and shaved, had a bite of food and were called out on parade bringing with us all the things we had decided to take with us. We were counted and found all present and correct. Now accompanied by the commandant and all the guards we marched out of camp making our way to the woods about a mile away on the hills near the town. On arrival there, we selected a spot on high ground which gave us a view over the railway marshalling yards and could see our barrack. We had not long settled when the fore-alarm sounded and a few minutes later the full alarm.

We heard the drone of the approaching aircraft, getting louder as they came into view: a whole formation of American Flying Fortesses. They came straight towards the Falkenberg marshalling yards and immediately dropped their bomb loads on the target. There were a series of loud explosions raising dust clouds high in the air, and having completed their mission, the planes turned and started their homeward flight. There had been no sign of any anti-aircraft fire at them nor of any German fighters. They had had complete freedom of the sky. After the 'all-clear' had sounded and the dust had settled, some of us made our way back to the camp to see what damage had been done. The whole marshalling yard had been wrecked. Our barrack was completely ruined, having received one or two direct hits – all that was left was just a shell. We all thanked God we had escaped. Had we been in the barrack I doubt anyone would have survived. The commandant said he was very thankful he had listened to us. We rummaged around the ruins for anything we could salvage but there was not very much. I lost all my architectural books but found a cricket ball. I left it there as I did not think we would be playing again!

16

Into the Woods and on to Freedom

We returned to our patch in the woods: we had no camp, no home. The guards located a large barn and the commandant said we would use this as a temporary home until he was given some orders from district headquarters in Torgau as to what he should do. The barn proved to be our final prison camp in Germany. We discovered there were other German soldiers sheltering in the woods and quite a number of civilian refugees.

We had not been the only people rummaging through the debris of our camp. Amongst them was a Russian POW or forced labourer; how he managed to get there, I have no idea. He had found a few small items which were of no value to us, so we told him he could have them.

Later on, it seems, he was arrested for looting and taken up into the woods and handed over to a group of German officers who tried to interrogate him. They told him he had been caught looting for which the punishment was death: he would be taken away and shot immediately. This took place just outside 'our' barn and as we were standing nearby we heard what was going on. We decided to intervene and told the German officers that he had not been looting because we had given him the goods they had found in his possession. The senior officer in the group dismissed our protests and ordered him to be taken away and shot. We then said to him that we had made a note of his and the other officers' ranks and their regiments, from the insignia they were wearing. We warned him that the war was almost over and if he persisted in having an innocent man shot, he and his fellow officers would be reported to the Allied Command, sought out and tried as war criminals for murder. This was somewhat audacious of us, but it worked and they released the man. The Russian boy's life was saved, but for how long? After the war I learned how brutally the Russians treated any of their soldiers who had been prisoners of the Germans.

The weather in late April that year was good and warm so most of us slept outside. We awaited further developments. Rumours were rife that the Russians were rapidly closing in from the north-east and the Americans were approaching the River Elbe from the west. There were reports of shell fire being heard nearby; certainly we heard the distant rumble of artillery and daily we saw American planes flying over towards their targets to the east.

In the woods we found slit trenches that had been dug for shelter during air raids. We discovered they had been dug by German refugees from the Rhineland. They had been forced to leave their homeland due to the destruction of their towns and homes and had made their way eastwards to this part of Saxony to get away from the very heavy bombing of the Rhineland towns and cities. They had eventually made their way to south-east Saxony but were appalled at the attitude of the local people there who, they said, were completely indifferent to the refugees, refusing them shelter or help. We were surprised at their bitterness towards the local people and yet were quite friendly towards us, their enemies.

During one air-raid alarm, I found myself in a slit trench next to a German girl of about my own age and we got into conversation. This time I managed to converse reasonably well in German! She said she was from Düsseldorf and was training to be a dentist. She was a very pleasant girl, the first of my own age I had been close to for four years, and I suppose I was attracted to her. She said she felt the cold, so I gallantly gave her a tartan scarf I had received from home in a personal parcel. She was very grateful and thanked me. But our very brief friendship soon ended when the 'all-clear' was sounded and we went our separate ways. I have wondered, as one does, whether she survived the war and succeeded in becoming a dentist. The odds were stacked against these refugees because they were on the wrong side of the River Elbe, an area soon to be overrun by the Russians.

By now everywhere was chaotic; there was no more work for us as the marshalling yards were in a shambles and many of the civilians were fleeing.

We were all seriously short of food, and the refugees were even worse off than we were. Some of the our men had been wandering around to see what was going down at the railway yard and one of them came back and reported that there was a goods train which had recently arrived in the damaged marshalling yard and was now stranded in a siding. He thought it was carrying food supplies, probably for the Nazi hierarchy.

However, the problem was how to get a raiding party near enough to the train without being spotted by someone en route. There were some German soldiers, railway police and civilians around, so unattached groups of POWs would probably be stopped. After discussing the matter, we talked to the guards and it was decided our best chance was to have two guards escort the raiding party to within a hundred yards or so of the target, so it would look as if we were an official work party. This would, we hoped, ensure a safe journey to this point. The guards could disappear until the raid was over and later escort the raiders with their loot back to our position in the woods. When this plan was put to the commandant, he was very sceptical and said under no circumstances could he allow his guards to participate in a raid on a German train. We assured him the guards would escort us only and not take part in the raid on the train. He finally agreed.

I forget who was in the raiding party, but strong men were chosen who could carry plenty of loot so I was not one of them. As it turned out, everything went well and the men were not challenged or spotted. They brought back a variety of goods, the most important items for us were large bucket-sized tins of sweetened condensed milk, known as 'conny-onny', and crates of fresh eggs. The condensed milk was South African, so it probably had been captured in North Africa or Italy. Amongst the other goodies were bars of chocolate, packets of coffee, biscuits, cigars and fur coats which we gave to the female refugees as a spontaneous gesture of goodwill. The date of the raid, 21 April, seemed most appropriate as it happened to be Hitler's birthday, and his last.

We decided to have a bit of a party with the goodies the boys had acquired and invited the German refugees. They really enjoyed themselves and declared it to be the most enjoyable Hitler birthday they had celebrated and this thanks to the British POWs. I suppose, strictly speaking, this could be classed as fraternising with the enemy, but at the time we just felt we were all homeless refugees together. It was a spontaneous gathering of human beings in distressed circumstances sharing the fruits of our raid, allowing us to play at being Robin Hoods.

Despite the short-term euphoria over the train robbery and the celebration after, we were getting increasingly concerned with our situation. We were stuck in the woods listening to the faint rumble of artillery fire and had no doubt the Russians could only be a few days away. A day or so before we had seen Hungarian soldiers wearing khaki uniforms, who were fighting for the Germans, marching through Falkenberg. We were rather worried that if the Russians came across us in the woods they could well mistake us for Hungarian troops with dire consequences for us. The commandant did not seem to know what to do, so we told him it was high time we moved away from the Falkenberg area.

We told him it was becoming clearer every day that the war was nearly over and he and the guards would be taken as prisoners of war. We said they were lucky, unlike us, in having a choice of captors: Americans or Russians. We added under our breath, 'We only had you bastards.' Another officer from the district administration happened to be with us. The two considered what we said but they would not move without orders from Torgau; typical of German hierarchy, always afraid of the rank above. We asked them when they had last heard from Torgau, and they replied it had been about ten days previously. We said it seemed to us very unlikely that they would ever get any more orders because all means of communication were in such a shambles and clearly getting worse every day.

It took a lot of effort on our part to persuade them that we should move. We asked them their preference – Russians or Americans – knowing they would choose west and the Americans. It was decided we would move together as a unit of POWs accompanied by their commandant and guards. They could truthfully say to any German army units encountered on the way that they were evacuating a group of British prisoners whose camp had been bombed to a new location further west. This we considered a safeguard for us: it was better to have a military escort than to be on our own as escaped prisoners.

We started our preparations for the journey by discarding anything which was not absolutely necessary, although we did keep our few small personal items such as photographs, letters and so on. The most important thing was food: many of us had kept tins of food, bars of chocolate and dried fruit, and of course tea, for such an emergency. I packed my tinned food supplies in my small army side-pack. We also took our shaving and washing gear including, I remember, the tubes of German gritty toothpaste

(I do not recall having recently received any supplies of 'real' toothpaste from home). We had a good supply of fresh eggs, purloined from the German train, but difficult to carry uncooked. Using the empty condensed milk containers, we hard-boiled them. I reckoned I could eke out my store for about two weeks and hoped this would be long enough. For the first week our staple item was the eggs, several a day.

We encountered streams of refugees from the east (never from the west), mostly Germans but there were other nationalities such as Poles and Czechs. They trudged along the roads and tracks in almost continuous columns, carrying whatever they could, using whatever means of transport they could get hold of and manage. It was a very pathetic and moving sight.

On the one hand, this was just retribution for all the suffering the Germans and their allies had caused to the whole of Europe through Hitler and his glorious Third Reich (or as our men called it, the 'Turd Reich'). On the other hand, it was pure pathos, the tragedy of ordinary people caught up in events over which they had no control and never had had any possibility of controlling once they had elected the Nazis to power, hoping they would revive the German economy, create employment and improve their lives: it had all gone terribly wrong for them. Unfortunately since the end of the Second World War we have seen many similar refugee situations in many parts of Africa, Central America, Afghanistan and the Balkans. We now see these streams of refugees on our television screens and I think have become inured to the pictures. Unless one has actually experienced it, it is hard to grasp the utter degradation which can happen to our fellow human beings. I remember the similar streams of refugees in northern Greece as they fled southwards from the advancing German armies in early 1941. In retrospect I have a greater degree of sympathy for the poor Greeks.

The irony of the conquest of Russian territory was that at the beginning of the war the Germans and Russians had been allies, carving up Poland between them. The Germans had only made this alliance to protect their backs whilst they attacked Western Europe. Now the tables were turned and they were reaping the rewards of their blatant aggression. On this Eastern Front they were facing advancing Red Armies, red with blood, more ruthless, more brutal and much less disciplined than their own armies; they were absolutely panic-stricken, scared of what would happen to them if the red hordes caught them.

One realises, as always, there were plenty ordinary, decent people who had never endorsed the Nazis, but the vast majority of the Germans had gone along with them. Now the tide had completely turned and they were absolutely terrified, having heard stories of Russian atrocities from soldiers coming back from the Eastern Front.

The next morning, as soon as everyone was ready, we set off west, expecting in due course to reach the River Elbe. The commandant, sensibly, decided we should avoid main roads which were clogged with refugees and army vehicles and stick to minor roads and tracks through the woods, which abounded in this part of Saxony. We also avoided as far as possible any contact with German army units: in fact we saw hardly any sign of the German forces. Somehow along the way we had acquired one or two handcarts on which we were able to put some of our baggage to avoid carrying it. We slept in the open as we were, without undressing, and made what ablutions we could in the mornings before brewing some tea, having a bite to eat and resuming our trek.

One morning we had not gone very far when there was a lot of moaning from Joe Potter (of dried peas fame) who said his feet were hurting so much he could not go any further; we could not stop, so we decided he would have to be given a ride on one of the handcarts. Joe sat up there on the cart still moaning about his sore feet and we moved on. Then one of the men pushing the cart looked at Joe's feet. In his usual early morning panic, Joe had put his boots on the wrong feet: no wonder his feet hurt! He was made to change them round. This solved the problem and he was told, in no uncertain terms, to continue on foot like the rest of us.

As we made our way through the woods, from time to time we came across groups of German civilians including some young women who usually passed the time of the day and went on their way. However, we noticed that Blondie Stead was often missing and was not available when the commandant and guards wished to communicate with him to give us instructions. Blondie was off into the woods chasing girls, no doubt in exchange for a bar of chocolate or a packet of cigarettes. The men were getting exasperated with Blondie's antics and asked if I would take over again as man of confidence, or more realistically as leader of the group. The commandant had no hesitation in agreeing, so I once again took over as liaison with the commandant and guards, not that there was really very much to do. Thus I ended up my POW days as the leader of the men from our camp.

We reached the Elbe in about three days. Our challenge – the most difficult of the march to freedom – now was to cross it and it would involve a bit of collaboration with the enemy. Most of the bridges over the Elbe had been destroyed by Allied bombing. We moved along the bank and after some miles eventually arrived at a pontoon bridge which had been erected by German army engineers.

There was considerable confusion at the bridge. There were queues of military vehicles, lorries, tanks and men on either side of the bridge waiting to cross. It seemed as if the Germans were retreating in both directions: those on our east bank were fleeing the Russians and those on the west bank were trying to evade the advancing American forces. The two German groups could not agree as to which direction should have priority in crossing. The commandant went down to the officer on guard on our side of the river to make arrangements for us to cross. He was given an immediate rebuff: no way would any prisoners of war be allowed to use the bridge to cross the river; it was solely for the use of the German forces.

We waited; the chaos continued unabated; we looked along the river but there was no indication of anywhere else to cross and we gathered there were no other bridges in this area. We were becoming very despondent, wondering if we would ever be able to get over the river before the Russians arrived which we did not fancy at all. There was no way we could swim across: the currents were much too strong, and it was not long since three of our colleagues had drowned in this treacherous river.

Then we noticed a lot of commotion on the bridge. A German army vehicle carrying a heavy anti-aircraft gun going from east to west had broken down and was blocking the bridge. There was a complete impasse, no movement at all across the bridge in either direction.

We did some quick thinking. We decided to volunteer to push the vehicle across the bridge manually for them, not as a gesture to their war effort but just as a means to get over the Elbe. It was with some reluctance that the officer in charge of the bridge agreed to the offer. Of course, it took all of us to move the vehicle right across as the river was very wide at this point, but we eventually pushed it over to the western bank and we all got across safely. We were unconcerned about this small act of collaboration: the vehicle we had pushed was still broken down and useless. Having all arrived safely on the west bank, we formed up and resumed our weary march westwards, together with the commandant and the guards, including our friend Schmidt.

A day or so afterwards in the evening we met up with another group of British prisoners and exchanged news. We settled down for the night near the other group on a hillside with light tree cover. We made our evening meal which included, as usual, some hard-boiled eggs, then settled down to go to sleep under the stars, using our greatcoats for blankets and improvising pillows. I used my small side-pack containing my food supply as a pillow; I felt the pack would be safe under my head. I was very tired after the day's walking and soon slept soundly, unusual for me because I am normally a very light sleeper. When I woke up in the early morning I was horrified and very distressed to discover my pack of food had been stolen from under my head. I noticed that the other group of British prisoners had already left by this time. Whether it was one of this other group who was the thief or possibly one of the refugees who were also around, I shall never know, but I am certain it was not one of our own men – it would have been hard to hide the evidence.

Sometime in the early morning on the same day we heard some sporadic rifle fire nearby, and I recall seeing one poor refugee or escapee staggering by with half his face shot off and then collapsing. There was nothing we could do for him. Luckily for me I did not go short of food as my muckers, Charlie and co., always helped out. However, there were problems with some of the men who had earlier demanded the issue of all the food parcels and had eaten all their supplies before the camp was bombed and now expected the prudent ones to share their food with them and were unpleasant if refused.

The other group of British prisoners who were on their own had been critical of us for having German guards with whom we were on good terms, almost, they said, as if we were comrades. We had explained our strategy. Indeed our guards several times when challenged had claimed to be moving us to a new location. Escaping prisoners on their own were still liable to be shot at by any German soldiers they encountered and German soldiers were rather trigger happy at this stage of the war. Our commandant, the other district officer and the guards now knew very well they would be taken prisoner by the Americans, so it was in their own interests to be handed over to them as, in effect, our prisoners.

We continued westwards; the other group had already completely disappeared. From this point onwards we rarely encountered anyone; there were no further incidents with other escaping prisoners, refugees or German soldiers.

Some days later we reached another river and looked for a place to cross when we saw, in the distance, an iron railway bridge. When we reached it, we saw that it had been bombed and was in a tangled mess. However, it still spanned the river and it was possible for us to scramble across to the other side through the wreckage.

We were about halfway across when we heard a shout to halt and identify ourselves in an American accent. It was an American soldier, wanting to know what the hell we were doing wandering about in the front line. When he was satisfied we were genuine British prisoners of war, he allowed us to cross the tangled bridge saying, 'Get the hell out of here, this is dangerous, it is the front line and not safe for you.' This struck us as very amusing as for several days we had been moving across his so-called front line and had not encountered any sign of fighting and did not feel we were in any more danger than usual. Nevertheless, we were very pleased to be in contact at last with the Americans, even if it was in the form of one lonely, fidgety soldier guarding a useless, bombed railway bridge.

We felt so close to the end. We picked our way through the tangled ironwork of the bridge to the other side and made our way into a town square. There we met more American soldiers, who told us we were in Wurzen, on the River Mulde, a tributary of the Elbe. It appears that we had done a considerable detour from Falkenberg to reach this town. As we made our way into the town square we noticed a whole crowd of rather dejected German soldiers who were now prisoners of war. They were being guarded by American soldiers and had been disarmed; all their rifles and side-arms lay in a large untidy heap in the middle of the square. We approached the American officer who seemed to be in control and explained to him that we were British ex-POWs who had made our way to freedom bringing our camp commandant and guards with us. I handed over the commandant, the other German officer and the guards to the American officer informing him we had been treated correctly according to the Geneva Convention by these Germans and suggested they deserved to be treated reasonably well now it was their turn to be POWs. In particular I commended Corporal Schmidt who had always gone out of his way to be kind and helpful; he was, as I have said, a 'good' German. That was the last we saw of them. I hope they survived the war and settled down in their own homes after their spell as POWs.

The American officer reiterated that Wurzen was too dangerous and that he was arranging for trucks to collect us as soon as possible and take us to a safe place behind the lines. Some trucks arrived shortly afterwards and some of the men began to climb on board but Charlie Whitaker, Steve Donaghue, Chalky White, Harry Layden, Pete Yeomans, Fred Howlett and myself had other ideas: we felt we should celebrate our freedom.

We could see no sign of any fighting or danger and instead of getting on a truck, we wandered off down the street until we located a German *bierhaus*. We went in and told the landlord we were British prisoners who had just gained our freedom and so we intended to celebrate and further-more all the drinks would be on the house. He did not really have any alternative but to comply which he did without any fuss. We stayed there for two or three hours drinking the dark brown sweetish *Malzbier* and enjoying our newly won freedom, toasting each other, our country and the Yanks, all at the innkeeper's expense. Having drunk to our freedom we left the *bierhaus* and went off to find the Americans who soon produced a truck and off we went.

I must say the Americans were not particularly friendly, clearly consider-ing us a bit of a nuisance interfering with their fighting – although we had yet to see them do any fighting. Maybe we were naïve expecting them to welcome us with open arms when we were disrupting their job of work. Our war was over, but they still had a job of work to do. Their casualness annoyed us somewhat and, we were glad to move on and no doubt they were pleased to be rid of us.

Incidentally, it was just about this time that the American and Russian ground forces met up for the first time at Torgau. I have often wondered what happened to RSM Parslow and his staff. I would think he also was liberated by the Americans, as the town was on the west side of the Elbe. Not so Stalag IVB at Mühlberg which was, I later learned, liberated first by Cossacks on horseback and later by Russian officers. It was said to have been chaos. The Russians did not supply any food, the ex-prisoners having to scour the surrounding countryside which had already been stripped almost bare by marauding groups of undisciplined Russian soldiers. Eventually I believe that the British POWs were marched to Riesa and handed over to the Americans from whence they were taken to Halle before repatriation. Some of this is recounted in *Jenny's War* by Jack Stoneley.

We were taken to a small town called Naumburg on the river Saale. It was, and no doubt still is, a delightful place, with a large central market square surrounded by charming four- or five-storeyed buildings with mansard roofs, an imposing *Rathaus* (town hall) and a magnificent baroque cathedral. Like so many small German towns, it was an example of the very best in town planning. Without any doubt, the Germans excelled in building the most delightful town squares on a human scale, something so lacking in most post-war development. There was no sign of bomb damage. The town was probably of no great strategic importance and had no doubt been overrun without opposition by the rapid advance of the American forces.

Our arrival was unexpected and we were taken to hastily organised quarters. We were housed in what appeared to be a disused warehouse. There we slept on the floor, as usual using our greatcoats for blankets. There must have been some organisation because on a letter home my address is given as block 18 room 67 or perhaps it was ironic, because as far as I remember,

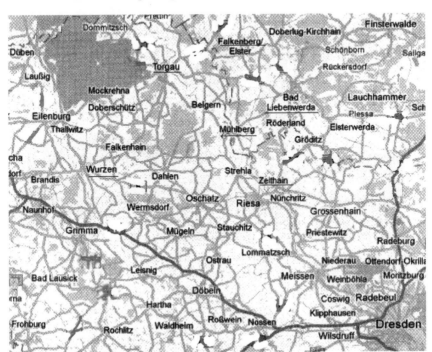

Views of Naumburg-Saale, showing the marketplace and cathedral.

our building was just one independent warehouse, but it was good to be able to communicate with home.

We were taken over to the American army mess for our meals where we were segregated from the American soldiers, quite understandably. We saw them eating their meals of steaks and other meats with fresh vegetables, and a variety of puddings all of which they had together on tray-like plates. It made our mouths water, but we soon found out there was none for us. We were handed packets of K-rations, the field rations used where there were no cooking facilities. We felt as if we were being treated as second-class people or refugees and felt hard done by; it certainly was not the welcome we had expected. Looking back, one realises we were an unexpected burden on these army units near the front line. Their priority was to fight a war and their fresh food catering was calculated for their numbers and probably much of it brought from America and not obtainable locally, therefore the only sustenance they could offer us was in the form of dry rations. On the other hand, they must have known of the POW camps dotted around Germany and should have had some contingency plans to deal with any released prisoners they encountered, which should have included feeding them – maybe the planning was not as thorough as we thought it would be.

There was quite a lot of resentment amongst the ex-POWS about our reception and treatment by the Americans. Despite the K-rations, we were still rather hungry and decided to scout around to find some extra food to fill our empty bellies. Someone discovered a warehouse which was said to be a food store. We decided to raid it and help ourselves to anything available inside. As we approached it, the American military police warned us off and said if we tried to enter the warehouse they would open fire on us for looting. We ignored them and went up to the doors and started to open them, at which the military police fired some shots into the air. We called their bluff and opened the doors. All we found inside were sacks of sugar and rice. The Yanks did not interfere, they just melted away.

We took the 'acquired' goods back to our warehouse where we were able to cook the rice and have it with plenty of sugar and milk. We had obtained some fresh milk, by barter with chocolate and cigarettes, from the local dairy shop. The word was that one could get 'the services' of a German girl for a tin of bully beef, a tin of condensed milk, a packet of cigarettes or a couple of candy bars. I had no interest in such transactions. We now had so much sugar that I remember one man saying, 'Would you like some rice on your sugar?'.

The Americans did supply us with cigarettes, either Camels or Lucky Strike, quite a different taste from our Virginia cigarettes. They also supplied us with their ubiquitous Hershey bars. As the days passed, the Americans became more organised, the food they supplied improved considerably and by the time we left Naumburg it was excellent.

By this time, there were around 3,000 British ex-POWs at Naumburg awaiting repatriation. Amongst them I met up with quite a number I had known in earlier camps. It was good to see they had survived the ordeal and we were able to exchange stories about work and life in the camps.

We were able to write letters home but were not provided with any stationery. I wrote mine on sheets torn out of a notebook which I was able to 'buy' from a local stationery shop. I wrote to my mother and to Stella and still have two of the letters written to Stella, the first written very faintly in pencil, dated Sunday evening 29 April, the day we arrived in Naumburg. The other was in ink (so I must have acquired a pen) dated Wednesday 2 May. I wrote about the number of us awaiting repatriation; also that the Americans were claiming to be repatriating 8,000 French ex-prisoners by air each day.

During the first week at Naumburg we were permitted to go out around the town. We found a photographer and decided to have our photographs taken. I still have two of them: one of myself and the other of a group with Harry Layden, Fred Howlett and myself.

For some unknown reason I am wearing spectacles in one but not in the other. Harry and I are shown wearing collars and ties, recording for posterity my prowess at tailoring. I also had a red and blue flash on my sleeve to represent the Royal Engineers, all quite irregular but we looked smart. I cannot recall there was any reaction to our collars and ties by the reception staff when we landed in England. I have a feeling such things were just overlooked.

From time to time we were told we would soon be moving and after the first week were confined to the camp to ensure we were ready to move at a moment's notice. We did feel it somewhat hard to be penned up again after four years of captivity, but no doubt it was sensible to keep us together. In my letters to Stella I noted we were short of books and games to help pass the time. I wrote that the food was now good but did not include bread, butter, tea and milk and that there was just coffee to drink. Although the letters were written on 29 April and 2 May, the American army postal service stamp is 10 May for both of them.

One of our main concerns was clothing, especially underwear, as many of us had lost our changes of underwear in the bombing of our camp and had nothing to change into. Had we moved on quickly it would not have mattered, but hanging around for a week or two it became a rather smelly problem. If we took them off to wash them, then we had to wait for them to dry which took some time. If we were suddenly called it would have been, to say the least, a little awkward. The weather, as I mentioned in my letters home, was unseasonably dull, cloudy and wet. During our years in Germany, May had been a lovely month with plenty of warm sunshine; luckily it had been fine during our journey from Falkenberg to Wurzen.

By this time, the war in Europe had ended, but we heard little about the cessation of hostilities and had no idea there had been VE celebrations in London and all over Britain – an event we all missed out on.

The weather was, we were told, partly responsible for the delay in our repatriation. Eventually we were asked to get ready to move and were taken by truck to an airport at Merseburg, a town to the west of Leipzig, and from there flown to Reims in France by the American air force on Saturday 12 May. It was the first time I had ever been in an aeroplane, a Dakota I think; I remember enjoying the experience. We were taken to a transit

Harry Layden, Fred Howlett and myself.

Lance Corporal Sydney Litherland, alias Lord Junak.

camp to await a plane to take us home. We were allowed out into Reims and so I was able to visit the Cathedral of Notre Dame, one of the great Gothic cathedrals that I had studied for my examinations on the history of architecture, so it was a great pleasure to see it in all its glory. The American air force personnel at Reims were very friendly, treating and feeding us very well indeed. On the third day we were taken to the aerodrome where RAF planes were waiting to take us back to England. We queued up and were counted into groups and assigned to the planes which were to take us home.

17

Back to England and Demobilisation

We climbed into the plane – a Lancaster bomber – in an orderly fashion. They packed in as many as safety would allow. I was directed to sit on the floor in the nose of the plane; I was told this was the bomb aimer's position. I was very lucky as I had a clear view through the transparent nose of the plane of the way ahead. This was my second flight and a most important one. It was a most comfortable flight. We were all very excited, especially when we saw and then passed over the white cliffs of Dover. I had never seen them before but they were quite unmistakable. We landed at an RAF aerodrome at Tring in Hertfordshire where we got off the plane to a great reception from the RAF, WRAF and, I think, the WVS. We were directed into the dining room and given tea, sandwiches and cakes and generally fêted.

This was 15 May 1945. I had left England on 12 September 1940: I had been away a long time.

It was not long before we were handed over to the 'care' of the army and taken away to a reception camp. I immediately wrote to Stella to let her know I was back in England. My letter to her that day is headed Amesbury, Hertfordshire, which is clearly wrong. I am pretty certain the journey from the aerodrome was not as far as Amesbury, which is in Wiltshire; I rather suspect the camp was probably at Amersham.

Now we came smartly back to reality with a bang. Sergeants and corporals ordered us around with all the red tape and bullshit of the regular army. Of course there had to be organisation to sort us out. Our details were taken down: army unit, service number, rank and so on. Some of us, including me, still had their army service and pay books, and that smoothed the process. Then we all had the usual cursory medical checks. I was again graded A1 which I thought very satisfactory considering what we had been through. We were issued with new uniforms, battledress and other clothing and equipment. Our POW clothes were taken away and I suppose were destroyed – the end to our wearing collars and ties, what a pity!

The food we were given, although adequate, was very inferior to that of the Americans, especially compared to that we had been given at Reims. I soon came to realise that England was suffering from severe food shortages and that there was strict rationing. This came as somewhat of a surprise because rationing was only just beginning when I had left England in 1940 and had, at that time, made little impact. Rationing was to last until sometime after Stella and I had departed for Southern Rhodesia in 1949.

We were given some pay and issued with railway warrants to our home town and given two weeks' leave. We were told we would be informed before the end of our leave where we would then have to report. It was here I took leave of my muckers and other friends from the POW camps. I had and still have many of their addresses but lost touch with them, except for a few years with Lindsay Nicholls in New Zealand and Mr Barker, the YMCA man.

One of the first letters I wrote on arrival back in England was to the chairman of the British Red Cross to thank him and all the Red Cross staff for all their help during my years in captivity; I felt this was something I had to do. I received a nice letter of acknowledgement from Major-General Sir Richard Howard-Vyse, which I still have.

I had written to Stella to say I intended to go straight to Longbridge Deverill near Warminster, where she was still, I thought, working in the land army. However, the rail ticket I was issued was to Burton-on-Trent – my official home address – so I wrote to ask her to join me there. I then learned she had left the land army because of illness and returned to her home in Salisbury. In due course I caught my train to Burton and on to Berry Brow in Efflinch Lane, Barton-under-Needwood. I think it was my brother Dick who collected me at Burton station and so I arrived home on 17 May 1945.

With two exceptions the whole family was there to welcome me home. The two missing were brother Charles, who was still in the forces and somewhere in Mesopotamia in the RAF, and Mary, who was now married and living in Reading. Charles, I heard, was shortly to return to England.

I was soon brought up to date with news of my school friends, learning that my closest friend Maurice Jackson, serving in the RAF, had been shot down and killed over France (his mother, later, sent me a photograph which I have still of his grave in France). Another good friend, Norman Carfoot, had also been killed serving as a pilot in the RAF. I felt a sense of guilt that they had gone whilst I, as it were, was sitting out the war safely in a prison camp. I also learned my grandfather Litherland had died. Aunt Olive said he had prayed he would be spared to see my safe return, but sadly he had died just a few months earlier. I learned that my granny Clark had also died at the ripe old age of ninety-nine.

Although I was pleased to be home I was overwhelmed by all the fuss. I just wanted to be quiet for a while and adjust to the new reality of freedom. I was told a dance had been arranged at Barton Village Hall to welcome me home but I did not want to go. The family could not understand my attitude and felt that I was not appreciative of all their efforts to welcome me back. Maybe much of my attitude was due to my eagerness to be with Stella who had been such a strength to me with all her regular, loving letters to the camps. Zilpah, our maid/housekeeper seemed particularly resentful of me. She was, to me, a strange woman, who had been with the family since I was about six and was well entrenched in running the household and very protective of my youngest sister Ruth. Aunt Olive had said she believed she had had an affair with my father, although I found that hard to believe. She certainly had one with George Gilbey our chauffeur/gardener, as I had caught them at it in one of the greenhouses before the war.

I think the family thought I would come back and settle back into the same life in Barton as before the war. They did not seem to appreciate that I had changed, grown up. I now had a much wider vision of the world; I had met a whole range of men from very different backgrounds and had seen them in all sorts of situations. I had travelled and my whole attitude to life had changed. Of course, I had a lot of catching up to do in studying for my career in architecture, having lost nearly five years. Perhaps I felt life in Barton was much too parochial, or perhaps I was somewhat muddled and would take some time to recover. I also missed the camaraderie of the men I had been with all those years. Clearly life at Barton was not for me.

Stella came up to Barton two or three days after my homecoming and I was so pleased to be with her again. Zilpah, especially, resented her, spying on us when we were just talking together in my bedroom to see if anything untoward was going on.

I think it must have been at this stage I finally began to feel my future was away from Barton. My mother welcomed Stella but I sensed the others were put out that all my attention was given to her and not to them. Soon after she arrived we went into Burton to buy an engagement ring in Clarke's the jewellers, just opposite the market place in High Street. They were very helpful and Stella chose a simple diamond ring, which she still wears. Somehow or other I scraped the money together to pay for it, quite an achievement on a lance corporal's pay.

Out of my small army pay I had paid, ever since my enlistment, a small allowance to my mother. I felt an obligation to help her as far as my resources would allow, which were now rather precarious. Soon afterwards, Stella went back to Salisbury, disillusioned at the attitude of my family, with the exception of my mother who was always very kind to her. This saddened me because Stella had been a tower of strength with her constant stream of letters to me, revealing a tremendous loyalty from a young girl who had not been officially engaged to me and no doubt had been subjected to temptations from other soldiers, especially the Americans who abounded around Salisbury. My mother had also constantly supported me throughout. I wished it was just her and Stella I could be with. The other member of the family who was always kind to me and Stella was Aunt Olive, and we later became very close to her.

I felt I no longer had anything in common with the village people, although they had been my friends before the war. I do know that my brother Dick's wife Molly really annoyed me. She said she was not having me and 'that girl' coming back to Burton expecting to take over the architectural practice which her Dick had built up. That was nonsense: the practice had been built up by my father; there had been little going on during the war – Dick had just kept it ticking over. I vaguely understood he had purchased the practice from my mother. If so, I knew none of the details. I did not know if he did anything to support mother. By taking over the practice at 10 High Street, Burton, he did acquire quite a number of small works of art which father had always kept in the office and that I felt was rather unfair.

Why did I never keep in touch with my fellow POWs, having taken the trouble to record their addresses? I do not know the answer. Perhaps

I just wanted to put the whole of the experience behind me and get on with my future life. In the same way, I rather consciously more or less severed close connections with my family and decided to make my future with Stella who had supported me so much during the dark days. In any case, I soon became very busy getting my professional qualifications and then we went to Southern Rhodesia (now Zimbabwe) in 1949 to start a new life.

My leave came to an end much too soon. I received instructions, including my railway warrant, to report to a camp near Horsham in Sussex. The camp – another bloody camp – had been set up as a rehabilitation and retraining centre for former POWs. The idea was to teach us how to be disciplined soldiers once more, how to carry out drill on the square and all the bull that entailed. It even included how to salute officers correctly and we were to be retrained in weapon handling, including some new weapons developed during our 'temporary' absence and with which we would be unfamiliar. There was also physical training including route-marches and sessions in the gymnasium intended to make us fit again.

All we were looking forward to was getting out of the army as soon as possible. This, however, was dependent on one's age and length of service. The time of discharge was calculated from one's age and the date of enlistment; you were then allocated a number and you had to wait until your number came up.

Most of the officers and some of the instructors at Horsham were younger than we were and most of them had not seen active service. Some officers were only just out of OCTU, so we felt we could give them a run for their money; our attitude was, 'Get a bit of service in.'

My mother had given me a large box of cigars from father's store, untouched since he died in 1937. They were good Havana cigars, Henry Clays. I took them to Horsham with me and shared them with my new colleagues. We had seen a Movietone newsreel of Churchill smoking a cigar whilst inspecting troops and puffing away as he walked along the ranks. One day we were called out on parade, now back to columns of three. Three of us took our places in the front rank with lighted cigars behind our backs and as soon as the young officer started his inspection we started puffing at our cigars. The officer was taken aback; the RSM exploded in a rage: how dare we be so insolent as to smoke cigars on parade? 'Sir,' we explained, 'Mr Churchill who is chief of the armed forces smokes cigars when inspecting military parades, we are only following his example. Surely if he can smoke on parade, we are entitled to do the same and it cannot be wrong or an offence?' Of course all the other soldiers were laughing out loud; it was bedlam. Eventually having had our fun, we had to put them out and order was restored but no action was taken against us.

One of my fellow smokers was Sapper Pozzi, a real wag. When we were being instructed in how to salute properly, he would bring his hand up and wave it up and down before completing the salute. I remember one young officer who was in charge of the parade, still with his feet wet just out of Sandhurst, corrected him saying, 'Pozzi, you do not wave your hand up and down like that, you keep it quite still. Whoever taught you to salute like that?' Sapper Pozzi replied, still wiggling his hand, 'Sir, I was taught to salute like this by my commanding officer, Lt Colonel X, Sir, at Dunkirk, Sir, 1940, Sir,' putting great emphasis on the Dunkirk. There were loud guffaws from everyone on parade. The poor young officer, who had not seen any active service went red in the face with embarrassment and had to let the matter drop.

On another occasion we had just completed a period of physical training in the gymnasium and were given ten minutes to change and get on the parade ground for a much hated drill session. Several of us decided to have a shower first as we were rather sweaty and as a consequence were somewhat late on parade. 'Where have you been, what the hell have you being doing? You know very well you are given ten minutes to get on parade,' roared the sergeant major. We replied, 'But, sergeant major, surely it is most unhygienic to come straight from sweating in the gymnasium and change into battledress without first having a shower. We have always been taught, in the army, that personal cleanliness is of paramount importance and were just obeying those instructions.' He was completely nonplussed, muttered away to himself, telling us to be quicker in future. We took the mickey out of them on every possible occasion, regarding the whole rehabilitation and retraining course as a bit of a joke.

On another occasion we were taken out to a firing range to see a demonstration of the PIAT anti-tank gun, which was unfamiliar. The gun was ceremoniously set up and a target of a large white sheet placed about forty or fifty yards away. The RSM and one officer were in attendance. The instructor explained the mechanism of the gun, showing us how it was loaded and the procedure for firing. He said he would give a demonstration after which some of us could try our hand. He carefully loaded the gun, pulled the trigger and fired it. The projectile came out of the end of the barrel and just flopped down on the ground about three feet in front of the gun. This really amused us all, and there was much laughter and clapping and some rude and uncomplimentary remarks, in particular from Sapper Pozzi. The RSM was not at all amused and picked Pozzi out, telling him to step forward and if he thought he could do better, to do so. Up strolled Pozzi; quite nonchalantly he reloaded the gun and fired: lo and behold, the projectile shot out and went straight through the centre of the target! There were cheers from every quarter and considerable embarrassment for the instructor, the officer and the RSM. That was the end of the demonstration; I never saw a PIAT gun again and I doubt if any of the others did.

We had missed out on the celebrations for VE Day; however, we were still at Horsham when VJ (Victory over Japan) Day was announced on 15 August. There were celebrations in Horsham which we attended; regretfully I remember very little about the festivities. I understood that they were a bit of an anti-climax after the earlier festivities for VE day – those had apparently been huge and nationwide.

We were given weekend passes to go to London, travelling from the small village station near the camp with only one elderly ticket collector who was always rushed by the men catching the train and leaving it on their return. He never had a chance to check or collect tickets; as a result the majority never bothered to buy tickets.

Towards the end of August our rehabilitation training came to an end. I suppose it had had some effect on us, but in the main we had enjoyed playing fun and games with the young officers. We now had to be posted to our units. I was posted to Doncaster to a Royal Engineers depot, the only one to go there. I was informed the reason was that I was required to undergo a trade test as an architectural draughtsman – which again seemed to me a complete waste of time. I had already passed the intermediate examination of the Royal Institute of British Architects which, according to the rules of the Establishment for Engineer Services, entitled me to be promoted to the rank of warrant officer class 2, the rank just above staff sergeant. I had only learned of this in POW camp. I had written to the army from the camp to seek my promotion only to be informed that this was only for regular army soldiers, a typical army excuse. Had I been able to get the promotion it would have entitled me to go to a non-working camp and it would also have given me a very substantial pay rise; I felt I had been cheated.

I was issued with my railway warrant, regimental route and some pay for the journey. Off I went to London, to Charing Cross station, then over by tube to Euston station, and caught my train to Doncaster. On arrival and having sought directions, I found my way on foot, carrying my kit, to the Royal Engineers depot, arriving there in the early evening. I reported to the guard room who, as usual, knew nothing about my posting, adding that the office was already closed. However, eventually someone gave me some instructions as to where to find a billet for the night, telling me to report back in the morning when the office would certainly sort things out. Their directions meant nothing to me.

As I picked up my kit ready to move on, into the guard room walked an RSM. He immediately hailed me by name: it was none other than Fred Bray, the architect from Penzance who had served with me at Moascar Camp in the canal area in Egypt. He asked me what I was doing there. I told him and added that I was looking for a billet for the night, but doubted if I could find my way around the camp.

Fred told me he had been offered a commission but refused it because he did not want to serve in a field regiment, preferring to stay as a warrant officer doing the architectural work for which he was qualified. He had stayed in Moascar for a while before being transferred to the engineer-in-chief's office in Cairo where he had spent the rest of the war; he was now in Doncaster awaiting his release from the army – being older than me his number was shortly to come up. He then said I was not to worry about finding the junior NCOs' mess but to go with him and he would find me a bed in the warrant officers' mess. I protested that I could not possibly do that as I was not entitled to be there, but he insisted that it would not be a problem: he would fix it with the mess management on the grounds of my having been a POW and a close friend of his. And so I stayed in the warrant officers' mess for the whole of my short stay at Doncaster. I was made welcome by most of the WOs. My main object in telling this story is that as I walked into their mess and put my kit by the bed Fred had found for me, who should be there but my old *bête noire* RSM Morris! I am certain he must have recognised me, but he immediately turned away and ignored me for the duration of my stay but, surprisingly, he never questioned my presence in the mess; perhaps he thought I had been promoted. Despite the niggle for me of having Morris around, all the other warrant officers made me very welcome. Fred and I spent hours reminiscing and exchanging news and views.

I duly took the revision course in architectural draughtsmanship which I did not find at all onerous and was passed. I had no idea what would happen next.

It was now mid-September and approaching my twenty-sixth birthday on 20 September. Stella and I had decided to get married on my birthday but finding this to be a Thursday we decided to change the date to Saturday 22 September. The wedding was to be at Stella's parish church of St Martin's in Salisbury, just around the corner from her home. All the arrangements were made and invitations had been sent out. I purchased the wedding ring, again from Clarke's in Burton whilst on a weekend leave. I had gone to Barton to be present in St James church when the banns of marriage were called as it was a requirement for me to be there on at least one occasion. My brother Charles, now back in England awaiting his demobilisation, had agreed to be my best man. I had applied for leave as soon as I had arrived at Doncaster to cover the wedding and our honeymoon, which I had already booked. I was told there was no problem and the leave would be granted.

Then quite out of the blue, on 16 or 17 September, I was suddenly posted to Ripon. I asked about my leave for the wedding and was told I would have to make a fresh application when I arrived at Ripon. This really upset the apple-cart. I arrived at Ripon in a panic. Here was I with all my wedding arrangements made, not knowing if I would be given leave by the new commanding officer at Ripon. I have only the faintest recollections of the camp at Ripon. I do not recall where I was accommodated or what work, if any, I was given; my whole mind was given to the problem of my leave and forthcoming marriage. For the first time I sought advice from the camp padre, who was very helpful and said he would immediately contact the CO and request him to grant me my leave straightaway, and thankfully he was successful. My leave to cover the wedding and honeymoon was granted almost immediately. I was given my railway warrant and other relevant papers were issued, and I then made my application for my marriage allowance – could not forget that.

I left Ripon never to return. There had been one hitch: as required by the Anglican Church, our banns had been called at my home church of St James at Barton-under-Needwood and at St Martin's in Salisbury, but the certificate from Barton had not been sent, as I had requested, to Salisbury. There was not much I could do about it as I was in Ripon. However, the vicar at St Martin's managed to make an urgent telephone call to the vicar at Barton, who arranged for its arrival in the nick of time – without it we could not have been married.

I arrived in Salisbury in the early afternoon, 21 September, and booked into the County Hotel in Fisherton Street. I phoned Stella's sister Heather to say I had arrived safely and also spoke to her father. I had no stag night; I spent my last night as a bachelor entirely on my own at the hotel. Charles had been due that evening but had not arrived, so I had a very lonely night. The next morning he still had not arrived and I began to get really worried. I thought I would probably have to ask Stella's brother to be best man. I had my lunch at the hotel, quite alone, with still no sign of my brother Charles. Then just about an hour before the time of the service, he turned up at the hotel and we were able to set off for the church and arrive there on time. We wore our battledress in contrast to Stella who looked beautiful in her splendid wedding dress. Stella's sister Heather and a friend were the bridesmaids. The service was conducted by the Rev. Harry Bloomfield. It was a delightful service with a full choir, the ring was put on her finger and we signed the register with witnesses and became man and wife and still are, some sixty-six years later.

The reception was held at a school hall only a few yards from the church. Despite the food rationing, Stella's family and friends were able to put on an excellent wedding feast enjoyed by everyone. My brother Charles was, sadly, the only member of my family present. My mother was ill and unable to travel on her own; apparently no one else wanted to bring her. My sister Mary would have come but she was in hospital. It was sad that the rest of my family just ignored the wedding – did not even send greetings. I think it hurt Stella more than it did me, I was so very happy to have Stella as my wife.

I had booked us into the Trossachs Hotel on Loch Katrine in Scotland for two weeks. I have no idea how I managed to find the money for the hotel, let alone the rail fares; it must have been out of the back pay I received on my return from Germany. It was very difficult to make ends meet on a lance corporal's pay, and I was still making a small allowance to my mother. I had no capital and my few possessions consisted mainly of my clothes and some books. Now that I was married I had to discontinue the allowance to my mother; I just could not afford it with a wife to support.

Stella's family and friends had miraculously found the ingredients for a good wedding cake. After cutting the cake and enjoying the joyous reception we were driven to Salisbury station to start our journey to Scotland. I was still in uniform and Stella in her going-away outfit. We travelled up to Waterloo station and across London by Underground; I remember Stella being terrified of the escalator, her first, and I more or less had to force her to use it: I just could not understand what all the fuss was about. We got across London to King's Cross station and caught the train to Scotland. We travelled third class overnight and thus our wedding night was spent in a crowded railway compartment – not so very romantic! Having changed at Stirling we arrived at Callander in the morning and took a taxi out to the 'fairy tale' Trossachs Hotel, so our honeymoon proper started on Monday 24 September.

Stella at first experienced some difficulty in remembering to sign as Litherland, her hesitation gave the game away, so the staff knew immediately we were on our honeymoon, not that we really minded. So at the Trossachs we first got to know each other, and for the first time, intimately. We had a lovely time spent walking in the beautiful countryside along the loch and in the hills.

Then as we were having afternoon tea on Friday, 28 September, the receptionist came into the lounge and announced there was a telephone call for Mrs Litherland. After her name had been called a couple of times, Stella realised the call was for her. She answered the telephone call and came back to tell me it was to tell her that her aunt Muriel's husband, Maurice, had unexpectedly arrived home in Plymouth after having been a prisoner of war of the Japanese on the island of Java.

Maurice had been a chief petty officer in the Royal Navy serving on HMS *Exeter* when the ship was sunk by the Japanese in the Java Sea. He had subsequently been reported missing in action. There had been no evidence of whether he was alive or dead.

As soon as he was reported missing, his wife Muriel's marriage allowance was stopped. She had two young children to bring up on her own and now with no help whatsoever from the Royal Navy. It was almost as if she was being punished for his being missing. Such was the Welfare State at that time, very unfair and seemingly callous. Muriel had taken the children to Salisbury where she was living with Stella's mother, her sister, and it was Stella's family who supported her during this horrendous period of her life. She was so poor that, Stella told me, she always washed out the milk bottles with a little water to extract the last drop of sustenance. Nothing whatsoever had been heard of Maurice until his miraculous return.

Maurice said he had managed to get ashore onto the island of Java where he was taken prisoner with other survivors from the ship. They were most horribly treated by their Japanese captors. He had spent most of the time in a workshop making coffins for his many fellow prisoners who had died of starvation or as the result of beatings and ill treatment. When the Australians liberated Java he was taken to Australia in an almost comatose state. He had recovered slowly and when he was sufficiently well had been repatriated. It was only on his arrival that the family knew that he had survived.

Stella's brother Martin had also served on the *Exeter* earlier in the war and taken part in the Battle of the River Plate, during which battle the ship was badly damaged as they tried to sink the German battleship *Graf Spee*. Now there was great rejoicing at Maurice's homecoming, safe but not completely sound.

Stella said she would very much like to go to see him and I agreed, although this meant shortening our honeymoon. I informed the hotel of the circumstances and they agreed to our leaving early and adjusted our account accordingly. We managed to book seats on a train from Stirling for the evening of Saturday 29 September and arranged for a taxi to take us to Callander for the local train to Stirling, where we caught the train to King's Cross. From London we would continue our journey onwards to Plymouth.

There were no sleepers available on the train: we were told they were all reserved for members of the staff of the Royal Household who were travelling back to London. We managed to get seats in the corner of the last compartment of the second carriage of the train, the first containing sleepers. Our seats were facing the engine. The train was very crowded and there were people who could not get seats standing or crouching in the corridor. I clearly remember seeing a soldier handcuffed and under arrest for desertion with a military police escort. It was a long, hot night as we cuddled together trying to sleep but with little success. Eventually, early in the morning, we steamed into Crewe Station, after a long, boring but smooth journey overnight.

At Crewe there was a change of crew. At the time there was a train drivers' strike – I do not know why, no doubt something to do with pay. The replacement driver who boarded the train at Crewe was a volunteer driver because the usual driver was on strike. He was reported to have said, 'London and back before lunch.' The early morning was quite bright and sunny but with patches of fog from time to time.

Sadly our driver never got back home to Crewe. At about 9 a.m. on the morning of Sunday, 30 September, when the train was at Bourne End near Watford, there was a sudden braking and shuddering; there were sounds of things smashing, then there was more jolting and swaying, and an almighty noise as the train left the rails and plunged down the embankment on the left, the side on which we were sitting. It all happened so very quickly it was impossible to remember the exact sequence of the disaster or really describe precisely how it took place. Then, after all the noise of splintering wood and smashing glass, the train gave a final great shudder and came to a rest.

For a few seconds there seemed to be a deathly quiet but then, suddenly, I could hear voices shouting both in our compartment and outside. Some were shouts of terror, some screams, some people were moaning and others trying to give instructions. I heard someone shout that they could smell petrol and the train was about to catch fire and burn. I was very dazed and Stella appeared to be asleep.

I heard some movement near me inside our compartment. I looked up and saw that one of the soldiers had managed to clamber out of the compartment through a shattered window; he then helped another soldier out and they began to try to get others in our compartment out of the wreckage. They said they would help me out first and then get Stella out. They told me first to stretch my right arm forward and get hold of the window frame and pull myself up, this I did, then I was to grasp another piece of wreckage with my left hand. Mentally I gave the instruction to the arm but it was not obeyed; the arm just did not move, obviously damaged. The soldiers had to drag me out and sat me down on the ground clear of the train. I was very shaken and dazed for a few minutes before regaining some composure. After that they gradually helped the others out and then turned their attention to Stella, who was unconscious. They very carefully dragged her out. There was a train door lying on the ground nearby so they carefully laid her down on the door.

Eventually everyone was helped out and was standing, sitting or lying at the bottom of the embankment in various degrees of shock. The next thing I remember was a naval officer coming along who identified himself as a doctor. We indicated Stella lying unconscious on the door whom he quickly examined. He said he thought she had broken her back, gave her an injection, got out his fountain pen and wrote on her forehead the dosage of morphine he had injected into her, then moved on to attend to others towards the front of the train.

It was now a fine sunny morning as we waited amidst the debris and chaos. There were items of luggage strewn all around. The next thing I recall was a lady from the WVS asking me if I would like a cup of tea, that great English restorative. When I said, 'Yes please, I'd love one,' she replied, 'Have you got a mug?' I thought what an extraordinary thing to say in the circumstances, as if we were all expected to have a cup or mug in our pockets. I suddenly remembered we did indeed have two plastic beakers which were in a valise. I looked around and spotted the valise lying a few feet away – it had been thrown out of the train in the crash. I was able to retrieve it, get out a beaker and have a most welcome cup of strong tea. I gave the other beaker to one of the soldiers so that he could also have some tea. I was amazed at how very quickly the WVS ladies had appeared on the scene, although I had no idea really of how much time had passed since the crash. I was lucky to have found the valise and retrieved it as it contained the few pieces of jewellery Stella possessed. Our cases were still missing but at the time I gave no thought whatsoever to them. I suppose I was in a state of shock.

Sometime afterwards we were informed that the train had been travelling at full speed when it came into a foggy patch. Along this stretch of line there was a signal switching the train onto a slow line. The driver must have missed the signal in the fog as he did not brake or slow down and hit the points guiding the train onto the slow line at an excessive speed and, sadly, it became derailed and plunged down the embankment. The engine and the first two carriages took the full impact of the crash. As far as I can remember, some of the carriages further back had stayed on the track above. There were a large number of casualties: thirty-two killed including the driver and eighty-two injured, according to the *Daily Mail* of 1 October. Most of the fatal casualties were in the two front carriages. The paper goes on to say, 'Three people are detained at Watford Peace Memorial Hospital. Two, Mr and Mrs S. Litherland are seriously ill, while the third is unconscious and not yet identified.'

Ambulances began to arrive and Stella was carefully put on a stretcher and loaded into an ambulance, together with another young woman who was also unconscious. I followed with the valise, but the ambulance crew did not want me in the ambulance and I had to plead with them, saying I was Stella's husband and we should not be parted. They relented and we were whisked away to the Peace Memorial Hospital at Watford. It was lucky that I went with her because I learned later that only the three of us were taken to this hospital. Most of the injured were taken to the hospital at Hemel Hempstead or to Ashridge Hospital. If I had not been in the ambulance, we would have ended up in different hospitals.

On arrival, Stella and the other young woman, both still unconscious, were quickly put on trolleys and wheeled away to a female ward. I clambered out of the ambulance, saying I was quite able to walk but the nurses insisted that because I was in shock I must be put on a trolley too and was taken to a men's ward. I was taken to a bed, the curtains drawn around and I was undressed and my clothes taken away. I was sponged down and put into hospital pyjamas.

When the curtains were drawn back, Sunday lunch was being served, the main item of which was roast beef. A nurse asked me if I would like something to eat, I said, 'Yes please,' as I was very hungry: 'I would love some roast beef and vegetables.' She replied it would be better if I did not have the roast meal but I could have some jelly and custard. I was very disappointed; I could not understand the reluctance to give me the proper meal but when I put a spoonful of jelly to my mouth I realised why. My mouth was full of grit and fragments of glass and I just could not eat anything. I had to call the nurse to come and clean out my mouth. Even then I had difficulty; I could not eat properly until my mouth had healed a couple of days later. I, then, finally accepted that I was in shock. I had not realised there was anything wrong with my mouth, not even when I drank the tea at the scene of the crash. In retrospect it is interesting to note that there was no system of a preliminary examination and assessment on arrival as there is today in a modern accident and emergency unit.

The other thing I knew was that my left arm was injured because I could not lift it at all. A doctor soon came and said that I had most likely torn the deltoid muscles in my left shoulder; he did not think there was any breakage but as a precaution I should have an X-ray, which confirmed his diagnosis. The treatment for the torn muscles was rest and a prolonged period of physiotherapy until they mended. I did slowly get the use of my arm back, but I have never been able to extend the left arm fully upwards.

The hospital was quite modern and the ward I was in was pleasant and spacious. Some of the other patients were servicemen of around about my age. Those on the mend were very lively and up to all sorts of tricks and games and naturally they flirted with the nurses. I remember one young serviceman, I think an airman, was going for an operation. When he was put on a trolley, we placed a bunch of white lilies on top of him as he as wheeled off, saying we did not expect to see him again, but luckily for him we did. I was very soon mobile, a walking patient.

Early the next morning I was taken to see Stella. It had quickly been established by the staff that we were a honeymoon couple, so always on my visits the nurses in her ward would smile and draw the curtains to give some privacy. The first time I saw her she was lying there with her head bandaged and still unconscious. I could only sit there and look at her, whilst holding her hand; it made me so sad. The nurses and doctors said they did not know how long she would be in this state or even if she would come out of the coma at all. She was unconscious for over a week. The doctors thought she had a fractured skull, and said she must lie flat. She was not X-rayed because they did not wish to move her. Her back was probably damaged, even broken; however, everything in time healed.

When we did not arrive at Salisbury on our way to Plymouth, Stella's parents were worried and when they heard that there had been a rail crash, they contacted the police who made enquiries for them and eventually found out that we had survived and were in hospital in Watford. Stella's mother, father and her younger brother Stephen immediately set out to come to the hospital. When they arrived at Watford they were given a police escort to the hospital and given brandy before being allowed to see her. Even so, Stephen passed out when he saw her. I was told that one of the popular papers had a headline on Monday 1 October 1945: 'Parents rush to bedside of dying bride.'

For the first few days the doctors had not known if she would survive. It was a very harrowing time; I was myself still in quite a daze. We had both survived the war, bombs and bullets and Stella had steadfastly supported me through the years of incarceration. Now, as we were about to embark on our married life, disaster had struck. It seemed so unfair, but we were lucky not to have been killed, saved most probably because we had travelled in the last compartment of the carriage.

The next visitors were my aunt Maud, my mother's sister, and her husband George Lawson, who lived at Harpenden so they were quite close to Watford. Uncle George worked for the railways and asked me if we had any missing luggage as, he said, there was a lot of unclaimed luggage recovered from the wreckage. I described the two cases we had lost which he was able to locate and return to me; he and Aunty Maud were a great help. They were amongst our regular visitors and were very kind. My sister Mary came from Reading to see us on several occasions, as did Stella's sister Heather. We had letters from my mother but she was not well enough to visit us. I quickly recovered my general health but still could not use my left shoulder. I had daily physiotherapy and was given other exercises to do. Very gradually movement came back. Once Stella was conscious, she began her slow recovery. We were in the Peace Memorial Hospital for about six weeks. We had received excellent care.

After six weeks, Stella was allowed to go to her parents' home at 2 St Martin's Terrace, Salisbury, to recover. I was transferred to a military hospital on the outskirts of Salisbury to continue my treatment which allowed me to be near Stella. I was allowed out of hospital to visit her two or three times a week, but had to be back in hospital on time. This seemed a strange arrangement. Stella was incapacitated and confined to bed at home and I, being completely mobile, was required to stay in hospital just to get my daily exercises. The hospital was very efficient, run on strict military lines, headed by a matron who was a great disciplinarian and out of the top drawer, her name the Hon. something Guest. The whole staff and patients lived in awe of her and dreaded her inspections, which were often twice a day.

My shoulder slowly mended and in early 1946 I was told I would be soon discharged as fit for duty and posted back to my unit. As Stella was still far from well I put in a request, on compassionate grounds, for a posting near Salisbury to be near Stella. I assumed the Southern Command Engineer Services were still around in Salisbury or at Wilton and that I might be posted there. In the customary unsympathetic manner of the army in those days, my request was completely disregarded and I was posted to Darlington in County Durham, an area under the Northumbria

Command. I had to make my farewell visit to Stella, not knowing when I would be given leave to see her again.

I was issued with my railway warrant, given some pay and so on. I set off by train to Darlington. On arrival, I was instructed to report to the CRE's (Commander of Royal Engineers) office which was in a house called Blackwell Grange on the outskirts of Darlington.

After a longish walk carrying all my kit, I found the grange and reported, only to be informed, just like my arrival in Salisbury all those years ago, that I would have to find my own accommodation/billet somewhere in the town. However, this time I had been expected. It turned out to be difficult to find any accommodation; all the places on the list of billets I was given, seemed to be full. For the first few days I stayed at the YMCA in Darlington.

I soon settled down in the office with the rest of the staff who all seemed congenial and were welcoming. I remember John the chief draughts-man, probably a sergeant, Muriel an ATS clerk who was very friendly and helpful, and Captain Yates with whom I made many trips out into the countryside.

Accommodation was still a problem; I was only allowed to stay three nights at the YMCA. The grange was some distance from Darlington and it was a bind having to hike to and fro, although I had most of my meals in the NAAFI. John, faced with the same problem, had decided to camp out in the office and suggested I do the same. So instead of looking for a billet in Darlington I managed to find a camp bed and some blankets and set up 'home' in the office. We stored our camp beds and bedding away during the day and we had a very spacious quiet office/bedroom at night. In this way we solved the accommodation problem at no cost at all, an important consideration in those impecunious days. We were able to save our accommodation allowance which we still received. Officially no one knew about it, but I suspect they all, including some of the officers, knew. We had breakfast in the office. We had a kettle so could make tea and from the NAAFI we were able to buy packets of cereal, milk, bread, butter and marmalade. I do not think the CRE himself ever knew we were camping out in the office.

Having a quiet office to ourselves during the evenings and nights, I was able to get down to some swotting for my RIBA finals. I had enquired about what further architectural education was available under the army schemes for returning soldiers and was told I could apply for a university place.

One of the places on offer to study architecture was at Liverpool University, at the time considered to be excellent, perhaps the best architectural course in the country. However, it would mean a three-year course, at least. I would have to live on a very small allowance from the government. I would not be on full army pay as by the time I started at Liverpool I would have been demobbed. On this pittance I would have to support Stella. We would have to put off starting a family until after completing the course and finding a job. I was tempted, but instead decided once again to sign up for the correspondence course with Professor L. Stuart Stanley based at the Bartlett School of Architecture, London University. This course, including the cost of textbooks, was also supported by the army scheme and therefore would cost me nothing. My objective was, if possible, to take my RIBA finals at the first possible opportunity in July 1946, which would mean some very hard work. If I passed, I would be able to find a job with enough salary to support Stella and perhaps start a family. So I enrolled on the course with Professor Stanley.

John's and my daily routine was to get up, wash and shave, have our breakfast and clear everything away well before the rest of the staff arrived. We then worked until lunchtime and walked to the Darlington NAAFI for lunch, unless I was out on a survey in the field, then walk back to Blackwell Grange and work until the office closed at 5 p.m. This allowed me to do an hour or so of study before returning to the NAAFI for supper, and then back again to Blackwell Grange for the night. I would continue to study until getting the camp bed out at around 11 to 11.30 p.m. As I completed each paper of the course I sent it off to Professor Stanley for marking. I got good marks for all my papers, which was encouraging as I had put in a lot of hard work. I had no distractions such as the cinema or the pub. I made good progress and completed a good part of the course before leaving Darlington.

Out of the subsistence allowance I received for living in a billet, I was able to pay for all my meals at the NAAFI, buy my breakfast food and have some money left over: the first savings I had been able to make since our marriage. I used the NAAFI for my meals because it was not only the cheapest place in Darlington but also the only place where one could get a decent meal; all the other restaurants were very restricted by rationing and had little to offer.

There were two NAAFIs in Darlington, one for the men and the other, restricted to the ATS, for the women. We were allowed to have afternoon tea at the ATS NAAFI, but not allowed to use their shop or have other meals there. Stella had asked if I could get her some cosmetics; she did not like asking her sister Heather, who was in the Wrens, to get them. It was almost impossible for civilians to buy good cosmetics in the shops. As I could not use the ATS NAAFI shop myself, I asked one of the girls to buy them for me, either Muriel from the office, or a driver named Effie. All the drivers at the CRE office were female. I was able to get various brands such as Coty, Elizabeth Arden, Helena Rubinstein, and Max Factor, and Innoxa and Hinds face creams, none of which were available in the civilian shops.

Muriel was able to get me a Penelope tablecloth for Stella to embroider and also a rug canvas. She and the other ATS girls were very kind. I had told them about Stella's injuries in the train accident, so they were eager to help out. I was also able to buy chocolates from our NAAFI and post them to Stella in Salisbury: there was still strict rationing of sweets and chocolates for civilians. I also posted my dirty laundry to Stella for washing and ironing; postage by Forces Mail was quite cheap.

As I had three days' leave at Easter, I decided to visit Barton to see my mother and the rest of the family there. Mother was not at all well. She was only in her mid-sixties but was beginning to fail very quickly. Afterwards I returned to Darlington for the last days of my army service.

Despite being a long way from Stella and really missing her, I enjoyed the atmosphere in the office at Blackwell Grange as the staff from the CRE down were all very pleasant and easy to work with. Most of my work was with Captain Yates. Our job was to go out into the surrounding countryside to do a reconnaissance of all road and rail bridges in the Northumbria Division, measuring them and noting their type of construction and materials. Back in the office I made drawings of them and then Captain Yates made calculations of the amount of explosives which would be required to demolish them. To me this seemed to be a rather pointless exercise, as the war was over and I could not visualise any circumstances when these bridges, many of them in very remote places, would ever need to be demolished. The work may have been of some use to the local highway authority, although they would no doubt have their own records. I guess our work when completed was just tucked away in army records and archives, completely forgotten until the time came to destroy the plans and reports. Possibly it was just an exercise conceived for training purposes and to give the men something to do whilst awaiting discharge from the army. For Captain Yates, our driver Sapper Effie and I, it was most pleasant to be out in the dales and see, the first time for me, the lovely countryside of Durham and Northumberland. In particular I remember St John's Chapel, Stanhope and Wolsingham in Weardale. We also visited Barnard Castle and other small towns and villages in the area. The weather was very good so we were able to enjoy the spring flowers. Most days we were able to picnic in the country and then pop into a local pub for a drink. We could not eat in the pubs at that time because very few served any food.

In those days, all negative drawings – or tracings as we called them – if required to be kept for any length of time had to be done on tracing linen. This was a special linen, stiffened with some sort of starch, usually pale blue in colour. There were a large number of rolls of this tracing linen in the office, together with many out-of-date tracings already set aside for eventual destruction. At the time tracing linen was being replaced by a new plastic tracing material and we were instructed to use it instead, making the tracing linen redundant. I and others in the office collected these unwanted tracings and also the rolls of linen which we were told were no longer to be used, parcelled them up and sent them home. The material was then laundered to remove all the starch thus providing valuable pieces of linen which could be used for making sheets, pillowcases, tablecloths, handkerchiefs and other useful items.

All material was still scarce and rationed, available only with special coupons. People had to use all possible means to get hold of things that were in short supply. Whilst we were still in the army we could purchase items in the NAAFI which were not available to the general public and naturally took advantage of that facility. Seventy years later our profligate waste saddens me. I wrote to Stella every day (she still has some of the letters), detailing my last few days at Blackwell Grange.

My release number had now come up and I could begin preparations to leave the army. I parcelled up all my books and other personal possessions and posted them off to Stella in Salisbury. When I had been at Barton over Easter I had taken the opportunity to pack up all my few personal belongings there, also sending them off to Salisbury. I ordered a new drawing board and tee-square to be delivered to Salisbury ready for use after my release. I still had a considerable amount of design to undertake as part of my architectural study course. I bought a very large notebook in which to start the draft of the thesis I was required to submit to the RIBA for approval after I had, I hoped, passed the final examination. My thesis had to be accepted before I could be elected as an associate member of the institute. Even at this early stage, I was looking beyond architecture and wrote to Professor Stuart Stanley to obtain details of his course on town planning in which I was very interested. This course was also available under the army scheme and I signed up for it, leading to membership of the Town Planning Institute (later called the Royal Town Planning Institute).

I was informed I would be released at the beginning of May 1946. The CRE called me into his office, told me he was very pleased with my work and asked me if I was prepared to stay on in the Royal Engineers. He said he was prepared to recommend me for a commission and would back me to the hilt if I decided to stay. I considered the offer but not very seriously. I decided I had had quite enough of the army, with all its bull and bureaucracy, and declined his offer. Had I stayed, I would have probably been embroiled in Korea and Malaysia, but I think, on balance, I have had a more interesting life.

All the rigmarole of discharge from the army now got underway. I still have my release document on its khaki-coloured paper, signed by a Captain Weston on behalf of the chief engineer Northumbria Division. My 'military conduct' is stated as 'exemplary'; no doubt that was fairly standard. My 'testimonial' reads: 'Lance Corporal Litherland is an architectural draughtsman of outstanding ability. He was taken prisoner on Crete and so missed the rapid promotion which he undoubtedly would have received. He is an able assistant to any architect.' There is a big stamp 'UK release', and there is an Aldershot stamp dated 2 May 1946. There is another stamp dated 9 December 1947, presumably the date when the release document was eventually sent to me. The document says, 'release leave expires on 27 June 1946'. The main significance of that date is that it informed me when my army pay would cease. From then on, I would be left to my own devices, a most daunting prospect for an impecunious newly-wed.

Following the train accident, my brother Dick asked whether we had made a claim for compensation from the railway company in respect of Stella's injuries. I replied that we had not; I do not believe we had even thought about claiming. He told me that a friend of his, Harold Timms, a solicitor in Burton-on-Trent, would be prepared to act on Stella's behalf. We agreed and Harold went ahead with the claim. He negotiated with the railway company, who accepted liability in principle and said they would require their doctor to examine Stella.

One day their doctor arrived, unannounced, to see her. She happened to be alone. He asked her how she felt; she replied that she was beginning to feel better. He made a very cursory examination – with no one else present – quite unethical. Then without further ado, he produced a document which he asked her to sign. The document was not read to her nor explained, neither was her signature witnessed. It later transpired that she had certified that she would make no further claim against the railway company on health grounds. This was all highly irregular, from the examination without a third person, the unwitnessed signature to the pressure put on a young girl, unused to legal documents, to sign. The outcome was the railway company paid her compensation of, I recall, about £1,000 in full and final settlement of any claim she had against the company. It was a very dirty trick as she signed away her right to any further money should she have any further problems. It never occurred to me that I also might have a claim in respect of my own injuries; I suppose I felt that the army were looking after my health and that was that. Nowadays, I would have a huge claim for all the distress I suffered – how times have changed! Nevertheless the money she received was quite a godsend for us and helped as we started out on our real married life after I left the army.

My release from the army was not just a matter of leaving Darlington and going home. First I had to go to Aldershot to a demobilisation centre where I would be required to hand in all my army equipment: rifle, tin hat, various packs, army clothing, even my water bottle and mess tins. I would be charged for any missing items. I recollect we were allowed to keep one battledress uniform. Having handed in all our army goods and chattels we would then be issued with some civilian clothes.

I was given a railway travel warrant to Aldershot including the times of the trains I was expected to catch. I said farewell to those of my colleagues at Blackwell Grange who happened to be in the office very early that morning, 1 May 1946. I had several hours to spare in London so I was able to call at the headquarters of the RIBA at 66 Portland Place to finalise my application to sit for the final examination in July 1946. I was also able to call on Professor Stuart Stanley who had an office not far from Portland Place. I caught a train to Reading where I stayed the night with my sister Mary, her husband Frank and their two children.

On the morning of 2 May I caught an early train to Aldershot. After a bit of a trek, I arrived at my destination and reported to the guard room. I was directed to the office dealing with discharges from the army, where I would end the six years which had been taken from my life. It was my last direct experience with the army.

The atmosphere at the discharge centre was more relaxed than usual, understandably so. I duly handed in my rifle together with all the other pieces of army equipment and army property; there was nothing missing, so there was no surcharge. Then I was issued with my 'demob' clothes and changed into the suit and shirt. I was given a cardboard suitcase for the items I was not wearing and my other odds and ends, including the battle-dress uniform I was permitted to keep. The 'demob' clothes consisted of one suit – 'off the peg' – and of rather poor quality, like those then available at the Fifty Shilling Tailors (one of the high street outfitters in those days), two shirts, a tie, some underclothes, socks, a pair of shoes and a grey trilby hat. The final item was a rather thin overcoat. The clothes were all what were called 'utility': they were neither smart nor very attractive; perhaps similar to what one might expect in a Communist country. I went back home in these clothes but rarely wore them afterwards. Putting the rest of my possessions in the suitcase, I, with others, was marched off to my last pay parade, received and signed for my pay and then moved on to be given my last railway warrant to take me to Salisbury. And so I walked out of the Aldershot barracks a civilian once more. I caught a train to Woking where I changed platforms to catch the train to Salisbury. My faithful Stella was there to meet me. Thus ended the six years' wartime service of 'The Good Soldier Sydney', alias Lord Junak.

Index

If you enjoyed this book, you may also be interested in …

Survivor of the Long March
CHARLES WAITE WITH DEE LA VARDERA

Private Charles Waite lost his freedom in May 1940. He wasn't rescued until April 1945, near Berlin after having walked 1,600km from East Prussia.

Silent for seventy years, Charles writes about all he saw and suffered in his five lost years, including the Long March. There are simply no memoirs of that terrible trek – except this one.

978-0-7524-6519-7

Ein Volk, Ein Reich
LOUIS HAGEN

Louis Hagen saw his family flee their home and many of his relatives died at the hands of the Third Reich. To understand why, he interviewed nine people he had known before the war who represented a wide spectrum of German society, tracing their experiences of Nazism from the first hopeful days until the horrors of the Russian occupation of Berlin.

978-0-7524-5979-0

Jungle Journal:
Prisoners of the Japanese in Java 1942–1945
FRANK AND RONALD WILLIAMS

This is the story of Lieutenant Ronald Williams, held as a prisoner of war in the Japanese-occupied Dutch East Indies from 1942–45. Told through diaries and papers, *Jungle Journal* includes many cartoons and poems produced by the prisoners, as well as extracts from the original 'Jungle Journal', a newspaper created by the men under the noses of their guards.

978-0-7524-8721-2

Visit our website and discover thousands of other History Press books.

www.thehistorypress.co.uk

The History Press